29 95
68c

FAULT TOLERANCE
Principles and Practice

FAULT TOLERANCE
Principles and Practice

T. Anderson & P. A. Lee
Computing Laboratory, University of Newcastle Upon Tyne, England

ENGLEWOOD CLIFFS, NEW JERSEY   LONDON   NEW DELHI
SINGAPORE   SYDNEY   TOKYO   TORONTO   WELLINGTON

To Pat and Jude

Library of Congress Cataloging in Publication Data

Anderson, T
    Fault tolerance, principles and practice.

    Bibliography: p.
    Includes index.
    1. Fault-tolerant computing. I. Lee, P.A.,
1950-   joint author. II. Title.
QA76.9.F38A53   001.64   80-29619
ISBN 0-13-308254-7

British Library Cataloguing in Publication Data

Anderson, T.
    Fault tolerance.
    1. Fault-tolerant computing
    I. Title   II. Lee, P.A.
    501.64   QA76.9.F38
    ISBN 0-13-308254-7

© 1981 by PRENTICE-HALL INTERNATIONAL, INC.

All rights reserved. No part of this publication may be reproduced, stored in a retrieval system, or transmitted, in any form or by any means, electronic, mechanical, photocopying, recording or otherwise, without the prior permission of Prentice-Hall International, Inc., London.

ISBN 0-13-308254-7

PRENTICE-HALL INTERNATIONAL, INC., *London*
PRENTICE-HALL OF AUSTRALIA PTY., LTD., *Sydney*
PRENTICE-HALL CANADA, INC., *Toronto*
PRENTICE-HALL OF INDIA PRIVATE LIMITED, *New Delhi*
PRENTICE-HALL OF JAPAN, INC., *Tokyo*
PRENTICE-HALL OF SOUTHEAST ASIA PTE., LTD., *Singapore*
PRENTICE-HALL, INC., *Englewood Cliffs, New Jersey*
WHITEHALL BOOKS LIMITED, *Wellington, New Zealand*

Printed in the United States of America

10 9 8 7 6 5 4 3 2 1

CONTENTS

FOREWORD   ix

PREFACE   xi

1 INTRODUCTION   1

FAULT PREVENTION AND FAULT TOLERANCE   4
ANTICIPATED AND UNANTICIPATED FAULTS   5
BOOK AIM   9
REFERENCES   10

2 SYSTEM STRUCTURE AND RELIABILITY   13

SYSTEM STRUCTURE   15
    System Model   17
    Software/Hardware Interaction   26
    Interpreters and Multilevel Systems   29
    Atomic Actions   36
SYSTEM RELIABILITY   39
    Failure and Reliability   39
    System Specification   42
    Multiple Specifications   44
    Erroneous Transitions and States   46
    Component/Design Failures   50
    Errors and Faults   52
SUMMARY   58
REFERENCES   59

3 FAULT TOLERANCE   63

FAULT TOLERANCE: HOW   64
    Principles of Fault Tolerance   64
    Redundancy   67
FAULT TOLERANCE: WHERE AND HOW MUCH   70
    Quantitative Reliability Evaluation   72
A FRAMEWORK FOR IMPLEMENTING FAULT TOLERANCE   77
    Exceptions and Exception Handling   78
    Exception Handling in Multilevel Systems   83
    Summary of Exception Handling   87
REFERENCES   89

4 FAULT TOLERANT SYSTEMS 93

ESS NO. 1A   94
    System Description   95
    Reliability Strategies   97
SIFT AND FTMP   98
    SIFT System Design   99
    SIFT Reliability Strategies   101
    FTMP System Design   102
    FTMP Reliability Strategies   102
SYSTEM R   104
JPL-STAR   105
PLURIBUS   107
TANDEM 16   107
REFERENCES   110

5 ERROR DETECTION 113

MEASURES FOR ERROR DETECTION   114
    Replication Checks   118
    Timing Checks   123
    Reversal Checks   124
    Coding Checks   126
    Reasonableness Checks   128
    Structural Checks   130
    Diagnostic Checks   133
MECHANISMS FOR ERROR DETECTION   135
STRUCTURING ERROR DETECTION IN SYSTEMS   139
REFERENCES   143

6 DAMAGE CONFINEMENT AND ASSESSMENT 147

MEASURES FOR DAMAGE CONFINEMENT   148
MEASURES FOR DAMAGE ASSESSMENT   152
MECHANISMS FOR DAMAGE CONFINEMENT   155
    Protection Mechanisms   158
    Protection in Multilevel Systems   163
MECHANISMS FOR DAMAGE ASSESSMENT   166
SUMMARY   168
REFERENCES   169

7 ERROR RECOVERY   173

MEASURES FOR ERROR RECOVERY   174
    State Restoration   177
    Forward and Backward Error Recovery   179
MECHANISMS FOR ERROR RECOVERY   179
    Checkpoints and Audit Trails   186
    The Recovery Cache   190
RECOVERY IN MULTILEVEL SYSTEMS   197
    Inclusive and Disjoint Recovery   200
RECOVERY IN CONCURRENT SYSTEMS   208
    Concurrent Processes   208
    Recovery for Competing Processes   210
    Recovery for Cooperating Processes   213
    Distributed Systems   223
SUMMARY   224
REFERENCES   225

8 FAULT TREATMENT AND CONTINUED SERVICE   231

FAULT LOCATION   233
SYSTEM REPAIR   236
RESUMING NORMAL SERVICE   244
SUMMARY   247
REFERENCES   247

9 SOFTWARE FAULT TOLERANCE   249

THE RECOVERY BLOCK SCHEME   251
    Implementation of Recovery Blocks   258
    The Utility of Recovery Blocks   259
    Acceptance Tests   263
    Run-Time Overheads   269
    Summary of Recovery Blocks   272
THE DEADLINE MECHANISM   273
THE N-VERSION PROGRAMMING SCHEME   275
    Implementation of N-Version Programming   276
    Voting Check   278
    Summary of N-Version Programming   279
    Comparison with the Recovery Block Scheme   280
SUMMARY   286
REFERENCES   288

10 CONCLUSION 293

METHODOLOGY AND FRAMEWORK FOR FAULT TOLERANCE 295
Ideal Fault Tolerant Components 297
Failure Exceptions 300
Critical Components 302
THE FUTURE 303
REFERENCES 305

REFERENCES 307

ANNOTATED BIBLIOGRAPHY 325

MULTIPLE SOURCES 325
FAULT TOLERANT SYSTEMS 326
COMTRAC 326
COPRA 327
C.vmp 328
ESS Systems (Bell Laboratories) 329
Fault Tolerant Multiprocessor (FTMP) 332
Fault Tolerant Spaceborne Computer (FTSC) 333
HIVE 336
IBM 9020 337
JPL-STAR Computer 338
Plessey System 250 339
Pluribus 341
PRIME 342
Software Implemented Fault Tolerance (SIFT) 343
Space Shuttle Computer Complex 345
Tandem 16 346
SOFTWARE FAULT TOLERANCE 348
Recovery Blocks 348
N-Version Programming 352
Other Software Fault Tolerance Papers 352
Exception Handling 356

AUTHOR INDEX 359

SUBJECT INDEX 363

FOREWORD

The notion of incorporating means for tolerating faults in order to improve the reliability of a computing system has become well established since the original work on this topic by von Neumann in the mid-1950s. The extent to which such techniques are actually used has of course varied as computer hardware technologies have changed, and has depended on the stringency of the reliability requirements that have had to be satisfied. Nevertheless, as ever more computers have been employed on highly critical tasks, so the use of fault tolerance has increased and spread from the military and aerospace community (which funded much of the early development) into more general industrial and commercial environments.

Originally, fault tolerance techniques were designed solely to cope with predictable malfunctions of individual hardware components. However, as computing systems have been put to use in increasingly complex situations, so system complexity itself has become one of the major barriers to achieving the extremely high levels of reliability that are often required. Since much of this complexity is, for good reasons, found in the software rather than the hardware components of a computing system, the need has arisen for a fresh and more general system viewpoint on fault tolerance, encompassing both hardware and software. Two particularly important questions must be considered. First, how should measures for fault tolerance be incorporated so that they do not themselves exacerbate the situation, by contributing excessive additional complexity (rather than reliability) to a system? Second, how can fault tolerance measures contribute to the problem of coping with the residual design faults that all too often exist as evidence of the designers' inadequate mastery of the complexity of their system?

It was thoughts such as these that led the writer and his colleagues to set up a broad-based research project on system fault tolerance at the University of Newcastle upon

Tyne some nine years ago. The present book is, in many ways, one of the major results of this research. The authors, leading members of the research project, have achieved an admirable synthesis of the major hardware and software issues in, and of the best current practice concerning, the design of fault tolerant computing systems. They have done this through a carefully balanced yet very readable discussion of basic ideas and concepts, and of the technical details of a number of important contemporary fault tolerant computing systems. Their text has clearly benefitted from the considerable experience both authors have had of presenting seminars and advanced courses on the material, to academic and industrial audiences in the U.K. and the U.S.A. I can therefore warmly recommend it for use both as a university-level text book, and by the designers of all computing systems on which any great degree of reliance is to be placed - and what other worthwhile systems are there?

Brian Randell

Computing Laboratory
University of Newcastle upon Tyne

March 1981

PREFACE

Fault tolerance is not a new topic; since the 1950s fault tolerance techniques have been adopted in computing systems in order to achieve highly reliable hardware operation. Although considerable effort has been devoted to the development of techniques which provide tolerance for specific hardware component faults, much less attention has been paid to more general aspects of fault tolerance. In particular, techniques capable of providing tolerance to faults in the design of either hardware or software are rarely incorporated in a system - indeed, in most fault tolerant systems the design is assumed to be free from faults. However, we feel that a general approach to fault tolerance (one which is appropriate even for design faults) is now essential, for two reasons. Firstly, software is, and will remain, a critical part of any highly reliable computing system; the importance of software-fault tolerance techniques can only increase. Secondly, the growing complexity of hardware design possible through the advent of VLSI technology will make design faults a problem which, hitherto, has had little impact on hardware systems. VLSI technology is already detracting from the effectiveness of many of the specific fault tolerance techniques designed for discrete component systems.

Since 1972 the Science Research Council (SRC) of Great Britain has sponsored an ongoing programme of research at the University of Newcastle upon Tyne investigating reliability in computing systems. Two major projects, directed by Brian Randell, were initially concerned with techniques for tolerating faults in software systems, but subsequently generalized these techniques to provide an overall systems approach to fault tolerance. This book is an outgrowth of the work of these projects.

This book is unique in that, to our knowledge, it is the only book which concentrates solely on the fault tolerance approach to computing systems reliability. Moreover, the book presents a general approach to fault tolerance which encompasses the specific techniques that have been applied in hardware systems while covering the more powerful techniques necessary to tolerate faults in the software and design of a system. The book examines the principles which underly all fault tolerance techniques and the means by which these principles can be implemented in practice. The importance of structure is stressed, and a framework is presented within which a structured and coherent approach to implementation can be undertaken. Throughout the book, examination of the principles and techniques is illustrated by means of practical examples taken from state-of-the-art fault tolerant systems.

The book contains ten chapters covering the following topics. Chapter 1 is introductory in nature, discussing why fault tolerance is necessary in many computing systems, and stating some of the basic premises adopted in this book. Chapter 2 establishes a model of system structure which provides a basis for the discussions of fault tolerance in subsequent chapters. This chapter also introduces basic terminology - for example, terms such as *fault, error* and *failure* are given precise but general definitions. Chapter 3 examines the fundamental principles of fault tolerance, discussing the role and use of redundancy, and introducing a framework to support the implementation of fault tolerance in computing systems. To place the material presented in perspective, Chapter 4 describes seven fault tolerant systems which are used to exemplify the topics discussed in subsequent chapters.

Chapters 5 to 8 are concerned with the four constituent phases of fault tolerance. Each chapter discusses the measures that can be implemented, and the mechanisms that can be provided to assist an implementation. Following these, Chapter 9 presents recent developments in the area of software-fault tolerance, that is, methods of constructing software systems capable of tolerating the effects of software 'bugs'. This novel area of research is likely to be of increasing importance as computing systems are used in ever more critical applications. The final chapter, Chapter 10, draws together some of the conclusions from the earlier chapters.

Each chapter contains its own comprehensive set of references which are listed (in order of citation) at the end of the chapter. An extensive annotated bibliography supplements these references, and contains three sections. The first section covers overall references to conference proceedings, books and articles which discuss fault tolerance in general. The second section provides comprehensive, annotated references for the 15 major fault tolerant computing systems known to the authors. The final section covers the field of software-fault tolerance. A complete reference list sorted alphabetically by author (over 200 entries in total) follows Chapter 10.

This book will be of direct benefit to teachers, practitioners and researchers of fault tolerance. Courses on system reliability are becoming a common and important part of university computer science curricula at both undergraduate and postgraduate level, and the fault tolerance issues covered by this book will be directly relevant to such courses. (Indeed, the book should support the development of new specialized courses based on fault tolerance, for final year undergraduate or postgraduate teaching.) Practitioners will, we hope, benefit from our distillation of the principles of fault tolerance which can serve two purposes. Firstly, the book provides a starting point for the design of a fault tolerant system, identifying the topics which must be addressed. Secondly, the principles may be used to examine and develop existing systems by providing a new approach to viewing the provision of fault tolerance and perhaps exposing deficiencies in an existing design. Researchers workers in the area of fault tolerance will also benefit from the comprehensive set of references provided and from the annotated bibliography.

The material contained in this book owes much to the work of past and present members, too numerous to mention individually, of the aforementioned SRC projects, many of whom have helped us by reading drafts and providing valuable comments. In particular we would like to thank Ron Kerr and Brian Randell for their diligent reading of earlier versions. The financial support of the SRC (latterly under the Distributed Computing Systems programme coordinated by Rob Witty), and access to their facilities for producing camera-ready copy, are gratefully acknowledged. Without sustained pressure from Henry Hirschberg of Prentice-Hall we would not have embarked on, or completed, the writing of this book. For help in its production we are indebted to: Julie Lennox who typed our almost illegible drafts; Colin Prosser of the SRC Rutherford Laboratories who programmed a minor miracle to enable camera-ready copy to be generated; and Ron Decent of Prentice-Hall who guided us through the quagmire of typesetter's jargon.

Despite all of this assistance, no doubt some faults still still remain in this book. We hope our readers will tolerate them.

Tom Anderson
Pete Lee

Computing Laboratory
University of Newcastle upon Tyne

March 1981

1

INTRODUCTION

There have been many technological advances in the organization and construction of computing systems, and developments are still progressing at a great pace. Hardware developments are producing systems with ever decreasing cost and size, and with increasing power and complexity. Since computers are an inherent part of many aspects of present day life it is clear that these advances and developments will give added impetus to the utilization of computer systems in many different areas.

Computing systems are already used in a wide variety of applications, such as: defense systems, flight systems, air traffic control, roller coaster control, banking systems, airline seat reservation systems, telephone systems, household appliances, TV games, and so on. Applications as diverse as these would have widely differing consequences resulting from a malfunction of their embedded computing system. Hence there are widely differing requirements for the reliability and availability of computers. At one extreme, wrong outputs from a computer may simply be inconvenient; at the other end of the spectrum, where human lives and/or vast sums of money may be at stake, erroneous outputs or no outputs at all simply cannot be tolerated.

At present there are few systems where human lives are absolutely dependent on a computing system. For example, computers in civil aircraft normally provide useful but non-critical functions. In the event of a computer malfunction the crew can intervene and take over the responsibilities of the computer. However, as more and more complex applications need to be automated it will be necessary to rely more heavily on computing systems; eventually manual intervention will no longer be a feasible backup measure. Some examples of this are already to be seen. The Space Shuttle is a vehicle which is *totally* dependent on the proper operation of its computers; a mission cannot even be aborted if the computers fail. Other examples are likely to arise from the Aircraft Energy Efficiency Program being sponsored by the National Aeronautics and Space Administration (NASA), where computer control will be essential to provide the fine degree of control surface actuation required to maintain the stability of fuel-efficient aircraft, a degree of control which the crew could not achieve.

Most applications of computing systems do not have the absolute requirement for reliability of the above examples, where incorrect computations or loss of service would be totally unacceptable. In some applications the reliability requirements place emphasis on the integrity of the data entrusted to the computing system. For example, in data base systems used to retain valuable information, the main reliability requirement is that the data should not be lost or corrupted; short losses of service may, however, be quite acceptable. In other applications the availability of the facilities provided by the computer system may be of paramount importance. For example, in computer controlled telephone switching systems there is a prime requirement for maximum availability of the computer, although it is permissible for a small percentage of telephone calls to be incorrectly handled (the assumption being that customers will tolerate infrequently arising faults).

The provision of a degraded service in the presence of faults may be adequate for some applications. For instance, if part of the backing store holding the data base for an airline seat reservation system failed, the system could still accept a reservation although delaying the issue of tickets until the fault had been repaired and the reservation confirmed (or cancelled). Even in apparently non-critical areas reliability will be an important consideration - no one will want to buy an automobile with an engine controlled by

INTRODUCTION

a microprocessor which fails, albeit safely, every few hundred miles.

It seems clear that there are already applications in which the reliability of the computing system is of the utmost importance, and other critical applications are being developed. Also it is likely that the availability of highly reliable computing systems would further promote their consideration for other critical applications, and for achieving greater efficiency in areas which, hitherto, have been limited by the capacity of manual or mechanical operators.

How then is reliability to be achieved in computing systems?

Unreliability in any system, computing or otherwise, is a consequence of *faults* in the system. Computing systems are by their nature very complex objects; they contain large numbers of sub-systems and components with complex interrelationships, implemented in both hardware and software. Consequently, there are many things that could go wrong in a computing system and hence often do go wrong, usually in a variety of ways. In order to provide reliable computing systems there are two complementary approaches which can be adopted. The most obvious and direct course of action is to attempt to ensure that a computing system is, and remains, free from faults. This requires that potential faults are avoided in the first place, that any faults which remain are exposed and eliminated before reliance is placed on that system, and that new faults do not develop. This approach is termed *fault prevention* since the aim is to prevent faults from being present in the operational system. The second approach accepts that an implemented system will not be perfect, and that measures are therefore required to enable the operational system to cope with the faults that remain or develop. This latter approach, termed *fault tolerance,* forms the subject matter of this book.

FAULT PREVENTION AND FAULT TOLERANCE

The traditional approach to achieving reliability in computing systems has been largely based on fault prevention, the goal of which is to prevent system failure by ensuring that all possible causes of unreliability have been removed from the system before reliance is placed on its operation. There are two aspects to fault prevention, namely *fault avoidance* and *fault removal*.

Fault avoidance is concerned with design methodologies and the selection of techniques and technologies which aim to avoid the introduction of faults during the design and construction of a system. The use of reliable components and proven interconnection technology, methodologies for coping with the complexities of hardware and software designs, formal methods for verifying logic designs and proving programs, are all examples of techniques for fault avoidance.

Despite the adoption of fault avoidance techniques, faults are usually present in a constructed system, for instance, because of the unavailability (or cost) of fault-free hardware components, or because the enormous complexity inherent in computing systems results in oversights and faults in their design. Fault removal is concerned with checking the implementation of a system and removing any faults which are thereby exposed. For example, a system can be extensively tested to reveal faulty hardware components and faults in the design of the hardware and software. Following fault removal, the system will be put into operation. Of course, if faults develop (or remain) then system failure is likely to ensue, and manual intervention will then be required to cope with the situation. (Systems with this characteristic are sometimes labelled fault-intolerant.)[1]

The application of fault prevention techniques to a system has not, in general, proved sufficient for the attainment of high reliability. In particular, fault avoidance and removal were found to be insufficient for reliable operation of the hardware in computing systems because physical components age and deteriorate and can therefore become faulty. It was recognized that *fault tolerance* was often required, at least to protect the system against such hardware component faults.

Fault tolerance at the hardware level in a system is by no means a new concept, and as early as 1956 there were proposals for adding extra (redundant) hardware components to systems to achieve higher reliability,[2] proposals made necessary by the unreliability of the components from which early machines were constructed. Following the development of semiconductor technology, hardware components became intrinsically more reliable and the need diminished for tolerance of component failures in general purpose computing systems. Nevertheless, fault tolerant hardware was still necessary for some specialized applications which had reliability requirements such that fault prevention alone was insufficient. For example, a requirement for one computer controlled telephone switching system was that there should be less than two hours down-time in 40 years.[3] In consequence, the theory and practice of fault tolerance for hardware is now well established and several fault tolerant systems have been designed and built, some of which will be discussed later. Given this expertise, why then is a book on fault tolerance in computing systems required? This is discussed below.

ANTICIPATED AND UNANTICIPATED FAULTS

An examination of the computing systems that have been proposed or built and which include fault tolerance strategies will reveal that such strategies have only been adopted to provide protection against those faults that had been *anticipated* during the design of the system. The only faults that could be anticipated with any degree of accuracy were those arising from the failures of hardware components, for which quantitative measures were available (at least for the discrete components from which early systems were constructed). Given the expected probabilities of component failures, it was relatively straightforward for the system designer to identify those failures likely to occur in the operational system. Once identified, the consequences of a failure could be anticipated, and appropriate fault tolerance measures incorporated in the system to detect when (if) the failure occurred and to ensure that correct system operation could be maintained.

While the anticipation of faults has been successful in the past for hardware, the present trend towards very large scale integration is already casting doubt on the validity of the assumption that all component failure modes are known. The failure modes of, say, a diode are easy to anticipate and its limited set of inputs and outputs simplifies the strategies required to detect and deal with such failures. In comparison, there are millions of ways in which a microprocessor chip could fail and it becomes impossible to enumerate all failure modes and anticipate their consequences, let alone design specific measures to cope with each failure. It follows that *unanticipated faults* are likely to arise in hardware systems, and will certainly require tolerance in high reliability applications.

However, there is a much more important and insidious reason for the occurrence of unanticipated situations. If there are *faults in the design* of a system then the effects of such faults will be unanticipated (and unanticipatable!).

Design faults at the hardware level of a computer correspond, for instance, to wrong or missing interconnections between components, or even to the wrong choice of components. If tolerance for such faults was necessary, there would then be a need to cope with the unexpected. Fortunately, the designs of hardware systems have been sufficiently simple that standard fault prevention techniques have largely ensured that design faults were eliminated from the system, although design faults in hardware systems are by no means unknown. (When found, such faults are often regarded as features of the system!) Methods have been developed for designing hardware circuits so that a (limited) set of test patterns can be automatically generated and used to provide the equivalent of exhaustive testing, so that the correctness of a design can be substantiated. Formal methods of verifying the intended operation of a hardware design have also been devised. (A detailed discussion of these techniques is given elsewhere.)[4] In consequence, existing fault tolerant systems rarely, if ever, provide measures to tolerate design faults.

While design faults may have been uncommon in hardware systems, the only type of fault that can be introduced into a non-physical system, such as a system implemented in software, is a design fault (this will be discussed in more detail in Chapter 2). Applications of the fault prevention techniques that have been successful for exposing design faults in hardware systems have only met with limited success when applied to software. Given the relative complexities of the hardware and software in computing systems this is not surprising. Hardware systems have been comparatively straightforward, with limited and constrained interconnections and simple interactions between components. In contrast, software systems can be enormously complex, with a vast set of possible states making exhaustive testing impossible to achieve, and with complicated designs which currently defeat efforts aimed at proving programs to be correct by formal methods.

Nevertheless, fault prevention has remained the standard approach for attempting to produce reliable software systems. Indeed, the majority of developments in the software field have aimed to improve the fault prevention approach to software reliability - requirements definitions, precise specifications, design methodologies, structured programming techniques, proving, testing, documentation techniques, the development of high level programming languages, and software management all attempt to prevent mistakes being made and thereby eliminate the presence of faults from the run-time system.[5,6,7,8]

Despite such developments it has become widely recognized that faults in software are a major cause of failures in computing systems. For example, the Apollo series of lunar missions involved one of the most carefully planned and executed software projects that has ever been undertaken. Despite the no-expense-spared approach (approximately $660 million was spent on software for Apollo) almost every major problem in the series was the direct result of software design faults.[9] Another spectacular example of a failure caused by software occurred in 1971 during a French meteorological experiment involving 141 atmospheric balloons. Instruments in each balloon responded to two commands: a read command which caused the data that had been collected to be relayed to a satellite for subsequent transmission to ground stations, and an abort command in case a balloon went astray, which caused the balloon to explode. Unfortunately, a fault in the software controlling the experiment caused an erroneous abort signal to be sent, and as a result 72 balloons were destroyed.[10] (Boehm[11] and Myers[5] give some other examples.)

Since the major part of the complexity of a system to be implemented on a computer is left to the software designer, and given the difficulties that seem to be inherent in the production of fault-free software, it is not surprising that operational software systems contain design faults. What is surprising is that, until recently, tolerance for software faults has not been advocated and that almost all software research has been applied to chasing the elusive goal of producing perfect software. If attainable, perfect software has the attractive property that if left alone it will always remain free from faults; this may have been one reason for the exclusion of fault tolerance. Another reason may simply have been the pragmatic observation that it is difficult to cope with the unpredictable consequences of design faults. Clearly, the problem of design faults in software must be mastered if reliable computing systems are to be achieved. While it can be expected that the effectiveness of fault prevention approaches to software construction will continue to improve, it is highly unlikely that complex software systems will ever be completely free from design faults. Moreover, software systems are rarely static and, due to the comparative ease with which they can be changed, are continually being modified and enhanced with the risk that new design faults are thereby introduced.

Design faults are not solely a software problem, but a problem that occurs in all complex systems. Unmastered complexity at any level in a system will give rise to design faults. Very large scale integration technology is enabling the complexity of hardware to be increased to such an extent that the well-established techniques for preventing design faults will no longer be adequate, and design faults will therefore be a further cause of unanticipated faults in future hardware systems. A basic premise of this book is that tolerance of design faults or, more generally, tolerance of unanticipated faults, will be necessary for the provision of highly reliable computing systems.

BOOK AIM

To summarize the previous sections, reliability in computing systems may be enhanced by fault prevention and by providing measures to tolerate those faults which remain in the operational system. In the past, fault tolerance has only been applied to computer hardware, specifically to cope with the anticipated situations arising from component failures. However, the preceding section has argued that tolerance for unanticipated faults will also be required. Unfortunately, the techniques which have been developed and adopted for coping with anticipated faults do not suffice if unanticipated faults occur, since measures designed for specific situations cannot be expected to cope with the unpredictable consequences of faults which have not been foreseen. New and more general fault tolerance techniques are required.

This book attempts to describe a general approach to the principles and practice of fault tolerance, encompassing both the existing work on tolerance for anticipated faults and recent developments for tolerating unanticipated situations, such as those arising from design faults. The book discusses the overall design of fault tolerant computing systems and examines the implementation issues that arise. The principles that are described are applicable to all aspects of a computing system, both hardware and software. This, it is felt, is of particular importance since the distinction between hardware and software is becoming more and more blurred (one man's hardware is often another man's microprogram).

To place the material presented in this book in perspective, a series of state-of-the-art systems which have been designed to be fault tolerant will be examined. The specific approaches adopted in these systems will be used throughout the book to provide exemplification of the various techniques as they are discussed.

It is not the purpose of this book to discuss at length or in detail the techniques which have been successfully used for the provision of hardware component fault tolerance. Many publications on this subject are available - extensive reference lists are provided by Carter[4] and by Avizienis.[12]

Moreover, technological advances are, as mentioned before, invalidating many of the assumptions on which previous work has been based. The book also omits detailed discussion of the many fault prevention techniques which have been applied to both software and hardware systems. This is not to say that fault prevention will play no part in the attainment of high reliability. Fault prevention is of course highly praiseworthy, and its importance in the provision of high reliability cannot be overstressed. However, very high standards of reliability can only be achieved through the application of both fault prevention and fault tolerance; a basic assumption made in this book is that despite the application of fault prevention, complex systems will always be affected by faults. The book therefore concentrates on fault tolerance, with particular emphasis given to the techniques necessary for tolerating unanticipated faults, an area which has received little attention until recently.

REFERENCES

1. A. Avizienis, "Fault-Tolerant Systems," *IEEE Transactions on Computers* **C-25**(12), pp.1304-1312 (December 1976).
2. J. von Neumann, "Probabilistic Logics and the Synthesis of Reliable Organisms from Unreliable Components," pp. 43-98 in *Automata Studies*, ed. C.E. Shannon and J. McCarthy, Princeton University Press, Princeton (NJ) (1956).
3. R.W. Downing, J.S. Nowak, and L.S. Tuomenoksa, "The No. 1 ESS Maintenance Plan," *Bell System Technical Journal* **43**(5), pp.1961-2020 (September 1964).
4. W.C. Carter, "Hardware Reliability," pp. 211-263 in *Computing Systems Reliability*, ed. T. Anderson and B. Randell, Cambridge University Press, Cambridge (1979).
5. G.J. Myers, *Software Reliability: Principles and Practices*, Wiley, New York (1976).

REFERENCES

6. D.E. Morgan and D.J. Taylor, "A Survey of Methods of Achieving Reliable Software," *Computer*, pp.44-53 (February 1977).
7. R.T. Yeh and K.M. Chandy (eds.), *Current Trends in Programming Methodology (Volumes 1-4)*, Prentice-Hall, Englewood Cliffs (NJ) (1978).
8. T. Anderson and B. Randell (eds.), *Computing Systems Reliability*, Cambridge University Press, Cambridge (1979).
9. E. Ulsamer, "Computers - Key to Tomorrow's Air Force," *Air Force Magazine* **56**(7), pp.46-52 (July 1973).
10. Anon., "Blown Balloons," *Aviation Week & Space Technology*, p.17 (September 20 1971).
11. B.W. Boehm, "Software and its Impact: A Quantitative Assessment," *Datamation* **19**(5), pp.48-59 (May 1973).
12. A. Avizienis, "Fault-Tolerance: The Survival Attribute of Digital Systems," *Proceedings of the IEEE* **66**(10), pp.1109-1125 (October 1978).

2

SYSTEM STRUCTURE AND RELIABILITY

Most computing systems are extremely complex, as is evidenced by the intricacy of their implementations. This complexity is to some extent a consequence of the many and various requirements which are routinely imposed on these systems: requirements for general purpose facilities, and at the same time for highly specialized facilities; requirements to provide service to numerous users with diverse demands, and to provide this service simultaneously (or seemingly so); requirements for extremely sophisticated facilities, and for simple and convenient access to those facilities; requirements for prompt and timely service, and for efficient, economical and reliable operation. It can be persuasively argued that modern computing systems constitute the most complex artifacts ever constructed. Given the complexity of these systems, and accepting that their design and construction are susceptible to the inherent fallibility of those who design and construct, it would be surprising indeed if a modern computing system provided its intended service with perfect reliability.

To obtain substantial gains in reliability it is essential that the level of complexity of systems is brought under control. The designers of hardware for computing systems have made a virtue out of necessity by accepting the constraints imposed by physical factors (e.g. limits on the number of components which can be interconnected). By adhering to strictly enforced design disciplines applied to components having relatively simple interfaces an enviable degree of control has been maintained over the complexity of hardware systems. However, these disciplines may well prove inadequate as advances in VLSI expose hardware designers to the problems of complexity which have always confronted software designers.

Software has one great advantage over hardware, and that is the ease with which it can be constructed and subsequently modified. Software systems are built, extended and adjusted to meet changing requirements simply by typing appropriate characters on a key-board (the difficulties all lie in selecting those characters). The relative difficulty and cost of making belated design changes in hardware systems has meant that the complexity of most computing systems is largely to be found in their software. For this reason much ongoing research is concerned with mastering software complexity. Techniques such as structured programming,[1] step-wise refinement,[2] top-down development,[3] information hiding[4] and separation of concerns[5] have a common thread in that they all embrace the principle of divide and (hope to) conquer. The notion of abstract data types and the programming languages which provide, to a greater or lesser extent, encapsulation mechanisms by which a programmer can define his own data types,[6] are founded on the same principle. All of these techniques try to ensure that a system is not constructed as a monolithic entity.

It is now widely accepted that systems should be designed and implemented so that they are well-structured, being built up as a coherent assembly of component subsystems, which are themselves built up from smaller components, and so on. Ideally, each stage of combining a set of component systems to form some larger system should be kept sufficiently simple for it to be easily comprehended, in order to minimize the risk of mistakes in design. Although such an approach cannot be expected to eliminate all faults from an operational system, the identification and imposition of structure when the system is being designed and constructed should greatly reduce the number of residual faults.

It is particularly necessary to maintain system structure when fault tolerance techniques are considered. If the structure which the system designer envisaged is indeed present in the actual implementation of a system, and if the constraints implied by that structure are enforced during the operation of the system, then assumptions may be made which greatly simplify the provision of fault tolerance. Furthermore, a well-structured approach to the design and inclusion of fault tolerance techniques is a prerequisite for their success; an unstructured approach could easily reduce system reliability by introducing more faults than those to which tolerance was provided.

System structure can be seen to have a major impact on system reliability in general, and on fault tolerance in particular. Indeed, many issues concerning the reliability of a system can only be discussed with respect to certain basic notions of structure. The first section of this chapter establishes terminology for these basic notions, and presents a framework in which issues of fault tolerance are discussed in subsequent chapters. An elementary model of a system is introduced for this purpose.

Terminology is also the concern of the second section of the chapter where precise, but informal and (it is believed) intuitively satisfying, definitions are given for a number of reliability concepts. Accurate isolation and identification of the relevant concepts is crucial for much of the discussion in the following chapters.

SYSTEM STRUCTURE

The notion of a system is extremely general, and has a role in all disciplines. Even when attention is restricted to computing systems there is enormous variation; for example, in cost, power and complexity (from a simple pocket calculator to a Cray super computer) and in requirements, utility and implementation (from the software of a military command and control system to the electronic circuitry of a TV game). This section examines a very simple model for systems which, by virtue of its simplicity, is believed to be very widely applicable. In consequence it suffers from certain limitations, but nevertheless provides a basic framework with respect to which various aspects of structure, reliability and fault tolerance can be examined.

Before embarking on the presentation of the system model it is appropriate that the notion of a system should be given a more precise meaning. A beginning can be made by asserting that a *system* is any identifiable mechanism which maintains a pattern of behavior at an interface between the mechanism and its environment. An *interface* is simply a place of interaction between two systems.

The word 'interface' is sometimes used with a different meaning (particularly in the context of hardware systems). The second meaning (which is *not* used in this book) is that any apparatus used to connect two devices constitutes an interface. Since the apparatus is just as much a device as those it connects, and device is merely a synonym for system, it should be clear that opportunities for confusion abound if the second meaning is used as well as the first. The definition adopted here has the merit of specializing the original meaning: a surface forming a common boundary.

A system is said to interact with its *environment*, and responds to stimuli at the interface between the system and the environment. The environment of a system is another system which provides input to and receives output from the first system; thus the system can provide service in response to requests from the environment. The external behavior of a system can be described in terms of a finite set of states, the external states of the system. At discrete instants of time the system makes a transition from one external state to another, and thus moves through a sequence of external states.

Thus, a system maintains behavior at the interface between the system and its environment. An asymmetric view of this interface concentrates on the behavioral properties of a given system, taking as understood that these properties are only determined with respect to a second system operating as its environment. In this way it is legitimate to refer to the interface of a single system, when a more strict interpretation would always require an interface to be between two systems.

SYSTEM STRUCTURE

Since a system can exhibit behavior in many different forms, it is often convenient to limit attention to a subset of the behavior of a system. A curtailed view of a system can be defined by applying a simple abstraction function to the system interface. It is often appropriate to consider disjoint subsets of the behavior of a system as corresponding to separate interfaces of that system (strictly, the separate interfaces should be thought of as sub-interfaces of the single interface between the system and its environment). A large computing system maintains an immensely complicated interface with its environment, but some simplification can be obtained by considering the system to support a number of disjoint interfaces. Among these interfaces will be: interfaces for receiving input from card and paper tape readers; interfaces for producing output on line-printers and graph-plotters; interfaces for interaction with operators and users at terminals; interfaces for maintenance and support by service staff. Many of these interfaces are usually envisaged as being further subdivided. For instance, a user at a terminal will regard the operating system command language interface as a means of gaining access to a wide range of other system interfaces which provide facilities such as file editing or message passing; further interfaces are those supported by the various language processors and application packages available. Finally, there are interfaces to the system which are perhaps of limited interest, such as the interfaces to the air conditioning unit, the power supplies and the fire alarms. All of these interfaces exhibit selected subsets of the overall behavior of the computing system.

System Model

The above attempt to characterize systems in terms of what they *do* (i.e. support behavior at an interface) is only concerned with the external characteristics of a system. A model of the internal structure of systems must address the issue of what a system *is* by stipulating the way in which systems are built up from their constituent parts.

Following Melliar-Smith and Randell,[7] a *system* is defined to consist of a set of components which interact under the control of a design. A *component* of a system is another system. Indeed, the *design* of a system is also a system, but has special characteristics which are discussed below. Although definitions are often circular, the recursion involved is not usually as explicit or as deliberate as that employed here. A justification for this circularity is that any implemented system will be founded on some physical system, and the physical sciences seem to suggest that physical systems may well incorporate just such a recursion.

"Great fleas have little fleas upon their backs to bite 'em,
And little fleas have lesser fleas, and so *ad infinitum*."[8]

As a special case (and to avoid infinite recursion) a system may be considered to be *atomic*, with the implication that any further internal structure of the system cannot be discerned, or is not of interest and can be ignored.

The external behavior of a system is the manifestation of internal activity within the system, and for a non-atomic system this activity can be examined in more detail. The *internal state* of a system is defined to be the ordered set of the external states of its components; the external state of a system is simply an abstraction of its internal state. Note that the state of a system is defined without reference to the design of the system. This is intended to distinguish the ongoing activity of the system from its internal organization (which is usually fixed).

A system will move through a sequence of internal states as a consequence of changes of state by its components; these changes are determined by interactions between the components. The pattern of these interactions is established and controlled by the design of the system, which also determines the way in which interactions between the system and its environment impinge upon the components. It must be stressed that throughout this book the *design* of a system refers to that part of the system which actually supports and controls the interactions of the components, and does *not* refer to either the abstract concept of a system design as envisaged by its designer (e.g. as embodied in a blueprint) or to the process by which the system was designed. This rather strict interpretation is adopted to ensure that a deficiency in the design of a system (discussed in the next section) refers to a deficiency which is actually present in the system, and hence can affect its operation.

Thus, a system contains a set of component subsystems, which cooperate so that their combined activity generates the external behavior of the system. The design of the system should be thought of as whatever else is present in the system which enables, directs and sustains the cooperation between the components, and their relationship to the system environment. In general, the design must ensure that each component receives as input an appropriate subset of the outputs from all of the other components. Furthermore, the design is responsible for channelling system input to the components, and also for generating the system output as an abstraction of the component outputs.

The system definitions adopted here are intended to be sufficiently general that they are applicable to any real system. In particular they cover computer systems considered as assemblies of physical components, and can be applied at many different levels in such systems. A single circuit board can be regarded as a system - the components are the electronic components soldered to the board while the design is implemented as the tracks and wires which provide their interconnection. A CPU can be considered as a system with components such as registers, logical and addressing units, with a design consisting of the control units and data highways linking them. A complete computer system has as components the central processor, primary and secondary storage, and peripherals, with the design implemented as the data buses and cabling which interconnect them.

It can certainly be argued that in all of the above examples what has been asserted to constitute the design could be regarded as just another component (or set of components). For example, the control units of a CPU may be regarded as components and not part of the design (indeed, the data highways could also be regarded as components). However, no matter what set of components are selected there must still exist some means by which these components interact, and this will form the design. If desired, a physical system can be regarded as a collection of components whose interactions are determined solely by their geometrical disposition, with interconnection effected by juxtaposition. The design is then merely the positioning of the components and as such is perhaps rather trivial. In many systems it is very unnatural to adopt such an extreme position, which could involve regarding a large number of blobs of solder as separate components in a computer system. Furthermore, physical juxtaposition is not available in an abstract system (such as a software system).

To apply the system model to software systems a more abstract view of a computing system must be adopted. From this viewpoint, the activity of the system is not generated by physical components but by abstract components usually referred to as *processes*. The activity of a process can be thought of as the sequence of actions generated when a program or set of programs is executed (Horning and Randell[9] present a detailed formal treatment of the notion of a process). Thus, a software system can be viewed as a single comprehensive process which, in general, can be structured as a set of interacting processes forming the components of that system. Each process, in turn, may consist of a further set of (sub)processes, and so on. The means by which processes interact (e.g. message passing or shared variables) and the mechanisms which control their interactions (e.g. semaphores or monitors) constitute the design of the software system. In this context, process is a synonym for component or system; all of the discussion on system structure can be related to processes. The dependence of a process on the underlying hardware to sustain its existence is disregarded here, but will be returned to later in this section when structure internal to a single sequential process is examined.

It is useful to have a pictorial representation for systems modelled as a set of components and a design. A simple *system diagram* is shown in Figure 2.1 for a system with n components $c_1, \ldots, c_n$ and design d. The line connecting each component to the design indicates that the component sends its output to and receives its input from the design. The line connecting the design to the outside world indicates that system input and output is handled by the design. Although this representation has the virtue of being general purpose, it is rather uninformative since the only system specific information it conveys is the number and names of the components, and the name of the design.

SYSTEM STRUCTURE

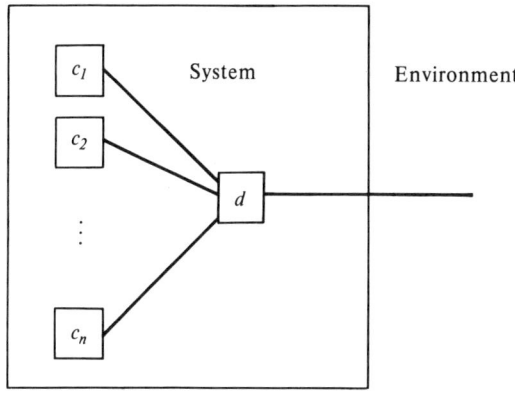

Figure 2.1 General System Diagram

A more useful representation, which is widely used in practice, omits the design but displays the interconnections between components. A diagram of this type will be called an *interaction diagram* because it conveys some information about the pattern of component interactions enforced by the design. In an interaction diagram, any two components which interact are shown connected by a line (with arrows indicating input and output). Lines entering the system from outside indicate which components receive system input; lines leaving the system indicate which components produce system output. An (artificial) example of a system with four components c_1, c_2, c_3, c_4 is represented in this way in Figure 2.2. Although an interaction diagram presents useful information about which components interact, it obviously does not completely describe their interactions. To obtain more detailed information it would be necessary to examine the design of the system.

An interaction diagram corresponds quite closely to the intuitive concept of a system as a collection of interacting components, particularly for physical systems. The only systems for which the general system diagram is more appropriate are those in which the design is actually implemented as a form of switching network. For such systems, the system diagram becomes an interaction diagram if the

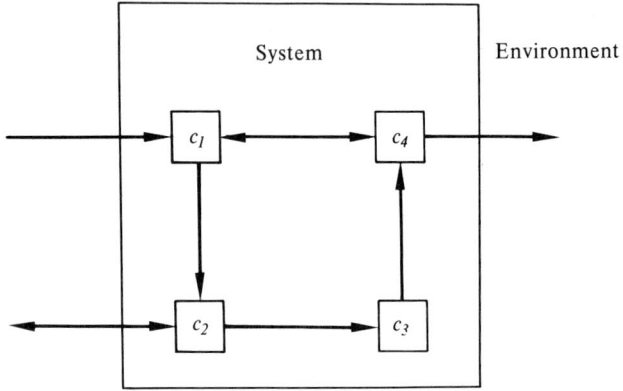

Figure 2.2 Example Interaction Diagram

design is regarded as a component of the system (of course, the resulting system still has a design - that indicated by the lines in Figure 2.1 when it is considered to be an interaction diagram for a system having $n+1$ components).

Interconnections between components correspond to internal interfaces within the system, and this is a natural interpretation for the lines in an interaction diagram. Labels are often attached to these lines, either to name an interface or (more commonly) to indicate the form of interactions which take place on an interface.

An interaction diagram for a physical system could often be referred to as an interconnection diagram since the design of a physical system is often implemented as a set of interconnections between components - very much as is indicated by an interaction diagram. Complicated combinations of processors, storage, peripherals etc. are easily portrayed in this way. As an example, Figure 2.3 depicts the main computing system at the University of Newcastle upon Tyne. Several other examples are given in Chapter 4. Interaction diagrams can also be used to exhibit lower level structure in a computing system, such as the internal organization of a CPU or the layout of a circuit board. Circuit diagrams for electrical and electronic circuits are very similar to interaction diagrams.

SYSTEM STRUCTURE

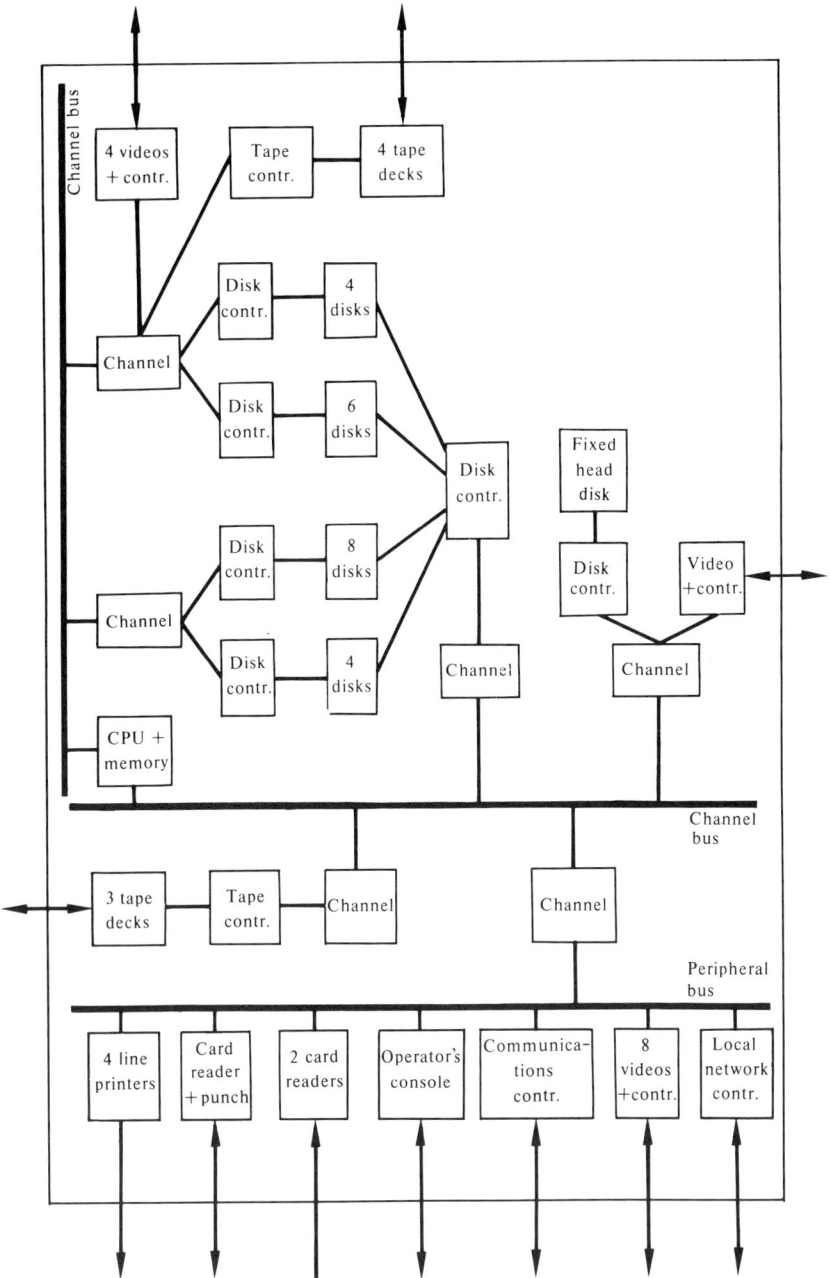

Figure 2.3 University Computing System

The pattern of interaction between the processes of a software system (e.g. the processes which provide the facilities of an operating system) could also be indicated by means of an interaction diagram. However, the lines linking processes (components) would then represent logical communication paths rather than physical connections. A form of interaction diagram is an important element in the MASCOT[10] approach to constructing software for real-time systems.

Only one level of the structure of a system can be depicted in an interaction diagram, but further structure can be presented by means of interaction diagrams for each component of the system. This elaboration can be continued until atomic components are reached. The set of interaction diagrams produced in this way are clearly related in the form of a tree. Each separate interaction diagram indicates how a set of components are assembled to form a system whereas the tree structure indicates how a (possibly very large) set of atomic systems can eventually be combined, after a number of intermediate stages of assembly, to form the overall system. (System structure is presented in exactly this form by Ross,[11] who also stipulates that no system should have more than six components.)

The full system structure model with multiple levels is established as follows in terms of an *assembly tree*. Each node of an assembly tree denotes a system. The root of the tree is the node which denotes the overall system whose structure the tree represents. The leaves of the tree denote systems which are considered to be atomic. An upward (towards the root) edge from *node1* to *node2* indicates that the system denoted by *node1* is a component of the system denoted by *node2*. An interaction diagram can be given for the system denoted by any non-leaf node (derived from the design of that system), indicating the interconnections between the component systems denoted by the immediate descendants of that node. However, many other interaction diagrams can be constructed by replacing any component in an interaction diagram by its own interaction diagram. In this way an interaction diagram can be produced for any non-leaf node in terms of nodes forming a cut across the subtree rooted at that node. (A cut across a subtree is a subset of the nodes of the subtree such that (i) every leaf in the subtree is either in the cut or is a descendant of a node in the cut, and (ii) no node in the cut is a descendant of a node in the cut.) The most comprehensive interaction diagram depicts the overall system as the collection of atomic systems denoted by the leaves of the tree.

For systems as defined here, the structuring depicted by an assembly tree will be fixed and unique. However, these systems are intended only as models for real systems. A real system implemented as a multilevel assembly from n atomic systems could have its structure described by any assembly tree with n leaves (there are more than $(n/2)^n$ such trees). Although very few of these trees would depict a suitable structure for a given system, it will often be possible to find more than one structure which is appropriate, albeit in different contexts.

Furthermore, there can be no guarantee that an appropriate assembly tree will be selected - in relation to real systems, structure may be like beauty, and reside only in the eye of the beholder. For an assembly tree and the associated interaction diagrams to model the structure of a real system it is clearly necessary for interactions in the real system to conform to those prescribed by the model. Indeed, it can be argued that structure is only present in a real system to the extent that it is actually enforced by constraints on the interactions between components. Thus in a physical system, structure can usually be identified as a consequence of physical constraints and physical boundaries - the absence of any electrical connection between two peripheral devices of a computing system is a fairly effective constraint on their direct interaction. On a large enough scale, physical structure can often be ascertained simply by looking at a system. Structure in an abstract system (such as a software system) is correspondingly more tenuous.

Structure is the basis of methodologies for designing and constructing both hardware and software for computing systems. When structure envisaged by the designer is absent from an operational system because constraints are omitted or ineffective the consequences can gravely impair the reliability of the system. Two cables in a communications network may be intended to be components in distinct subsystems of the network, but if interaction between signals carried by the cables is possible because of crosstalk the structure of the network will differ from that which was planned. An operating system may be designed to support the execution of separate processes, but if no protection facilities are available a single aberrant or malicious process could overwrite all the others (and the operating system too) with dramatic impact on and implications for the structure of system software.

Software/Hardware Interaction

The system model present above is intended to be appropriate for both hardware and software systems. As indicated by the examples, its application to computing systems viewed either as physical systems (entirely hardware) or as abstract software systems is straightforward. In practice, however, software cannot always be considered in isolation from hardware. Interaction between the software and hardware of a computing system can be viewed (and modelled) in a number of different ways. In this sub-section an approach is presented which has the benefit of enabling the static structure of program texts to be modelled within the standard system framework. Because this approach is a little unconventional, the following sub-section develops a more conventional approach based on interpretive interfaces.

Consider a simple computing system which, viewed as a hardware system, has four components: a card-reader, a line-printer, a memory unit and the CPU. A single program (and its data) is loaded in the memory and executed by the CPU. Regarded as a software system, this computing system can be modelled by a single sequential process encompassing the activity generated by executing the program. In order to examine the internal structure of this process it is necessary to consider the relationship between the hardware and software. An assembly tree for the system in which the leaves represent hardware components is not directly relevant, since the software of the system would not appear as a component. From a hardware viewpoint the software only exists as part of the state of the memory unit and remains essentially passive; programs only differ from data values because of the way they happen to be used by

SYSTEM STRUCTURE

the CPU. An attempt to examine the structure of the software from such a viewpoint is not very illuminating. An examination of the hardware component storing the software would reveal that the software is represented as an addressable sequence of memory words - a valid structure certainly, but hardly a useful one. More detailed examination of the component would merely uncover the internal organization of storage at the bit level.

The approach proposed here is that program text (as represented in memory) should be regarded as the design of an abstract system in which the components are the objects manipulated by the program when executed. A system diagram for this view of the simple system outlined above is presented in Figure 2.4.

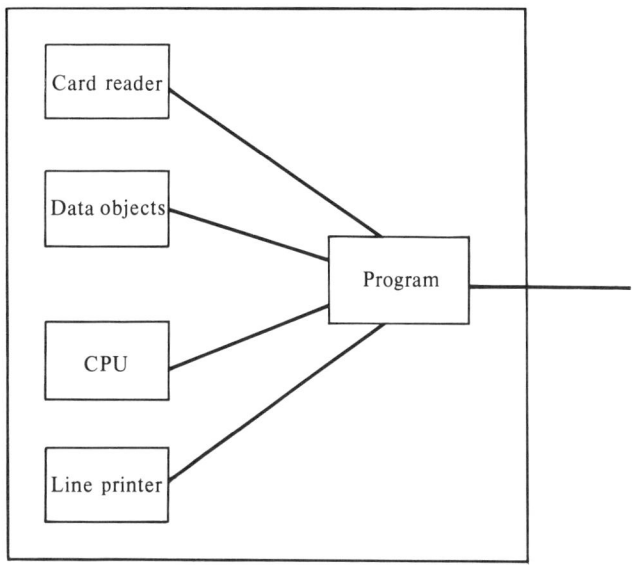

Figure 2.4 Abstract Representation of a Computing System

In this abstract system the components correspond closely to the hardware components of the physical system (as is intended). The card-reader and line-printer are direct images of the actual devices; the data objects are program variables stored in the memory unit; the CPU of the abstract system performs the arithmetic and logical operations provided by the hardware CPU. Note, however, that the abstract CPU does not execute the program; the program is regarded as controlling the interactions between the abstract components.

Internal structure of the abstract components can be modelled by examining the structure of their hardware counterparts. More interestingly, it is possible to model the structure of the program since this also is a system - the design of the abstract system of Figure 2.4. Two points should be noted however.

Firstly, the program to be modelled will consist of binary machine code. As such, its structure may not correspond exactly with that desired by the designer of the program. Much of the structure present in source code is often lost when a program is compiled. Further aberrations may result from mistranslation by the compiler or from corruption due to memory failure. These problems are not avoided by modelling the activity of the system in terms of the language in which the program was coded. Rather they are concealed - which could be dangerous.

Secondly, since the program forms the design of a system, the state of the program itself should not change (in the absence of memory failures). Self modifying programs were proscribed long ago and should certainly not be found in reliable systems. Therefore, interest only attaches to the way that the software is divided into components built up from basic instructions. In an assembly tree for a program, the root corresponds to the program itself while the leaves represent the individual instructions contained in the program. The structure of the assembly tree identifies a hierarchical decomposition of the program and, in principle, any tree with the requisite number of leaves could be used as a structural model of the program. However, such a model will only be useful to the extent that it clarifies some aspect of the organization of the program. Appropriate assembly trees will presumably reflect textual structure present in the source code version of the program, and in this way can portray the basic structure imparted to a program by the use of techniques such as top-down (or bottom-up) design methodologies. Beneficial structure is

SYSTEM STRUCTURE

more likely to be found in programs written in high level languages providing features which encourage modularity - constructs such as subroutines, procedures, classes, forms, clusters, etc.

Interpreters and Multilevel Systems

The most important aspect of the relationship between the hardware and software of a computing system is that the hardware maintains an interface on which the software is executed. As a consequence of the general purpose facilities provided by a hardware computer interface, it is (in principle) possible to construct in software an abstract version of any desired system. The behavior of the computing system can then be regarded as being generated by the abstract system, ignoring the existence of the hardware. This sub-section discusses hardware/software interactions in terms of the interface on which the software is executed, and examines systems in which a hierarchy of such interfaces can be identified.

Consider a system C with two separate interfaces, one for receiving stimuli and the other for producing responses:

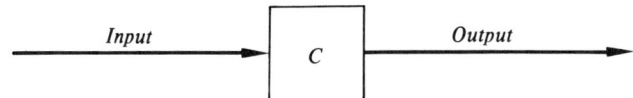

Suppose that C can be decomposed into two components H and S in the form illustrated in Figure 2.5. If the system C has the property that its behavior can be described for all inputs given *only* the behavior of the component S then i is said to be an *interpretive interface*, H is said to be an *interpreter* and S is said to be *interpreted*.

Whenever an interpretive interface can be identified in a system it is possible to adopt a viewpoint which considers the interpreted component as operating autonomously at a new abstract level (as shown in Figure 2.4). Within this new level, the structuring model of this chapter can be reapplied. Because of the importance of the abstraction involved in this change of viewpoint, a simplified *interpreter*

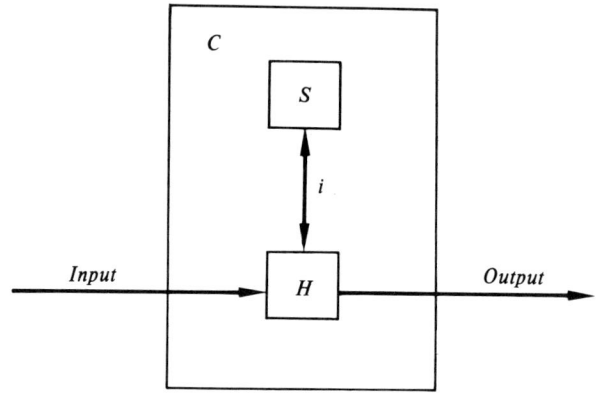

Figure 2.5 Interpretive Interface

diagram is used to emphasize the role of the interpretive interface:

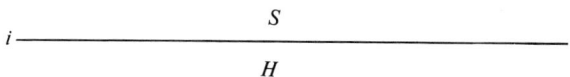

When C is a computing system, S can be identified with the memory containing the program (and data) controlling the system, and H will then comprise the rest of the hardware. The interpretive interface is characterized by a language providing objects and operations to manipulate those objects; this is the machine language of the hardware computer. (The name i may be used to refer to either the interface or the language.) Machine language programs stored in S are executed by fetching, decoding and obeying the individual instructions which make up the programs. Figure 2.6 is a typical example of an interpreter diagram for a computing system.

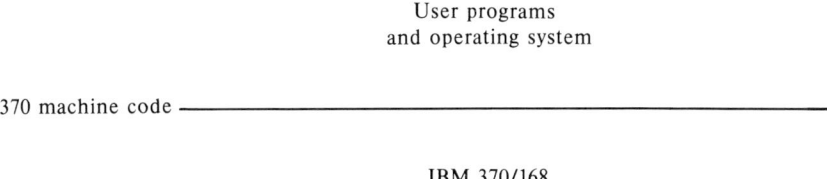

Figure 2.6 Interpreter Diagram

One interesting possibility, and one which does occur in practice, is that a further interpretive interface (or interfaces) can be identified within an interpreted system. A system which contains a hierarchy of interpretive interfaces is termed a *multilevel interpreter system* and is conveniently represented by combining the separate interpreter diagrams. The paradigm of such a system is a computer supporting an APL interpreter, and this is illustrated in Figure 2.7.

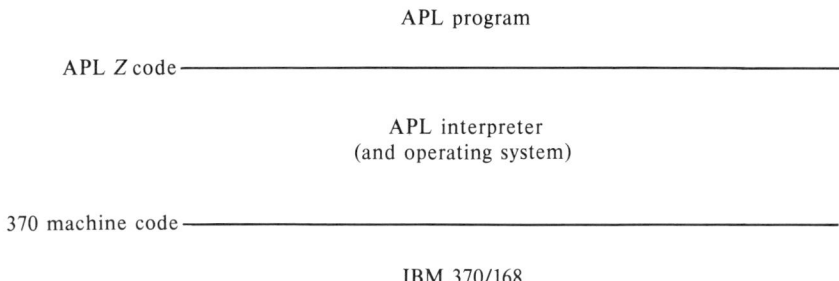

Figure 2.7 Multilevel Interpreter System

Microprogrammable computers[12] provide further examples of multilevel interpreter systems. In the Burroughs B1726 computer, user programs are compiled into an appropriate intermediate language and stored in main memory. These programs are executed by means of an interpreter written as a microprogram which resides in a control store. In turn the interpreter is itself interpreted by hardware. The NANODATA QM-1 has an extra level; machine language instructions in main memory are executed by microprograms in control store, and microinstructions are executed by what are termed 'nanoprograms' in a lower level control store (called the nanostore), and the nanoinstructions are finally executed by hardware.

Although an envisaged system may be structured into many levels for design purposes, implementation considerations often prohibit supporting multiple interfaces by means of interpreters (which must decode and obey every instruction of an executed program) because of the overheads incurred by the use of this admittedly very powerful technique. Instead, the following approach is often adopted.

Suppose that an interface L_0 is available but that a system is needed to support an interface L_1. One possibility would be to construct a full interpreter for L_1 written in L_0, but this may not be necessary. If L_0 provides the necessary facilities, and if L_1 has many properties in common with L_0, then it may be possible to provide support for L_1 by *extending* the interface L_0. A system implemented in this way can be represented by an *interpreter extension diagram* as shown in Figure 2.8, where I is an interpreter for the language L_0, E is a program written in L_0, and P is a program written in L_1 (which is an extension of L_0).

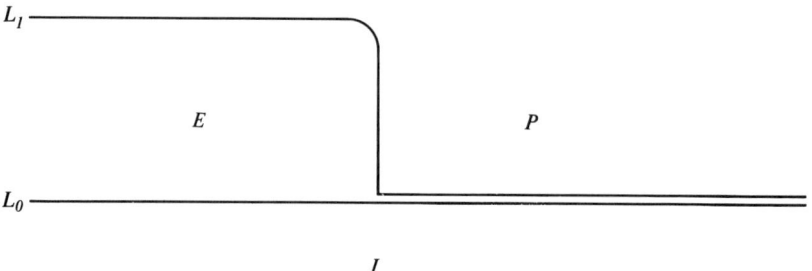

Figure 2.8 Interpreter Extension Diagram

The program E is referred to as an *interpreter extension*, and must provide support for the facilities of L_1 which are not available from L_0.

When an instruction from the program P is executed on the L_1 interface it is first examined by the interpreter I, which determines whether the required operation is directly supported by I itself (i.e. whether it is an L_0 operation and hence does not involve the facilities provided by the extension); if so, I performs the required actions. If not, the instruction must involve an operation for which the interpreter extension E provides the necessary support, and so I transfers control to E (of course, I must interpret E on behalf of P). When E completes whatever actions are required, I continues with the execution of P.

The interpreter extension diagram of Figure 2.8 is simply the diagram of a two level interpretive system modified to indicate the difference in implementation and the overlap in properties of the interfaces L_0 and L_1. There is no necessity for any user of the interface L_1 to be aware of the separate existence of E and I since together they provide an interpreter for L_1.

A run-time subroutine or procedure mechanism can be regarded as a simple extension facility which is available in some form on most computers. More powerful extension mechanisms could allow the addition of new data types and new notations, as well as permitting the removal (by concealment) of features of the L_0 language. Most operating systems form an interpreter extension since they provide an interface to user programs by extending a basic hardware interface by means of 'supervisor call' instructions. An operating system usually prevents user programs from invoking certain 'privileged' instructions supported by the hardware, for example, the instructions which control peripheral devices and (in most systems) the instructions which provide facilities for implementing an extension.

If the extension facilities provided by the underlying interpreter are sufficiently powerful it will be possible to construct a sequence of new interfaces, each an extension of its predecessor, and each enabling further extensions to be made. A system implemented in this way is called a *multilevel extended interpreter system*. An example system containing three extensions is shown in Figure 2.9, where lines indicating overlapping interfaces are coalesced.

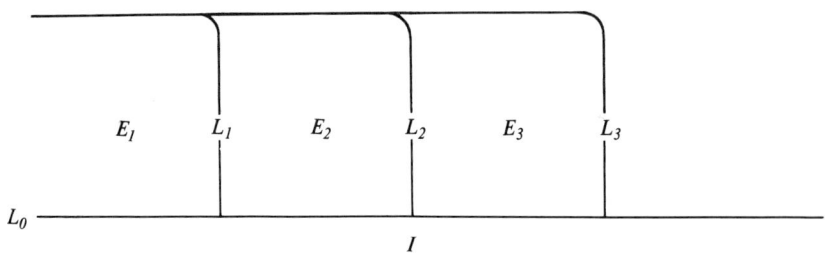

Figure 2.9 Multilevel Extended Interpreter System

Each interpreter extension E_i contributes to the support of interface L_i and is itself executed on the interface L_{i-1}. When a program is executed on interface L_i, the interpreter I determines for each instruction whether support can be provided directly, or if not, which of the available interpreter extensions E_j $(j \leq i)$ provides support. Thus, the program P can make use of objects and operations provided by any extension or the underlying interpreter.

The benefit to be gained from using interpreter extensions to implement new interfaces in preference to further levels of interpretation is in greatly reducing the overhead involved. If program P in Figure 2.9 makes infrequent use of facilities provided by the extensions it is easy to ensure that P can use operations from the L_0 interface without any overhead being incurred. Although existing systems only support fairly limited extension facilities, current research into the use of abstract types to achieve modularity in software systems suggests that interpreter extensions may be much more prevalent in the future.

The software of a computing system is often thought of in terms of multilevel diagrams, even when an examination of the software would reveal that the levels were not actually implemented by an explicit extension mechanism. Often the intended structure is removed by the compilation process. Nevertheless, the simple linear hierarchical structure which these diagrams exhibit has been found to be very useful in constructing complex software systems; examples are the 'THE' multiprogramming system[13] and the Venus operating system.[14]

An interpretive interface (supported either by an interpreter alone or in conjunction with an interpreter extension) forms an important structural division in a computing system. It enables two different levels of a system (e.g. hardware and software) to be considered as distinct systems for design purposes. Of course, the two systems are linked by the interpretive interface; the interpreter must maintain the operation of the interface since the interpreted system relies on the facilities provided for its very existence.

In subsequent chapters it is very convenient to distinguish facilities provided by an interpreter from those which are explicitly programmed in the interpreted system. To enable this distinction to be clearly drawn, two terms are adopted:

> a *mechanism* is a construction within an interpreter which implements a specific facility available on the interpretive interface;

> a *measure* is a group of instructions in the interpreted system intended to perform some specific task.

For example, consider a program which is required to search a table of values for some specific entry. A subroutine for that purpose could be included as a measure in the program. This would not be necessary if the hardware included a mechanism supporting an instruction to search a vector for a given value. These terms can also be applied in the more general framework of the basic system model:

> a *mechanism* refers to the means by which a component performs some task for a system;

> a *measure* would be implemented by the design of the system in order to combine the activities of a number of components.

However, the term 'mechanism' will be principally used in interpretive systems.

Techniques implemented as a mechanism can be expected to have rather different characteristics to those implemented as measures, particularly in the context of an interpretive interface. In keeping with the nature of a general-purpose interpretive interface, mechanisms are likely to employ simple strategies which have wide applicability, since they will usually be designed in advance of the routines which will make use of them. Specialization can only be achieved by making a priori assumptions about the needs of these routines. In contrast, measures in a system can derive benefit from knowledge of the aims and purpose of the system. As a result they will usually be system dependent and specialized rather than generally applicable. Mechanisms provided by the interpreter, either automatically initiated or invoked explicitly, can be utilized by a measure, and supplemented by further actions if required - mechanisms are often designed to facilitate or optimize the operation of measures in the interpreted system.

Later chapters (particularly Chapters 5-7) discuss the use of measures and mechanisms to provide fault tolerance in a system. Whenever possible these chapters place emphasis on *mechanisms* for fault tolerance because these provide efficient general-purpose techniques which could be implemented in any computing system. Furthermore, because they are included at a lower level in the system, it may be possible to implement mechanisms more reliably than measures. One reason is that mechanisms are likely to be simpler. Another is that since a mechanism is likely to remain unchanged over long periods it can be constructed with meticulous care. Measures will often be more complex and much more ephemeral.

Atomic Actions

All of the preceding discussion on system structure has only been concerned with the way in which a system can itself be subdivided, and as such has dealt with *static* (or *spatial)* structure. Interest also attaches to the pattern of interactions between the components of a system, and to the identification of *dynamic* (or *temporal)* structure in this internal activity. The concept of an *atomic action,* as developed by Lomet,[15] can be used to rectify this omission.

The activity of a system component is defined to be the sequence of external state transitions of the component.

SYSTEM STRUCTURE

Each transition is regarded as primitive and indivisible, and takes place instantaneously (in principle). A single state transition constitutes the simplest atomic action. Clearly, there can be no interaction between the component and the rest of the system for the duration of a single transition (since this is assumed to be instantaneous). The absence of interactions can be taken as the criterion for atomicity:

> The activity of a group of components constitutes an *atomic action* if there are no interactions between that group and the rest of the system for the duration of the activity.

To the rest of the system, all of the activity within an atomic action appears to be indivisible and could have occurred instantaneously at any time during the atomic action.

Figure 2.10 shows the activity of three components partitioned into a number of atomic actions indicated by the curved lines, with vertical lines used to indicate interactions between processes.

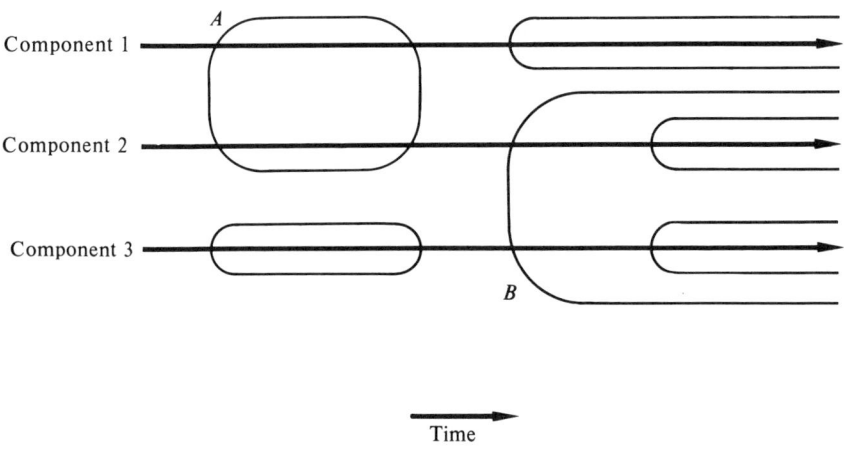

Figure 2.10 Atomic Actions

Initially components 1 and 2 interacted in atomic action A while the activity of component 3 formed a private atomic action. After a short interval during which all three components could interact, component 1 entered a private atomic action while components 2 and 3 interacted in atomic action B. Subsequently, components 2 and 3 both entered private atomic actions nested within B. Note that within each atomic action many more nested atomic actions could have been shown; in each case only the atomic action of longest duration has been illustrated.

Formal treatments of the atomicity of system activity, such as that of Best,[16] are based on precise notions of information flow and dependency between events. These formal approaches permit certain limited interactions between an atomic action and the rest of the system; interactions are permitted if they have no impact on the activity of the atomic action and do not provide the rest of the system with any information concerning the progress of the atomic action. The definition of atomicity adopted in this book is more restrictive, in that no interactions are permitted between an atomic action and the rest of the system. This simplifies the determination of whether or not the activity of a group of components forms an atomic action.

Atomic actions provide the designer of a system with a useful conceptual tool for factoring and organizing the interactions between system components. This tool is particularly effective when atomic actions can be enforced by imposing constraints on component interactions, thereby imposing structure on the flow of information within the system. Techniques for enforcing atomicity range from the use of physical separation (e.g. use of separate processing units) to controls on facilities for component (usually process) interaction (e.g. locking of shared objects). These issues are discussed in more detail in Chapter 6.

Mechanisms which enforce atomicity in software systems have received considerable attention, particularly in the area of data base systems. The widely employed notion of a *transaction*[17,18] enables the user of a data base system to arrange that a sequence of interactions with the data base will constitute an atomic action. Davies[19] discusses the way in which the very general concept of a *sphere of control* can be used to specify atomic actions (as well as resource allocation, recovery, auditing, ...). Lomet[15] suggests some simple programming language constructs for defining and using atomic actions.

SYSTEM RELIABILITY

A major obstacle to any examination of the reliability of systems, and in particular to a discussion of techniques for fault tolerance, is the lack of agreed terminology for the relevant concepts. Several alternative definitions have been proposed for the reliability of a system,[20,21,22,23,24] while a range of different (but rarely distinguished) terms are used to describe the causes of system unreliability. Attempts to isolate or combine issues arising from the hardware/software dichotomy can introduce further difficulties. This section provides a set of terms together with precise, though informal, definitions for various concepts relating to system (un)reliability. These concepts enable definitions to be supplied for the widely (but often indiscriminately) used terms *failure, error* and *fault*. The terminology presented conforms to conventional usage as much as possible and is equally applicable at all levels of a system, whether implemented in hardware or software.

Failure and Reliability

Any definition of the reliability of a system must involve distinguishing between acceptable and unacceptable behavior of the system. In principle, such a distinction can be made in an arbitrary manner since once it is placed in service the behavior of a system is determined solely by its implementation, and is not influenced by user requirements - a computer which halts at seemingly arbitrary intervals, disrupting all processing, is still behaving in accordance with its construction, but possibly in response to some internal phenomenon that the manufacturer of the computer did not envisage. In practice, however, all systems are designed and built to be used, and therefore support interfaces which provide facilities required by their users.

One criterion by which the acceptability of system behavior might be judged is that of user satisfaction;[22] behavior which the users of the system consider to be satisfactory could be taken to constitute acceptable behavior. The principal objection to this criterion is that the classification of behavior as acceptable is dependent upon the expectations of users of the system, expectations which may be unjustified and are open to change (e.g. as experience with the system is gained). Behavior which the system was specifically designed to provide can still be considered unsatisfactory by an ill-informed user, while misuse of the system (such as demands for services which the system was never intended to provide) may well produce behavior which the user regards as unsatisfactory. However, an objective assessment of system reliability should not be adversely influenced by users' misapprehensions. It is therefore essential to distinguish between unsatisfactory behavior which is a consequence of misunderstandings by users of the system from unacceptable behavior due to deficiencies in the system itself - that is, to distinguish misplaced reliance on a system from genuine unreliability of the system. For this to be possible a *specification* of the intended behavior of the system is needed.

Before any system can be designed and built some form of specification of required behavior must be prepared. During the course of design and construction, numerous changes may be made to the specification; for example, a potential user may change his requirements, the designers and implementors may insist on amendments, or financial restrictions may necessitate changes. Eventually, however, a specification of system behavior should be available which is acceptable to users (and purchasers), and which is acknowledged as appropriate by the implementors (and vendors) of the system.

When a specification of acceptable behavior is available it provides a standard against which the behavior of the system can be judged:

> A *failure* of a system occurs when the behavior of the system first deviates from that required by its specification.

Clearly it is necessary for a specification to stipulate what constitutes a deviation, that is to specify what tolerances are imposed on the various outputs from the system.

This definition does not require a failure to be identified or even observed; all that is required is that a failure *could* be identified by a rigorous application of the specification. It is possible for a system to fail without having any damaging effect on its environment. For example, an airline reservation system could fail by inadvertently deleting all reservations for a flight from Chicago to New York. The failure would have no impact on passengers if the flight was cancelled due to a thunderstorm. Of course, it is more likely that a system failure *will* adversely affect its environment, with possibly catastrophic consequences. An airline reservation system could fail by booking passengers on a non-existent flight from Chicago to New York, with the adverse effect of forcing a number of passengers to stay overnight in Chicago (the passengers concerned might regard this as a catastrophe). The outcome of a failure of an aircraft auto-landing system could be much more serious.

Note that it is not possible (with the above definition of failure) to build systems capable of undoing their *own* failures since this would imply that, by some means, behavior which deviated from that required by the specification could be transformed (after it had occurred) into behavior which conformed to the specification. Although it is feasible that a system could receive some indication that it had failed and, in response, take remedial action, the failure would still have occurred. For example, if an aircraft auto-landing system received an indication of failure (e.g. undercarriage jammed) it could respond by causing the aircraft to climb and by requesting manual intervention. Nevertheless, a failure to correctly deploy the landing gear would still have occurred and could not be undone. Remedial action can at best only mitigate the further consequences of a failure and thereby reduce what could be termed the severity of the failure. This is not to say that such actions are futile, but it can be argued that they are more appropriately performed by the environment of the failing system whenever this is possible.

Clearly, the reliability of a system must be inversely proportional to the rate at which failures occur. A precise characterization of the *operational reliability* of a system can be given as a record of the occurrences of failure over a particular period of time. Although such a record is completely factual, it is necessarily influenced by the specific inputs received by the system over the relevant period. Consequently, recordings of operational reliability can give a misleading indication of subsequent system reliability, particularly if there are variations in the pattern of system usage.

A more general notion of system reliability can be expressed in terms of the (un)likelihood of failure.

> The *reliability* of a system can be characterized by a function $R(t)$ which expresses the probability that the system will conform to its specification throughout a period of duration t.

The nature of this definition is such that $R(t)$ cannot be known for any system; at best, the use of reliability modelling techniques will enable the form of $R(t)$ to be predicted and estimates made of the relevant parameters. The theory of reliability modelling is now well established;[20,25] an overview of its application to computing systems is provided in Chapter 3. In order to have a single numeric value indicating the reliability of a system the average interval between failures can either be measured or predicted. This value, the Mean Time Between Failures (MTBF), is probably the most widely used indicator for the reliability of a system.

System Specification

The above definitions of failure and system reliability are given with respect to a specification of acceptable behavior for the system. (The situation is, of course, analogous to the notion of 'correctness' of a program, which can only be defined with respect to a specification of correct behavior for the program.) Most of the subsequent definitions of this section derive from the definition of a failure and so they too are with respect to a specification. In view of the fundamental role played by specifications it is appropriate to elaborate on the desirable characteristics of a specification.

A specification for a real system must serve many purposes: those of designers, builders, vendors and users of the system. As a result, specifications are often imprecise, incomplete, inconsistent, subject to question and change, and may even be undocumented. In circumstances such as these the determination of whether a system failure has occurred will be equally imprecise, incomplete, and subject

SYSTEM RELIABILITY

to acrimonious debate. To ensure that system behavior can be judged definitively, the specification for a system should be what is referred to here as an exact specification.

An *exact specification* for a system is consistent, complete and authoritative, and can be applied as a test in all circumstances to determine whether the behavior of the system is or is not acceptable. Thus, an exact specification can always be used to allocate responsibility for any undesirable behavior of a system. If the behavior of the system conforms to the specification then any blame must be directed at the user of the system. Only if a failure has occurred can the system be criticized.

The need for *consistency* in a specification is obvious. If a specification is inconsistent then in certain circumstances it cannot be adhered to by any system. A specification which imposes requirements that cannot be met, or even requirements which are unrealistic in practical terms, must be regarded as excessively stringent.

Ideally, a specification should be *complete* so that the behavior of the system is defined for all possible input sequences. Otherwise circumstances will exist in which acceptable and unacceptable behavior cannot be distinguished. In practice, specifications are usually incomplete; they rarely define system behavior for unforeseen inputs, of for inputs considered to be impossible (or highly improbable). However, if a system receives input for which its behavior has not been specified then no matter what behavior is produced the system cannot be held to have failed. In effect, an incomplete specification is supplemented by a rider stipulating that in circumstances not explicitly covered by the specification any behavior from the system must be considered acceptable. Alternative ways of obtaining complete specifications (such as requiring specific behavior to be produced in all circumstances) yield specifications which could not be adhered to by any practical system. No system can produce desirable behavior in the face of all possible catastrophes. For example, if a specification does not explicitly prescribe what is acceptable behavior for a computing system when it is struck by lightning then after being thus stricken the system can (and probably will) behave in an arbitrary fashion. This arbitrary behavior cannot be considered unacceptable (according to the specification) despite the fact that users of the system are most unlikely to regard arbitrary behavior as satisfactory.

When a specification provides a *test* for acceptable system behavior it can itself be regarded as a system. Viewed in this way, a specification E for a system S receives, as its input, information concerning the behavior of S over some period of time (i.e. a record of the interactions which took place on the interface between S and its environment). The only valid responses from E are 'Yes, acceptable' or 'No, failure'. To arrive at one of these conclusions E must perform some form of simulation of the desired operation of S and determine whether there is a conflict between the actual behavior of S and that predicted by the simulation. When there is a conflict, the behavior of S could be defended by claiming that the specification E was defective. Such a claim is usually substantiated by modifying the specification (instead of the system) and appealing to some higher authority that the revised specification is what was really intended from the outset. To avoid debate in this situation the specification should be *authoritative*. A specification which is authoritative cannot be questioned, admits no higher authority, and brooks no debate - not even in the aftermath of a thunderstorm.

Exactness of specifications is a characteristic that should always be sought, but is rarely achieved in full. Very few practical systems have their behavior prescribed by an exact specification but an important area of current research has as its goal the production of improved system specification techniques.[26,27,28,29] When a system failure is suspected an inexact (or non-existent) specification cannot always be used to determine whether a failure has occurred or not, in which case some external authority (usually human) will have to adjudicate.

Multiple Specifications

It may be necessary to have more than one specification for a single system, since different aspects of the behavior of a system may be subject to different specifications. For instance, one specification applied to a system could describe the desired functional relationship between inputs and outputs, another could be concerned with performance criteria (e.g. limits on response times), while a third could impose requirements on the availability of service from the system. Of course, a single specification could be applied to the system, imposing requirements on all of these separate aspects of behavior.

The relative severity of failures can be indicated by means of multiple specifications, each in turn imposing less stringent (but more important) requirements on the system. The last specification in this hierarchy imposes only essential requirements - in consequence a failure is correspondingly severe. The first specification is comprehensive - behavior which deviates from this specification but from none of the others will constitute a relatively minor failure. As an example consider the following hierarchy of three specifications for a data base system.

(i)   All commands must be correctly obeyed.
(ii) All commands must either be correctly obeyed, or ignored (producing a warning message).
(iii) Information recorded in the data base must not be corrupted.

If the system fails to meet specification (iii) then a severe failure has occurred due to a loss of information. If the system meets specification (iii) but not specification (ii) then a less severe failure has occurred; despite an arbitrary response from the system no information has been corrupted. If specification (ii) is met but specification (i) is not met then a minor failure has occurred; a command has been ignored by the system but no information has been corrupted.

In the same way, a hierarchy of specifications can be used to define desirable behavior from a system which has failed. Often, this will just be to stipulate that, if possible, a failing system should generate some indication of failure (e.g. sounding an alarm or turning on a lamp). For instance, in the data base example above, a fourth specification could be added to the hierarchy.

(iv) If any information in the data base is corrupted, all users must be informed.

As noted by Gall,[30] "When a fail-safe system fails, it fails by failing to fail safe".

It is often necessary to specify the standard of reliability which is demanded of a system. For example, an avionics computer system for use in civil aircraft may be required to have a failure rate which is less than 10^{-9} per flight hour.[31] To define a standard of reliability two specifications will be needed. The first specification defines acceptable behavior of the system in the normal way. The second specification can then be expressed in terms of system reliability requirements with respect to the first specification. It is then important to distinguish a failure of the system with respect to the first specification from a failure with respect to the second 'reliability' specification. The latter is likely to be a much more serious event. For example, a system used to manufacture integrated circuits may be said to fail when a circuit is rejected by a comparison check. An individual failure in this context is almost irrelevant. Of much greater significance is a specification of reliability which stipulates the required overall yield (e.g. 5% per shift). If the yield falls below the specified value then the system fails with respect to the reliability specification.

Erroneous Transitions and States

Whatever specification of acceptable behavior is imposed on a system, the assumption that this specification is authoritative implies that any examination of the causes of failure need only concern the internal operation of the system itself (since the specification cannot be challenged). Only two basic concepts are essential in discussing the causes of failure; these may be thought of intuitively as an event which should not have occurred and a condition (or state) which should not have arisen. In relation to the internal operation of a system these two concepts are termed an *erroneous transition* and an *erroneous state*, respectively. This sub-section provides precise definitions for these deficiencies in the internal operation of a system, and examines their relationship to (external) system

SYSTEM RELIABILITY

failures and to (internal) failures of either the components or the design of a system. The outcome of this examination is (as can be expected) that a system failure must be a consequence of either a component or a design failure.

Consider a system producing external behavior in response to a sequence of interactions at the interface between the system and its environment. The system passes through a sequence of external states which are merely a more abstract representation of a sequence of internal states s_1, s_2, s_3, ... Assume that while the system progresses through states s_1 to s_{n-1} its external behavior conforms to the system specification, but that on entering state s_n the external behavior conflicts with the specification. That is, the system fails when it reaches the internal state s_n. In this situation it seems natural to seek a 'cause' to which the 'effect' of failure can be attributed - that is, to identify some earlier (internal) event which can be held responsible for the failure. The internal state transitions are the obvious candidates.

Since the system was (presumably) not intended to fail, at some point the sequence s_1, ... , s_n must have diverged from that which was intended. Suppose that this divergence occurred when the system entered state s_i. The transition from s_{i-1} to s_i must then be considered responsible for the eventual failure of the system, and can therefore be regarded as erroneous. All of the other transitions can be considered to be valid since they are not held responsible for the failure of the system. States s_1, ... , s_{i-1} are clearly valid but all of the states s_i, ... , s_n are erroneous since the system should not have entered those states. In a file system, for example, an erroneous transition would occur if, by some means, an entry in the catalog of files was corrupted. Failure of the system would not occur until the corrupted entry was accessed, which could be much later. The state of the file system would be valid prior to the damage to the catalog, and erroneous subsequently.

The above discussion is intended to reflect the situation when, after a system failure, the history of system activity is scrutinized in order to identify the cause of that failure. A post-mortem of this nature will often proceed by observing that the internal state at the time of failure is clearly erroneous, that the initial state of the system (or some other state prior to the failure) was valid, and that there must therefore have been an erroneous transition at some stage. Symbolic debugging systems for software are usually designed to assist a programmer to locate an erroneous transition by searching for the stage in a computation at which there is a transition from a valid state to an erroneous state.

It may seem from the above that an erroneous transition could be defined to be a transition to which a failure is attributed, and that an erroneous state could be defined to be a state which leads to a failure. Unfortunately, such simplistic definitions are inadequate. To be satisfactory, the definitions must take account of some additional complications. The precise definition of an erroneous transition will be established first since the identification of erroneous transitions is necessary to determine whether an internal state is erroneous or valid.

Intuitively, an erroneous transition places a system in an internal state from which a failure could ensue. However, the definition must allow for the possibility that a potential failure does not actually occur. For example, consider a computer memory word as a system which records an integer value. The internal state of this system consists of a sequence of bits. A spurious inversion of one of these bits would constitute an erroneous transition since it would be responsible for a failure of the system if the word was subsequently read to obtain the integer value. However, there are a number of ways by which failure might be averted. Firstly, the word could be overwritten with a new integer value before it was read. Secondly, another spurious inversion of the same bit could occur before the word was read. Thirdly, the system could contain special circuitry to ensure the return of a correct value even in the presence of an incorrect bit. The following definition takes account of possibilities such as these.

> An *erroneous transition* of a system is an internal state transition to which a subsequent failure could be attributed. Specifically, there must exist a possible sequence of interactions which would, in the absence of corrective action from the system, lead to a system failure attributable to the erroneous transition.

SYSTEM RELIABILITY

If an internal state transition is not erroneous then it is said to be *valid*. Note that a transition is valid if it cannot be blamed for any possible subsequent failure; there is no implication that valid transitions only occur when a system is operating as it was intended.

As might be expected, the definition of an erroneous state is very similar to that of an erroneous transition.

> An *erroneous state* of a system is an internal state which could lead to a failure by a sequence of valid transitions. Specifically, there must exist a possible sequence of interactions which would, in the absence of corrective action by the system and in the absence of erroneous transitions, lead from the erroneous state to a system failure.

If an internal state is not erroneous then it is said to be *valid*. These definitions ensure that a system cannot fail subsequent to a valid state if no erroneous transitions occur.

The role of these definitions is illustrated schematically in Figure 2.11, in which the arrows indicate possible transitions between internal states of a system.

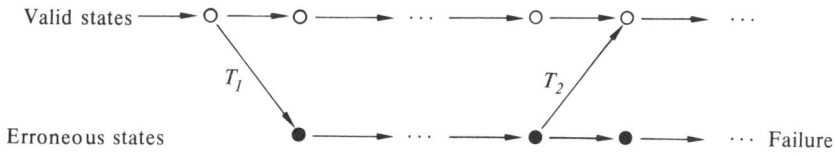

Figure 2.11 Erroneous Transition and Erroneous States

All transitions are assumed to be valid with the exception of the transition labelled T_1. Transition T_1 is erroneous because of the possibility of a subsequent system failure. The status of T_1 is not affected by the possibility of the system returning to valid operation via transition T_2, which could occur because of the particular interactions actually experienced by the system, or because of corrective action from the system. Corrective action could take place as a consequence of some highly fortuitous component failure or, more likely, be a deliberate and carefully planned activity performed by the system in response to the detection of an erroneous state. It could be argued that when the system itself ensures that failure is averted by taking corrective action, the transition T_f should not be regarded as erroneous. However, this would mean that states in which corrective action was taken could not be considered erroneous - in which case corrective action would not be necessary!

It should be noted that for any system the decision as to which aspects of the activity of the system are regarded as providing corrective action is essentially subjective. Clearly, this decision has an impact on which transitions can be considered erroneous. If 'error-correcting' circuits on memory are regarded as providing normal rather than corrective action (as their designer might wish to assert) then a spurious inversion of a single bit cannot be regarded as an erroneous transition since the situation does not lead to a failure (from this viewpoint the 'error-correcting' circuits do not 'correct errors', they merely make a necessary adjustment to the memory). Techniques for providing corrective action are discussed in Chapter 7.

Component/Design Failures

When an erroneous transition has been identified as the cause of a (possible) failure, it is natural to ask what caused that transition to be erroneous. Internal state transitions are determined by the components of the system in conjunction with the design. Hence the components and the design of the system are (the obvious) candidates for the cause of an erroneous transition.

One explanation for the occurrence of an erroneous transition is the simultaneous occurrence of a failure of a component of the system. If one (or more) of the components fails to meet its specification this could certainly place the system in an erroneous state. The above discussion can then be applied to the failing component, considering it as a system in its own right: the component has failed and must therefore have passed through a sequence of (internal) erroneous states as a result of some earlier erroneous transition within the component. For example, a failure of a computing system to read a file from disk could be a consequence of an erroneous transition which resulted in an invalid block of data being recorded on the disk. This erroneous transition could be due to a failure of the disk controller when writing to the disk, which could be due to a failure of the circuitry driving the disk heads, which could be due to a failure of an integrated circuit, and so on. The ultimate cause of a failure can be pursued as far as is considered worthwhile.

If, however, all components meet their specification when an erroneous transition takes place, the problem must lie in the design of the system. An obvious (implicit) specification of behavior for the design of a system is that it should ensure that all internal state transitions of the system are valid in the absence of any component failures. If there is an erroneous transition and no components have failed then the design of the system must have failed.

Considered as a system which has failed, the design must be in an erroneous state. Since the state of the design of a system is usually not intended to change, the design will in most cases have been erroneous from the outset (i.e. the initial state of the design was erroneous). This can be attributed to the occurrence of an 'erroneous transition' at some point during the design process (e.g. because of a misunderstanding by a designer) or during the construction of the system (e.g. because of a wire being connected to the wrong pin, or because of an incorrectly punched or compiled program). Another possibility is that during the operation of the system an erroneous transition within the design results in a previously valid design becoming erroneous. For example, consider the tracks and wires used to implement the design of a system constructed on a printed circuit board. The design may initially function correctly, but tracks can creep, contact at a dry soldered joint may be lost, or a wire could be dislodged. Each of these events is likely to constitute an erroneous transition causing the design to enter an erroneous state and subsequently fail. Similarly, when the design of a system is implemented as software stored in memory, any inadvertent change to the software, whether caused by a program or by a memory failure, is likely to constitute an erroneous transition within the design.

Thus, an erroneous transition must be the outcome of a failure of either a component or the design of the system. This seems quite natural: a system consists of a set of components together with a design; a failure of a system must be a consequence of a failure of either a component or the design. Although the occurrence of a component failure can, in principle, be determined objectively by recourse to the specification for the component, the identification of a design failure necessarily involves a subjective decision. Such an identification must envisage a modification to the design of the system which is intended to ensure that subsequently all internal transitions are valid. The changes which can be made to correct a defective design will rarely be unique; a judgment must be made as to the most appropriate correction. This subjective decision can influence the identification of which transition is deemed to be erroneous. As a trivial example consider a program which fails when executed because a variable was not assigned an initial value. Identification of an erroneous transition in this situation requires a decision on where in the program the variable should have been initialized.

Errors and Faults

Although the notions of an erroneous transition and an erroneous state have been carefully defined, they are not particularly convenient for discussing deficiencies in a system which could affect its operation. (The reader will have noted that this book is not entitled 'Erroneous Transition Tolerance'!) This is because the concept most often referred to in such discussions is that part of an erroneous state which is actually erroneous. It is common practice to use the terms error or fault for a specific defect within a system and this terminology is established below.

When a system is in an erroneous state, an examination of the external states of the components of the system will enable a decision to be made as to which components have external states that would have to be changed to make the internal state of the system valid. The states of such components are said to be errors in the system. Thus:

> an *error* is a part of an erroneous state which constitutes a difference from a valid state.

Even though the external state of a component may be an error in the system of which it is a part, that component need not be in an erroneous state when it is considered as a system in its own right. The internal state of the component may be perfectly valid but not be compatible with the states of other components of the containing system. There are two ways in which this can arise. Firstly, if the error is a consequence of a design failure then clearly the component could be in a valid state; it need not have failed. Secondly, the error may be a consequence of interaction with another component which is in an erroneous state; errors can propagate within a system even though components conform to their specifications. For example, a memory word storing the value of a variable could fail by always returning the value zero. (An incorrect value in a variable is clearly an error in the state of a computation.) However, the failing memory word is unlikely to remain the only error in the system. The value of any other variable calculated using the original error would also be an error.

Nevertheless, if a system is in an erroneous state then this must be as a result of either a design or a component failure. Errors in components or in the design can lead to errors in the system. In order to distinguish between errors at different levels in a system, to facilitate discussion of cause and effect relationships between errors, and to conform to established usage:

> An error in a component or the design of a system will be referred to as a *fault* in the system. A *component fault* in a system is an error in the internal state of a component, and a *design fault* in a system is an error in the state of the design.

A component fault can result in an eventual component failure and a design fault can lead to a design failure. Either of these internal failures will produce an erroneous transition in the operation of the system and this transition can be referred to as the *manifestation of a fault*. The manifestation of a fault will produce errors in the internal state of the system, which could lead to a system failure.

As an example, consider a banking system which maintains the personal checking accounts for the bank's customers. One component of the system is a master file which stores the current balance of each customer. The system design is a suite of programs which perform and record the transactions applied to each account. Suppose this system fails (dismally) by sending each customer a statement on which all transactions are entered correctly, but the current balance is listed as zero. Subsequent examination of the erroneous state of the system reveals that the only error is the external state of the master file which specifies that all balances are zero. One possible explanation for this error could be a design fault, such as a 'bug' in the program for closing an account which has the effect that all balances are cleared instead of just one. The 'bug' would be an error in the state of the design - a design fault in the system. Alternatively, the explanation could be a component fault, such as a defective internal register in a component used to perform arithmetic when calculating the balance for an account; this register is intended to provide the result of the calculation but always returns the value zero. The value of the register would be an error in the state of the component - a component fault in the system.

In the above example it should be noted that although the error in the system can be removed by replacing the correct balances in the master file, this does not remove any faults from the system. To remove the suggested design fault would involve correcting or replacing the program which closes accounts. The suggested component fault could be removed either by repairing the defective register or by replacing the entire component. The distinction between errors and faults and the different techniques for removing them are particularly important when fault tolerance strategies are considered in later chapters of this book.

Note however that the only difference between a fault and an error is with respect to the structure of a system; a fault in a system *is* an error in a component or in the design of the system. A fault is the cause of an error and an error is the cause of a failure, but the distinction between error and failure does not merely reflect system structure (though an error is part of an internal state while a failure relates to external states). Rather, the difference is that between a condition (or state) and an event. A system is in error (i.e. contains an error) when its state is erroneous, whereas a system failure is the event of not producing behavior as specified.

Examination of the possible causes of system failure has revealed an important dichotomy. On the one hand, a mistake made in designing or constructing a system can introduce a fault into the design of the system, either because of an inappropriate selection of components or because of inappropriate (or missing) interactions between components. On the other hand, if the design of a system is considered to be correct then an erroneous transition can only occur because of a failure of one of the components of the system. These two possibilities are the only sources of an erroneous transition, and thus of errors and consequent system failure.

It has been suggested[24,32] that erroneous interactions with a system can be considered to be faults which form a separate category. Within the framework developed in this section no such view can be taken. An interaction with a system whether correct or erroneous, permitted or not, cannot be a cause of failure. Either the system specification explicitly determines the response to the interaction, in which case any failure must be attributed to a fault within the system; or it does not, in which case there can be no failure since the system is at liberty to produce an arbitrary response. Certainly it is by means of interactions between the components of a system that errors are propagated within the system; this is discussed at some length in later chapters. Any component subject to an 'error propagating' interaction is by definition a part of some overall system, and in that system a fault can be identified which bears the responsibility for causing the unwanted interaction to occur.

As is discussed in Chapter 1, design faults require more powerful fault tolerance techniques than those needed to cope with component faults. This is largely a consequence of the different characteristics of the two classes of faults. Design faults are unpredictable, their manifestation is unexpected and they generate unanticipated errors. In contrast, component faults (particularly those in physical components) can often be predicted, their manifestation is expected, and they produce errors which can be anticipated. Analysis of the failure modes of physical components, based on experience with identical or similar components, can give invaluable guidance. However, design faults are usually eliminated once they are found; experience of the last design fault uncovered is not a very reliable guide to the untoward effects of the next one.

Hardware component faults are often classified by extent, value and duration.[33] *Extent* applies to whether the errors generated by the fault are localized or distributed; *value* indicates whether the fault generates fixed or varying erroneous values; *duration* refers to whether the fault is transient or permanent. A *transient fault* is a fault which is present in a system for only a limited period of time (less than some threshold) after which it spontaneously disappears from the system. A recurring transient fault is often referred to as being *intermittent*. Any fault which is present for longer than the threshold period is said to be *permanent*. Design faults are usually permanent, but faults resulting from physical degradation can often be transient. Classification of faults by their duration should not be confused with the frequency of their impact on a system. A fault can easily be permanent but have the characteristics of a transient fault if its manifestations are very infrequent. Examples are a 'stuck-at-1' fault on a line which should almost always have that value anyway, or a 'bug' in a rarely executed statement of a program.

One aspect of the distinction between a component fault and a design fault is usually apparent when they are exemplified. It is easy to give precise and explicit examples of hardware component faults (e.g. a diode which has failed open-circuit) but explicit examples of software design faults usually seem both trivial and contrived (e.g. an attempt to exchange the values of variables X and Y using the program $X := Y; Y := X$). However, here is a genuine example, if only slightly less trivial, originally presented by Anderson and Kerr:[34]

$$A_i := A_i - A_j; \quad A_j := A_j + A_i; \quad A_i := A_j - A_i$$

This program is intended to exchange the values of variables A_i and A_j without using an auxiliary variable, but will fail if the values involved are such that arithmetic overflow occurs. In fact the program contains another design fault:

if $i=j$ the value of A_i will be lost. Despite being elementary this example typifies the vast majority of design faults in being due to an oversight on the part of the designer concerning some exceptional case where special action is required.

A comment which is often made is that software is only prone to design faults, since programs are not physical and do not deteriorate with time in the way that is expected of hardware systems. The comment is true, but the reasoning is superficial. Here it is argued that all failures are caused by design faults, but these may be observed as component faults at some level of abstraction. Failure of any system is either due to a design fault or is a result of a component failure. The failure of a component is in turn attributable either to a design fault within the component or to a failure of a sub-component. Eventually, at some level, the original system failure will be attributed to a design fault, unless a failure of a component which is considered to be atomic is held responsible. (Even failure of an atomic component may be considered to be due to a design fault in that a component with inadequate reliability was selected.)

The only feature which distinguishes between physical and abstract systems is that physical systems have failure modes which can be attributed to the ravages of time (corruption due to moth, rust, electron migration, and the like) whereas abstract systems have the attractive property of remaining indefinitely in the same pristine (or otherwise) condition in which they were constructed. Consequently, abstract systems are only prone to faults introduced by their designers. However, for an abstract system to be used it must be given a physical representation. (A software system can only be used when it is stored in the memory of a computer.) Faults can be introduced in constructing the representation of the system. Furthermore, time can impinge on the physical representation of the abstract system; alpha particles can (indirectly) influence a software system if it is stored in VLSI memory. The only *direct* impact the passage of time can have on an abstract system is that changing demands may be placed upon it. Efforts to adjust the system to cope with these demands are even more liable to introduce design faults than the process of originally creating the system. Belady and Lehman[35] argue that any system that is used undergoes continuing change, and that as a result its structure inevitably degenerates. The outcome is often that, to its users, even a software system can appear to age and exhibit all the characteristics of physical deterioration.

SUMMARY

The primary aim of this chapter is to establish a framework and terminology which are adopted throughout the remaining chapters. In order to facilitate subsequent reference the most important of the definitions supplied in this chapter are repeated here, in a shortened form when appropriate.

> A *system* is a set of interacting components together with a design which prescribes and controls the pattern of interaction.
>
> An *interface* is a place of interaction between systems.
>
> A *measure* is a construction within the design of a system (e.g. in the program of an interpreted system) intended to perform a specific task.
>
> A *mechanism* is a construction within an interpreter which provides a specific facility.
>
> A *failure* occurs when the behavior of a system first deviates from that specified for it.
>
> An *erroneous transition* is an internal state transition to which a possible failure could be attributed.
>
> An *erroneous state* is an internal state which could lead to a failure by a sequence of valid transitions.
>
> A defective value in an erroneous state of a system is referred to as an *error* in the system.
>
> A defective value in the state of a component or in the design of a system is referred to as a *fault* in the system.

REFERENCES

1. O.-J. Dahl, E.W. Dijkstra, and C.A.R. Hoare, *Structured Programming*, Academic Press, London (1972).
2. N. Wirth, *Systematic Programming: An Introduction*, Prentice-Hall, Englewood Cliffs (NJ) (1973).
3. R.A. Snowdon and P. Henderson, "The TOPD System for Computer Aided System Development," pp. 338-354 in *Tutorial: Software Design Strategies*, ed. G.D. Bergland and R.D. Gordon, IEEE Computer Society, Long Beach (CA) (1979).
4. D.L. Parnas, "On The Criteria to be Used in Decomposing Systems Into Modules," *Communications of the ACM* **15**(12), pp.1053-1058 (December 1972).
5. E.W. Dijkstra, *A Discipline of Programming*, Prentice-Hall, Englewood Cliffs (NJ) (1976).
6. R.T. Yeh and K.M. Chandy (eds.), *Current Trends in Programming Methodology (Volumes 1-4)*, Prentice-Hall, Englewood Cliffs (NJ) (1978).
7. P.M. Melliar-Smith and B. Randell, "Software Reliability: The Role of Programmed Exception Handling," *SIGPLAN Notices* **12**(3), pp.95-100 (March 1977).
8. A. de Morgan, *A Budget of Paradoxes*, Longmans Green, London (1872).
9. J.J. Horning and B. Randell, "Process Structuring," *Computing Surveys* **5**(1), pp.5-30 (March 1973).
10. K. Jackson and C.I. Moir, "Parallel Processing in Software and Hardware - the MASCOT Approach," *Proceedings of 1975 Sagamore Computer Conference on Parallel Processing*, Sagamore (NY), pp.71-78 (August 1975).
11. D.T. Ross, "Structured Analysis (SA): A Language for Communicating Ideas," *IEEE Transactions on Software Engineering* **SE-3**(1), pp.16-34 (January 1977).
12. A.K. Agrawala and T.G. Rauscher, *Foundations of Microprogramming*, Academic Press, New York (1976).

13. E.W. Dijkstra, "The Structure of the 'THE' Multiprogramming System," *Communications of the ACM* **11**(5), pp.341-346 (May 1968).
14. B.H. Liskov, "The Design of the Venus Operating System," *Communications of the ACM* **15**(3), pp.144-149 (March 1972).
15. D.B. Lomet, "Process Structuring, Synchronization and Recovery Using Atomic Actions," *SIGPLAN Notices* **12**(3), pp.128-137 (March 1977).
16. E. Best, "Atomicity of Activities," pp. 225-250 in *Lecture Notes in Computer Science 84*, ed. W. Brauer, Springer-Verlag, Berlin (1980).
17. J.N. Gray *et al.*, "Granularity of Locks and Degrees of Consistency in a Shared Data Base," pp. 365-394 in *Modelling in Data Base Management Systems*, ed. G.M. Nijssen, North-Holland, Amsterdam (1976).
18. K.P. Eswaran *et al.*, "The Notion of Consistency and Predicate Locks in a Data Base System," *Communications of the ACM* **19**(11), pp.624-633 (November 1976).
19. C.T. Davies, "Data Processing Spheres of Control," *IBM Systems Journal* **17**(2), pp.179-198 (1978).
20. R.E. Barlow and F. Proschan, *Mathematical Theory of Reliability*, Wiley, New York (1965).
21. G.J. Myers, *Software Reliability: Principles and Practices*, Wiley, New York (1976).
22. P. Naur, "Software Reliability," pp. 243-251 in *State of the Art Report on Software Reliability*, Infotech, Maidenhead (1977).
23. T. Gilb, *Software Metrics*, Winthrop, Cambridge (MA) (1977).
24. B. Randell, P.A. Lee, and P.C. Treleaven, "Reliability Issues in Computing System Design," *Computing Surveys* **10**(2), pp.123-165 (June 1978).
25. R.E. Barlow and F. Proschan, *Statistical Theory of Reliability and Life Testing*, Holt Rinehart and Winston, New York (1975).

REFERENCES

26. B.H. Liskov and S.N. Zilles, "An Introduction to Formal Specifications of Data Abstractions," pp. 1-32 in *Current Trends in Programming Methodology, Vol. 1*, ed. R.T. Yeh, Prentice-Hall, Englewood Cliffs (NJ) (1977).

27. P.M. Melliar-Smith, "System Specification," pp. 19-65 in *Computing Systems Reliability*, ed. T. Anderson and B. Randell, Cambridge University Press, Cambridge (1979).

28. D.R. Musser, "Abstract Data Type Specification in the AFFIRM System," *IEEE Transactions on Software Engineering* **SE-6**(1), pp.24-32 (January 1980).

29. J.V. Guttag and J.J. Horning, "Formal Specification as a Design Tool," *Conference Record of Seventh Annual ACM Symposium on Principles of Programming Languages*, Las Vegas (NV), pp.251-261 (January 1980).

30. J. Gall, *Systemantics: How Systems Work and Especially How They Fail*, Pocket Books, New York (1978).

31. G.E. Migneault, "Software Reliability and Advanced Avionics," *AFIPS Conference Proceedings 1980 NCC* **49**, Anaheim (CA), pp.715-720 (May 1980).

32. A. Avizienis, "Fault-Tolerance: The Survival Attribute of Digital Systems," *Proceedings of the IEEE* **66**(10), pp.1109-1125 (October 1978).

33. A. Avizienis, "Fault-Tolerant Systems," *IEEE Transactions on Computers* **C-25**(12), pp.1304-1312 (December 1976).

34. T. Anderson and R. Kerr, "Recovery Blocks in Action: A System Supporting High Reliability," *Proceedings of 2nd International Conference on Software Engineering*, San Francisco (CA), pp.447-457 (October 1976).

35. L.A. Belady and M.M. Lehman, "A Model of Large Program Development," *IBM Systems Journal* **15**(3), pp.225-252 (1976).

3

FAULT TOLERANCE

Reliability is a desirable feature for any computing system, and a necessary requirement for some systems as discussed in Chapter 1. While operation without failure is the goal, it cannot be guaranteed that a system will be free from faults and their effects during its operational lifetime. Even in the absence of financial considerations, quality assurance cannot absolutely ensure that system components do not fail, and fault prevention is unlikely to succeed completely in eliminating design faults from a complex system. In order to provide reliability despite the presence of faults, measures for *fault tolerance* must be adopted.

The wide spectrum of requirements imposed on systems, coupled with rapid changes in hardware technology and costs, mean that definitive rules for the application of fault tolerance cannot be provided. What this chapter, in conjunction with the following chapters, attempts to do is to present the range of options open to a system designer.

Any system must be designed to match the computational requirements of the intended application; this will not be considered here. Given a proposal for a system with the desired computing power and functional characteristics the questions pertaining to fault tolerance concern *how, where* and *how much: how* fault tolerance can be implemented in the system; *where* it should be deployed; and *how much* is actually necessary in order to achieve the desired reliability. These are some of the basic issues to be considered here.

The implementation of fault tolerance in any particular system will be inexorably linked with the design and characteristics of that system, often to the extent that the features for fault tolerance and the features for normal system operation cannot be easily distinguished. Thus, a description of one fault tolerant system, with its own particular terminology and set of assumptions, does not serve to answer the question of how fault tolerance can be achieved in general. An overall discussion of the design and implementation of fault tolerant computing systems requires consideration of three factors. Firstly, it is necessary to identify the basic principles which underly all fault tolerant systems, principles that will be applicable at all levels in a computing system and not just, say, to the hardware. Secondly, the measures and mechanisms to support and implement techniques based on these principles must be investigated. Thirdly, a framework is required to support a well-structured and coherent approach to fault tolerance in order to ensure that the additional complexity introduced by the implementation of fault tolerance techniques does not reduce, rather than increase, the reliability of the system. The first and third of these factors are discussed in this chapter. Measures and mechanisms for implementing fault tolerance in computing systems are described in detail in Chapters 5-9.

FAULT TOLERANCE: HOW

Principles of Fault Tolerance

In this book four constituent phases of fault tolerance are identified which, taken together, provide the general means by which fault tolerance can be implemented to prevent faults from leading to system failures. The four phases are (i) error detection; (ii) damage confinement and assessment; (iii) error recovery; and (iv) fault treatment and continued system service.

(i) *Error detection*: In order to tolerate a fault in a system its effects must first be detected. It should be clear from the definition of fault adopted in this book that while a fault cannot be directly detected by a system, the manifestation of the fault will generate errors somewhere in the system. Thus the usual starting point for fault tolerance techniques is the detection of an erroneous state. The measures and mechanisms that can be adopted for error detection are examined in detail in Chapter 5.

(ii) *Damage confinement and assessment*: When an error is detected much more of the system state may be suspect than that initially discovered to be erroneous. Because of the likely delay between the manifestation of a fault and the detection of its erroneous consequences, invalid information may have spread within the system, leading to other errors which have not (yet) been detected. Thus before any attempt is made to deal with the detected error it may be necessary to assess the extent to which the system state has been damaged. This assessment will depend on decisions made by the system designer concerning damage confinement, and on run-time measures and mechanisms for identifying damage; all of these topics are discussed in Chapter 6.

(iii) *Error recovery*: Following error detection and damage assessment, techniques for error recovery must be utilized. These techniques will aim to transform the current erroneous system state into a well defined and error-free state from which normal system operation can continue. Without such a transformation system failure is likely to ensue. Hence, error recovery is one of the most important aspects of fault tolerance and is one of the areas in which most work has been done. This work is described in Chapter 7.

(iv) *Fault treatment and continued service*: Although the error recovery phase may have returned the system to an error-free state, techniques may be required to enable the system to continue providing the service required by its specification, by ensuring that the fault whose effects have been recovered from does not immediately recur. One problem in fault treatment is that the detection of an error does not necessarily serve to identify the fault. The relationship between faults and errors can be complex - even in simple systems it is often the case that more than one fault can give rise to the same error. For example, a parity error on a read from memory may be indicative of a faulty memory unit, a faulty transmission bus, a faulty memory power supply, a faulty parity check, and so on. Thus the first aspect of fault treatment will be to attempt to locate the fault accurately. Following this, steps can be taken to repair the fault or to reconfigure the rest of the system to avoid the fault; alternatively, no action may be needed if the fault was thought to be transient. Techniques for fault treatment are examined in detail in Chapter 8.

These then are the four constituent phases which form the basis for all fault tolerance techniques and thus can and should form the basis for the design and implementation of a fault tolerant system. There can be considerable interplay between the various phases which tends to blur their identification in a particular system. For example, a protection mechanism usually provides one form of error detection and can also play an important role in the design and implementation of the damage assessment phase. Similarly, any damage assessment undertaken by a system will be based on the adoption of exploratory measures to identify possible damage, measures which will themselves use error detection techniques. The provision of error recovery will normally be dependent upon the damage assessment provided (or assumed) in the system, although some forms of error recovery attempt to minimize the need for damage assessment. Finally, fault location is usually based on the use of diagnostic checking, a form of error detection.

The order in which the phases are undertaken may also vary from system to system. Error detection is the normal starting point for fault tolerance. Following this, the other three phases can be in any order, although it is usual for any damage assessment to precede error recovery and fault treatment, since these are likely to depend on the extent of the damage incurred.

It is not necessarily the case that all four phases will actually be operational in a fault tolerant computing system. Often, decisions made during the design of the system can preclude the need for run-time measures and mechanisms within the system. This is usually the case for damage assessment and for the fault location aspect of fault treatment since these exploratory or heuristic techniques are difficult to implement efficiently (and reliably!). Although these phases need not be present in a particular system,

FAULT TOLERANCE: HOW

this does not mean that they are unimportant as far as fault tolerance is concerned. Rather, this simply reflects the fact that they can be considered at system design time, and assumptions made so that the need for run-time measures and mechanisms is precluded. The assumptions will be based on which faults have been foreseen and on the structure presumed to be present in the operational system. For example, in a system containing a protection mechanism for isolating processes from each other, the damage assessment phase might simply assume that the structure imposed by the protection mechanism prevents the spread of damage from an erroneous process to other processes, and not consider the possibility of the protection mechanism itself having failed.

One design decision which precludes the need for measures within the system is to rely on manual intervention. The repair of faults is the obvious example of an activity which is usually performed manually.

Despite these observations, the four basic phases form a useful starting point for the design of a fault tolerant system, identifying the general principles and basic techniques by which fault tolerance can be achieved. Thus one of the steps in the design of a fault tolerant system will be to decide how these phases are to be applied in the implemented system or to what extent the design of the system precludes the need for run-time measures and mechanisms. Before this can be determined the system designer must identify *where* fault tolerance is actually required and assess *how much* is necessary, questions which concern the provision of redundancy in the system.

Redundancy

All techniques for achieving fault tolerance depend upon the effective deployment and utilization of *redundancy*, that is, extra elements in the system which are redundant in the sense that they would not be required in a system which could be guaranteed to be free from faults. The methods by which redundancy has been introduced into a computing system have, in the past, been classified in various ways. A common early classification, derived from systems which provided tolerance only for hardware component faults, naturally separated hardware redundancy from software redundancy. Hardware redundancy was concerned with extra transistors, logic gates, memory units, power supplies and the like, while software redundancy referred only to the extra programs provided to integrate the hardware redundancy into the complete fault tolerant system.

Hardware redundancy has been categorized further into *static* (or masking) redundancy and *dynamic* redundancy.[1] For static redundancy, redundant components are used within a system to provide fault tolerance so that the effects of a component failure are masked from, and not apparent to, the environment of that system. In contrast, dynamic redundancy is employed just to provide an error detection capability within a system, and has to be supplemented by redundancy elsewhere in order to achieve fault tolerance. For example, the use of error correcting codes in memory units can be regarded as an application of static redundancy, while a simple parity code can be viewed as dynamic redundancy since tolerance of a memory fault would require redundancy elsewhere, for instance in the code of the operating system.

The canonical example of the use of static redundancy is Triple Modular Redundancy (TMR). In its standard application, TMR is used to provide tolerance against hardware module failures. Thus, to tolerate a failure of module A in Figure 3.1(a), A could be replaced by the TMR system illustrated in Figure 3.1(b) consisting of three copies of module A (each of identical design) and voting circuits V (i.e. error detecting and recovery circuits) which check the outputs of these modules and select the value of the majority. The system in Figure 3.1(b) is therefore designed to tolerate the failure of any single copy of module A by only producing output on which at least two modules agree.

A more abstract approach leads to another view of redundancy. Given that any system contains a set of components which interact at a number of interfaces, then redundancy within that system may be identified in three forms. Firstly, a component (and therefore all of its interactions) may be redundant; secondly, an interface between two essential components may be redundant; finally, *temporal redundancy* may be utilized in a system, in

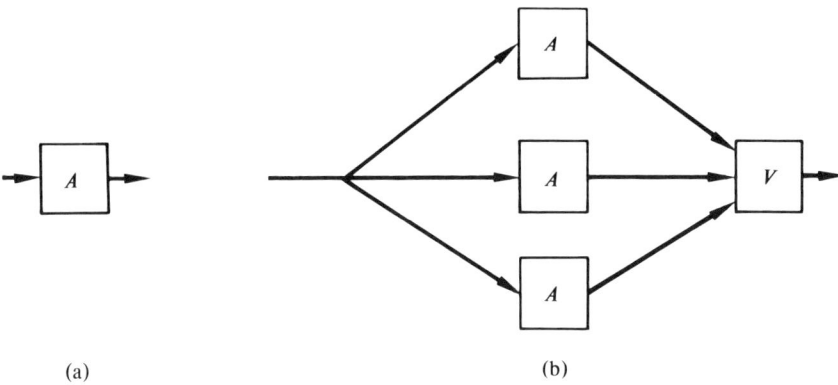

Figure 3.1 Triple Modular Redundancy

that repeated use (which is redundant use in the absence of faults) may be made of a component - of course, additional redundant components will be required to effect the repetition.

The classification of redundancy as either static or dynamic is absolutely dependent upon the structure imposed on the system, and not just on the use made of the redundancy. Different abstract views of a fault tolerant system can lead to different classifications of the redundancy within that system. For example, a parity check coupled with an operating system that kept backup copies of memory pages could be viewed by a user as an application of static redundancy. The reason why static and dynamic are appropriate classifications for hardware redundancy is that physical boundaries tend to dictate the view that can be taken of hardware systems, and hence of their redundancy. In software systems, where structuring tends to be more subjective, this classification is not usually adopted, although it is equally applicable.

FAULT TOLERANCE: WHERE AND HOW MUCH

There are many factors which influence *where* redundancy should be deployed in a system and *how much* is actually required. The governing factor will obviously be the reliability requirements of the particular application, requirements which should form the basis of an accurately documented specification of reliability. Other factors of importance will usually involve some limitation on costs, whether this is expressed in monetary terms to cover the implementation of fault tolerance, or in terms of power, weight and space constraints (as might be the case for air or space borne systems), or even in terms of the time overhead incurred through the use of fault tolerance (likely to be an important factor in real-time systems). Such costs will have to be measured against the possible cost of system failure. Clearly, where a multi-million dollar spacecraft or aircraft is at stake, extensive fault tolerance features are likely to be justifiable; when human lives are involved no technique which could enhance reliability can be excluded from consideration.

The design of a fault tolerant system will be an iterative process, involving identifying the possible faults that could affect a system and evaluating the alternative methods of implementing fault tolerance. The aim of such iterations will be to minimize the redundancy used while maximizing the reliability provided, subject to constraints on the cost of the system. A general view of the alternatives available to a system designer for the provision of fault tolerance follows directly from regarding a system as being constructed from a set of components and a design. From this viewpoint, the faults that could affect the system can only be design faults or component faults. However, component faults can result from design faults within that component or from subcomponent faults, and so on. This recursion can be continued, until atomic components are reached (i.e. components which are treated as being indivisible). Thus, the options open to the system designer for the placement of redundancy relate to the level at which a fault is identified.

To provide reliability in the face of design faults, a system designer must utilize (static) redundancy within the system to provide fault tolerance. Component faults could be dealt with in a similar manner; however, an alternative is to enhance the reliability of the components, by examining their internal structure in order to include redundancy within those components. This, of course, constitutes a shift in viewpoint, regarding the component as a system whose service must be provided reliably, and hence this discussion (and all of the techniques to be described) can then be applied to the component. Redundancy included within a component to improve its reliability can be tailored to suit the specific needs of that component. Indeed, it is widely recognized amongst hardware designers that hardware redundancy is more effective when applied to components rather than to the containing system.[2] Hence, redundancy deployed at low levels within a system can be very economic and effective, but only against particular classes of fault. In contrast, redundancy at the system level to cope with the unreliability of the component will be more expensive to provide, but can be much more general in its ability to contend with a range of faults.

If a fault and its effects can be accurately predicted then specific measures will be more efficient and require less redundancy than global measures provided to tolerate the same fault. However, if unexpected faults are encountered or if the assumptions about a particular fault were unjustified, then global measures are likely to be much more effective. For example, semiconductor memory sometimes suffers from a failure of one storage element, resulting in a single-bit error in a word of the memory. Error correcting codes can be implemented within the storage unit to provide tolerance against such faults at a cost overhead of the order of 25%. However, triplication of the memory unit in a TMR structure, while requiring an overhead of at least 300%, would guard against multiple-bit errors in a word as well as failure of the memory accessing circuits and other related components.

An assumption in the above discussion has been that static redundancy is used within, say, a component to mask the effects of faults from the system of which it is a part. It is also possible to include dynamic redundancy within a component solely for the purpose of error detection. If techniques for the other phases of fault tolerance are not implemented within the component then error detection serves only to warn of the impending failure of the component and thereby enable fault tolerance in the system to be invoked, exactly as if that system had itself detected an error. Further discussion of this point is given in Chapter 5.

The danger of incorporating redundancy into a system is that the overall system reliability could be reduced, due to the increased number of components. In addition, if the redundant components are not themselves sufficiently reliable, there will be little hope of improving the reliability of the system. One of the reasons for requiring a framework within which fault tolerance can be achieved was to separate the components concerned with fault tolerance from the rest of the system, to minimize any increase in complexity. A second reason is that such a separation enables identification of some of the *hardcore* of the system, that is, the critical components which support the fault tolerance activities of the system and which must operate reliably if system failures are to be prevented. Since these components will themselves be systems, their reliability can be enhanced by the use of fault prevention techniques, and by applying fault tolerance internal to those components. If the size, complexity and construction of such critical components are comparable with those of the system for which they are supporting fault tolerance, there will be cause for concern. For example, Wakerly[3] notes that to construct a voting component for three microprocessors in a TMR structure could conceivably require 14 integrated circuit packages constructed from the same (unreliable) technology as the three microprocessor packages, and hence would lead to a system with lower reliability than that of a single microprocessor chip. Clearly the critical components must be such that their reliability can be assured.

Quantitative Reliability Evaluation

In order to determine the extent to which fault tolerance should be adopted within a system and the extent to which critical components may influence the overall system reliability, it is obviously highly desirable that accurate predictions can be made for the reliability of any proposed design. The hardware components in a system are an obvious starting point for reliability evaluation for two main reasons. Firstly, the reliability of any system incorporating software will be very dependent upon the reliability of the hardware components providing the interpretive interface - for example, few programs will get very far if instruction fetching and decoding is unreliable. Secondly, the component failures which can affect a physical system can in principle, and often in practice, be predicted and assessed. Indeed, the traditional approach to fault tolerance, concerned only with hardware component failures, has led to the development of various quantitative models for predicting the reliability of the hardware units in a system. (In these models, reliability is defined to be a function of time, specifying the probability that a system will not have failed by time t assuming fault-free hardware at time 0.)

Hardware reliability predictions are based on a knowledge or presumption of the failure rates of the basic components from which the hardware units are constructed, information which has been derived from data accumulated during component testing. For example, it has been observed that, following an initial 'burn-in' period, electronic components usually fail at a constant rate and their reliability can be modelled by

$$R(t) = e^{-\lambda t}$$

In general, the reliability of hardware systems without redundancy (and without design faults) can be modelled by this equation, where λ is the sum of the failure rates of all of the constituent components.

Since this definition produces an estimate of reliability dependent upon time, another commonly used metric is the Mean Time Between Failure (MTBF) defined as

$$\text{MTBF} = \int_0^\infty R(t)dt.$$

(This evaluates to $1/\lambda$ for a non-redundant system, as might be expected.) A comparison of the MTBF of several competing system proposals will enable the proposal with the most promising reliability to be selected. Alternatively, systems with a fixed 'mission time' (e.g. a 10 hour flight) can be compared by evaluating their probability of failure at the end of this time period using the above equation for $R(t)$, or by calculating the time at which the system will have a specified probability of failure (e.g. the time t' for which $R(t') = 0.95$).

Another metric often quoted for hardware systems is the Mean Time To Repair (MTTR). This is of particular importance in systems which rely on manual intervention to repair faulty units so that a system can be restored to its full capacity. An example of this can be seen in the ESS No. 1A system, where calculations have shown that duplication of critical units is sufficient to enable the reliability requirements to be met, given that a MTTR of less than two hours can be achieved.[4]

If the calculated reliability of a non-redundant system is judged to be insufficient, as is likely to be the case for critical applications, the system designer has two choices: either to improve the inherent reliability of the system through a reduction in the number of components (and/or the use of better components), or to incorporate redundancy and make use of fault tolerance (the options for which were discussed in the previous section).

The analysis of hardware systems employing static or masking redundancy has formed the basis of, for example, many books[2,5,6,7] and papers.[8,9] More recent techniques, particularly for computing systems employing dynamic redundancy, have been based on Markov modelling schemes.[10,11,12] The analytical study of the reliability of hardware systems is an area in which much research is being actively pursued, either to refine existing techniques or to remove some of the assumptions on which previous techniques were based, or even to try and catch up on advances in hardware construction.[13] Recent papers in this area will be found in the IEEE Transactions on Reliability and in the proceedings of the Annual International Symposium on Fault Tolerant Computing.

While mathematical techniques for evaluating the unreliability of computer systems suffering from physical faults are well established, less success has been achieved with techniques intended to be appropriate for systems containing design faults, for example, software systems. If one compares the nature of physical faults to that of design faults, this is not very surprising. For instance, software systems do not wear out (there are many users of manufacturer's operating systems who do not think this is a virtue!). Quantitative measures concerning physical faults are based on three main assumptions:-

(i) component failures will occur independently in independent replicated units;

(ii) the behavior of a physical component can be predicted from data gathered from observations of other components that are assumed to be similar;

(iii) the design of the system is free from faults.

None of these assumptions seems justifiable in a system with design faults (especially the last!). If a system contains a design fault then that fault will be present in all copies of that system - for example, if the design of component A in Figure 3.1 was faulty, the triplicated system would reliably produce wrong results since its design assumes fault independence.

Design faults and their erroneous effects cannot be predicted, except for the gross prediction that a complex component is likely to contain design faults. If the presence of a design fault could be accurately predicted then that fault would be removed from the system, rather than measures being provided to tolerate it. The eradication of a design fault will be permanent, while a physical fault may recur. Furthermore, observing the behavior of components is unlikely to provide data on design faults that is directly applicable to other components with different designs - in contrast, physical component faults are usually assumed to result in failures with a particular frequency distribution (such as a Poisson distribution) applicable to other components.

Despite these difficulties, a number of models have been proposed for reliability evaluation and prediction of software systems. Surveys of over twenty software reliability models have been published elsewhere.[14,15,16] Early models were developed from the well established techniques for hardware systems, but based on assumptions intended to be appropriate for software systems. Some models try to predict the future behavior of the system from its past behavior, trying to estimate the remaining number of faults ('bugs'). Other models use data obtained during system testing and debugging for this prediction; yet others have suggested planting known faults into a system, subjecting the system to testing, and then estimating the remaining number of (unknown) faults from the proportion of known and unknown faults that were exposed during the testing.

Approaches based on 'fault' counting make many assumptions about faults in software systems. For example, one major assumption is that there is a direct relationship between the characteristics and numbers of exposed and undiscovered faults. The problem with this assumption, a standard method of predicting a population from a sample, may be illustrated by considering the estimation of, say, the number of deer in a forest. A caught sample might reflect the total number of deer; more likely it would provide an estimate for the number of deer which were most easily caught, for example those with three legs, and would not be representative of the population as a whole. Similarly, one would not release marked three legged deer in the forest, round up a sample, and use the proportion of marked to unmarked deer to estimate the total (3 and 4 legged) population.

A second important assumption made in several models is that the unreliability of the system will be directly proportional to the number of faults which remain. While it is possible for a fault to lead to a system failure, this need not be the case. For example, a system with a single fault in an infrequently executed piece of code would be expected to be more reliable than a system with a single fault in code executed frequently. Many reliability models for software do not (and cannot) take the operational behavior of the system into account, and hence would not distinguish between these two circumstances.

The development of software reliability models remains an active research area with new models, such as those based on Bayesian techniques,[17] being developed to remove suspect assumptions on which earlier models were based. The models currently proposed for quantitative assessment of the reliability of systems with design faults seem to be based on assumptions which have yet to be justified for real systems. Similar doubts have been expressed elsewhere.[18,19] Empirical investigations of several models[20,21] also casts doubts on their accuracy. The only safe prediction that can be made about design faults is that they will be found in complex systems unless extremely stringent measures are taken to preclude them.

A FRAMEWORK FOR IMPLEMENTING FAULT TOLERANCE

One of the consequences of adding redundancy to a system is that the size and complexity of that system are increased, factors which could lead to a decrease, rather than an increase, in reliability. Since redundancy is necessary for fault tolerance, its incorporation and use within a system must be carefully structured and controlled to minimize any increase in complexity. What is needed is a framework within which the four constituent phases of fault tolerance can be implemented, and the abnormal activities of the system (i.e. the measures for fault tolerance) separated from normal activity and automatically invoked as required.

Consider the system model developed in Chapter 2. A component will receive inputs, which will be requests for service, and will produce responses when the service has been completed. The responses from a component can in fact be separated into two distinct categories, namely normal and abnormal responses. As might be expected, these two categories correspond respectively to those situations where the component has (apparently) provided its normal service satisfactorily, and to those where it has not. As will be discussed below, abnormal responses are usually signalled when there is a fault in a system, and as such are directly appropriate for the initiation of fault tolerance.

The abnormal responses from a component are commonly referred to as exceptional responses or *exceptions*, particularly in software systems, and this terminology will be adopted in this book. Exceptions and facilities for exception handling form the basis of the framework suggested in this book for the implementation of fault tolerance.

Exceptions and Exception Handling

The basic issues concerning exceptions and exception handlers can be discussed from two viewpoints. The more abstract viewpoint would provide further consideration of exceptions in the system model, as begun above. A more practical viewpoint for computing systems is to consider the various issues with respect to an interpretive interface between the 'hardware' and 'software' of a system. The latter viewpoint will be adopted here, for two main reasons. Firstly, this is the most common and perhaps best understood use of exceptions and exception handling mechanisms. Secondly, since the tolerance of 'hardware' faults is often achieved by software techniques, the handling of the hardware component exceptions signalled on an interpretive interface can be of vital importance to the fault tolerance in a system.

However, although the main concepts will be examined with respect to a simple interpretive system, it is claimed that the concepts are useful as a framework for fault tolerance in other forms of system, for instance, in multilevel software systems (discussed in the following section) or within hardware systems. Fault tolerance in hardware systems is not usually explained in terms of exceptions and exception handling. Nevertheless, tolerance within a hardware system of anticipated component failures is often achieved by techniques which may be identified with the handling of exceptions, although the mechanization of the relevant facilities is different to that adopted, say, for an interpretive interface.

Consider a simple system consisting of an interpreter and a program. The interpretation of each instruction in the program can result in one of two types of response from the interpreter: a normal response when execution has proceeded satisfactorily, or some form of exceptional response when something appears to have gone wrong. In the latter case the interpreter is said to *signal* an exception to the program; the program (or more accurately the instruction in the program) which resulted in an exception is said to have *raised* an exception on the interface on which it is executing. As its name suggests, an *exception* is an indication that something out of the ordinary has occurred which must be brought to the attention of the program which raised it. Typical examples of exceptions signalled by interpreters are division by zero, arithmetic overflow and underflow, illegal instruction, protection violation and the like.

Measures that are provided within the program for dealing with an exception are termed the *handler* for that exception, and the signalling of an exception will result in the handler for that exception being invoked. There are various methods by which this could be achieved. One mechanization would be for the interpreter to set a flag which could be interrogated by the program. However, there are two main disadvantages of this approach. Firstly, there is no way to force the program to interrogate the flag and invoke a handler. Secondly, the inefficiency of having to test for exceptions, essentially after every instruction, is likely to discourage the frequent testing that is expedient. It is more usual (and desirable) for the interpreter to support an *exception mechanism* which automatically invokes a handler by forcing a change in the flow of control of the program. For example, an interrupt mechanism is commonly used for this purpose in many computers.

An interpreter will be able to signal several (possibly many) different exceptions to a program, each of which will have a unique name as well as further parameters containing information for use by the handler. It is therefore necessary to provide some means whereby a program can associate a handler with a particular exception. Since there is a fixed set of exceptions which can be signalled by an interpreter (and that set will form part of the specification of the interpretive interface) most present day machines have a static scheme for the association of handlers with exceptions; for example, an interpreter may force a control flow change (a trap) to a prespecified location in response to a particular exception. As will be seen later, a more general scheme for associating handlers with exceptions and for declaring new exceptions is desirable.

The examples of exceptions listed above have the characteristic that they are all signalled by the interpreter when a program has attempted to misuse the interpretive interface, for example, by attempting to divide a number by zero. (This topic is discussed in more detail in Chapter 5.)

Exceptions with this characteristic will be referred to as *interface exceptions*. An interface exception will be signalled when the interpreter detects what is regarded as an error in the program being interpreted, which in many cases will be indicative of a design fault in that program. However, this need not always be so. For example, a read request to a magnetic tape controller may result in an end-of-tape exception being signalled. If the program containing the read request was attempting to read what it erroneously expected to be a valid block of a file then the exception will indicate the presence of a fault in that program. However, if the program had been designed to read files of unknown length from a tape, using the end-of-tape exception to signify the end of the file, then the raising of the exception would be regarded by the designer of the program as part of its normal behavior and not indicative of a fault. Similarly, an illegal instruction exception normally indicates a faulty program, except perhaps in a diagnostic program which was checking the exceptional responses of the system.

While the above examples show that the signalling of an interface exception cannot always be assumed to indicate the presence of a fault, a further class of exceptions can be identified which *must* be associated with faults. Suppose the memory of the simple interpreter system contains a single bit parity check and no further redundancy (i.e. dynamic redundancy is used within the memory). If the parity check in the interpreter detects a parity error when a word is accessed (i.e. one or more bits of the word have been erroneously stored or altered) then there will be nothing the interpreter can do to correct this situation. The usual pragmatic response is for the interpreter to signal an exception in the hope that the program can provide the necessary measures to tolerate the faulty memory. This exception indicates failure of the memory word (and of the interpreter); exceptions signalled in such situations will therefore be classified as *failure exceptions*.

While the handling of a failure exception will be necessary for the fault tolerance activities of a system, interface exceptions can be used for both normal and fault tolerance activities within a program. Indeed, Goodenough[22] proposes exception handling for use as a normal programming construct to handle unusual but valid situations, as in the end-of-tape example above. However, it does not seem appropriate to indiscriminately use an exception mechanism for both abnormal activities and normal processing - a clear separation of these activities is necessary to ensure a coherent approach to fault tolerance. Thus, this book will not consider the use of an exception mechanism for the normal activity of a program, but will assume that exceptions and their handlers are used solely for the implementation of fault tolerance. (Restricting the use of an exception mechanism to fault tolerance is also advocated by others.)[23,24]

A more general view of exceptions, their handlers, and their use for fault tolerance derives from the abstract model of a system. An interface exception will be signalled by a component as a response to an illegal request for service. A failure exception will be signalled by a component if dynamic redundancy within the component detects an error in the internal state of that component, or if fault tolerance (static redundancy) within the component does not succeed in dealing with a fault. For example, the voter in Figure 3.1(b) could signal a failure exception if the outputs from all three copies of module A were different. A failure exception should therefore be signalled if a component determines that for some reason it cannot provide its specified service. Strictly speaking, a failure exception does not necessarily indicate that a component failure has occurred, since the event of failing can only be determined by the system of which that component is a part. However, it will be assumed that the signalling of a failure exception does indicate a failure of a component, which will be attributed to a *component fault* in the system; the associated handler must therefore implement measures appropriate for tolerating that type of fault. In contrast, an interface exception will usually be indicative of a *fault in the design* of the system, and the handler associated with an interface exception should implement measures which provide tolerance for design faults.

Although the classification of an exception as either an interface or failure exception can be useful it is inappropriate for an interpreter to enforce any distinction between the two classes, largely because of the uncertainty involved in associating exceptions with types of fault (this point is elaborated in Chapter 5). Thus the only distinguishing characteristic of an exception signalled by an interpreter will be its name. The specification of the interpretive interface should provide further details of the circumstances in which a particular exception will normally be signalled (e.g. classifying it as an interface or failure exception). Indeed, a complete characterization of the behavior of an interface in terms of objects and operations available must include the exceptions that can be signalled.[25,26] However, it will be the responsibility of the handler in the program to determine the responses appropriate for an exception.

It cannot be guaranteed that a fault in a system will lead directly to a component signalling an exception, and it is therefore necessary to include measures for detecting errors within the system itself. A measure performing a diagnostic check of a component can be used to reveal component failures, while a check on the state of the system can detect errors caused by design faults. When a mechanism for exception handling is available it seems eminently sensible to use that mechanism for structuring the response of the system to any errors it detects. Referring to the simple interpretive system used as the basis of the earlier discussion, what is required is a mechanism which enables the program itself to invoke a particular exception handler if that program detects an erroneous state. To satisfy this requirement, it will be assumed that the interpreter provides an instruction

raise <*exception name, other parameters*>

which can be used by the program to achieve the desired effect. The *other parameters* field of the instruction enables further information to be passed to a handler. (The instruction is called **raise** by analogy with interface exceptions which are said to be raised by the program.) The term 'raising' an exception will be used to describe both explicitly raised exceptions (i.e. through use of the **raise** instruction) and implicitly raised exceptions (i.e. signalled exceptions). The **raise** instruction requires a small generalization of the exception mechanisms supported by an interpreter, essentially to allow a program to define new exceptions to be added to the static set provided by the interpreter, and to allow the association of handlers with these exceptions.

It may also be useful to change the handler associated with an exception as a program proceeds (particularly for interface exceptions). It will be assumed that the exception mechanism provides this facility, allowing a program to **enable** and **disable** handlers for particular exceptions. A simple scope rule such as that applied in block structured languages may be appropriate: a handler for an exception could remain enabled until a new handler for the same exception is enabled, with the disabling of the new handler resulting in the (automatic) enabling of the previous handler. Alternatively, a simpler exception mechanism could require explicit disabling of handlers, perhaps signalling an interface exception if two handlers were enabled for the same exception. The current set of handlers enabled by a program will be referred to as the *handling context* of the program.

While exception handling is an accepted concept in software systems (not always for fault tolerance, it must be noted), few software systems have the simple one level structure in which exception handling issues have so far been discussed. Issues pertaining to exception handling in multilevel systems, in particular those with multiple software extensions, are examined in the following section.

Exception Handling in Multilevel Systems

Exception handling in multilevel interpretive systems is, as might be expected, a straightforward application of the issues discussed in the previous section. Exception handling in multilevel extended interpreter systems raises some new issues which are worthy of consideration. These issues will be discussed with respect to a simple example of an system with a single extension, shown in Figure 3.2, from which further generalizations are straightforward.

Figure 3.2 illustrates a system in which it is assumed that the basic interface L_0 has been extended by an extension F to include 'files' as abstract objects together with their associated operations (e.g. $F.op$ in Figure 3.2). Since F extends the L_0 interface with new objects and operations, it is also desirable that F extends the set of exceptions on L_0 to include new exceptions relevant to operations supported by F. Just as the interpreter will provide checks on the use

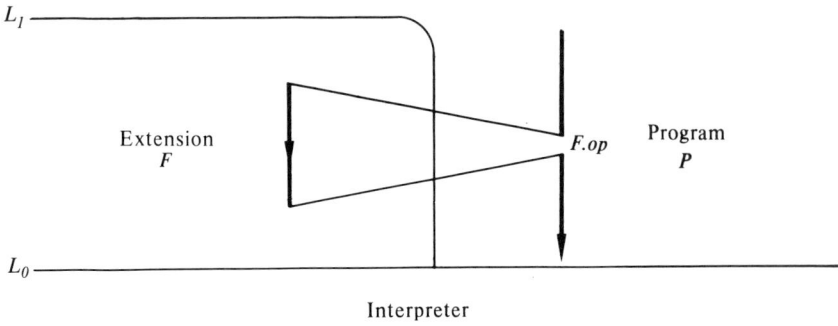

Figure 3.2 A Simple Extended Interpreter System

of the L_0 interface, so F should include checks on the use made of its facilities by P. F should therefore be able to signal interface exceptions to P just as the interpreter can. Similarly, F should be able to signal a failure exception to P should F be unable to provide its specified service.

The signalling of exceptions from F to P could be supported by means of specific arrangements between F and P, but since P need not be aware of the existence of F it is clearly preferable to have a unified exception handling mechanism supported by the interpreter. Thus an interpreter should provide an instruction to enable an extension to signal an exception

signal <*exception name, other parameters*>

When this instruction is executed by an extension (e.g. F) the named exception will be signalled to the caller (e.g. P) of that extension. (As before, the caller is said to have raised the exception.) By this means, a program will not have to distinguish between an exception signalled by an extension and one signalled by the interpreter.

It must be noted that the **signal** instruction is different to the **raise** instruction introduced in the previous section, and both are required. Superficially, both operations may appear to perform similar functions since both are used to initiate fault tolerance by means of exception handling. However, **signal** allows an extension to signal an exception to a calling program *at a higher level of abstraction*, invoking the handler within the calling program; **raise** enables a program to raise an exception *at its own level of abstraction* in order to invoke a handler within that program. For example, in Figure 3.2 F can **signal** an exception to P, invoking a handler provided within P; F can also **raise** an exception which will be dealt with by a handler provided within F and which will not be part of the interface seen by P. The distinction being drawn here between **signal** and **raise** corresponds precisely to the distinction made between **signal** and **exit** in the CLU language.[23]

The existence of multiple levels of abstraction leads to issues concerning the automatic propagation of exceptions from one level to another. For example, suppose that during the execution of F the interpreter signals an exception. If a handler had been provided within F for that exception then there would be no difficulty. However, if there was no handler within F, should the interpreter search the handling context of P for an appropriate handler? Several published opinions on this question[23,24,27] propose the answer 'no', and for sound reasons. The signalling of an exception when an instruction is executed will only have meaning to the program which contained that instruction, and will be meaningless to a program which invoked that program. For example, if P calls F to perform a 'file read' operation, a 'disk read parity' exception signalled by the interpreter during the execution of F would be meaningless to P, since P need not (and should not) be aware of the concrete representation of a file involving the disk. Thus a rule that signalled exceptions are not automatically propagated is appropriate. One of the actions of a handler in F may be to signal a new and different exception to P; however this should be the responsibility of the handler in F and not of the interpreter.

There may be some exceptions raised during the execution of F for which the handlers in F do not have adequate fault tolerance responses. The only sensible response in this situation will be for the handler to signal a failure exception to P in the hope that P contains measures appropriate for dealing with this failure of F. Conceptually, an extension such as F ought to handle all of the exceptions that could be raised during its execution, signalling further exceptions as necessary. Clearly it is also appropriate for the interpreter to signal an exception to indicate to P the failure of F, as a default response should an exception be raised during the execution of F for which F has not in fact enabled a handler.

An exception handler which itself signals an exception exemplifies one aspect of an important and contentious issue in exception handling which concerns the flow of control that follows the termination of a handler. Since this issue is a natural part of the techniques for the phase of fault tolerance concerned with the provision of continued service, discussion of this issue is postponed to Chapter 8.

In the discussion so far an exception signalled by an extension has been assumed to follow what Parnas[28] refers to as the 'calls' hierarchy, that is, the exception is signalled to the program which called the extension. (This may in turn result in the signalling of a different exception further up the call chain, as discussed previously.) Levin[27] proposes a more complex exception mechanism in which an additional set of handling contexts may be searched for appropriate handlers, based on the 'uses' hierarchy.[28] The uses hierarchy associated with an extension identifies that set of programs which have been using the objects and operations supported by an extension. These programs need not be in the calls hierarchy at the time an exception is signalled by the extension. If there is only a single process in the system then there will be little distinction between the calls and uses hierarchy when an exception is signalled. However, if the system supports multiple parallel processes which make shared use of objects maintained by extensions, an exception signalled by an extension may need to be directed to all of the processes that have used that extension, even though those processes may not be on the call chain at that time. Essentially, the propagation of exceptions in the uses hierarchy allows an extension to forewarn all of its users that further calls for service from the extension are likely to result in an exception (at least, until some corrective action has been undertaken) rather than signalling an exception on subsequent calls from the processes concerned.

While the uses hierarchy may be convenient for signalling exceptions in some special situations, Liskov and Snyder[23] conclude that these situations are rare, and solutions can still be implemented (albeit with more complexity) with a mechanism utilizing the calls hierarchy. It does not seem that the extra complexity inherent in the implementation of Levin's mechanism justifies its preference over an exception mechanism using the calls hierarchy, at least as far as fault tolerance is concerned.

Summary of Exception Handling

To summarize, exceptions and exception handling provide a suitable framework for structuring the fault tolerance activities incorporated in a system. This framework allows a clear separation of the abnormal (fault tolerance) activities of a system from its normal activity, which is necessary if the complexity of a system is not to be unduly increased by the addition of redundancy to the system. The detection of an error will result in an exception being raised, with the handler corresponding to the exception being automatically invoked to implement measures necessary for the other phases of fault tolerance.

The interpretive interface between hardware and software is one of the most important places for the provision of exceptions and exception handling mechanisms. Ideally, an interpreter will signal *failure* exceptions indicating the presence of *component faults* and *interface* exceptions when interface violations occur (normally indicative of a *design fault* in a program), and will support an exception mechanism by providing instructions which permit

(i) new exceptions to be declared;

(ii) named exceptions to be raised and signalled, with parameters allowing further information to be passed to a handler;

(iii) handlers for exceptions to be enabled and disabled.

The implementation of these facilities by an interpreter is relatively straightforward. Declaration of an exception merely involves the interpreter making an entry in a symbol table of exception names, in which the exceptions that can be signalled by the interpreter will form a fixed part. If the raising of an exception is expected to be a relatively infrequent event, as should certainly be the case when exceptions are used to support fault tolerance, then enabling a handler need only involve recording information in the appropriate handling context to indicate the availability of a handler. When a program explicitly raises an exception, the interpreter must perform a search of the handling context of that program to locate a handler. The signalling of an exception will cause the interpreter to search the handling context of the program containing the instruction which (implicitly) raised the exception. In the event that no handler exists a failure exception will be signalled by the interpreter.

Several recent papers on exception handling in software systems have proposed features similar to those described in this section, albeit within a programming language framework.[22,23,24] Indeed, programming languages such as Ada,[29] PL/I,[30] Mesa[31] and CLU[23] appear to provide many of these facilities (although not always supporting the manner in which this section has suggested exception handling be used). However, a close examination of an implementation of such language oriented features usually reveals that they are not implemented by an underlying mechanism, but that measures are (automatically) incorporated in a program by a compiler to obtain the desired effects. While there is nothing intrinsically wrong with this approach, the increased efficiency and security of interpreter-provided mechanisms is desirable, particularly when exception handling is used for fault tolerance. Compiler generated measures are required because of the inflexibility of current, hardware implemented exception mechanisms. If, as is suggested here, exception handling can play a vital part in the implementation of fault tolerance in a system, consideration of the issues discussed in this section could lead to architectures tailored for fault tolerance with mechanisms for the direct support of suitable exception handling features.

REFERENCES

1. R.A. Short, "The Attainment of Reliable Digital Systems Through the Use of Redundancy - A Survey," *IEEE Computer Group News* **2**(2), pp.2-17 (March 1968).
2. R.E. Barlow and F. Proschan, *Statistical Theory of Reliability and Life Testing*, Holt Rinehart and Winston, New York (1975).
3. J.F. Wakerly, "Microcomputer Reliability Improvement Using Triple-Modular Redundancy," *Proceedings of the IEEE* **64**(6), pp.889-895 (June 1976).
4. P.W. Bowman et al., "Maintenance Software," *Bell System Technical Journal* **56**(2), pp.255-287 (February 1977).
5. R.E. Barlow and F. Proschan, *Mathematical Theory of Reliability*, Wiley, New York (1965).
6. M.L. Shooman, *Probabilistic Reliability: An Engineering Approach*, McGraw-Hill, New York (1968).
7. D.J. Smith, *Reliability Engineering*, Pitman, London (1972).
8. W.G. Bouricius et al., "Reliability Modeling Techniques for Fault Tolerant Computers," *IEEE Transactions on Computers* **C-20**(11), pp.1306-1311 (November 1971).
9. J.A. Abrahams and D.P. Siewiorek, "An Algorithm for the Accurate Reliability Evaluation of Triple Modular Redundancy Networks," *IEEE Transactions on Computers* **C-23**(7), pp.652-692 (July 1974).
10. Y-W. Ng and A. Avizienis, "A Reliability Model for Gracefully Degrading and Repairable Fault-Tolerant Systems," *Proceedings FTCS-7: Seventh Annual International Conference on Fault-Tolerant Computing*, Los Angeles (CA), pp.22-28 (June 1977).
11. J.H. Wensley et al., "SIFT: Design and Analysis of a Fault-Tolerant Computer for Aircraft Control," *Proceedings of the IEEE* **66**(10), pp.1240-1255 (October 1978).

12. J.H. Lala and A.L. Hopkins, "Survival and Dispatch Probability Models for the FTMP Computer," *Digest of Papers FTCS-8: Eighth Annual International Conference on Fault-Tolerant Computing*, Toulouse, pp.37-43 (June 1978).
13. A. Avizienis, "Fault-Tolerance: The Survival Attribute of Digital Systems," *Proceedings of the IEEE* **66**(10), pp.1109-1125 (October 1978).
14. D. Swearingen and J. Donahas, "Quantitive Software Reliability Models - Data Parameters: A Tutorial," *Workshop on Quantitative Software Models*, Kiamesha Lake (NY), pp.143-153 (October 1979).
15. J.-C. Rault, "The Many Facets of Quantitative Assessment of Software Reliability," *Workshop on Quantitative Software Models*, Kiamesha Lake (NY), pp.224-231 (October 1979).
16. V. Vemuri, "The Current State of Software Reliability Modeling," *Workshop on Quantitative Software Models*, Kiamesha Lake (NY), pp.232-238 (October 1979).
17. B. Littlewood, "A Bayesian Differential Debugging Model for Software Reliability," *Workshop on Quantitative Software Models*, Kiamesha Lake (NY), pp.170-181 (October 1979).
18. B. Littlewood, "How to Measure Software Reliability and How Not To," *IEEE Transactions on Reliability* **R-28**(2), pp.103-110 (June 1979).
19. P.B. Moranda, "Software Quality Technology," *Computer* **11**(11), pp.72-78 (November 1978).
20. A.N. Sukert, "Empirical Validation of Three Software Error Prediction Models," *IEEE Transactions on Reliability* **R-28**(3), pp.199-204 (August 1979).
21. R.M. Reiss, "A Prediction Experiment with Three Software Reliability Models," *Workshop on Quantitative Software Models*, Kiamesha Lake (NY), pp.190-200 (October 1979).
22. J.B. Goodenough, "Exception Handling: Issues and a Proposed Notation," *Communications of the ACM* **18**(12), pp.683-696 (December 1975).

23. B.H. Liskov and A. Snyder, "Exception Handling in CLU," *IEEE Transactions on Software Engineering* **SE-5**(6), pp.546-558 (November 1979).

24. F. Cristian, "Exception Handling and Software-Fault Tolerance," *Digest of Papers FTCS-10: 10th International Symposium on Fault-Tolerant Computing Systems*, Kyoto, pp.97-103 (October 1980).

25. F. Cristian, "Robust Data Abstractions," *Acta Informatica* (To Appear).

26. M.E. Majster, "Treatment of Partial Operations in the Algebraic Specification Technique," *Proceedings of Conference on Specifications of Reliable Software*, Boston (MA), pp.190-197 (April 1979).

27. R.A. Levin, "Program Structures for Exceptional Condition Handling," Ph.D. Thesis, Carnegie Mellon University, Pittsburgh (PA) (1977).

28. D.L. Parnas, "On a Buzzword: Hierarchical Structure," *IFIP Congress 74*, Stockholm, pp.336-339 (August 1974).

29. D.C. Luckham and W. Polak, "Ada Exception Handling: An Axiomatic Approach," *ACM Transactions on Programming Languages and Systems* **2**(2), pp.225-233 (April 1980).

30. M.D. MacLaren, "Exception Handling in PL/I," *SIGPLAN Notices* **12**(3), pp.101-104 (March 1977).

31. J.G. Mitchell, W. Maybury, and R. Sweet, "Mesa Language Manual (Version 5.0)," CSL-79-3, Xerox Palo Alto Research Center (CA) (April 1979).

4

FAULT TOLERANT SYSTEMS

In the chapters that follow, the measures and mechanisms which can be implemented to support the four constituent phases of fault tolerance are illustrated by practical examples taken, in the main, from fault tolerant systems that were actually constructed and put into operation. In order to set the scene for subsequent discussion of these examples, this chapter provides an overview of the seven systems from which the majority of examples have been taken.

The example systems have been chosen to illustrate the range of fault tolerance techniques adopted in response to the different reliability requirements imposed on these systems. Information on the example systems has been obtained solely from the referenced papers. In consequence, when the new terminology and insight which it is hoped this book provides is applied to some systems, possible inadequacies in those systems appear which may simply be a reflection on the documentation available for a system. It is not the aim of this book to present a detailed critique of any particular system, but to illustrate techniques and ideas and the utility of the proposed framework and terminology. While no attempt has been made in these chapters to cover every fault tolerant system, the bibliography at the end of the book provides annotated references to the important fault tolerant systems that have been proposed or built.

Seven systems are examined in some detail in this chapter and in those that follow. These systems are the ESS No. 1A, SIFT, FTMP, System R, JPL-STAR, Pluribus and the Tandem 16 system.

ESS NO. 1A

One application area in which computers are playing an ever increasing role is in the control of telephone switching systems. This application is well exemplified by the Bell Systems Electronic Switching Systems (ESS) which have been under development since 1953. Continuous commercial operation commenced in 1965 with the No. 1 ESS, a system supporting large telephone offices of up to 65000 lines and capable of handling 100,000 calls per hour. Since that time over 1000 No. 1 ESS systems have been put into service and other ESS models have been developed for smaller switching offices. (An overview of the development of the ESS systems is given by Toy.)[1]

The reliability and availability requirements for the ESS systems are extremely stringent: down-time of the total system is not supposed to exceed 2 hours over a 40 year period, with not more than 0.02% of calls being handled incorrectly. The computer system (referred to subsequently as the processor, to conform with the terminology used by Bell) is the crucial part of the system; failure of the processor results in a total loss of system function. In consequence, a design objective for the processor is that its down-time should not exceed two thirds of the total system down-time. This limits the processor to being out of service for not more than 2 minutes per year, in a system which is expected to be operational 24 hours a day, 365 days a year. In order to achieve this high level of reliability and availability, extensive redundancy has been incorporated into the ESS processors to provide tolerance against hardware faults and to allow necessary (manual) repair activities to take place, without disrupting the operation of the system. The discussion here will concentrate on the features incorporated in the ESS No. 1A,[2,3] the successor to the No. 1 ESS.

System Description

An overview of the hardware units which constitute the No. 1A processor is given in Figure 4.1. As can be seen, the processor is constructed from four main types of units:

(i)   the central processing units (CPU0 and CPU1);

(ii) the program stores;

(iii) the call stores;

(iv) the auxiliary units.

The CPUs are connected to all other units by the three buses shown in Figure 4.1. These buses are in fact duplicated although this has been omitted from the figure for clarity.

Figure 4.1 shows that the main form of redundancy in the No. 1A hardware is the replication of critical units. The CPU, being at the heart of the system, is fully duplicated (CPU0 and CPU1). During normal system operation one of the CPUs is designated as the *active* unit and controls the activity of the system, with the other *(stand-by)* CPU monitoring the active CPU, ready to assume the role of active unit if trouble is encountered. The timings for the rest of the system originate from a digital clock in the active CPU. This clock also provides timing signals for both the active and stand-by CPUs which therefore operate synchronously.

The program stores, as their name suggests, hold the programs being executed by the CPUs. To simplify the provision of spares and the introduction of new software releases, the program stores in the No. 1A are constructed from core stores, a departure from the No. 1 ESS which relied on read-only program stores. Redundancy for the program stores is provided by so-called rover stores, which are stand-by spare units that can be put into service as program stores if necessary. The information necessary for processing and routing telephone calls is held in the call store complex, which is also constructed from core stores in the No. 1A processor.

The random-access memory in the system is divided into protected and unprotected areas. This division is enforced by the active CPU, which contains the mapping registers defining these areas, and which provides different instructions to write to the different areas. The mapping

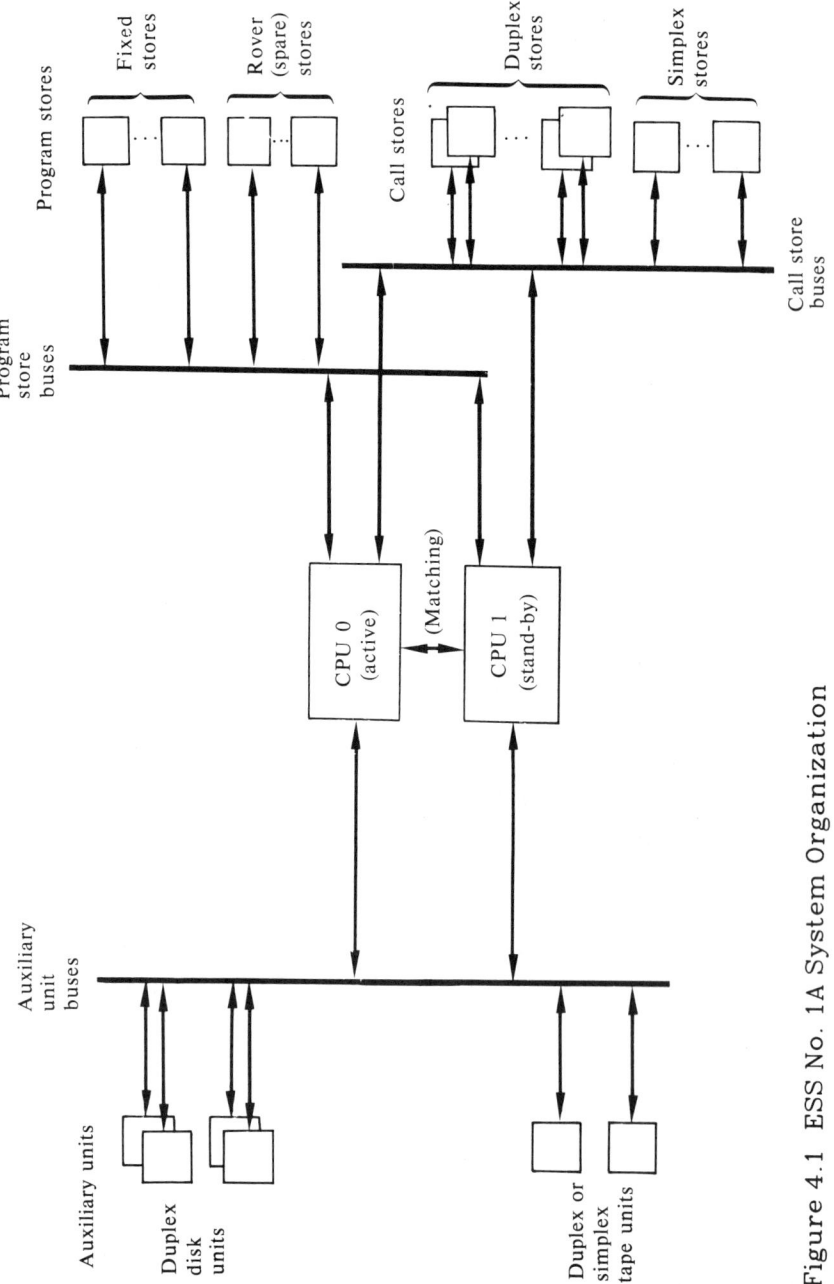

Figure 4.1 ESS No. 1A System Organization

registers are software controlled via other (special) write instructions. Basically, the protected area contains the parts of the memory that are not duplicated (e.g. the program stores), as well as those locations which vitally affect the operation of the system (e.g. the internal registers of the CPUs).

The auxiliary units consist of bulk storage devices and their controllers, essentially disk and tape units. The disks provide a file store for the system, used mainly for retaining backup versions of programs and data and for holding infrequently used programs. The tape units are used to record the accounting information which is generated for completed calls, as well as infrequently used portions of the system data base. All of the auxiliary units operate autonomously, competing with the CPUs for access to the core stores.

The call processing programs are divided into two classes, deferrable and non-deferrable. The deferrable programs are those for which data is already in the system, and these programs are not therefore critically time dependent. The non-deferrable programs (e.g. input/output programs) are those which must be executed according to a strict schedule and are activated by a clock interrupt. For example, the program that detects and receives dial pulses has to be run at regular intervals.

Reliability Strategies

The accumulation of experience from the earlier ESS systems has enabled the designers of the 1A processor to identify four main categories of problems likely to cause system down-time. The four categories and their expected contributions to system down-time are as follows:

(i) hardware unreliability - 0.4 minutes per year

(ii) software unreliability - 0.3 minutes per year

(iii) procedural faults - 0.6 minutes per year

(iv) fault tolerance deficiencies - 0.7 minutes per year

Hardware unreliability covers the faults that prevent a working system configuration from being established. All critical units in the ESS No. 1A are duplicated to minimize this cause of down-time. *Software unreliability* is expected to cause almost as many problems as hardware, even though some of the thoroughly-tested programs from the No. 1 ESS are used. *Procedural faults* arise from manual interactions with the operation of the ESS No. 1A, since manual intervention by operators and maintenance personnel can override much of the protection that has been built into the system. For example, having isolated a faulty CPU a maintenance engineer might erroneously pull circuit boards out of the active CPU and hence bring the system down.

Tolerance of hardware faults is achieved by a combination of hardware and software techniques. In the main, error detection is implemented in hardware (e.g. operation of the active CPU is checked against that of the stand-by CPU by matching circuits) with exceptions being signalled by means of an interrupt mechanism to invoke the fault treatment programs which form a major component of the fault tolerance techniques. *Fault tolerance deficiencies*, which are expected to be the major cause of system down-time, concern the deficiencies in these programs.

Tolerance of software faults is limited to attempts at maintaining the consistency of the data base. The programs that perform these error detection and recovery actions are referred to as the *audit programs*.

SIFT AND FTMP

In commercial aircraft, computers are usually used to provide a variety of services such as navigation, semi-automatic landings, flight control and stability augmentation. However, these services are not critical and the safety of the aircraft is not dependent upon the computer; the crew are always available to provide manual backup if computer failure occurs.

As part of a program investigating the design of new aircraft which are intended to be much more efficient in their use of fuel than those currently in service, NASA is studying aircraft which would operate with greatly reduced stability margins and would as a result be totally dependent on computer control for the safety of a flight. Computer systems used in this way will be required to have reliability characteristics comparable to those specified for other aircraft parts. A typical figure is that the probability of failure should be less than 10^{-9} per hour for a 10 hour flight, during which no maintenance will be available.

NASA are sponsoring two independent research projects investigating the design and implementation of a computer system to match these requirements. The two architectures under development are SIFT (Software Implemented Fault Tolerance)[4] which has been designed at SRI International, and FTMP (Fault Tolerant Multiprocessor)[5] at the C.S. Draper Laboratory. At a superficial level both systems have features in common; for instance, both systems are similar in their provision of redundancy at the hardware level, containing at least three times the resources nominally required for the critical tasks. Despite their similarities, each system embodies a different approach to the implementation of a fault tolerant computing system capable of meeting the above reliability requirements.

SIFT System Design

The three main hardware sub-systems in a SIFT system, as illustrated in Figure 4.2, are:
(i) main processing modules;
(ii) input/output (I/O) processing modules;
(iii) buses.

The computational power for the applications programs is provided by the main processing modules, each of which consists of a CPU and some memory, connected by a high bandwidth direct link. In a production system, the memory would consist of read-only areas in which programs would be permanently stored, and read-write areas for data storage. The current design of SIFT supports up to eight processing modules in one system. The I/O system is structurally similar to the processing modules, but has smaller computational and memory capacity. The processors in the I/O system are connected to the sensors and actuators of the aircraft. Up to five I/O processors can be incorporated in one system.

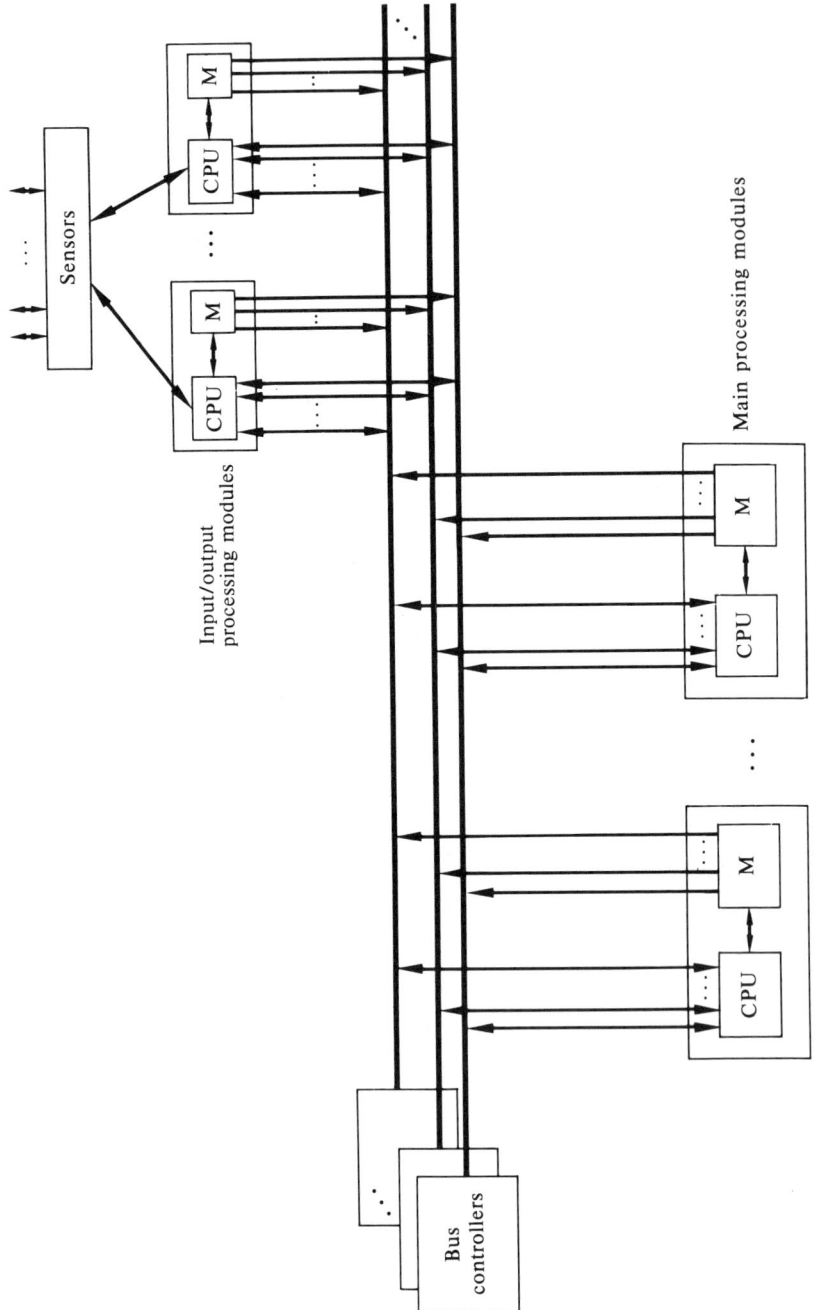

Figure 4.2 SIFT System Organization

Processing modules are interconnected by a bus system which consists of multiple buses (up to five) and their controllers. Every processor and memory module is connected to all of the buses. Each processor can therefore read, by an explicit command, from any memory module via any bus. Writing to memory via the buses is not permitted; the processor in a processing module can only write to its own memory, not to the memory of other modules.

The software system of SIFT consists of two main parts; the applications software and the executive software. The applications software is responsible for the actual computations associated with flight control, and is structured as a set of iterative tasks, each of which has a particular iteration rate. In each iteration a task will normally: obtain its inputs from the executive software; calculate the necessary output values; and make its outputs available for input to the next iteration via the executive. The multi-computer organization of the SIFT system is not visible to the applications software.

The executive software is responsible for scheduling the application tasks and controlling their inputs and outputs as mentioned above. The executive software is structured into two parts: a global executive concerned with system-wide functions, and a local executive concerned with the functions local to a particular processing module.

SIFT Reliability Strategies

One of the main aims of the SIFT design has been to utilize standard units in the system wherever possible. The only units that required special design were the bus system and its associated interconnection devices. Moreover, the processing modules and the I/O processing modules do not contain special hardware provisions for implementing fault tolerance - even simple techniques such as parity checks on the memory are not included since (it is claimed) such techniques would not significantly improve the reliability of the system.

The basic aim of SIFT is to provide the applications task with an extremely reliable interpretive interface with *no* failure exceptions. The approach is based on NMR with each task iteration being executed in parallel on at least three processing modules. The processors operate in loose synchronization, with the executive simply ensuring that the iterations do not get out of step with each other. The input to a task iteration is chosen by its local executive, voting on all of the outputs produced by the previous executions of that task and selecting the value of the majority.

The implementation of the NMR structure of software execution is the responsibility of the executive software, as suggested by the system name 'Software Implemented Fault Tolerance'. Of course, this means that the executive is a critical component of the system since design faults in the executive are likely to result in system failures. In an attempt to ensure that the executive software contains no faults, the SIFT designers intend to give a rigorous mathematical proof of its correctness.

FTMP System Design

FTMP is a multiprocessor system consisting of a number of processing modules, global memory modules, and input/output modules, connected together by multiple buses. An engineering prototype will contain 10 of each module interconnected by five buses. A processing module consists of a CPU, and a small private memory acting as a high-speed buffer for items accessed from the global memory. For example, programs are loaded from the global memory into the buffer memory for execution.

FTMP Reliability Strategies

In common with SIFT, the aim of FTMP is to provide an applications program with a highly reliable interpretive interface by replicating the execution of a program in different processors. However, FTMP differs from SIFT in three main ways. Firstly, the replicated executions of a program occur in tight synchronization, with the processors operating in bit-synchronization. Secondly, FTMP supports only TMR replication, whereas the more general NMR strategy is possible in SIFT (although TMR is expected to be the most common). Thirdly, and most importantly, FTMP differs from SIFT in the implementation of the replication. While the SIFT designers have adopted a software controlled implementation, the FTMP designers have provided specialized hardware support to enable three modules of the same type to be configured to operate together in what is termed a *triad*.

A simplified view of an FTMP module is given in Figure 4.3 (the module may be a processing module, a global memory module or an input/output module).

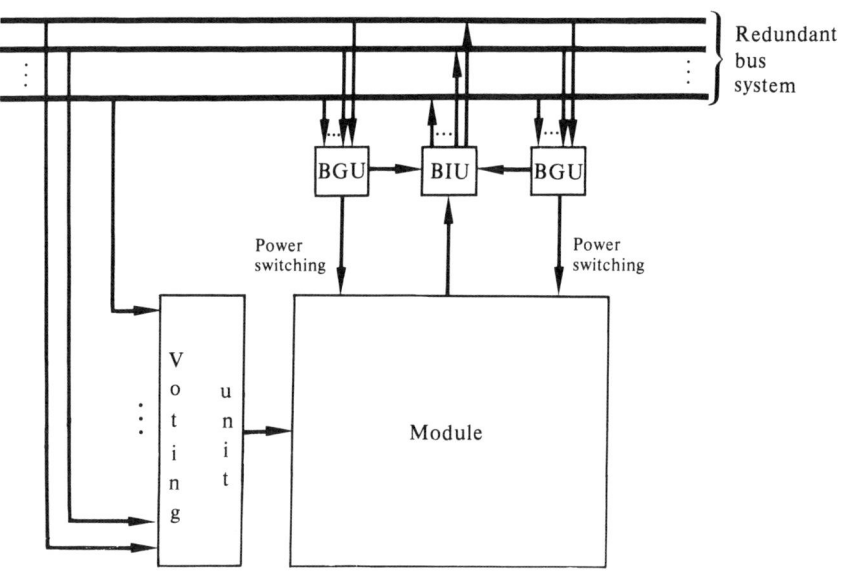

Figure 4.3 FTMP Module

The status of every module is controlled by special hardware units called Bus Guardian Units (BGU). The responsibilities of these units include control of the power supplied to the module and selection of the bus on which the module is permitted to transmit. All Bus Guardian Units are addressable and are controlled by messages sent to them by the operating system executing on a processor triad. The BGUs, being a critical part of the system, are duplicated for enhanced reliability. The Bus Isolation Unit (BIU), which actually connects the outputs of a module to the redundant bus system, is controlled by the BGUs. The Voting Unit of each module compares data transmitted redundantly to a unit over several buses and selects that value agreed on by the majority.

SYSTEM R

In many computer systems it is vital that the information entrusted to the system is not lost or corrupted. Thus fault tolerance has been adopted as a means of providing reliable storage in many data base systems, particularly for the purpose of providing tolerance to failures of the hardware units on which the data was stored, and against system stoppages which could leave the data base in an inconsistent state.

System R[6] is an experimental relational data base management system designed and implemented at the IBM San Jose Research Laboratory. (Many novel aspects of System R and its query language do not impinge on its fault tolerance and will not therefore be considered in this book.) There are two main software components of System R, called the Relational Data System (RDS) and the Relational Storage System (RSS). These components are implemented as extensions to an IBM 370 machine and its operating system, as illustrated in Figure 4.4.

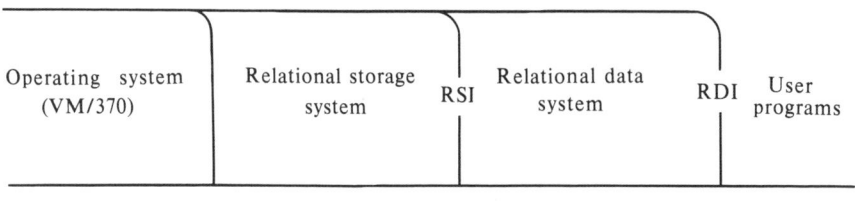

Figure 4.4 System R Organization

SYSTEM R
105

The Relational Data Interface (RDI) implemented by the RDS is the principal interface between a user and the data base, providing high-level features for data retrieval, manipulation and definition, as well as mechanisms to assist in the provision of fault tolerance at the user level. The RDS is built upon the Relational Storage Interface (RSI) provided by the RSS. The RSS provides access to the raw data in the data base, by controlling devices, buffer and space allocation and the like. Measures for fault tolerance are also included in the RSS, particularly to provide for recovery to a consistent state following a system crash.

JPL-STAR

One of the first major investigations into many aspects of fault tolerance was undertaken at the Jet Propulsion Laboratory (JPL), resulting in the design and implementation in 1969 of the JPL-STAR (Self Testing and Repairing) computer.[7] The JPL-STAR was designed as a general purpose computer whose main characteristics were chosen to match the requirements of a spacecraft guidance, control, and data acquisition system to be used on long unmanned space missions of 10 or more years duration. The redundancy incorporated in the JPL-STAR and the fault tolerance techniques adopted reflected the no-maintenance-available environment in which it was expected to function, in contrast to the other systems described here for which manual maintenance could always be provided.

A simplified diagram of the JPL-STAR is shown in Figure 4.5. The TARP (Test And Repair Processor) was one of the main features of the system, implementing in hardware the majority of the fault tolerance techniques. TMR was used to provide highly reliable operation of the TARP; three copies were operational at all times with stand-by spares to replace copies identified as being faulty. The CPU in the JPL-STAR was partitioned into a number of separate units, with stand-by spares for each unit. Stand-by spares were maintained in an unpowered condition. Redundant buses were used to interconnect all units.

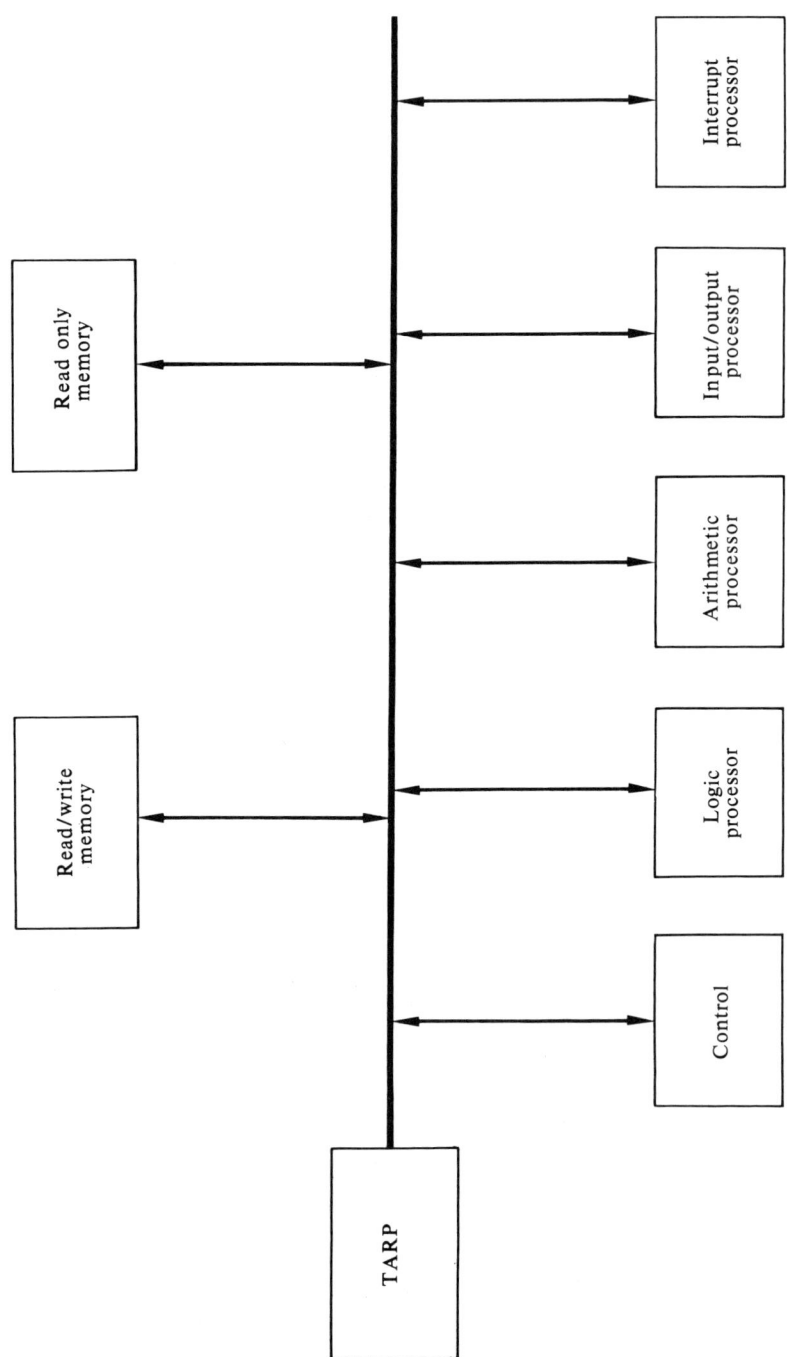

Figure 4.5 JPL-STAR System Organization

A single extension (the STAREX operating system)[8] was provided which assisted in the implementation of some aspects of fault tolerance, dealing with memory failure exceptions signalled by the TARP and providing recovery to the applications programs.

PLURIBUS

The Pluribus[9] is a multiprocessor system, designed by Bolt, Beranek and Newman, originally to serve as an interface message processor (IMP) for the Advanced Research Projects Agency (ARPA) computer network ARPANET. Essentially, the IMPs act as communications processors, providing a message transmission facility between nodes of the network, implemented as a store-and-forward packet switching system. The activities of an IMP are concerned with packet receipt, routing and retransmission as well as connecting host systems to the rest of the network. An IMP is only a component of a larger system (the network) which itself incorporates some fault tolerance features; for instance, if a sending IMP does not receive an acknowledgment after the transmission of a packet, then retransmission via another IMP and communications line (if one exists) can be attempted. Thus the reliability requirements for an IMP place emphasis on availability, rather than fault-free operation. Occasional losses of a packet or message, or short periods of down-time, are considered to be acceptable.

TANDEM 16

The Tandem 16 system[10] is one of the first commercially available fault tolerant systems. The system was designed to provide high availability for applications such as on-line data base transaction processing systems. The basic philosophy of the Tandem system is that no single hardware component failure should result in a system failure. To this end, the system has been designed as a multiprocessor system with redundant interconnections between processors and their peripherals. A typical system configuration is shown in Figure 4.6. A Tandem system can have between 2 and 16 processing modules, each containing its own main memory, power supplies and input/output channel. Two interprocessor buses (the dynabus) provide a high bandwidth communications path between all processors. Peripheral controllers can be attached to two separate input/output channels. An extension, the Tandem operating system,[11] implements the responses of the system to faults, providing reconfiguration to avoid faulty units and permitting on-line repair and maintenance of the hardware.

TANDEM 16 109

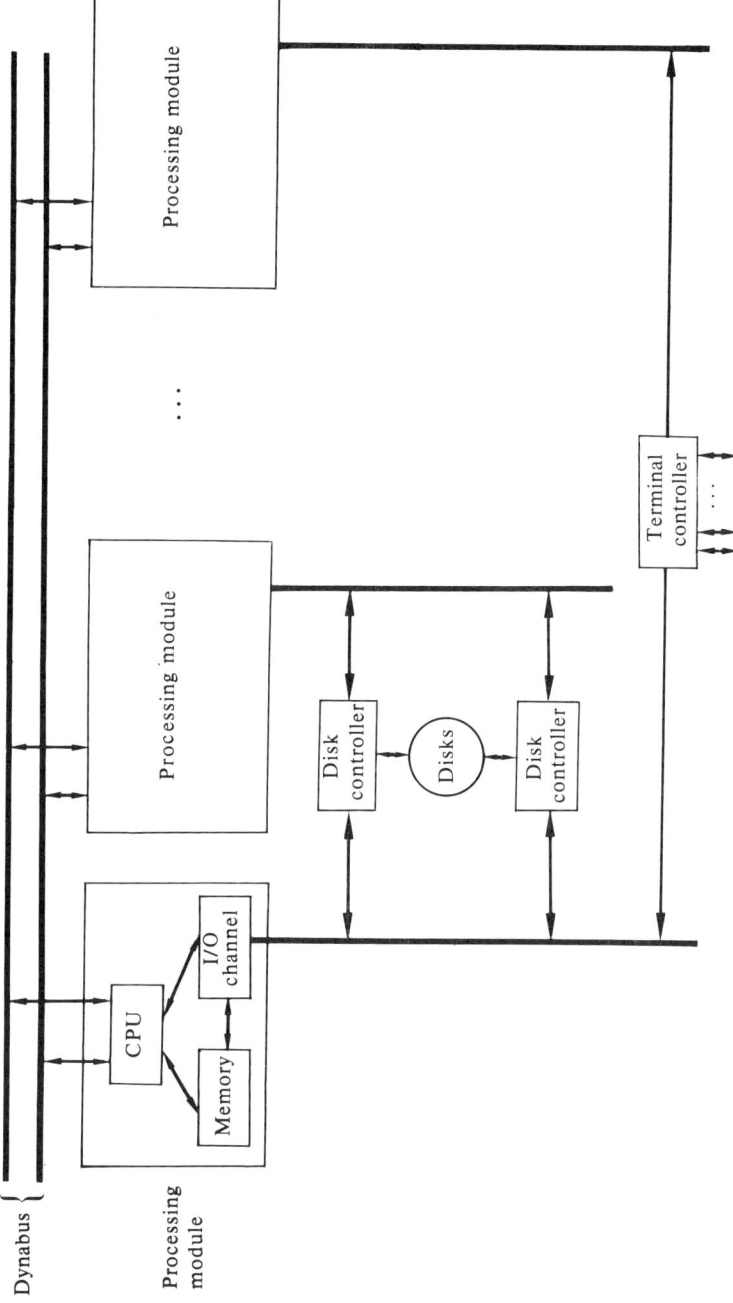

Figure 4.6 Tandem 16 System Organization

REFERENCES

1. W.N. Toy, "Fault-Tolerant Design of Local ESS Processors," *Proceedings of the IEEE* **66**(10), pp.1126-1145 (October 1978).
2. G.F. Clement and R.D. Royer, "Recovery from Faults in the No. 1A Processor," *Digest of Papers FTC-4: Fourth Annual International Symposium on Fault-Tolerant Computing*, Urbana (IL), pp.5.2-5.7 (January 1974).
3. Bell Laboratories, "ESS No. 1A Processor," *Bell Systems Technical Journal* **56**(2) (February 1977).
4. J.H. Wensley et al., "SIFT: Design and Analysis of a Fault-Tolerant Computer for Aircraft Control," *Proceedings of the IEEE* **66**(10), pp.1240-1255 (October 1978).
5. A.L. Hopkins, T.B. Smith, and J.H. Lala, "FTMP - A Highly Reliable Fault-Tolerant Multiprocessor for Aircraft," *Proceedings of the IEEE* **66**(10), pp.1221-1240 (October 1978).
6. M.M. Astrahan et al., "System R: Relational Approach to Database Management," *ACM Transactions on Database Systems* **1**(2), pp.97-137 (June 1976).
7. A. Avizienis et al., "The STAR (Self-Testing and Repairing) Computer: An Investigation of the Theory and Practice of Fault-Tolerant Computer Design," *IEEE Transactions on Computers* **C-20**(11), pp.1312-1321 (November 1971).
8. J.A. Rohr, "STAREX Self-Repair Routines: Software Recovery in the JPL-STAR Computer," *Digest of Papers FTC/3: 73 International Symposium on Fault-Tolerant Computing*, Palo Alto (CA), pp.11-16 (June 1973).
9. D. Katsuki et al., "Pluribus - An Operational Fault-Tolerant Multiprocessor," *Proceedings of the IEEE* **66**(10), pp.1146-1159 (October 1978).
10. J.A. Katzman, "A Fault-Tolerant Computing System," *Proceedings of Eleventh Hawaii International Conference on System Sciences*, Honolulu (HA), pp.85-102 (January 1978).

11. J.F. Bartlett, "A 'NonStop' Operating System," *Proceedings of Eleventh Hawaii International Conference on System Sciences*, Honolulu (HA), pp.103-117 (January 1978).

5

ERROR DETECTION

The starting point for all fault tolerance strategies is the detection of an erroneous state, that is a state which, in the absence of any corrective actions, could have led to a failure of the system. Thus the success of any fault tolerant system will be critically dependent upon the effectiveness of the techniques for error detection.

In principle, the more error detection is utilized in a system the better it will be for reliable operation, since if all errors were detected and appropriate techniques were applied to recover from those errors, then no fault could lead to system failure. In practice there will be limitations to the amount of error detection that can be provided. Obvious limitations are the cost of the redundancy needed for error detection and the overheads incurred at run-time by extensive checking. Other limitations will be discussed subsequently.

The first two sections of this chapter will discuss error detection with respect to measures and mechanisms; measures that can be incorporated into any system consisting of a set of components; and mechanisms that can be implemented in an interpreter to provide error detection on behalf of programs executing on the interpretive interface. The aims of these measures and mechanisms will be to raise exceptions (see Chapter 3) following which the other phases of fault tolerance provided within exception handlers will be automatically invoked. As can be imagined, the characteristics that are assumed for a particular exception will play an important part in determining the subsequent activity of the handler and the fault tolerance techniques it adopts, for instance, whether specific or general purpose recovery is appropriate. Therefore the final section of this chapter will examine the important role played by structuring the incorporation of error detection in a system so that the specific exceptions that are raised result in appropriate responses from their handlers.

MEASURES FOR ERROR DETECTION

Design faults and component faults in a system will lead to the generation of erroneous states. This section will examine the measures that can be incorporated in a system to perform the checks necessary to detect errors and consequently **raise** exceptions.

As with most measures, there is a wide spectrum of alternatives available. Ideally, the checks incorporated in a system will be so exhaustive that if no errors are detected then none exist, and the operation of the system can be guaranteed to have conformed to its specification. At the other extreme such checks might be minimal, with reliance being placed instead on mechanisms for error detection (which are the subject of the next section). The following discussion will concentrate first on the ideal approaches to error detection, and will then examine the practical limitations which necessitate the adoption of less stringent measures.

Consider a system S which has been designed to provide a specified service. If the behavior of S does not conform to that prescribed in the specification then S has failed. Since the purpose of fault tolerance is to prevent failures, it follows that useful measures for error detection can be based on intercepting the outputs produced by S and checking whether those outputs would in fact conform to the specification. In effect, this results in a new system S' consisting of S (as a component) with extra components to perform the check, as shown in Figure 5.1.

MEASURES FOR ERROR DETECTION

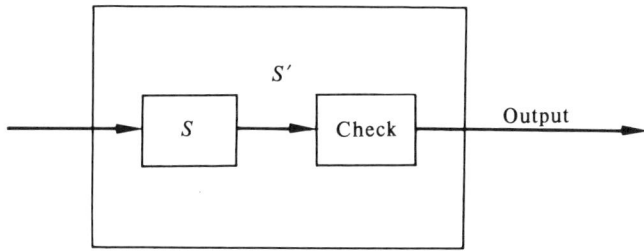

Figure 5.1 System With Check

A first criterion for an ideal check is that it should be based *solely* on the specification, and should not be influenced at all by the internal design and implementation of S. Checks based on the internal construction of S can of course be useful, as will be discussed subsequently. However, the design of S will reflect the service that its designer thought should be provided, which may not be exactly what had been defined in the specification. Thus ideal checks will treat the system as a 'black box', the internals of which have not influenced those checks.

In order to check whether the outputs of S would meet the specification, it will be necessary to provide an alternative implementation to model the required service and against which the activity of S can be compared. The success of the check will depend upon the thoroughness and accuracy of this model. From this a second criterion for an ideal check follows, namely that the model used should completely and accurately represent the specification, and hence the check can be *complete*.

It is clear that a check can only be guaranteed to be successful if there is no possibility of there being a common point of failure between the system and its check (i.e. a fault which affects both the system and its check) which would prevent or invalidate the error detection. For example, such a problem could arise if the system and the check had components in common. Similarly, if the system designer also designed the check, a common design fault would be possible. Therefore, a third criterion for an ideal check is that it should be *independent* of the system with respect to its susceptibility to faults.

To reiterate, three criteria for ideal checks have been identified: firstly, that the check should be derived solely from the system specification; secondly, that the check should be a complete check on the behavior of the system; and thirdly, that the system and its check should be independent. If checks can be designed and implemented to satisfy these criteria then a powerful error detection capability can be provided.

In practice, such rigorous checking cannot be attained for most systems. It may not be possible to satisfy the first criterion if the specification of the system is not an exact specification (discussed in Chapter 2), and often this leads to checks having to be based partly on the implementation of the system. Even if a specification is exact, it will not usually be feasible to perform a complete check on all aspects of the specification. The complexity of such a check is likely to result in faults in the check itself, as well as imposing unacceptable financial and performance overheads on the overall system. For example, while it is simple to check that the output of a sorting routine is indeed in order, it is much more expensive to check that the output is a permutation of the inputs (to ensure that no input values have been lost or changed).

Furthermore, the independence between a system and its check cannot be absolute, for two main reasons. Firstly, the check will obviously require access to the information to be checked, and may therefore have the ability to corrupt that information. Secondly, the implementation of any check will be based on assumptions about the structure of the system and hence about the type of faults that may (and may not) occur. For example, it might be assumed that the physical separation of a system and its check when these are implemented in hardware would provide the necessary independence. However, it is easy to envisage circumstances for which this assumption will be invalid, for instance, if a wire was dropped across the circuits.

For all of these reasons the provision of ideal checks for error detection is rarely practical, and most systems employ checks for *acceptability*. Acceptability is a lower standard of behavior than absolute correctness, with no guarantee of the absence of undetected errors. However, the aim of acceptability checks will be to detect the majority of erroneous situations and hence increase confidence in the operation of the system. Checks for acceptability will be based on assumptions about the behavior of the system and its environment and the possible faults which could arise. The success of acceptability checks will therefore depend on the degree of success with which the system designer has identified and precluded, either by good design or fortuitously, situations in which those assumptions would not hold. For example, to revert to the example above, it is unusual for wires to be dropped across circuits and it is therefore unlikely that a test would be designed to cope with this eventuality.

Checking that the outputs of a system are acceptable can take the form of a limited application of the criteria discussed above, with the check implementing some restricted model of the specification against which the activity of the system can be compared. An even more restricted check on a system would be whether specific erroneous situations had arisen, such as would be identified if dynamic redundancy was being used in the components of the system, rather than checking the whole system state for acceptability. This approach can only be used to detect specific anticipated erroneous situations; however, for those situations which can indeed be anticipated such checks will be much simpler and more efficient than a general check that the operation of the system appears to be satisfactory. For example, a check on a system consisting of a set of concurrent processes could be based on each process sending an 'I'm alive' message on a regular basis, rather than on a check of the complete state of the system.

There are various criteria which can influence where in a system error detection is employed. Two criteria support the adoption of last-moment checks, that is checks which are deployed after any results have been generated but just before those results are released from a system, such as for the system S' in Figure 5.1. Firstly, once results have left a system then fault tolerance within that system can no longer be applied (the system will probably have failed), and more global recovery is likely to be much more difficult and expensive. Secondly, a last-moment check ensures that none of the activity of the system remains unchecked. (Checks which are based solely on the system specification will of course meet these criteria.) However, it is also the case that there are some benefits to be gained by detecting errors at the earliest possible stage, that is, during the system activity which generates the results. Early checks will minimize the amount of system activity that is wasted (i.e. that activity between the erroneous transition caused by a fault and the application of the check), as well as being beneficial for fault tolerance since there will be less time for damage to spread within the system, and the actions necessary for damage assessment, error recovery and fault treatment are likely to be simplified.

Early checks should not be regarded as a substitute for last-moment checks. Since an early check will of necessity be based on a knowledge of the internal workings of the system, it will lack independence from the system, the consequences of which were discussed above. Therefore, both last-moment and early (internal) checks should be provided in a system, whenever possible, to achieve the benefits of both approaches.

The measures for error detection that can be incorporated in a computer system can take many forms. The majority of measures adopt checks which fall into the following broad classification:-

(i) replication checks;
(ii) timing checks;
(iii) reversal checks;
(iv) coding checks;
(v) reasonableness checks;
(vi) structural checks;
(vii) diagnostic checks.

Replication Checks

Replication checks provide one of the most powerful and complete measures for detecting errors in a computer system, but are among the most expensive in terms of the redundancy required. As the name suggests, replication checks involve some replication of the activity of the system being checked. The replication can be regarded as providing an alternative implementation of the system against which the activity of the system can be checked for consistency.

The type of replication utilized can take several forms, depending on the type of fault that has been anticipated. The most common use of replication checks is to detect the effects of component faults in a system, particularly faults in the physical components of hardware systems. If it can be assumed that the design of the system is correct and that component failures occur independently, then the replication can take the form of a separate but identical copy of the system which executes in parallel with the original system, with the two sets of results being compared by a simple equality test. If these assumptions are valid then no single fault in either version of the system can remain undetected. Moreover, it does not matter to the error detection whether the fault was in the system or in the copy, although the subsequent fault tolerance activities will need to identify which was erroneous. The only crucial aspect is the simple component which compares the outputs and indicates the presence of an error by raising an exception.

This type of replication check is one of the main error detection mechanisms in the ESS No. 1A system; the CPU is naturally a critical and complex component in that system, whose operation must be checked. Thus the CPU is completely duplicated (see Figure 4.1) with two identical CPUs normally operating synchronously within a single atomic action. The outputs from the CPUs are checked by *matching circuits* just before they are transmitted on the buses. In fact, there are two identical matching circuits associated with each CPU, and this last moment check is supplemented by earlier replication checks which compare the two CPUs at a number of internal points during the system operation. Furthermore, the matching circuits of the active CPU are used to compare different internal points to those checked by the matching circuits of the stand-by CPU. These measures provide further independence between the checks and enable some errors to be detected at an early stage, although increase the requirement for accurate synchronization between the systems. Assuming that the design of the CPU is correct and that identical components in the CPUs do not fail simultaneously and in the same manner then the two CPUs should never produce the same wrong result, and errors arising from a fault in any of the 50,000 or so gates that comprise the CPU will be detected. Further checks within the CPU are not therefore required (at least while the replication check is operational). The price paid for this highly effective error detection is the complete duplication of the CPU; however, since this duplication is necessary anyway because of the requirement for uninterrupted service and the criticality and inherent (un)reliability of the CPU, the replication check is cost-effective and practical.

Replication checks are also applied by the audit programs in the ESS No. 1A system to data which is stored in duplicate - for example, the contents of a program store can be checked against the backup copy on disk. Although other ESS No. 1A units are duplicated, this redundancy is used primarily for error recovery and not for replication checks. Other forms of checks (to be discussed subsequently) are used in the memory units and on the buses.

Replication in a system need not be limited to duplication, and multiple copies of a system may be used, for instance, in Triple Modular Redundant (TMR) systems. (When replication extends to three or more copies of a system the comparison check is referred to as *voting* to reflect the fact that erroneous outputs should be masked by selecting the output agreed on by a majority of the copies.) As far as error detection is concerned higher orders of redundancy are no better than duplication, since the purpose of the comparison check is simply to indicate that a discrepancy has occurred between the outputs of the multiple copies of the system. However, since a check based on duplication cannot be used to identify which copy of the system is erroneous, more than two copies of a system may be used in order to obtain benefits in the implementation of the other phases of fault tolerance. Thus N-Modular Redundant (NMR) systems, the generalized form of TMR, are to be found in fault tolerant systems with extremely high reliability requirements. Fault tolerance in FTMP is based on TMR. Special hardware circuits are used to form 'triads' which consist of three identical modules operating together. Every module contains a decision element to check (and correct) the data received over three active buses. TMR was also the basis for the organization of the TARP processor in the JPL-STAR, since the provision of fault tolerance in the STAR depended totally on the reliable operation of the TARP.

Replication checks are also the major form of error detection in the SIFT system. Since the replication is controlled by software, SIFT is not limited to a fixed level of replication, and different orders of replication can be adopted as necessary; TMR is expected to be the most usual case. Replication checks are also employed in the Space Shuttle computer complex, where four computers are normally used so that up to two (independent) computer failures can be tolerated.[1]

Clearly, the replication checks discussed so far, based on identical copies of a system, will not detect the consequences of design faults, which would affect all copies of the system. If design faults are expected, replication must be provided using versions of the system with different designs. This is the basis of two methods discussed in Chapter 9 for providing tolerance for software faults, one of which explicitly employs a replication check. It should be noted that all of the fault tolerant systems discussed above which use replication checks employ identical copies of a system (hardware and software); the designers of SIFT intend to use formal verification techniques to try to ensure that there are no design faults in the software which could diminish the protection provided by the replication.

A replication check is suggested by Ayache *et al.*[2] as a means of checking the flow of control in systems of concurrent processes. The check is based on two implementations of the control structure of the operational system: that embodied in the processes executing the functions of the system, and a Petri-net based model of the high-level control flow expected from that system. The check can reveal any discrepancies between the expected control flow and that observed in the run-time system, for instance, as a result of design faults in the processes.

Another, much more limited, application of replication checks can be implemented by means of repeated use of the same system. Of course, this will only be effective against faults which are transient and affect only one set of results generated by the system.

Replication checks can provide an extensive and powerful, but simple, error detection capability, albeit at a high cost in terms of the redundancy required. Since few assumptions need to be made about the cause of an error, replication provides a general checking measure and there are few other checks which can provide equivalent detection power. In fact, in a system employing replication checks, it will usually be unnecessary to provide any further measures or mechanisms for error detection at lower levels in the system, that is, within the components from which the system is constructed. This is certainly the case if there is sufficient redundancy in the system to continue to provide the replication check despite component faults. For example, the SIFT and FTMP systems are designed to provide sufficient redundant modules that the replication check will be operational for the duration of a mission, even though failures of the replicated modules occur and maintenance is not available to replenish the supply of modules. These systems do not, therefore, provide lower-level checks such as parity checks in the memory. In other systems, such as the ESS No. 1A system, the redundancy provided is not always sufficient to maintain the replication check when component faults occur. Other measures must be adopted to enable errors to be detected when the replication check is not operational - for instance, when one of the No. 1A CPUs is being repaired. During the periods of reduced error detection capability, the system will be more vulnerable to faults, and the aim will be to recommence the use of replication checks as quickly as possible.

All of the forms of replication discussed so far have involved the provision of another implementation of the system under consideration which models *all* aspects of the behavior of that system and hence provides a complete check for errors. Much more restricted and limited models of the system can also be used to provide a replication of only some part of the specified behavior which will be used to judge the system as a whole. The most common use of this limited replication requires that a system provides some form of fixed response as well as its normal service.

MEASURES FOR ERROR DETECTION

This response will be taken to be a 'positive acknowledgment' that the system is operating correctly; the replication will involve an independent generation of this positive acknowledgment against which that of the system can be checked. For example, acknowledgments are extensively used in the ESS No. 1A between the CPUs and the other major units.

This type of replication was also employed by the TARP in the JPL-STAR in order to check the operation of the functional units of the STAR. Each functional unit generated status messages; this activity was independently replicated by logic internal to the TARP so that the responses actually received could be compared with the predicted responses. Thus the TARP could identify, for example, improperly activated units (if an unexpected message was received) and failed units (by the absence of an expected message).

Timing Checks

Timing checks are a particularly common form of the limited replication checks discussed above, and can be applied in both hardware and software systems. If the specification of a component includes timing constraints on the provision of service then a timing check can be provided in the system to determine whether the operation of the component meets those constraints. If the constraints are not met then the timing check can raise a 'timeout' exception to indicate the failure of the component.

While the raising of a timeout exception will be indicative of problems in the system, the absence of the exception is not usually taken to be an indication that the system is performing satisfactorily. Thus timing checks (and other limited checks) are usually used to reveal the presence of faults in a system but *not* their absence, and are used to supplement other checks on the operation of a system. For example, most computer systems implement a timing check on memory accesses, and while the raising of a timeout exception in response to a valid memory access will be indicative of a memory fault, the absence of an exception will only provide a positive indication that the contents of a memory location are accessible - other checks (e.g. a parity check) will be required to check for errors in the contents.

Timing checks are used in this manner on all of the major units in the ESS No. 1A.

Timing checks are also widely used in software systems, usually based on what are called 'watchdog timers'. The requirement imposed is that periodically the software must reset the watchdog timer as an indication that it is operating satisfactorily. If this updating does not occur due, say, to an infinite loop in the software, then the watchdog timer will raise an exception. The watchdog timer is usually provided as a mechanism by the underlying interpreter. In the ESS No. 1A this type of check is used to ensure that overall control in the system is not lost through a software or hardware malfunction. A similar check, but with a software implemented watchdog timer, is employed to ensure that various facilities of the system are not lost or locked out by programs that fail to complete. A timeout bit in the data structure associated with a particular facility is set by an audit program when the facility is in use, and cleared when it is idle. The audit program can then check whether a facility has been in use for a time greater than the maximum specified. A similar technique is employed in the IMP application program in the Pluribus to detect buffers which have been lost.

Timing checks form one of the major error detection measures in the Tandem 16. Every second each processor sends a special message to all other processors. Every two seconds a check is made to see whether messages have been received from all other processors. If a message has not been received then the corresponding processor is assumed to have failed, and the relevant exceptions are signalled. Timing checks are also performed on all input/output operations.

Watchdog timers also form the basic error detection mechanism in an approach proposed by Campbell et al.[3] for providing software fault tolerance in real-time applications. This approach will be discussed further in Chapter 9.

Reversal Checks

In many systems there is a complex (many-to-one) mapping between a set of inputs and the corresponding set of outputs, which can only be accurately checked by replication involving the generation of multiple sets of outputs. In other systems, where the relationship between inputs and outputs is one-to-one, an alternative check may be to use *reversal checks*. A reversal check takes the outputs from a system and calculate what the inputs should have been in order to produce that output - the calculated inputs can then be compared with the actual inputs to check whether there is an error. For example, in the ESS No. 1A a simple reversal check is applied to a magnetic tape write operation by reading back the data written to the tape and comparing it with the original data. Reversal checks were employed in the functional units of the JPL-STAR, where 'inverse microprogramming' was used to deduce from the active gating signals in the unit which operation had been requested; the deduced operation was then compared with that actually requested. The SERF fault tolerant computer[4] used a reversal check on memory accesses to ensure that a selected word corresponded to the requested address.

Systems providing mathematical functions often lend themselves to reversal checks. For example, the obvious reversal check for a system intended to calculate square roots is to check that the square of the answer produced is equal to the input value. However, the finite precision of floating point numbers often precludes an exact equality test between the predicted and actual inputs.

A variant of the reversal check described above may be used in systems in which there is a fixed relationship between the inputs and outputs which can be checked. For example, the outputs from a system which solves a set of equations can be checked by back substitution. Similarly, the output of a system which is meant to invert a matrix can be checked by multiplying the input matrix by the output to see whether their product is the unit matrix. (A direct reversal check would be to invert the output matrix and compare it with the input.)

Clearly, reversal checks can only be applied to systems in which the inverse computation is relatively straightforward. However, for such systems the reversal check is likely to be simple and easy to implement, and will have the advantages of being independent of the system (both in its design and implementation) as well as being applicable as a last-moment check, the advantages of which have already been discussed.

Coding Checks

Coding checks are based on redundancy in the representation of an object (or set of objects) in use in a system. Within an object, redundant data is maintained in some fixed relationship with the (non-redundant) data representing the value of the object. Errors which result from a corruption of either form of data such that this relationship no longer holds can therefore be detected.

Parity checks are a well known example of a coding check, where a single redundant bit is associated with a set of bits (e.g. a word) such that the modulo 2 sum of all bits is 0 (even parity) or 1 (odd parity). Parity checks are to be found in the memory system of many computers, and are extensively used in the ESS No. 1A, Pluribus and the Tandem 16 to detect malfunctions in their storage systems and in transmissions between units. Faults which result in the inversion of an even number of bits will not be detected by a simple parity check, and more complicated coding schemes such as Hamming codes and M-out-of-N codes have been devised to provide recovery from single-bit errors and to detect multiple-bit errors, but of course require extra redundancy. For example, Tandem 16 systems which contain semiconductor storage have six check bits per 16 bit word to provide single-bit error detection and recovery, and double-bit error detection. Cyclic redundancy codes have also been developed to provide efficient error detection for blocks of data. For instance, a cyclic redundancy code check is used in the disk stores of the ESS No. 1A. (A detailed mathematical treatment of these and other coding schemes is given by Peterson and Weldon.)[5]

Another class of codes which have been used for error detection are arithmetic codes. These codes are based on remainder theorems for residue arithmetic and have the property of being preserved by arithmetic operations. Thus they can be used to check (some of) the operations of a CPU, as well as the operation of the storage and transmission systems. However, logical operations do not preserve the codes and therefore have to be checked by other means.

MEASURES FOR ERROR DETECTION

For example, the JPL-STAR employed arithmetic codes to check the operation of the arithmetic function units, but applied a duplication check to the unit providing logical operations. Arithmetic codes are rarely considered for use in contemporary fault tolerant systems since the present day trend towards inexpensive hardware and single-chip CPUs makes it inappropriate to treat logical and arithmetic operations separately. A detailed discussion of arithmetic codes is given by Avizienis.[6]

All of the coding checks discussed so far have been hardware oriented, for detecting errors expected to arise from hardware component faults. Coding checks are also applicable within the software of a system for detecting the erroneous effects of software (or hardware) faults. A checksum implemented in software can be used to check for errors in blocks of data. For example, software checksums are applied to blocks of the non-transient data in the ESS No. 1A, and are used in Pluribus to check for errors in the memories used to store programs. The VAX-11/780 computer provides an instruction (i.e. a mechanism) to allow a software system to evaluate cyclic redundancy code checks efficiently.[7]

When compared with other forms of check, such as replication, coding checks can be seen to provide an efficient and economical error detection measure, in terms of the redundancy required to implement the check. This is well exemplified by the JPL-STAR, where arithmetic codes were used (where possible) in preference to replication checks to reduce the cost of the overall system. However, coding checks are at best a limited form of acceptability check, based on assumptions about the types and consequences of faults which might affect the system. For example, a simple parity check may be suitable for core stores where the most commonly occurring faults give rise to single-bit errors but where multiple-bit errors are most unlikely; in contrast, a single-bit parity check is of little use for detecting the entirely different error characteristics affecting data transmitted over telecommunications channels, where multiple-bit errors are a common occurrence. Nevertheless, coding checks are often the only feasible method of checking the acceptability of large and complex amounts of data.

Reasonableness Checks

Other measures that can be adopted in a system to check for acceptability will usually be based on a knowledge of the internal design and construction of the system. These checks will test whether the state of various (abstract) objects in the system is 'reasonable', based on the intended usage and purpose of those objects as envisaged by the system designer.

A common check for acceptability is a range check which can determine whether the value of a particular object is in an acceptable range. For example: a word being used to hold an angle in degrees must be in the range 0 - 360; an array index must be within the bounds of the array; the voltage provided by the power company should be within specified limits.

While the range of values that can be taken by an object may be quite large, the successive changes in value of an object may be more limited and therefore more useful for error detection. For example, the velocity of a spacecraft could vary over a wide range - however, the incremental change in velocity between successive iterations of a guidance program would be expected to have a much smaller variation, and hence a range check on the change would produce a much more sensitive check than a test on the magnitude of the velocity. Objects may also be checked to determine whether they are consistent with other objects in the system - it should not be acceptable for the undercarriage of an aircraft to be retracted when the aircraft is stationary.

Many of the reasonableness checks applied in software systems are similar to the 'type' checking that is normally associated with programs written in high-level languages supporting abstract data types. It is clear that the redundancy provided in programs written in typed languages such as Pascal is highly beneficial for error detection. While many faults can be exposed at compile-time, run-time checks are also essential - for example, checks on the bounds of array accesses are usually satisfactory only as a run-time check. There can be no guarantee that those checks that can be performed at compile-time are sufficient to ensure that errors will not appear at run-time, for instance, because of faults in the interpreter or compiler. To quote Needham:[8] "All compile-time protection does is to assure one that the program used to be satisfactory; run-time protection gives some confidence that it still is".

Many run-time type checks have to be achieved by measures in a program, albeit generated automatically by the compiler. The redundancy and structure present in the source version of a program is usually absent from the compiled version since most interpretive interfaces do not have supportive mechanisms which require their retention. For example, a program might declare a variable to be an integer in the range 0 to 10, although this variable is represented in a 16 bit word at run-time; the structured control flow in a program is converted to an unstructured set of **goto** instructions. Worse still, the overheads of measures produced by a compiler to retain and exploit redundancy and structure for error detection at run-time are usually so high as to positively discourage their inclusion in programs, except perhaps in the early stages of testing. For example, IBM provide (at least) two compilers for PL/I - the checkout compiler which generates run-time checks, and the optimizing compiler which does not. Myers[9] compares several simple examples of PL/I statements compiled by these compilers and quotes overheads of typically 300% in the space and execution time requirements of the code produced by the checkout compiler. Other high-level language compilers provide an option to enable (or disable) the automatic production of measures for run-time checks.

Thus although run-time checks are usually included during testing, when their absence would do no harm, they are omitted when the system is put into operation, when for the first time they are really needed. The fact that such measures can place an intolerable overhead on the run-time performance (which is the reason for their suppression) is indicative of the mismatch that often occurs between the interface presented by the (hardware) machine and that required by the programmer. Since any suppression of checks can only be detrimental to the effective deployment of fault tolerance in a system, this is obviously one area in which mechanisms should be provided by the underlying machine to remove the need for incorporating (inefficient) measures in the system.

Unfortunately, such mechanisms are not common and it is of interest to note that, despite the development and promotion of high-level languages, the impact on computer architectures has been minimal. Few architectures have been designed with mechanisms which attempt to match more closely the requirements of programs written in typed high-level languages, particularly where error detection is concerned. (Some examples will be discussed in the following section on mechanisms for error detection.) Unless computer hardware improves in performance to such an extent that the inefficiency of compiler-generated measures for error detection is no longer a problem, it is to be hoped that supportive mechanisms for checking the execution of programs written in high-level languages will be developed, at least for those applications where fault tolerance is required.

Explicit checks for reasonableness included in software systems are sometimes termed *assertions* (or **assert** statements). An assertion is a logical expression implementing a reasonableness check on the objects in a program, and is evaluated at run-time. The logical expression is expected to evaluate to **true** if the state is not erroneous, and to raise an exception otherwise. For example, run-time assertions on the reasonableness of data read from sensors were used by Andrews[10] to detect the consequences of hardware faults.

Structural Checks

There are two forms of check which can be applied to the data structures in a computing system. Checks on the semantic integrity of the data will be concerned with the consistency of the information contained in a data structure, and will apply checks of the forms described above. Checks on structural integrity will be concerned with whether the structure itself is consistent.

Structural checks are particularly applicable to complex data structures which consist of a set of elements linked together by pointers, for instance, lists, queues and trees. Redundancy in these structures can be of three main forms: firstly, there can be counts of the number of elements that there should be in a structure; secondly, redundant pointers can be incorporated in a structure; and thirdly, the elements in a structure can contain status (or type) information. For example, Figure 5.2 illustrates an example of a list structure where the list head contains a (redundant) pointer to the last element in the list, and the elements contain status information. A check that the last element identified by the list head corresponds to that identified by following the chain of 'next element' pointers can detect structural errors in the list.

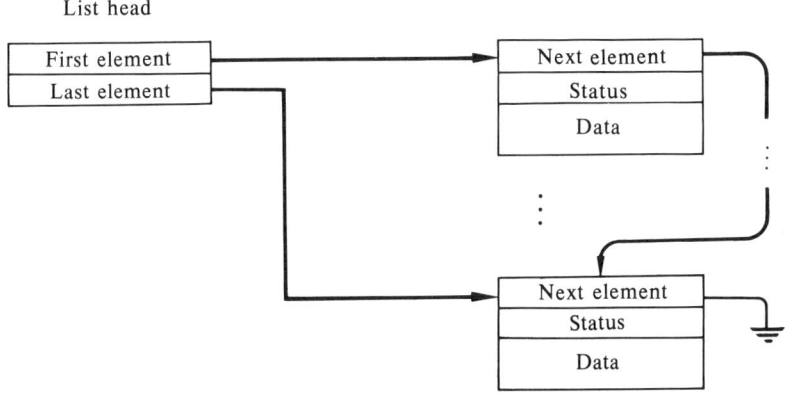

Figure 5.2 Redundancy in a Linked List

While the use of a single redundant pointer enables some structural errors to be detected it will provide little assistance for damage assessment and error recovery strategies. For this reason, further structural redundancy may be included; for instance, doubly linked lists in which each element contains a pointer to the previous element as well as a pointer to the next element would simplify the recovery required after a single pointer had been corrupted.

Since a list structure is usually employed to link together elements which have some characteristic in common (e.g. a list of memory segments not currently allocated) redundancy can be incorporated into each element to represent such characteristics, for example, to indicate the status of the element as in Figure 5.2. A check can then detect whether the status of the elements on a list conforms to that expected. Checks of this form and others based on structural redundancy are extensively used by the audit programs in the ESS systems, in Pluribus and in the Tandem 16.

Some recent research into the addition of redundancy to data structures to enable structural checks to be performed and recovery provided has been reported by Taylor et al.[11,12] (Recovery aspects of this work will be discussed in Chapter 7.) Central to this research is the notion of a *change*, which is an atomic operation which updates part of the representation of a data structure - for the purpose of this discussion, regarding each write to memory as a change will suffice. Basically, if N changes are required to validly transform a structure to a new valid state then all faults which result in N-1 (or less) erroneous changes to that structure will be detectable. For example, a single change is sufficient to transform the list shown in Figure 5.2 to a new valid state. Consequently a fault which changed the first element pointer to point to a subsequent element of the list could not be detected by a structural check. However, if the redundant pointer to the last element was replaced by a count of the number of elements on the list (requiring the same amount of redundancy, it should be noted) then two changes would be needed to achieve a valid transformation (to the count and the first element pointer). A single erroneous change to any part of the structural representation would therefore be detectable.

The theoretical results of this work not unnaturally give the worst case performance for error detection, indicating that for a structure requiring N changes to achieve a valid transformation, only N-1 or less erroneous changes can be detected. However, it would take a fortunate sequence of N or more erroneous changes to transform a structure into an erroneous state which would not be detected by the structural checks - for instance, the single undetected erroneous change to the list in example above would have to change the first element pointer to point to a valid list element; changing the pointer to some random location could be detected by other checks, such as type checks on the pointer and status fields. The reported experimental results[13] confirm that in practice the level of detection is better than that predicted by the theory.

The theory developed by Taylor *et al.* suggests that the more changes are required to validly update a data structure, the better it is for error detection (and error recovery). However, it can be appreciated that a large number of changes implies the use of a complex data structure with the inherent risk that the complexity of the updating programs could itself introduce errors. Nevertheless, the development of a theory which can be used to guide a system designer in the effective placement and utilization of redundancy in data structures should improve on current approaches which are guided only by intuition.

Diagnostic Checks

Diagnostic checks differ from the measures discussed so far in that they are concerned specifically with checking the behavior of the components from which the system is constructed, rather than checking the behavior of the system itself. A diagnostic check involves exercising a component with a set of inputs for which the correct outputs are known. The outputs actually obtained from the component can then be compared with the expected values, with a discrepancy indicating the likely presence of a fault within the component being tested. During the interval between the applications of the diagnostic check (and in the absence of failure exceptions from the component) the component is assumed to be working satisfactorily. If this assumption does not hold there is the likelihood of damage spreading through the system until detected by some other check.

Diagnostic checks are usually implemented as programs which test for faults in the underlying (hardware) interpreter. Because of the general purpose nature of interpretive interfaces, diagnostic checks are usually expensive in terms of the time and resources required for their execution - for example, it may take several minutes to check even a moderately sized random-access memory thoroughly. In consequence, these checks are rarely used as a primary error detection measure (e.g. it would be impractical to perform a full diagnostic check on memory after every access) but instead may be run periodically (e.g. at system start-up time) or perhaps as a background job when the CPU would otherwise be idle. The latter strategy is used in systems such as Pluribus which have redundant units on which off-line diagnostic checks can be run.

Although diagnostic checks are not often employed as a main error detection measure, they are commonly used to try and locate more precisely a fault whose erroneous effects have been detected by some other measures or mechanisms in the system. Diagnostic checks will therefore be returned to in Chapter 8 when fault location is discussed.

The conditions under which a component is tested by a diagnostic check should be at least as stringent as the conditions that exist during the normal usage of the component. If this is not the case, a diagnostic check can fail to reveal the presence of a fault which nevertheless affects the normal operation. This is exemplified by the experience of the Pluribus designers who noted that the best diagnostic program for revealing faults in the hardware was the normal Pluribus software,[14] illustrating that the conditions generated by other diagnostic programs were not equivalent to those that occurred under normal system operation.

Testing hardware components under conditions more stringent than normal might involve exercising the components at full speed, or executing diagnostic programs while the voltage levels are reduced or increased from their nominal values in an attempt to show up components which have deteriorated. While such checks can be useful as a run-time measure for hardware systems which, due to their physical nature, can change with time, run-time diagnostic checks will be pointless for revealing faults in software systems, unless the software itself is subject to corruption. The only analogy that could be drawn between diagnostics for hardware and software systems is with the testing of software - for example, exercising a trigonometric routine with 'boundary case' values such as 0, 45, 90, 135, 180 degrees. However, since such checking will be performed before the software is relied upon and not as a run-time measure in the operational system, the analogy is somewhat strained.

MECHANISMS FOR ERROR DETECTION

Mechanisms for error detection are concerned with the techniques that can be implemented in an interpreter (or in an extension) to provide error detection for the programs being executed on the interpretive interface.

Some specialized mechanisms for error detection were mentioned in the previous section, for instance, support for timing checks and special instructions for evaluating coding checks. Other specific mechanisms could be provided to optimize the performance of the error detection measures in a program. However, this section will examine the more general forms which mechanisms for error detection can take.

An interface can be characterized by the set of abstract objects available on that interface together with their associated operations. Since all interactions on the interface will be in terms of those objects and operations, the interpreter can provide an *interface check* which will be concerned with checking whether the requested operation is legitimate, and whether the operands are valid and compatible with the requested operation.

As was discussed in Chapter 3, an *interface exception* will be signalled to the program if invalid usage of the interface is attempted. In many cases the exception will be attributable to a *design fault* in the program. Typical interface exceptions raised by interpreters in computing systems include illegal instruction, arithmetic overflow or underflow, protection violation and non-existent memory.

Interface checks are a very attractive form of error detection (at least as far as a program running on the interface is concerned) since they are performed automatically and efficiently - often in parallel with the execution of the requested operation - and cannot be suppressed by a programmer. If the abstract objects available on an interface exactly matched the requirements of a program's designer, or could be changed to match those requirements, then there would be little need for the inclusion of the problematical type checking measures discussed in the earlier section on reasonableness checks. Unfortunately, (general purpose) interpretive interfaces have tended to provide fixed objects, tailored to suit hardware constraints rather than assisting the detection of errors in programs. For example, most computers provide fixed length words which can be used indiscriminately to represent integers, characters, addresses, booleans, etc. Thus, an exception cannot be signalled if a program divides a word holding an address by a word holding a character and assigns the result to a word holding a floating point number, although an exception would presumably be highly desirable in this situation.

Tagged storage[15] is one mechanism for overcoming this problem. With tagged storage, a limited number of bits are associated with each word and are used to identify the type of object that word is currently being used to represent, for instance, integer, character or real. Appropriate interface checks can then be deployed to detect erroneous manipulations of such objects. The Burroughs B6700[16] is one of the few commercial machines to provide tagged storage. Others have been proposed.[9,17,18,19]

Accesses to single- and multi-dimensional arrays is another area in which mechanisms for error detection can be easily provided (although often are not) to ensure that accesses fall within the declared bounds of an array. Several machines provide a descriptor mechanism for this purpose. A descriptor characterizes a vector by indicating its bounds (and where it resides in store); indexing operations use the descriptor and can be checked for legality.

Range checks could also be useful even for simple objects such as integers. For instance, Pascal variables can be declared to be sub-ranges of integers such as

   var degrees: 0 .. 359;
   var arrayindex: 1 .. 10;

Ideally, a mechanism would be provided by an interpreter to support the declaration of such programmer-defined types of object and hence could enable the mechanization of runtime checks on the use of those objects. Kerr[19] describes an architecture providing such a mechanism.

The larger Burroughs machines[16] and more recently the ICL 2900 series[20] also provide mechanisms to support the addressing structure inherent in block structured languages, for example, containing stack and display mechanisms. Thus, on these machines much of the addressing structure present in the source language version of a program is retained in the compiled version, and checked at run-time.

Generalizing from the concepts of addressing and accessing objects, protection mechanisms are now well established as a means of constraining the activity of processes. Any constraint implies some form of checking; therefore protection mechanisms play an important role as a mechanism for error detection - an exception indicating an attempted protection violation is a common symptom of an errant program. However, since protection mechanisms structure the dynamic activity of a software system and confine possible flows of damage, a detailed discussion of protection mechanisms is best postponed until Chapter 6 which examines damage confinement and assessment.

Interface checks are not just provided by interpreters, but will be required whenever an interface is extended with new abstract objects or operations. Interpreter extensions will also need to implement interface checks and signal appropriate exceptions. For instance, an operating system extension could signal exceptions such as 'execution time exceeded' or 'non-existent file'. An exception mechanism supported by the interpreter allowing new exceptions to be declared and signalled provides natural support for this facility.

One system which effectively provides an extensible exception mechanism is System R.[21] The data definition facilities provided on the Relational Data Interface (RDI) of System R allow a user to create new abstract objects on the RDI which may then be accessed by other users. In order to prevent errors arising in these abstract objects, System R also allows the definition of assertions which are maintained with the objects and provide an (automatic) interface check on the use of those objects.

The form taken by the interface checks will naturally be dependent on the particular abstract objects to which they are applied, but will be similar to the measures discussed in the section above on 'Reasonableness checks'.

Here they will be illustrated by considering the assertions that could be defined for a data base composed of (abstract) objects used for the customer records of a bank.

In System R an assertion can be defined to check the state of either individual tuples (e.g. a customer's overdraft must not exceed his overdraft limit) or sets of tuples, checking the relationships between groups of objects (e.g. the sum of the balances of all accounts must be positive). Assertions may also be defined to check the permissible transactions in the data base (e.g. the interest rate charged on an overdraft must never decrease). In System R this is aided by the availability of the NEW and OLD values of tuples (i.e. before and after a transaction) for use in these assertions.

The other factor that can be controlled in System R is the point at which the assertion is evaluated. By default, an assertion is evaluated whenever a change is made to the associated tuples. However, this can be refined by specifying that the assertion is to be checked only when a new tuple is inserted, or changed, or updated, or any combination of these (e.g. when a customer account is closed the balance must not be negative). Furthermore, while assertions on individual tuples may be evaluated as soon as a tuple is changed, assertions which relate to sets of tuples may only be applicable after a set of changes have been made. For instance, a program running on the RDI may withdraw money from one account and deposit it in another, requiring changes to be made to two tuples. After the first tuple has been updated but before the second is changed, an assertion over the set of tuples concerning the balancing of accounts would not hold. This necessitates the provision of support for atomic actions as a mechanism available on the RDI so that a group of interactions on the interface can be treated as a single unit. In data base terminology these atomic actions are referred to as *transactions*. In System R, the default time for the execution of an assertion is at the end of a transaction (i.e. a 'last-moment' check), although an assertion can be specified to be evaluated immediately, which would be appropriate for single tuple assertions.

The other class of exceptions that can be signalled on an interpretive interface are *failure exceptions*. As noted in Chapter 3, failure exceptions will be signalled when dynamic redundancy within the interpreter detects an error, or when the fault tolerance techniques at the interpreter level do not succeed in dealing with a fault. For example, whenever a simple one-bit parity check reveals an error, a failure exception would have to be signalled, whereas an error correcting code could enable single-bit errors to be tolerated although multiple-bit errors could result in the signalling of a failure exception. In consequence, a failure exception will indicate to the program that there is a *component fault* in the interpreter, and that it will be necessary for the handler in the program to provide the necessary measures to tolerate that type of fault.

STRUCTURING ERROR DETECTION IN SYSTEMS

So far it has been assumed that interface exceptions and failure exceptions indicated the presence of design faults (in the program) and component faults (in the interpreter) respectively. If this was always the case then the implementation of fault tolerance by the program would be much simplified since there would be a direct relationship between the type of a fault and a particular exception. As different techniques are appropriate for tolerating component faults and design faults, a handler could therefore directly apply the techniques relevant to tolerating the type of fault identified by the exception.

Unfortunately, the association of exceptions with faults may not be so straightforward in practice. Consider first the effects of design faults in a program. Obviously there can be no guarantee that such faults will lead to the signalling of an interface exception. The interface checks in the interpreter can only check for validity of use of the general-purpose interface it supports, and cannot check whether the usage is correct with respect to specific program-level criteria. For example, the addition of two integers (which did not cause overflow) would be regarded by the interpreter as a valid use of the interface, but would not be correct at the program level if one integer represented a speed in miles per hour while the other was a speed in centimeters per second. Thus, measures in the program for error detection will also be required to detect the consequences of design faults. These measures will **raise** exceptions which can be appropriately classified as interface exceptions to correspond to those signalled by the interpreter.

Some component faults in the interpreter will lead directly to specific failure exceptions being signalled to the program, as discussed in the section above. However, it is unlikely that all component faults will be signalled via failure exceptions. Not all components will contain redundancy, and those that do may not perform sufficient error detection to expose all internal faults. For example, a simple parity check could not detect the failure that would result if the value of two of the bits representing a word in memory were simultaneously inverted. Worse still, a component fault could lead to an interface exception being signalled. For example, an 'illegal instruction' exception could result if the failing memory word in the above example contained an instruction. (Since the memory component storing the program is effectively holding the implementation of the design of the program, as discussed in Chapter 2, an undetected memory fault would be expected to have characteristics similar to those produced by genuine faults of design in the program.)

Thus, while some component faults can be directly identified by failure exceptions being signalled, the relationship between other exceptions and faults in the system may not be so straightforward. One possible approach would be for the handlers of exceptions to perform a full diagnostic check to determine whether any component faults existed. For instance, following a mismatch between the two ESS No. 1A processors an exception is signalled by the comparison check to both processors, since the check cannot identify which processor is faulty. The first response of the handlers of this exception is to execute a diagnostic check to attempt to determine whether their processor is faulty.

It can be appreciated that this approach will not be practicable for the majority of exceptions because of the severe degradation of system performance which would be likely. The problem of identifying the type of fault is exacerbated by delays between the manifestation of a fault and the detection of its erroneous consequences, since such delays allow damage to spread and hence could give rise to other exceptions which could mislead the fault tolerance strategies. Measures for error detection usually incur such a delay, especially when utilized to detect the manifestation of component faults, since diagnostic checks are not usually used as a primary error detection measure. What is required is to design the placement of error detection in a system with the aim of minimizing this delay, particularly with respect to component faults.

The key to this placement is to provide interfaces in a system such that component faults (more accurately, those which have been anticipated) will always result in failure exceptions being signalled by the interpreter to the program executing on that interface - putting this another way, component faults should be uncovered by measures internal to the components rather than by measures in the system of which they are a part. If this can be achieved then all interface exceptions will be directly attributable to design faults in that program and, perhaps more importantly, the measures for error detection in the program will only need to be concerned with detecting the consequences of design faults. The benefits for fault tolerance noted at the beginning of this section can then be achieved.

There will not have to be a failure exception and appropriate redundancy for every physical component in the interpreter. All that is necessary is to indicate to the program that an exception is the result of a component fault in the interpreter rather than a design fault in the program. More accurate location of faulty components may be required subsequently, and it will usually be appropriate and easy to assist this location by providing specific exceptions to identify faults in the major units of the system (e.g. memory parity failure, disk read failure, CPU failure). For example, timing checks are used in the ESS No. 1A as a global check on the operation of the memory units in a system, with the timeout failure exception being used to invoke memory diagnostic checks for more accurate fault location.

Complete checking of an interpreter may not be as expensive or impractical as first impressions might suggest, particularly with the advent of VLSI. Carter et al.[22] report on the cost effectiveness of providing a complete check on the operation of an IBM/360 processor constructed from LSI, and conclude that complete checking is inexpensive (35% additional hardware over an unchecked processor; 6.5% additional to that normally incorporated in the IBM/360 processor) and does not degrade system performance. The relatively low costs of VLSI processors may well make complete replication checks of interpretive interfaces practicable for many systems - the Self Checking Computer Module for spacecraft systems described by Rennels[23] adopts this approach. However, the dangers of common design faults leading to undetected errors cannot be overlooked, especially in view of the ever increasing complexity of VLSI chips. Sedmak and Liebergot[24] describe the design of a generalized VLSI chip in which the functional logic is duplicated (using two independent designs) and the outputs compared by a replication check, thus enabling a large class of faults to be revealed and result in a failure exception being signalled. Indeed, Sedmak and Liebergot note that if this form of chip is adopted for the implementation of a general purpose computer "the large number of gates available in VLSI combined with limited input/output pins ... results in vastly superior fault-tolerance characteristics for a small cost increase".

Failure exceptions will not be limited to the interpreter/program (hardware/software) interface. In multilevel systems, failure exceptions can and should be signalled by extensions (which are components to the program making use of them) as was described in Chapter 3.

In those systems which do not contain sufficient redundancy and checking, some component faults will not result in failure exceptions being signalled. In these situations, subsequent exceptions caused indirectly by those faults may appear to indicate the presence of other types of fault, and the fault tolerance strategies may be misled, at least initially. As a last resort the system may have to try more desperate measures in an attempt to determine more precisely the location of faults.

REFERENCES

1. J.R. Sklaroff, "Redundancy Management Technique for Space Shuttle Computers," *IBM Journal of Research and Development* **20**(1), pp.20-28 (January 1976).
2. J.M. Ayache, P. Azema, and M. Diaz, "Observer: A Concept for On-Line Detection of Control Errors," *Digest of Papers FTCS-9: Ninth Annual International Symposium on Fault-Tolerant Computing*, Madison (WI), pp.79-86 (June 1979).
3. R.H. Campbell, K.H. Horton, and G.G. Belford, "Simulations of a Fault-Tolerant Deadline Mechanism," *Digest of Papers FTCS-9: Ninth Annual International Symposium on Fault-Tolerant Computing*, Madison (WI), pp.95-101 (June 1979).
4. J.J. Stiffler, N.G. Parke, and P.C. Barr, "The SERF Fault-Tolerant Computer," *Digest of Papers FTC/3: 73 International Symposium on Fault-Tolerant Computing*, Palo Alto (CA), pp.23-31 (June 1973).
5. W.W. Peterson and E.J. Weldon Jr, *Error-Correcting Codes*, MIT Press, Cambridge (MA) (1972).
6. A. Avizienis, "Arithmetic Error Codes: Cost and Effectiveness Studies for Applications in Digital Systems Design," *IEEE Transactions on Computers* **C-20**(11), pp.1322-1331 (November 1971).
7. R.S. Swarz, "Reliability and Maintainability Enhancements for the VAX-11/780," *Digest of Papers FTCS-8: Eighth Annual International Conference on Fault-Tolerant Computing*, Toulouse, pp.24-28 (June 1978).
8. R.M. Needham, "Protection," pp. 264-287 in *Computing Systems Reliability*, ed. T. Anderson and B. Randell, Cambridge University Press, Cambridge (1979).
9. G.J. Myers, *Advances in Computer Architecture*, Wiley, New York (1978).
10. D.M. Andrews, "Using Executable Assertions for Testing and Fault Tolerance," *Digest of Papers FTCS-9: Ninth Annual International Symposium on Fault-Tolerant Computing*, Madison (WI), pp.102-105 (June 1979).

11. D.J. Taylor, D.E. Morgan, and J.P. Black, "Redundancy in Data Structures: Improving Software Fault Tolerance," *IEEE Transactions on Software Engineering* **SE-6**(6), pp.585-594 (November 1980).
12. D.J. Taylor, D.E. Morgan, and J.P. Black, "Redundancy in Data Structures: Some Theoretical Results," *IEEE Transactions on Software Engineering* **SE-6**(6), pp.595-602 (November 1980).
13. J.P. Black, D.J. Taylor, and D.E. Morgan, "A Case Study in Fault Tolerant Software," *Software - Practice and Experience* **11**(2), pp.145-157 (February 1981).
14. D. Katsuki et al., "Pluribus - An Operational Fault-Tolerant Multiprocessor," *Proceedings of the IEEE* **66**(10), pp.1146-1159 (October 1978).
15. E.A. Feustel, "On The Advantages of Tagged Architecture," *IEEE Transactions on Computers* **C-22**(7), pp.644-656 (July 1973).
16. E.I. Organick, *Computer System Organization: The B5700/6700 Series*, Academic Press, New York (1973).
17. J.K. Iliffe, *Basic Machine Principles*, Macdonald, London (1968).
18. E.A. Feustel, "The Rice Research Computer - A Tagged Architecture," *AFIPS Conference Proceedings 1972 SJCC* **40**, Atlantic City (NJ), pp.369-377 (May 1972).
19. R. Kerr, "An Experimental Processor Architecture for Improved Reliability," pp. 199-212 in *State of the Art Report on System Reliability and Integrity*, Infotech, Maidenhead (1978).
20. J.K. Buckle, *The ICL 2900 Series*, Macmillan, London (1978).
21. K.P. Eswaran and D.D. Chamberlin, "Functional Specification of a Subsystem for Database Integrity," *Proceedings of International Conference on Very Large Data Bases* **1**(1), Framingham (MA), pp.48-68 (September 1975).
22. W.C. Carter et al., "Cost Effectiveness of a Self Checking Computer Design," *Proceedings FTCS-7: Seventh Annual International Conference on Fault-Tolerant Computing*, Los Angeles (CA), pp.117-123 (June 1977).

23. D.A. Rennels, "Architectures for Fault-Tolerant Spacecraft Computers," *Proceedings of the IEEE* **66**(10), pp.1255-1268 (October 1978).
24. R.M. Sedmak and H.L. Liebergot, "Fault-Tolerance of a General Purpose Computer Implemented by Very Large Scale Integration," *IEEE Transactions on Computers* **C-29**(6), pp.492-500 (June 1980).

6

DAMAGE CONFINEMENT AND ASSESSMENT

The design or component faults that affect a system will generate errors in the state of that system. Measures and mechanisms for error detection can hope to identify some errors but there can be no guarantee that all of the unwanted consequences of a fault (the *damage*) will be identified. In fact, there may be a substantial delay between the erroneous transition caused by a fault and the detection of any error, during which damage can spread through the system. For example, a fault in a program may result in the generation of erroneous values upon which other processes have subsequently based their actions. Thus, before error recovery is attempted it may be necessary for the system to adopt strategies for *damage assessment* in order to try to establish more precisely the extent to which the system state has been damaged. Appropriate recovery can then be undertaken.

Damage to the state of a system is caused by faults, and can then spread as a result of any subsequent flow of information. Strategies for damage assessment rely on the structure that the designer assumes will be present in the operational system, since it is this structure which enables the designer to identify the possible system activity that could have followed an erroneous transition, and the possible flows of information. The structure will itself be derived from the constraints that are known (or rather are assumed) to be placed on the flow of information in the system. The extent to which such constraints are present in the operational system and hence are able to *confine* the damage caused by a fault is an important consideration in the implementation of damage assessment. Thus the following section examines the measures for damage confinement that can be incorporated in a system.

Damage assessment, often involving subjective decisions about which information flows are significant and which objects have been damaged and are erroneous, will of necessity be system specific. An overview of the general measures that a system can undertake is presented in a following section. Since any measures for assessment will depend on the assumed structure in the system, and since any attempted confinement of information flow which is implemented by measures is unlikely to be dependable if that system (and hence that structure) is faulty, the section that follows concentrates on mechanisms for damage confinement, that is, on *protection mechanisms* for the implementation of atomicity. Finally, the support that mechanisms can provide for damage assessment is discussed.

MEASURES FOR DAMAGE CONFINEMENT

Damage confinement, concerned as it is with the structure of the activities within an operational system, forms the backbone of strategies for damage assessment. A useful concept for structuring the activity of a system and for examining the possible confinement of information flow is that of an *atomic action*, as defined in Chapter 2. For example, Figure 6.1 illustrates two processes engaged in atomic actions (represented by the curved lines) which have not yet completed. If process P_2 was detected to be in error at time t then an obvious strategy for damage assessment would be to assume that all of its activity since t_3 was suspect and that the changes to its state since then should be checked for errors (or abandoned). Under the assumption that the activity of P_2 since t_3 has been atomic, damage will not have spread to P_1. Similarly, if P_1 was detected to be erroneous then all of its activity since t_1 would be considered suspect, and because of the possibility of interactions with P_2 (between t_2 and t_3) all of the activity of P_2 from t_2 onwards would have to be treated with equal suspicion.

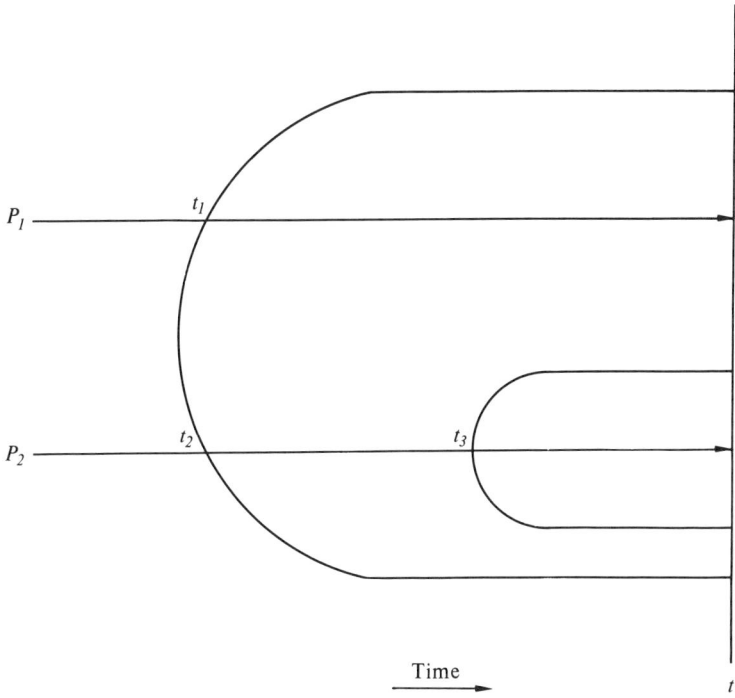

Figure 6.1 Atomic Actions

For some simple sequential systems containing a single activity the concept of atomic actions may not appear to be particularly useful. However, for such systems there may be a need to structure even that sequential activity into smaller atomic parts (e.g. such a structuring may be necessary for recovery purposes). Most practical systems, both hardware and software, do not contain just a single activity but support parallel activities. Parallelism exacerbates the difficulties of damage assessment since it can increase the ease with which damage may spread through a system. For example, one process may have based its decisions upon data which is subsequently detected to be erroneous by the process that generated that data. Thus the identification of atomic actions, and hence of the confinement of some activity, is an important structuring concept for damage assessment.

So far atomic actions have been discussed as a general notion for structuring the activities in a system. However, to be at all effective as a means of simplifying strategies for damage assessment it is essential that the structure atomic actions represent is embodied in the operational system and is not merely a figment of the system designer's imagination. Non-physical systems, such as software systems, could be constructed so that there are no run-time measures or mechanisms which enforce atomicity. Instead, the system designer might rely on his ability to design processes which are well-behaved and actually exhibit the atomic behavior that was envisaged during the design and on which the strategies for damage assessment have been based. For example, in a software system executed on an interpretive interface that provides no protection mechanisms, the assumed atomicity of processes may be dependent upon constraints imposed by the programming language in which that software was written. Strategies based on such (design-time) assumptions are clearly susceptible to the effects of run-time faults, and for atomic actions to be of practical benefit it is necessary to *enforce* atomicity by providing measures and mechanisms that confine the activities in a system. When atomic actions are enforced they impose clear constraints (or 'firewalls') which prevent unwanted information flow in the system. If these constraints can be maintained even when faults are present they will curtail the spread of damage through the system.

Measures may be deployed in some systems in an attempt to enforce constraints. For hardware systems some measures are provided implicitly - since air does not encourage electrical communications, physically separated components will not interact, under normal conditions at least. For example, a normally unstated assumption about a TMR system is that the three identical components will each operate atomically, and this is achieved by physically separating those components. Measures which enforce atomicity may be necessary in some circumstances, and a judicious application of insulating materials is usually included in hardware systems.

One of the advantages hardware systems have over software systems is that components normally operate atomically unless specific physical interconnections have been provided, and the visible structure of a hardware system dictates which information flows are and are not allowed. In contrast, interconnections in software systems are logical and have no directly visible form. VLSI is of course changing the size and complexity of the hardware component about which structural assumptions can be made. The possibilities of design faults and bridging faults causing totally unexpected and unforeseen communications between (internal) components highlights the problems of making assumptions about the behavior of VLSI components (and complex systems in general) and hence the problems of damage assessment. For example, it would be unwise to implement the three components and voter of a TMR system on a single chip since such an implementation could not provide the guarantees on the structure and atomic behavior of the relevant components that physical separation can provide.

Information flow in software systems can result from any use of shared variables. Measures to prevent such flows and hence to enforce atomicity are possible. These measures essentially have to emulate a protection mechanism, checking accesses to determine whether they are consistent with the desired behavior. Such measures are not particularly appropriate because of the run-time overheads that extensive checking will incur and, more importantly, because they are susceptible to the deleterious effects of design faults. Fortunately, mechanisms supporting protection schemes are well established and form the most important method of constraining software systems and enforcing atomicity. These mechanisms are the subject of the next but one section.

MEASURES FOR DAMAGE ASSESSMENT

The detection of an error, either by measures within a system or by mechanisms provided to the system, will result in an exception being raised. The name (and the assumed characteristics) of the exception will provide the handler with some initial information on the damage a fault has caused. The measures which can be adopted to obtain a more accurate assessment of the damage will depend on whatever structure the designer has assumed will be present in the operational system. If the designer decides to make no assumptions about the structure then any technique for damage assessment will of necessity involve an investigation of the state of the whole system. Since this will be impractical for most systems, reliance is usually placed on some aspects of system structure in order to delimit the set of objects involved. Thus the starting point for measures for damage assessment will be some initial estimate of the damage that has been anticipated beforehand by the system designer.

The simplest but most pessimistic technique for damage assessment is to assume that, in response to a particular exception, all of the objects within the initial estimate had been damaged. Such a damage assessment technique is *static* in the sense that it is specified at system design time. This approach is adopted in the Pluribus and ESS systems. When an error is detected in a (software) task in Pluribus it is assumed that the task executed atomically and that all of its activity since initiation is suspect and should be discarded. Similarly, the ESS No. 4 (a system which incorporates the No. 1A processor) adopts a pessimistic damage assessment approach based essentially on three initial estimates of the damage that might have been caused to the transient data in the call stores.[1] These estimates range from the assumption that small selected areas of transient data have been damaged (recovery from which affects no telephone calls), through estimates involving larger areas of data (resulting in the loss of calls which were being connected but not affecting established calls), to estimates which encompass all of the data (resulting in the loss of all calls). The estimate that is used depends on the particular exception that is raised. No further details are given in the referenced paper of the effects of (or prevention of) other flows of information resulting from the processing of calls, for example, that relating to the charging for calls.

Damage assessment in SIFT and FTMP is also static, based on assumptions about the structure present in the operational system. For example, in SIFT it is assumed that hardware measures ensure that a processor can only write to its own memory and cannot therefore damage objects held in other memories in the system. Although a process can read from other, possibly erroneous, memories it is assumed that the software implemented voting scheme on input data will mask any errors and hence prevent damage from spreading. Similarly, FTMP is dependent upon the Bus Guardian Units which implement its TMR structure. Both systems assume that damage will be confined to a particular unit and will not spread to the rest of the system. No attempts are made to refine the initial assessment of the damage within a unit.

A static approach was also adopted at the hardware level in the JPL-STAR, with a perhaps unnecessarily large initial estimate of damage. When an error was detected at this level it was assumed that all hardware units had been affected by the fault, even though the actions of many of these units could be regarded as being atomic. For example, each functional unit contained storage for the current operation code, its operands and results, and operated autonomously, apart from overall synchronization with the rest of the system. It would appear therefore that, once initiated, a functional unit would operate atomically. Hence, if error detection internal to that unit detected the consequences of an internal fault then any damage could be assumed to be confined to that unit and not to have contaminated other units. Similarly, the TMR-protected TARP appears to have operated atomically, with any faults and errors being masked from the rest of the system. Nevertheless, in both of these cases the pessimistic estimate was used, a particular consequence of which was that error recovery at the software level was always invoked (on the assumption that the state of the objects in the memory units had always been damaged).

Static damage assessment techniques have often been used for a priori damage assessment within hardware systems, where faults have been assumed to have particular error characteristics such that the damage caused by a fault could be assessed at design time. For example, simple hardware components were often expected to fail in a 'stuck-at-one' or 'stuck-at-zero' mode. From such assumptions, coupled with static and limited interconnections between components, the extent of damage resulting from a component fault (and also the error detection measures required) can be evaluated. However, the ever increasing complexity of hardware components, delays between the erroneous transition caused by a fault and the detection of its erroneous consequences, and parallelism in a system, can all combine to reduce the effectiveness of static assessments. As a result, responsibility for damage assessment (and error recovery) may need to be passed to the software, as in the JPL-STAR example discussed above.

Less pessimistic techniques for damage assessment may attempt to provide *dynamic* measures within the operational system to refine an initial estimate of possible damage. To implement such a technique it will be necessary to provide measures to explore, in some fashion, the data structures of the system. Since the purpose of this exploration is to detect errors, the measures will apply checks of the form described in the previous chapter on error detection, for example, by applying replication, coding, structural and other acceptability checks which enable the consistency of the data and its structure to be tested. Diagnostic checks may also be used for damage assessment, for example, when a hardware component failure has been identified. More usually, diagnostics are used to assist in fault location as will be discussed in Chapter 8.

Exploratory measures, which attempt to investigate the spread of damage, can be viewed as searching for and identifying atomic actions as and when necessary, rather than relying on atomicity imposed beforehand on the activity of the system. Atomic actions identified in this manner are termed *dynamically identified atomic actions*.

The audit programs in some of the ESS systems provide an example of exploratory damage assessment. These measures are based on the a priori reasoning that a fault will result in damage to the system data base which can be detected by replication checks (e.g. comparing the contents of a call store with a duplicated copy), coding checks (e.g. performing a sum-check on blocks of program stores to identify possible damage) or other consistency checks (e.g. checking the structure of doubly linked lists). The audit programs are executed on a routine basis as well as in response to exceptions.

Exploratory damage assessment measures, requiring heuristic strategies, are difficult to implement effectively in a computer system and are normally used only for simple and specific situations. In practice the complex and unexpected situations which can arise usually require some form of manual assistance for the accurate determination of the damage that will have been caused by a fault.

MECHANISMS FOR DAMAGE CONFINEMENT

It was noted earlier that any approach for damage assessment that depends on a priori reasoning by the system designer will be based on assumptions about the run-time structure that is expected to be present in the system. The mechanisms that are of most practical importance for damage assessment are those that enforce this structuring by confining the activity of a process, and hence provide constraints on the flow of information within the system and enable *planned atomic actions* to be specified and supported.

Planned atomic actions are atomic actions that have been planned during the design of the system. At run-time, the support for planned atomic actions must enable a process or group of processes to enter, execute, and then exit from an atomic action. As discussed in Chapter 2, atomic actions can be nested and the mechanisms for planned atomic actions should support this.

An action will not be atomic if, prior to its completion, there is a flow of information to or from processes external to that action. Information can only flow, of course, as a consequence of processes accessing common objects, either indirectly, through message passing mechanisms which take a copy of the object to be communicated and deliver it to the destination, or directly when the communicating processes access shared objects. Each of these will be considered below.

When communication between processes is only possible by using a message passing mechanism as, for instance, in the PRIME[2] and HIVE[3] systems, atomic actions can be implemented by ensuring that messages are sent only between processes participating in the same atomic action. This may be achieved by signalling an exception if an attempt is made from within an atomic action to send a message to, or receive a message from, a process outside that atomic action. An alternative implementation for the send message operation would be to retain any messages sent to external processes until the processes concerned exit from any atomic actions. Such a buffering mechanism was provided to processes in the HIVE system, although atomicity could not be guaranteed because an additional unbuffered message passing mechanism was also available.

In many computing systems, inter-process communication takes place through accesses to shared objects. In these systems the imposition of constraints on the accessing of objects must form the basis for implementing atomic actions. These constraints can take two forms: constraints on the execution sequences of the processes on the interface, and constraints on the accesses themselves. These will be examined in turn.

A flow of information into or out of an action would only be damaging if there was some conflicting concurrent activity. Therefore, a simple method of implementing atomic actions is to prevent such concurrency altogether, allowing just the process(es) within an atomic action to be executed for the duration of that action. Only when the atomic action has completed can any other processes be allowed to proceed. For example, many operating systems ensure that some of their actions are atomic by inhibiting interrupts to prevent interference from other activities.

In many systems it will not be feasible to implement atomic actions by constraining the available parallelism because of the degradation in performance and resource utilization that would result. It may be argued that if certain processes in a system operate on disjoint sets of objects they could be executed in parallel without violating any atomicity requirements. However, when atomic actions are provided by constraining concurrency no lesser restriction than the complete exclusion of concurrency should be adopted, unless other guarantees can be provided which ensure that unwanted process interactions do not occur. Guarantees implemented by measures in the processes concerned cannot be relied upon, especially in the presence of faults, and the only recourse is to provide mechanisms which enforce constraints on accesses to objects.

A gross solution to constraining the accesses made to objects would be to physically isolate those objects used within an atomic action from all other objects. Indeed, this forms the basis of 'periods processing'[4] (often employed in systems where highly confidential information is being processed) in which objects at different security levels are kept apart to the extent that the system is dedicated for specific periods to processing objects at a given security level. Following processing, the removable stores containing those objects are removed and the fixed stores are 'scrubbed' to ensure that no unintended information flows can occur. More generally, *protection mechanisms* are now well established as a means for constraining accesses to objects, and have been extensively studied. (An excellent survey of protection in computer systems is given by Saltzer and Schroeder.)[5] The aim of much of this work has been to provide protection against malicious processes, that is, processes whose intent is to breach the constraints that it was hoped were imposed on information flow. However, it is obvious that mechanisms to protect against malicious processes will also be effective against faulty processes which, by accident rather than by intent, attempt to violate constraints. It should also be noted that constraints on accesses to objects constitute rules for the usage of the interface on which those objects are available. Thus protection mechanisms (which implement the constraints) play an important role as interface checks for error detection, as well as in damage confinement.

Protection Mechanisms

There are in fact two aspects to protection mechanisms; that concerned with *intra-process* protection, and that concerned with *inter-process* protection. Intra-process protection is important to the dynamic structuring of a system. However, for the purpose of the present discussion, where support for planned atomic actions is being considered, attention will be concentrated upon inter-process protection. The next section will return to the topic of protection internal to a process.

Following Wilkes,[6] Saltzer and Schroeder[5] identify two general approaches to the implementation of protection mechanisms: list-based schemes, and ticket-based schemes. In list-based schemes, a list of authorized users is associated with each potentially sharable object. A process wishing to access such an object must possess a unique unforgeable identifier which is checked on every access against the identifiers on the list. With ticket-based schemes the right to access an object is associated with the process rather than the object - processes authorized to access an object are given an unforgeable ticket, possession of which essentially allows direct access to that object. For example, access to a private party could be list-based, implemented by a guard on the door checking names against a guest list, or ticket-based, implemented by a guard simply checking tickets, if tickets had been sent out only to those invited.

List-based schemes enable protection to be efficiently administered since there is a single list controlling all accesses to an object. However, the penalty paid is in the run-time overhead of checking each access. Ticket-based systems provide an efficient run-time implementation of protection, since possession of a ticket implies that an access is permitted, but are more complex to administer - for example, it may be difficult to prevent a process from passing the ticket to unauthorized processes. Protection in most computer systems is achieved through a combination of both schemes, although this chapter will concentrate on ticket-based implementations (in which the ticket is usually referred to as a descriptor or a capability) because of their importance as a run-time mechanism for structuring the accesses to shared objects.

Inter-process protection in ticket-based schemes is based on associating access rights with every process, specifying the objects to which the process has access and the manner in which each object can be accessed, for example, whether an object can be read, written to or executed. The set of access rights defines the *protection domain* for that process. Information may pass directly between processes if their protection domains overlap and hence allow some objects to be shared. Therefore, to implement atomic actions there is a need to prevent the overlapping of protection domains between the process(es) in an atomic action and the processes in the rest of the system, at least for the duration of the atomic action. This could be achieved directly by setting up the appropriate protection domains for each of the processes concerned to ensure that any object being accessed from within an atomic action is not present in the domain of processes outside that atomic action.

Recent work on protection has been concerned with *capability* mechanisms. A capability can be thought of as a protected ticket which supports two functions: naming a unique object, and listing a set of access controls applicable to that object. At any point in time a process will have associated with it a collection of capabilities maintained in a structure which is referred to as the capability list of the process. The existence of a capability in the list of a process provides the authorization for that process to access the object concerned but only in the manner specified by the capability. Thus the capability list defines the protection domain of a process. (As well as authorizing accesses, capabilities are used to implement the mapping that occurs between the name (or virtual address) of the object as generated by the process and the addresses that are employed in the underlying system. However, this topic is beyond the scope of this book. The interested reader is referred to the papers by Linden[7] and by Needham[8] for further details.)

Sharing of objects can occur when two or more processes possess a capability for the same object; capability systems usually provide a means whereby capabilities can be copied and passed between processes. It should be noted that it is necessary to prevent a process from forging or altering a capability and hence subverting the protection.

In consequence, it is essential that capabilities are dispensed and controlled by a mechanism rather than by a measure.

Capability mechanisms usually provide an efficient means of switching the protection domains of a process, based on a capability called the ENTER capability. ENTER is simply an access right applicable to executable (dynamic) objects just as READ and WRITE are access rights applicable to (passive) data objects. Thus an ENTER capability provides authorization to invoke a dynamic object. When a special 'enter' instruction is executed, the operand of the instruction specifies an ENTER capability. A field of the ENTER capability is used to specify a capability list which is to become the current capability list of the process, thus forcing the called process to execute in a different protection domain to that of the calling process. Coupled with this is a mechanism to enable capabilities to be passed as parameters from the caller to augment the new capability list. It can be seen that one method of implementing planned atomic actions would be to construct a capability list containing the capabilities needed for the shared objects and to then ensure that the processes involved in the atomic action enter this protection domain, passing as parameters any capabilities for objects that were to remain private to a particular process. It would also be necessary to ensure that processes outside the atomic action did not possess any capabilities for any of the objects encompassed by the atomic action. This might involve a temporary *revocation* (or withdrawal) of capabilities held by other processes. Redell and Fabry[9] discuss the difficulties and implementation of revocation in capability systems.

Another mechanism used to constrain accesses to objects and hence to implement atomic actions is based on the concept of a *lock*. Every sharable object in the system has a lock associated with it and when the lock is set only those processes which possess the corresponding key are allowed to access the object. (Essentially, the key can be regarded as being a simple form of capability authorizing all accesses to the object.) Hence, to implement an atomic action it is necessary to lock all of the objects to be accessed within the action, and to give the keys only to the processes concerned.

MECHANISMS FOR DAMAGE CONFINEMENT

Locking is widely used in operating systems to prevent unwanted parallelism between processes. This is achieved by establishing a gateway through which the competing processes must pass - the provision of a lock with a single key on the gateway enables the parallelism to be controlled, and schemes based on semaphores[10] and monitors[11,12] are now well established. These schemes usually assume the availability of a 'test-and-set' mechanism, that is, a primitive atomic operation which can be used to test whether a lock has been set and if not to set the lock (and take the key).

Data base systems such as System R also make extensive use of locking to enforce simple atomic actions (usually called transactions) and prevent the concurrent execution of multiple transactions generating inconsistencies in the data base. The inconsistencies that can occur are typified by the problem of the lost update. This is exemplified in Figure 6.2, where T_1 and T_2 represent transactions which are executed in parallel (instructions that are horizontally aligned are assumed to be executed simultaneously). As can be seen from this example, the interactions of T_1 and T_2 are such that the update of A by T_1 will be lost.

Figure 6.2 Lost Update

Eswaran et al.[13] have identified a 'two phase' strategy for lock acquisition and release necessary to implement atomicity. The two phases are a 'growing' phase, during which objects are acquired and locked but no object is unlocked, and a 'shrinking' phase when the locked objects are released and after which no more objects can be acquired. (Gray et al.[14] discuss a refinement of this scheme.)

Locking in data bases is complicated by the large number of objects available and by the desire to provide maximum parallelism while minimizing the overhead of executing the locking strategy. For example, locking individual records would enable maximum parallelism to be provided while incurring the largest overhead for lock management. At the opposite extreme, a single lock on the entire data base would minimize the locking overhead but would excessively constrain the concurrency possible. In System R a hierarchical locking scheme is provided to enable locking to be carried out at different granularities[14] (e.g. locking a tuple, or locking a relation which implicitly locks all of the tuples contained in that relation). As can be imagined, lock management in data bases is a complex subject, even though most data base systems do not permit parallelism within a transaction. Many of the issues are discussed in detail by Gray.[15]

A lock and key mechanism was also proposed for the PRIME system[2] to be used to constrain the accesses of processes to pages of memory and cylinders on the disks; for instance, each disk cylinder had associated with it a lock (called a class code) and only the process with the matching key was allowed to access a cylinder.

A further problem that can occur in systems employing locking strategies to implement atomic actions is that of deadlock.[16,17] Deadlocks occur whenever there is a circular dependency between processes for objects they have locked, for example, if process 1 has locked object A and requests object B while process 2 has locked object B and requires object A. Deadlock prevention may be attempted in some systems by imposing restrictions on the manner in which resources are acquired and released (e.g. by providing information at the start of an atomic action as to which objects will be required).[18] In practice deadlock prevention may be difficult and expensive to implement and is often not attempted. Instead techniques are provided to detect and cope with any deadlocks that arise during the operation of the system, for example, by recovering some of the processes involved in a deadlock.[15]

MECHANISMS FOR DAMAGE CONFINEMENT

While mechanisms have been used in existing systems to provide features similar to atomic actions, detailed examination of those mechanisms usually reveals that the full generality required for planned atomic actions is not provided. Protection mechanisms such as those based on capabilities perhaps come the closest but do not provide for synchronized entry to and exit from atomic actions, which is important for recovery as will be discussed in Chapter 7.

Protection in Multilevel Systems

The discussion so far has examined damage confinement with respect to the dynamic structure of systems, but has concentrated on mechanisms providing inter-process protection by constraining communications between processes. As mentioned above, intra-process protection is also highly relevant to the dynamic structuring of a system and hence to damage confinement and to measures for damage assessment. To illustrate the distinction between inter- and intra-process protection consider the multilevel system depicted in Figure 6.3.

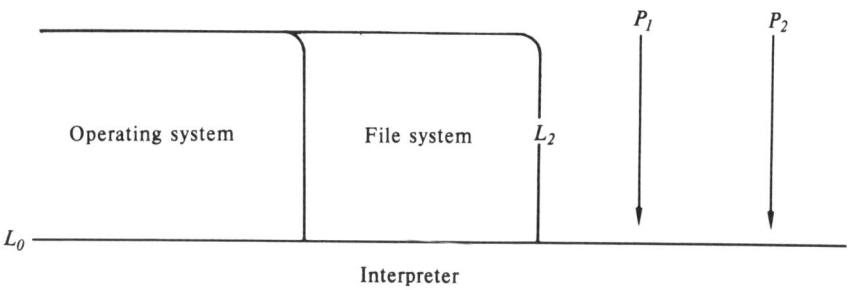

Figure 6.3 Protection in a Multilevel System

It is assumed that the interpreter implements the abstraction of separately executing processes. Each instruction executed on the L_0 interface will be associated with a particular process; the sequence of L_0 instructions executed for a process is referred to as the activity of that process. In the system depicted in Figure 6.3 the two processes P_1 and P_2 are executing on the same interface (L_2) and their activity can proceed in parallel (conceptually, at least). Many of the instructions executed on L_2 will be directly interpreted by the interpreter; other L_2 instructions will be interpreted by invoking the operating system and file system extensions. Thus the activity of a process $(P_1$ say) will be generated at several levels, arising from the execution of instructions associated with P_1 itself, supplemented by the execution of instructions in (lower level) interpreter extensions which implement some of the abstract objects being used by P_1. Intra-process protection is concerned with maintaining separation between these levels, involving all of the activity regarded as being internal to a process. Inter-process protection is concerned with maintaining the separation of the activities of the processes themselves, for instance, controlling the information flow between P_1 and P_2.

It can be appreciated that intra-process protection is of vital importance to the measures adopted by a process for damage assessment, since it is only by making assumptions about the behavior of the lower-level programs that reasonable measures can be designed. For example, it would be impossible for the designer of a process to provide rational measures for damage assessment to cope with the arbitrary errors that could arise if the file system was able to over-write instructions within the process.

It should be noted that the following discussion will not be concerned with protection between the interpreter and the processes it executes. Because of the powerful nature of interpretive interfaces it cannot be hoped to protect a process against the underlying interpreter. It must be assumed that the interpreter can be relied upon and will not be malicious. In the presence of failures of the components of the interpreter this reliance may be ill founded and the only recourse for any process will be to adopt exploratory (diagnostic) measures in an attempt to avoid further use of any instructions whose effects were suspect. However, the failures may prevent a process from attempting even this.

Furthermore, the notion of a process is an integral part of the structuring of the dynamic aspects of a system, and hence is of vital importance for damage assessment. Without this structuring the state of the whole system would have to be regarded as suspect following the detection of any error. Protection cannot be provided between a process and that part of the system which actually provides the abstraction of separate processes. In this section it is assumed that the interpreter implements this abstraction and hence the above comments follow directly. In other systems this abstraction may be the responsibility of the operating system interpreter extension (assisted by interpreter provided mechanisms, e.g. for protection and address mapping). Just as it is difficult to protect the state of a process from the interpreter which is executing the instructions of the process, it is difficult to protect a process against that part of the system responsible for its runtime manifestation.

The need for inter- and intra-process protection schemes was a consequence of the development of multiprogramming systems. In these systems, an operating system was primarily responsible for implementing the abstraction of multiple process execution and arranging the harmonious sharing of the resources provided by the interpreter between the processes. It was therefore necessary to prevent a process from corrupting the operating system and hence being able to take control of the whole system. This necessity led to the development of hierarchically organized protection mechanisms, in which the activity of a process at higher levels in the hierarchy is constrained to a more restricted protection domain than, say, the operating system at lower levels. For example, machines in the IBM 370 series (and many other computers) have a two level protection hierarchy in which the levels are called supervisor state and problem (or user) state. Other machines have a more general multilevel protection hierarchy. Multics, the first system to incorporate such a mechanism, provided eight levels (or rings) of protection,[19] while the ICL 2900 series provides 16 levels of protection.[20]

While hierarchical protection schemes can prevent a process from introducing errors into lower (more privileged) levels, the converse is not true since any given level usually has the potential for corrupting objects at all higher levels. For this reason, lower level programs (such as operating systems) have to be 'trusted' programs which must be carefully designed so as not to cause such damage. Since the main aim of a protection mechanism is to constrain information flow, hierarchical protection schemes are therefore less than satisfactory. Furthermore, the grain of protection in hierarchical systems is often fairly coarse and related to the management of the basic objects provided by the interpreter (e.g. to segments of virtual storage) rather than to the structuring that would be desired by extensions defining new abstract objects.

More recent developments which overcome these limitations have been based on the capability mechanisms introduced above. Capabilities allow a fine grained protection scheme to be implemented (even down to a single word) and provide tight encapsulation of the activity of a process. In particular, they support the principle of least privilege identified by Saltzer and Schroeder.[5] This principle states that any process should have access only to those objects it needs to perform its task. It is a lack of adherence to this principle which results in the problems that occur in hierarchically organized protection schemes, as indicated above.

Capability mechanisms also provide useful support for the creation of new abstract objects and their operations.[21] The ENTER capability (which is associated with an executable object), coupled with efficient switching of protection domains, provides a natural means for supporting abstract objects and providing protection between the calling program (which has no direct access to the concrete representation of the abstract object) and the called program (which cannot access any of the other objects in the protection domain of the caller).

MECHANISMS FOR DAMAGE ASSESSMENT

The earlier section on measures for damage assessment discussed static and dynamic damage assessment: static

MECHANISMS FOR DAMAGE ASSESSMENT

techniques imposed at system design time, and dynamic techniques involving exploratory measures by the system itself. Mechanisms for damage assessment can assist dynamic measures by monitoring and reporting on the inter-process information flow that actually occurred in a system.

In a single sequential program, information will flow due to the instructions which update the state of the variables of that program. Recording such updates can provide a record of the program's activity and hence of the damage that might have occurred. In practice such mechanisms are used, but normally form part of an error recovery mechanism and as such are not directly associated with damage assessment. Mechanisms which record state updates for recovery purposes, such as the recovery cache and audit trails, are described in detail in the next chapter rather than here.

Conventionally, inter-process communication is supported by a mechanism, implemented for instance by an operating system. If processes are constrained to use only this mechanism for communicating then a record of all communications can be accumulated dynamically. Although constructing the record is simple in concept there are limitations which reduce the practical usefulness of such a mechanism. One problem concerns possible interdependencies between communications. For example, if process A sends information to process B which subsequently communicates with process C, the mechanism cannot determine whether the communication between B and C was dependent or independent of the information sent between A and B. The worst case would have to be assumed.

The main problem of recording information flow concerns the quantity of information that must be retained. Clearly, such information cannot be collected and retained indefinitely, and there has to be some means for delimiting its retention. The termination of the processes concerned provides one point at which information can be discarded. More useful points can be related to the provision of recovery to the processes (this will be returned to in Chapter 7).

SUMMARY

Dynamic damage assessment is difficult to implement effectively in a computer system. Usually, damage assessment in a system will be static and based on gross, a priori decisions made during the design of the system. In some situations run-time measures can be provided to supplement the design decisions, although these will be limited to tentative explorations of the system state.

Of vital importance to any damage assessment strategy is the structure that the designer assumes will be present in the operational system, for it is this structure that enables the activity of a system and hence the flows of possibly bad information to be identified. Thus the mechanisms that are important for damage assessment are those that enforce structure at run-time, by providing constraints on the flow of information in the system. For this reason, the 'firewalls' that protection mechanisms provide against information flow, particularly against accidental information flow, are essential for damage confinement, and can also play an important role as an interface check for error detection. The more constraining the mechanism, the more beneficial it will be for damage assessment (and for error detection); for this reason capability protection mechanisms are very desirable.

Atomic actions have been shown to be a useful notion for considering the structure of the activity of a system, and mechanisms for enforcing atomicity have been discussed. Unfortunately, the full generality of nested atomic actions involving dynamically changing sets of processes is rarely supported, although capability mechanisms could provide a basis for an implementation.

Despite the advantages that capability mechanisms exhibit over more conventional protection mechanisms, it must be pointed out that capabilities have yet to be widely supported by computer manufacturers. Only two systems with hardware support for capabilities are known to the authors, namely the experimental Cambridge CAP computer[22,23] and the Plessey PP250 system,[24] although the descriptor scheme of Multics[25] and the larger Burroughs systems[26] have several features in common with capability machines. Other systems have been based on the capability concept, albeit implemented in software.[3,27]

There can be much interplay between the measures and mechanisms supporting damage assessment and confinement. For example, the provision of atomic actions will provide an encapsulation of the erroneous effects of a fault, thus identifying a portion of the state which is suspect and should be discarded, or in which it would be fruitful to concentrate exploratory measures. Mechanisms recording information flow can also assist any measures for damage assessment by providing information on the flow that actually occurred.

In practice, damage assessment is often a rather uncertain and incomplete aspect of fault tolerance, and is closely involved with error detection and recovery techniques. In most systems it is much easier to prevent damage from spreading than it is to determine after the event what damage an erroneous information flow might have caused. As computing systems become more distributed and decentralized, with multiple processors operating autonomously, it will become even more important to prevent the spread of damage and much more difficult to design system-wide strategies for dynamic damage assessment. Thus efforts spent in carefully deploying interface checks which try to limit the spread of damage by detecting errors at the earliest possible stage will be well worthwhile.

REFERENCES

1. M.N. Meyers, W.A. Roult, and K.W. Yoder, "No. 4 ESS: Maintenance Software," *Bell System Technical Journal* **56**(7), pp.1139-1167 (September 1977).

2. R.S. Fabry, "Dynamic Verification of Operating System Decisions," *Communications of the ACM* **16**(11), pp.659-668 (November 1973).

3. J.M. Taylor, "Redundancy and Recovery in the HIVE Virtual Machine," *Proceedings European Conference on Software System Engineering*, London, pp.263-293 (September 1976).
4. A.K. Jones, "Protection Mechanisms and The Enforcement of Security Policies," pp. 228-251 in *Lecture Notes in Computer Science 60*, ed. R. Bayer, R.M. Graham and G. Seegmuller, Springer-Verlag, Berlin (1978).
5. J.H. Saltzer and M.D. Schroeder, "The Protection of Information in Computer Systems," *Proceedings of the IEEE* **63**(9), pp.1278-1308 (September 1975).
6. M.V. Wilkes, *Time-Sharing Computer Systems*, Macdonald, London (1972).
7. T.A. Linden, "Operating System Structures to Support Security and Reliable Software," *Computing Surveys* **8**(4), pp.409-445 (December 1976).
8. R.M. Needham, "Protection," pp. 264-287 in *Computing Systems Reliability*, ed. T. Anderson and B. Randell, Cambridge University Press, Cambridge (1979).
9. D.D. Redell and R.S. Fabry, "Selective Revocation of Capabilities," *International Workshop on Protection in Operating Systems*, Rocquencourt, pp.197-210 (August 1974).
10. E.W. Dijkstra, "Cooperating Sequential Processes," pp. 43-112 in *Programming Languages*, ed. F. Genuys, Academic Press, London (1968).
11. C.A.R. Hoare, "Monitors: An Operating System Structuring Concept," *Communications of the ACM* **17**(10), pp.549-557 (October 1974).
12. P. Brinch Hansen, *Operating System Principles*, Prentice-Hall, Englewood Cliffs (NJ) (1973).
13. K.P. Eswaran *et al.*, "The Notion of Consistency and Predicate Locks in a Data Base System," *Communications of the ACM* **19**(11), pp.624-633 (November 1976).
14. J.N. Gray *et al.*, "Granularity of Locks and Degrees of Consistency in a Shared Data Base," pp. 365-394 in *Modelling in Data Base Management Systems*, ed. G.M. Nijssen, North-Holland, Amsterdam (1976).

REFERENCES

15. J.N. Gray, "Notes on Data Base Operating Systems," pp. 393-481 in *Lecture Notes in Computer Science 60*, ed. R. Bayer, R.M. Graham and G. Seegmuller, Springer-Verlag, Berlin (1978).

16. E.G. Coffman, M.J. Elphick, and A. Shoshani, "System Deadlocks," *Computing Surveys* **3**(2), pp.67-78 (June 1971).

17. R.C. Holt, "Some Deadlock Properties of Computer Systems," *Computing Surveys* **4**(3), pp.177-196 (September 1972).

18. D.B. Lomet, "Subsystems of Processes with Deadlock Avoidance," *IEEE Transactions on Software Engineering* **SE-6**(3), pp.297-304 (May 1980).

19. M.D. Schroeder and J.H. Saltzer, "A Hardware Architecture for Implementing Protection Rings," *Communications of the ACM* **15**(3), pp.157-170 (March 1972).

20. J.K. Buckle, *The ICL 2900 Series*, Macmillan, London (1978).

21. E. Cohen and D. Jefferson, "Protection in The Hydra Operating System," *Operating Systems Review* **9**(5), pp.141-160 (November 1975).

22. R.M. Needham and R.D.H. Walker, "The Cambridge CAP Computer and its Protection System," *Proceedings of 6th Symposium on Operating System Principles*, West Lafayette (IN), pp.1-10 (November 1977).

23. M.V. Wilkes and R.M. Needham, *The Cambridge CAP Computer and its Operating System*, North-Holland, New York (1979).

24. D.M. England, "Capability Concept Mechanisms and Structure in System 250," *International Workshop on Protection in Operating Systems*, Rocquencourt, pp.63-82 (August 1974).

25. J.H. Saltzer, "Protection and the Control of Information Sharing in Multics," *Communications of the ACM* **17**(7), pp.388-402 (July 1974).

26. E.I. Organick, *Computer System Organization: The B5700/6700 Series*, Academic Press, New York (1973).

27. W. Wulf *et al.*, "HYDRA: The Kernel of a Multiprocessor Operating System," *Communications of the ACM* **17**(6), pp.337-345 (June 1974).

7

ERROR RECOVERY

The previous two chapters have discussed in some detail the first two phases in the provision of fault tolerance in a system, namely, the detection of errors and the subsequent assessment of the extent of damage in the system state. These two phases are passive in the sense that they are not intended to effect any changes to the system. In contrast, the two remaining phases are active since they do change the system and thereby enable faults and their consequences to be tolerated. This chapter addresses the topic of *error recovery,* the aim of which is to eliminate errors from the system state. Chapter 8 discusses the fault treatment phase of fault tolerance which attempts to clear faults from a system so that continued service can be provided.

As defined in Chapter 2, a system state is *erroneous* if that state could lead to a failure of the system; the *errors* constitute those parts of the state which would have to be changed to prevent the failure from occurring. Thus, after an error has been detected and the damage assessment phase has produced an estimate of the extent to which the system state is erroneous, it will be necessary to eliminate those errors from the system state. Error recovery techniques have received considerable attention from research workers and system designers. The first section of this chapter discusses the measures which can be adopted in a system to transform an erroneous state into an error-free state. Mechanisms for error recovery are examined in the second section. Later sections extend the discussion to cover error recovery in multilevel systems and systems which contain concurrent processes.

MEASURES FOR ERROR RECOVERY

When an error is detected in a system, an exception will be raised to invoke an exception handler. The exception handler should include some method for eliminating errors from the system state, and this can only be based on the characteristics of the exception involved and on any available assessment of damage. For a particular exception (depending on the outcome of any damage assessment) the designer of a system may believe that an accurate prediction can be made of the errors actually present in the system. When this is the case the damage predicted is said to be *anticipated damage*. When an accurate prediction cannot be made the damage to the system is said to be *unanticipated*. The reason for making this distinction is that for anticipated damage it may be possible to implement error recovery very efficiently by making limited, but carefully selected, adjustments to the system state. An exception handler providing error recovery by means of selected adjustments must be tailored to deal with a specific erroneous system state and hence will be highly system dependent. The success of this approach obviously depends upon the accuracy with which damage is predicted (and assessed).

The following example shows that measures used to recover from anticipated damage are system dependent. Consider a calculation involving a floating point value which due to a complete loss of precision generates an 'arithmetic underflow' exception. Knowledge of the eventual use to be made of the value may allow the designer of the system containing the calculation to include a handler which provides recovery by supplying the value zero. In a different system, or even in the same system in other circumstances, a different response to the exception could be necessary - if the calculated value was to be assigned to a variable, an alternative handler could ensure that the variable was not updated. This might be appropriate in an iterative calculation making only small perturbations to the values of variables.

Another example illustrates the need for an accurate assessment of the location of errors in the system state. Measures for error recovery often make use of redundant information maintained by a system. Redundant data is sometimes available solely for fault tolerance purposes, but can also be provided in order to optimize the performance of a system. The latter is evident in the run-time organization for a block structured language when a 'display' is maintained to speed up accesses to variables held in the data stack. The designer of such a system may decide that if the exception 'corrupted display' is raised, the errors in the system will be confined to the display itself. Having thus anticipated the extent of the damage, one possible error recovery measure would be to reconstruct the display using pointers stored in the data stack. Although such a handler is attractive because of its directness and efficiency, its success obviously depends on the validity of the pointers in the data stack. If these pointers are erroneous then the approach cannot succeed.

Redundant data forms the basis of error correcting codes,[1] which are widely used in computer systems to provide recovery from anticipated damage in memory units. As noted in Chapter 5, the 16 bit words in semiconductor memory units of the Tandem 16 system are supplemented by a further six bits to provide single-bit error correction (and double-bit error detection). The program stores in the No. 1 ESS also utilize an encoding which provides single-bit error correction.[2]

A theory for the use of *structural redundancy* in data structures is being developed by Taylor et al.[3,4] They advocate the inclusion of redundant structural data such as extra pointers in list structures, count fields in composite structures, and run-time type information, as a means of aiding the provision of software fault tolerance. The redundant information can be checked for consistency, and the structure is corrected if inconsistent. Programs which provide this error detection and recovery capability are termed *audit programs;* these are executed periodically and/or when trouble is suspected. Audit programs are only concerned with structural inconsistencies - recovery from errors in the information actually recorded in the data structure must be provided by other methods.

When this work was discussed in Chapter 5 (under *structural checks)* the notion of a *change* to a structure was defined. A data structure is said to be *N-correctable* if there exists an algorithm which can recreate any valid state of the data structure which has been transformed by any set of N or fewer changes. For example, a doubly linked list is 1-correctable because it has two independent sets of pointers. If damage to an N-correctable data structure results from at most N changes then an audit program can provide recovery. (Note the analogy with N-bit error correcting codes for memory words.) An initial experiment in the use of structural redundancy for error correction has been performed[5] from which it is reported that about 90% of errors introduced by a 'mangler' (which randomly corrupts data structures) were corrected by audit programs. However, recovery overheads in the experimental system were rather high.

The use of audit programs in practical systems is very well exemplified by the Bell ESS systems. Their prevalence in those systems may be judged from the following: "all Bell System stored program switching systems have employed independent check programs known as audits".[6] Structural redundancy is included in the data structures which record the status of calls and lines in a switching system, and is checked for anomalies by audit programs which run at low priority until an error is detected. The audit programs are capable of correcting minor mutilations to the data structures but when damage is more severe, recovery is achieved by restoring damaged objects to their 'idle' state (some calls may be lost as a result). Field experience confirms the importance of the audit programs since they provide recovery for between 10 and 100 errors per day in a typical installation.[6] Almquist *et al.*[7] and Connet *et al.*[6] specifically examine the use of audit programs for error detection and recovery.

Error recovery based on the use of redundant data can only succeed if errors in the system do not overwhelm the redundancy; to that extent the damage must be anticipated.

In consequence, although these techniques can be effective in coping with errors due to known component failure modes (indicated by expected failure exceptions), in other circumstances recovery may not be achieved. For many of the exceptions raised by a system it will be impossible to predict or assess the exact location of all errors, and then little confidence can be placed in measures such as those used to provide recovery from anticipated damage. The approach of making selective adjustments to the system state is unlikely to succeed in eliminating all errors in the absence of accurate information concerning their location. More drastic measures are called for.

State Restoration

The only viable approach to recovery from unanticipated damage is to adopt a comprehensive approach to the removal of errors, namely to replace the entire state of the system. This is usually referred to as a *reset* of the system. The most basic reset strategy would, when invoked, place a system in some predefined state, for example an initial state of the system. Such a simple strategy is only likely to be successful for systems with special characteristics. For example, real-time control systems frequently return to an initial state in the normal sequence of computation, at what is often referred to as a 'frame boundary'.[8] Even for these systems, the specification would not have to be very stringent if emergency transitions to an initial state are not to introduce rather than remove errors from the system. Nevertheless, such basic reset techniques are used for recovery in both hardware and software systems.

Because of its simplistic approach, a fixed reset is often designed primarily to reduce the impact of a subsequent failure rather than attempt to prevent its occurrence. An example of this might arise in the use of a computer system to provide guidance, navigation and control of an aircraft. Should an unanticipated exception be signalled a possible response would be to reset the computer system to a fixed state from which it attempts to ensure continued safe flight by putting the aircraft into trim (a stable condition, flying level and under power).

Global recovery to a 'cold start' condition is employed in the HIVE system[9] using back-up copies of system software and data base files to reset the system state. Both software and hardware can be reset in the JPL-STAR which also has a cold start capability. In the Pluribus and ESS systems, components are reset as a means of error recovery. In both cases, some limited failures can result (the Pluribus may lose message packets, an ESS system may lose telephone calls) but the system will continue to provide service. These limited failures are acceptable because the environment of the system is able to tolerate them. Fault tolerance in the network protocols of the ARPANET ensures that lost message packets are retransmitted; customers of the Bell system can be expected to re-dial lost calls.

The main recovery tool in the No. 2 ESS is an 'initialization program' responsible for resetting data structures in the call stores.[10] Six levels of recovery are available, and are attempted in increasing order of severity until no further errors are detected. At level 1, hardware registers are reset. Levels 2-5 incrementally clear calls from the system, resetting the corresponding data structures. Recovery at level 6 consists of resetting all transient data in the call stores. Manual intervention is required to reset stable data associated with established calls.

The principal (and obvious) weakness of a reset to a fixed state is that a single state cannot take any account of the actual history of inputs to the system. Some alleviation of this weakness may be obtained by providing a set of states to which the system can be reset, the actual state used for any particular exception being selected by the exception handler. A much more significant improvement can be made to the basic reset strategy, and this is to reset the system to a state which has already occurred during the operation of the system. If the system can be restored to a state which it occupied prior to the manifestation of a fault then *all errors resulting from that fault must have been removed.*

For an error recovery technique to be able to restore a prior state of a system, some record of that prior state must have been preserved. To achieve this it is convenient to regard the system state as being comprised of a *normal* part and an *abnormal* part, corresponding respectively to that part of the state required for normal system operation and that required for fault tolerance. Thus, restoration of a prior state need only involve restoration of the normal part of the state, for which recovery information can be maintained in data structures in the abnormal part of the state. For example, a file editor can preserve a copy of a file which is to be edited, before any changes are made. This copy is part of the abnormal state of the system. Should a user of the editor accidently corrupt the file (e.g. by inadvertently deleting most of it - a not uncommon event) the editor is capable of restoring the file to its prior unblemished state. To avoid tedious repetition when discussing state restoration, the distinction between the normal and abnormal parts of the system state will usually be assumed rather than explicitly stated.

Forward and Backward Error Recovery

Because state restoration attempts to simulate the reversal of time it is referred to as *backward error recovery*. All other techniques for removing errors will be referred to collectively as *forward error recovery*. Backward error recovery techniques restore a prior state of a system without regard for the (normal part of the) current state, in the hope that the earlier state will be error free. In contrast, forward error recovery techniques manipulate some portion of the current state to produce a new state, again in the hope that the new state will be error free.

When recovery for anticipated damage was discussed earlier, it was noted that efficient and specialized recovery may be possible, but that this can only succeed if predictions concerning the location of errors are accurate. For this reason, forward error recovery measures are usually:

(i) dependent on damage assessment and prediction;

(ii) inappropriate as a means of recovery from unanticipated faults;

(iii) designed specifically for a particular system;

(iv)   impossible to implement as mechanisms.

The characteristics of backward error recovery could hardly be more different. As is substantiated below, backward error recovery is:

(i)   independent of damage assessment;

(ii)   capable of providing recovery from arbitrary faults;

(iii) a general concept applicable to all systems;

(iv)   easily provided as a mechanism.

Independence from damage assessment is a direct consequence of adopting the premise that any part of the system state may be in error. Backward error recovery must therefore achieve a complete replacement of the state - complete replacement means that damage assessment is unnecessary. In practice, backward error recovery strategies tend to be adulterated in the interests of economy and expediency, as will be seen in later sections of this chapter. The strategies can then only claim to be largely independent of damage assessment.

To assert that a recovery technique can guarantee recovery from errors due to any fault whatsoever is a bold claim, but with two provisos that claim can indeed be made for backward error recovery. All that is necessary is that the prior state must be successfully restored, and that the restored state preceded the manifestation of the fault which generated the errors. Clearly such a restoration will eliminate all of the errors produced by the fault; if the prior state was error free then the system will contain no errors after the backward error recovery is complete. Adoption of recovery techniques which perform less than a full state replacement necessitates a weakening of the guarantee.

State restoration is certainly a possible recovery method for any system, since the notion of state is inherent in that of a system. Furthermore, as a general concept, the requirements for a backward error recovery mechanism are easily met - particular methods of implementing such mechanisms are examined in the next section. However, this is not to say that state restoration is necessarily an appropriate, cost-effective, or even feasible recovery technique for all systems.

By far the most important of the four properties listed for backward error recovery is the ability to perform corrective action without making any assumptions about faults. It is this property which enables a system designer to provide recovery for a class of faults which would otherwise be difficult (if not impossible) to tolerate, namely, unanticipated faults such as faults in the design of a system. Most well established fault tolerance techniques are limited to providing tolerance for anticipated component faults. When, because of a need for high reliability, tolerance is required for unanticipated faults (in hardware or software systems) an error recovery technique can only make very limited assumptions about the errors with which it will have to contend. In this respect, backward error recovery has a substantial advantage over forward error recovery techniques.

Because backward error recovery has these properties, it is an extremely powerful recovery technique and will therefore be examined in considerable detail in this chapter.

From this discussion, backward error recovery may appear to have so many advantages that to even contemplate using forward error recovery seems surprising. To redress the balance, two drawbacks to state restoration as a recovery technique must be stressed. The first of these is to be found in the relative cost of the two forms of recovery. An exception handler providing forward error recovery will normally be much more economical than measures to restore a prior state, since adjustments need only be made to those parts of the system state which are (presumed to be) errors rather than to the entire state. Even when backward error recovery is implemented as a mechanism, its comprehensive adoption will incur penalties both in the speed of operation of the system and in the expenditure of resources for storing the information needed to permit the restoration of many prior states. As will be seen when recovery for systems containing concurrent processes is examined, these penalties can become so severe that some of the benefits of backward error recovery must be relinquished.

The second obstacle to the use of backward error recovery concerns objects which cannot be restored to their prior state. In any system in which backward error recovery is provided it is necessary to distinguish between *recoverable* and *unrecoverable* objects. Recoverable objects are those for which state restoration is available; any other objects are unrecoverable. Ideally, of course, all objects in the system should be recoverable, but in practice this may not be possible due to reasons of cost or physical constraints. For example, a peripheral such as a line printer is usually unrecoverable, since ink is difficult to remove from paper. (If it is essential to have a recoverable line printer this can be achieved by spooling the output until printing can be performed safely.) However, forward error recovery may also be applied to a line printer - erroneous printed output can be disposed of by sending a suitable request to the system operator. Such messages are said to provide *compensation* for errors, since the intention is to cancel out the damage in the system. It is possible in some situations to mechanize the provision of compensation in such a way that backward error recovery is achieved for a more abstract level in the system (Figure 7.7 provides an example later in this chapter).

The most obdurate type of unrecoverable object consists of objects external to the system, since the system can have no direct control over their values. If erroneous results are allowed to leave a system then external objects may enter unacceptable states. (The standard if somewhat extreme example here involves the erroneous launching of a missile causing a city to enter an unacceptable state.) Forward error recovery in the form of compensation is the only recovery method available (e.g. "Please ignore incoming missile").

MECHANISMS FOR ERROR RECOVERY

It has been argued that the only viable approach to recovery from unanticipated damage is to reset the state of the system, and that this reset should return the system to some prior state. Unlike forward error recovery techniques, which must be implemented as measures because they are

MECHANISMS FOR ERROR RECOVERY

system specific, the prior state restoration needed for backward error recovery can be provided either as a measure or as a mechanism. Backward error recovery is in effect a simulated reversal of time and can be more readily attained by a mechanism.

A backward error recovery mechanism can be constructed so as to place no reliance at all on the current system state and is therefore likely to be more secure than a measure which must depend to some extent on the current state. However, a mechanism which places absolutely no reliance on the current state will be particularly expensive to operate, and a number of mechanisms have been devised which are much more economical but only at the price of placing some minimal reliance on the current state. These will be discussed subsequently.

State restoration can be mechanized in a variety of ways, each offering different trade-offs in terms of costs in execution time and storage versus benefits of flexibility and security. However, the same set of basic recovery facilities must be supported by any implementation. These facilities are described below in the context of a single sequential process executed on an interpretive interface.

A point in time during the execution of a process for which the then current state may subsequently need to be restored is termed a *recovery point*. Replacing the current state of a process by the state it occupied at a recovery point is referred to as *restoring* the recovery point. A recovery point is *established* by arranging that appropriate information is preserved so that at any subsequent time it will be possible to restore the recovery point. This information is referred to as *recovery data*.

A flexible backward error recovery mechanism will permit more than one recovery point to be available. Clearly, if many recovery points are established, recovery data will have to be retained for each of them. The cost of maintaining the consequent accumulation of recovery data is such that in most implementations of backward error recovery it has been necessary to provide a facility which allows a recovery point to be *discarded*. Once a recovery point has been discarded it will not be possible for that recovery point to be restored. Hence a process which discards a recovery point makes a partial *commitment*. If all recovery points were discarded, the process would be completely committed, to the extent that no backward error recovery would be available from the interpreter.

A recovery point is said to be *active* from the time at which it is established until it is discarded. The period when a recovery point is active is referred to as the *recovery region* of that recovery point. Recovery regions can overlap; this is illustrated in Figure 7.1.

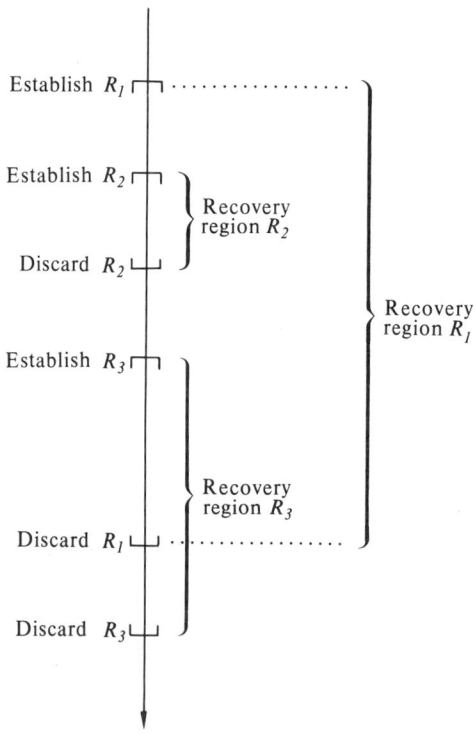

Figure 7.1 Overlapping Recovery Regions

If recovery points are discarded in the opposite order to that in which they were established (i.e. most recent first) then recovery regions will be properly nested, as are those of recovery points R_1 and R_2 in Figure 7.1.

To permit full and explicit control of a recovery mechanism by a process, the interpreter must provide operations to establish, discard and restore recovery points. Some means of identifying a specific recovery point will be needed in order to distinguish between multiple active recovery points. Responsibility for naming a recovery point could be left to the process or, alternatively, a unique identifier (such as a time-stamp) could be supplied by the interpreter.

The advantage of having the process control the operation of the backward error recovery facilities is that recovery points can be established at points in the computation where the system designer considers them to be most useful and effective. Similarly, recovery points can be discarded when they are no longer needed. Explicit restoration of a recovery point is available as a general purpose recovery action which can be initiated by an exception handler. Thus the provision of recovery can be linked to the structure and purpose of the process.

State restoration could also be initiated by the interpreter as an enforced response to any interface exceptions considered potentially dangerous, or as a default recovery strategy[11] to be adopted if an exception is raised which has no handler enabled. A policy would be needed to select which recovery point should be restored, such as the oldest active recovery point (giving the best chance of removing all errors) or the most recent recovery point (which would waste as little of the activity of the process as possible).

It is possible to construct a backward error recovery mechanism which operates independently of user processes, in which case the establishment, discarding and restoration of recovery points would be entirely under the control of the interpreter. For example, the interpreter could automatically establish recovery points at fixed intervals in time. If at any stage the amount of recovery data exceeded some specified threshold, then recovery points could be discarded until an adequate reduction in the amount of data was achieved. Some policy would have to be formulated to enable the interpreter to determine which recovery points should be discarded, with the aim of maintaining as comprehensive a recovery capability as possible. Although a completely automatic recovery scheme has the advantage of being transparent to user processes, it cannot provide recovery tailored to the structure of those processes. Instead, recovery schemes of this type are usually intended to provide tolerance to faults which are external to a process (e.g. memory corruption or hardware failure).

If recovery points are to be established at fixed intervals in time, the duration of these intervals must be selected. A high proportion of time will be spent recording recovery data if recovery points are established frequently. Conversely, if the interval between recovery points is large, the time needed for recovery and reprocessing may be excessive. Given an estimate of the frequency of recovery, the work of Young[12] and Chandy et al.[13] enables the interval between recovery points to be chosen so that the total time lost in recording recovery data, recovery and reprocessing is minimized. (Young's approximation to the optimum interval between recovery points is $(2tT)^{1/2}$ where t is the time taken to establish a recovery point and T is the mean time between recovery point restorations.) More recently, Gelenbe and Derochette[14] analyzed a model of a transaction oriented system, and obtained an estimate of the interval between recovery points which minimizes the average response time from the system. A general mathematical treatment of the problem of determining the optimum interval between recovery points is presented by Gelenbe.[15]

Checkpoints and Audit Trails

Backward error recovery mechanisms are most easily characterized in terms of the strategy they adopt for recording and preserving recovery data. Two basic strategies are available and have substantially different characteristics. The most direct strategy for ensuring that the state of a process can be restored is simply to take a complete copy of the state when a recovery point is established. When this is done, the recovery point is often referred to as a *checkpoint*[16] and the action of taking a copy of the state is then referred to as *taking a checkpoint*. In contrast, an indirect approach does not record any recovery data when a recovery point is established. Instead, the subsequent activity of the process is carefully monitored and a sufficiently detailed record of that activity is preserved to enable all changes to the state of the process to be reversed should restoration of the recovery point be required. The historical record of activity is known as an *audit trail*[17] or a *log*.[18] Many data base systems maintain an audit trail so that system activity can be (manually) certified as complying with legal and accounting regulations as well as for on-line recovery.[17]

When state restoration is provided by means of a checkpoint, the erroneous state is simply discarded and replaced by the version of the state recorded at the recovery point. Thus no reliance is placed on any of the values in the erroneous state, at the cost of a substantial overhead in the amount of recovery data which must be recorded at each checkpoint. In principle, a copy must be made of the contents of main storage and any secondary storage accessible to the process (including magnetic tapes if necessary). For many systems a complete checkpoint can only be taken infrequently, thereby incurring the risk that restoration of the most recent recovery point could involve a considerable loss of activity.

Restoration of a recovery point using an audit trail is achieved by processing the events recorded in the trail in reverse order, successively changing the state of the system so as to undo the effects of each event. This method of state restoration places some reliance on the erroneous state of the system since it depends on damage being confined to objects for which the audit trail can restore the prior value. Thus, an audit trail must keep a record of changes due to erroneous as well as valid transitions. However, an audit trail is an extremely flexible way of providing multiple recovery points. In effect, a recovery point is established as each event is recorded. For a recent recovery point, use of an audit trail as opposed to a checkpoint will greatly reduce the overhead associated with recording recovery data and the time needed for restoration, but obviously both will increase with distance in time from the recovery point.

One way of obtaining a compromise between the high storage penalty when many checkpoints are retained, and the cost in processing time of a long audit trail, is to combine the two techniques. If checkpoints are taken infrequently, additional recovery points can be established by maintaining an audit trail between each checkpoint. Should it be necessary to restore a recovery point between two checkpoints this can be achieved by restoring one of the checkpoints and then processing the audit trail - either forwards from the earlier checkpoint or backwards from the later one. Practical applications of such a combination are considered by Curtice.[19]

One account of this fairly common technique is presented by Boyd,[20] who describes a data base operating system in which an audit trail and checkpoints were used to provide independent methods of recovery for additional security. Every night a checkpoint was taken by dumping the entire data base onto magnetic tape. During the day, copies of all records that were to be updated during a transaction were saved on audit trail tapes. A copy was made of each record both before and after an update. Whenever a specified number of transactions had been completed a timing mark was placed in the audit trail. Four levels of error recovery were implemented for the files in the data base, and these were:

(i) undo the effects of a single erroneous transaction using the copies of records held in the audit trail for that transaction;

(ii) undo the effects of all incomplete transactions;

(iii) undo the effects of all transactions subsequent to a selected timing mark;

(iv) reload the data base from the dump tapes.

Recovery in data base and filing systems is often provided with respect to objects rather than processes. For example, a recovery point could be established for a file simply by taking a copy, often referred to as a back-up copy, of the file. The back-up copy provides a checkpoint for the file but is only a *partial checkpoint* for the system. A general discussion of recovery in data base systems is presented by Curtice.[19] Verhofstad[21] provides an extensive survey of data base recovery techniques, describing incremental dumping, careful updating, and differential files. Each of these techniques will be summarized in turn.

Incremental dumping is performed by making copies of any files which are changed by a process and retaining these copies in an archive - usually on magnetic tape. The copies

MECHANISMS FOR ERROR RECOVERY

are normally made after the process has completed a transaction with the data base, but may be taken more frequently for critical files. Incremental dumping is usually used in conjunction with the complete checkpoints produced by periodic (but infrequent) dumping of all files in the system. The incremental dumps then form a coarse-grained audit trail which provides recovery points between the checkpoints. The use of incremental dumping in the Cambridge University multi-access system is described by Fraser.[22]

Careful replacement takes the opposite approach to incremental dumping, in that a copy of the file is taken to establish a recovery point *before* changes are made to the file. If all changes are completed successfully the original version of the file can be (and often is) deleted, thus discarding the recovery point. Additional security can be provided by retaining the original version of the file, as was done in the HIVE system.[9]

A differential file is used to record changes which should have been made to a file so that the file itself can be left unchanged. In this way a recovery point is established since the unchanged original file provides a checkpoint. Any attempt to update the file must be intercepted so that details of the intended change can be recorded in the differential file. Similarly, attempts to read the file must first consult the differential file. Additional information can be stored in the differential file, such as time-stamps on the changes so as to obtain multiple recovery points. Periodically, the changes recorded in the differential file are applied to the original file, thereby discarding the recovery point(s). A differential file can be regarded as an audit trail for which the corresponding changes to the system have been held in abeyance. The technique is fully described by Severance and Lohman[23] who also present efficient hashing schemes intended to minimize the overhead of searching differential files.

Extensive recovery facilities are provided in System R.[24,25] Application processes manipulate files held in the data base by means of 'transactions' consisting of sequences of operations. Each transaction must start with a BEGIN operation and terminate with either COMMIT or ABORT. These operations are supported by the Relational

Storage System (RSS) described in Chapter 4, which provides all of the recovery facilities of the system. A recovery point is established by BEGIN, and is subsequently discarded by COMMIT or restored by ABORT. (Two other operations, SAVE and BACKUP, provide recovery internal to a transaction but have been little used in practice.)[25] Restoration of a recovery point is achieved by means of an audit trail (called a log in System R), and can be initiated either by an explicit ABORT or by the system in response to a problem such as deadlock.

The RSS uses a version of the differential file technique to provide recovery to files (at the file owner's option). When a page of a recoverable file is to be changed for the first time, both the original version and the changed version of the page are retained. Thereafter, changes are always made to the new version. The original version is called a 'shadow page' and ensures that a recovery point for the file is available. The recovery point can be discarded by discarding any shadow pages for the file, or restored by replacing changed pages by their shadow versions. At intervals, system-wide checkpoints are taken when the RSS is quiescent; at longer intervals a checkpoint is taken when System R is quiescent, and dumped to magnetic tape to guard against loss of disk storage.

The Recovery Cache

A partial checkpoint, introduced above in relation to recovery for files, provides a full system checkpoint until an object in the system is changed for which the partial checkpoint does not retain the prior value. If accurate predictions can be made as to which parts of the system state will be changed, a record of the current values of just those parts will enable the state to be restored. Since it may be impossible to predict accurately which parts of the state will change (particularly in the presence of faults), an alternative approach is to wait and see. As and when an object is about to be changed, its current value can be preserved as recovery data. In this way, recovery data can be accumulated to form a partial checkpoint incrementally, and predictions of which objects will be modified by a process are obviated. Instead, all changes must be monitored so that

MECHANISMS FOR ERROR RECOVERY

when an object is to be modified subsequent to a recovery point, its current value can be recorded in an *incremental checkpoint*.

A highly optimized incremental checkpoint mechanism has been designed to provide backward error recovery for recovery blocks (a technique for providing tolerance to software faults which is described in Chapter 9). The mechanism was originally called the recursive cache[26] but is now known as the *recovery cache*. (The word cache is used here with its dictionary meaning of a hiding place, and should not be confused with a high speed buffer.) An efficient state restoration mechanism is essential when programs containing recovery blocks are utilized, because they can be expected to establish many recovery points, and to do so relatively frequently.

The recovery cache mechanism yields a major economy in the retention of recovery data by not accumulating recovery data independently for each active recovery point. Instead, at any point in time recovery data is accumulated only for the most recently established recovery point (by monitoring changes to the system state). Furthermore, recovery data is only recorded for an object the first time that object is changed after the most recent recovery point.

Standard recovery cache mechanisms retain recovery data in a stack, in which the partial checkpoint for each active recovery point is held in what is termed a *cache region*. These are illustrated for a simple situation in Figure 7.2. A stack organization for the recovery cache is very convenient but only allows the most recent recovery point to be discarded. To enable an earlier recovery point to be discarded would entail the use of a more flexible data structure.

The operation of a recovery cache mechanism can be specified by describing the actions which are performed for each of four situations, namely, when a recovery point is established, when an object is to be updated, and when a recovery point is restored or discarded. The most recently established active recovery point will be referred to as the *current recovery point*, and the corresponding recovery cache region (at the top of the stack) as the *current cache region*. New recovery data is always recorded in the current

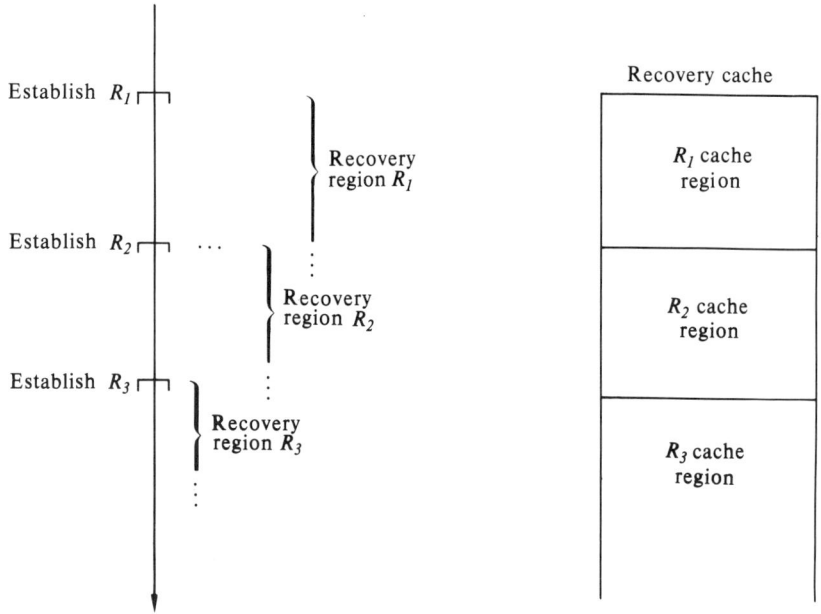

Figure 7.2 Recovery Cache Regions

cache region.

When a recovery point is established the recovery cache mechanism prepares to build up an incremental checkpoint for that recovery point in a new cache region. Initially, no recovery data is needed and the new cache region is empty.

When there is no active recovery point, objects are updated without interference from the recovery cache mechanism. Otherwise, whenever an object is about to be updated the recovery cache mechanism must determine whether the object is being updated for the first time after the current recovery point was established. If it is, the current cache region will not contain recovery data for the object and hence an entry for that object must be inserted. The entry must consist of a copy of the current value of the object (i.e. the value before the object is updated) together with the name of that object. Clearly, the value recorded will be the value that the object had at the time the current

MECHANISMS FOR ERROR RECOVERY

recovery point was established. Finally, the object can be updated since the current cache region now contains the information needed to restore the prior value of the object.

To restore the current recovery point, the recovery cache mechanism simply processes the recovery data stored in the current cache region. Each entry specifies the name of an object and the value to which it must be restored. If after restoration the recovery point is no longer required it should be discarded explicitly.

If there is only a single active recovery point it can be discarded by simply discarding the current cache region. However, if earlier recovery points are still active this will not suffice. The difficulty is that recovery data held in the preceding cache region (corresponding to the previous recovery point) will not be complete. Changes made to objects during the recovery region of the current recovery point (now being discarded) will have been recorded in the current cache region only, and not in the preceding cache region; this omission must be rectified. One approach is simply to combine the previous and current cache regions, but this can result in objects having more than one entry in a single cache region. When an object has an entry in both regions the one to be retained is that held in the earlier region; the current entry is no longer needed and should be discarded. Otherwise the amount of recovery data recorded is increased unnecessarily, and any subsequent restoration would have to ensure that the earlier value was restored. Thus, a recovery point is discarded by processing the entries in the current cache region, and supplementing the recovery data in the preceding cache region by the name and value of any object recorded in the former but not the latter. This merging ensures that the incremental checkpoint for the previous recovery point is brought up-to-date, and can be used for the subsequent accumulation of recovery data. The previous recovery point becomes the current recovery point.

As an example, Figure 7.3 indicates the contents of a recovery cache after the execution of the program shown alongside. Because two recovery points *(R_1 and R_2)* have been established the cache contains two regions. The current cache region contains an entry for both X and Y so that the current recovery point R_2 can be restored if

```
X := 10;  Y := 20;
establish R₁;
X := 30;
establish R₂;
Y := 40;  X := 50;
```

Recovery Cache

X	10
Y	20
X	30

Figure 7.3 Recovery Cache Example

necessary. However, the preceding cache region only contains an entry for X since Y was not changed while that region was current. To discard R_2, the current and preceding regions must be merged so that the combined region provides a checkpoint for R_1. This is achieved by transferring the entry for Y to the R_1 cache region and discarding the entry 'X 30'.

Note that the incremental checkpoint retained in the cache for an active recovery point corresponds to the stage in the computation at which the next recovery point was established. Only for the most recent recovery point does the recovery cache mechanism maintain an up-to-date partial checkpoint. However, this should not be considered a deficiency of the recovery cache; it was designed for use with recovery blocks and these ensure that only the most recent recovery point need be discarded or restored (since their recovery regions are nested). In any case, recovery to an earlier recovery point is easily obtainable by restoring each of the intermediate recovery points in turn, starting with the most recent.

Although the recovery cache mechanism can greatly reduce the storage overhead incurred in maintaining multiple active recovery points, to be practicable an implementation must also be efficient in terms of time. To this end, consideration must first be given to the actions performed when an object is to be updated, since this will occur much more frequently than the explicit recovery point operations (establish, discard and restore). The actual recording of recovery data when required is straightforward, but the determination of whether it is in fact necessary to record the prior value of an object is more difficult. Conceptually, a search of the current cache region is needed to ascertain whether a value has already been recorded for the object in question (and multiple searches are required when two cache regions are merged). Such searching could be very time consuming.

Most recovery cache implementations have expended additional storage to eliminate the need for a search every time an object is changed. The additional storage consists of a *recovery field* associated with each object for which recovery is to be provided. The first published design of a recovery cache mechanism[26] is based on the following economical strategy. The recovery field associated with each object is only a single bit, used as a flag to indicate whether a prior value of the object has already been recorded in the current cache region. Hence, to determine whether to record recovery data when an object is to be updated it is merely necessary to inspect the flag associated with that object. If the flag is clear then the update is the first to be applied to that object within the current recovery region - an entry must be inserted into the current cache region and the flag set.

When a recovery point is to be established or restored all of the flags must be cleared. If necessary, those which are set can be identified from the entries in the relevant cache region, since it is exactly those objects for which the flags will be set.

Discarding a recovery point is more complicated. Firstly, all flags must be cleared. Next, the flag must be set for each object with an entry in the preceding cache region. Finally, it is necessary to examine each entry in the current cache region, either to include it in the preceding cache region if no entry for that object is already present, or simply to discard it. No searching algorithm is needed since the decision for each entry can be made by examining the flag associated with the corresponding object. If the flag is already set the entry must be discarded; if not, the flag must be set and the entry included.

It is unfortunate that the residual inefficiency of this implementation occurs when a recovery point is discarded, since this can be expected to happen much more often than the restoration of a recovery point. Further optimization, with a further penalty in storage, eliminates this inefficiency but imposes an upper bound on the number of active recovery points. To obtain this optimization, a recovery field consisting of a vector of bits is associated with each object.[27] Each bit indicates whether an entry for that object is retained in one of the regions of the cache, with the first bit corresponding to the oldest recovery point and so on. The length of the vector fixes the maximum number of active recovery points. A counter is maintained of the number of active recovery points, which will be designated by RL (for recovery level, since it specifies the depth of nesting of recovery regions). Initially, RL is set to zero and all of the recovery fields are cleared.

To establish a recovery point it is only necessary to increment RL (checking that the maximum number of active recovery points is not exceeded). When an object is to be updated, bit RL of the recovery field of that object will be clear if an entry must be made in the current cache region, whereupon bit RL is set. To restore a recovery point, the value of the object specified in each entry in the current cache region is restored; at the same time bit RL in its recovery field is cleared. To discard a recovery point, for each entry in the current cache region, bit RL of the recovery field of the object identified is cleared. If bit $RL-1$ is set the entry is discarded; otherwise bit $RL-1$ must be set and the entry included in the preceding cache region. When all entries have been processed RL is decremented.

Another recovery cache mechanism has been designed[28,29] which operates almost identically to the bit-vector scheme just described, but with a storage overhead for recovery fields which is closer to that of the single-bit scheme. Each object has an integer recovery field which is used to indicate the greatest depth of nesting of recovery regions at which an entry has been made in the recovery cache for that object. The maximum value of this integer determines the maximum number of active recovery points permissible. For example, for a limit of seven active recovery points, the integer scheme would require a recovery field of only three bits whereas the bit-vector scheme would require seven bits. This reduction in storage overhead is offset to some extent by the need to record the prior value of the recovery field of an object in the recovery cache as well as the name and prior value of the object itself. Thus, when an object is to be updated its recovery field is compared with the current recovery level RL. If these are unequal then the name, value and recovery field of the object are stored in the current cache region. The object can then be updated and its recovery field set to RL.

To establish a recovery point, RL is incremented. To restore a recovery point, the value and recovery field of each object with an entry in the current region of the recovery cache must be restored. To discard a recovery point, for each entry in the current cache region the recovery field of the object identified is set to $RL-1$ and then the recovery field stored in the cache entry is compared with $RL-1$; if these are equal the entry is discarded but otherwise the entry must be included in the preceding cache region. After discarding a recovery point, RL is decremented.

Ideally a recovery cache should be implemented to operate at a similar speed to the objects for which it provides state restoration. Since the recovery cache is most likely to be used to provide recovery for computer memory, a hardware implementation has been designed and built by Lee et al.[27] Both the bit-vector and the integer recovery field mechanisms described above are supported by the hardware cache, which provides recovery for the memory of a PDP-11 computer. Performance measurements indicate that this cache imposes an average overhead of about 15% on accesses to memory.

RECOVERY IN MULTILEVEL SYSTEMS

This section examines the provision of error recovery in systems which have a multilevel structure (as defined in Chapter 2). Recall that the term 'multilevel system' refers to systems in which a hierarchy of interfaces can be identified, and where this hierarchy is implemented by a sequence of interpreters or interpreter extensions. In such systems it is useful to consider the extent to which recovery techniques at one level in the system can cooperate with those at other levels. Since forward error recovery techniques are specific to any level in which they are utilized, particular emphasis will again be placed on mechanisms which support backward error recovery.

The implementation of mechanisms to provide backward error recovery in a system organized as a hierarchy of interfaces supported by interpretation is straightforward in concept. For each interface on which backward error recovery is to be provided the interpreter supporting that interface must incorporate techniques for recording and maintaining recovery data to ensure the recoverability of abstract objects available on the interface. A variety of possible techniques have been discussed earlier in this chapter.

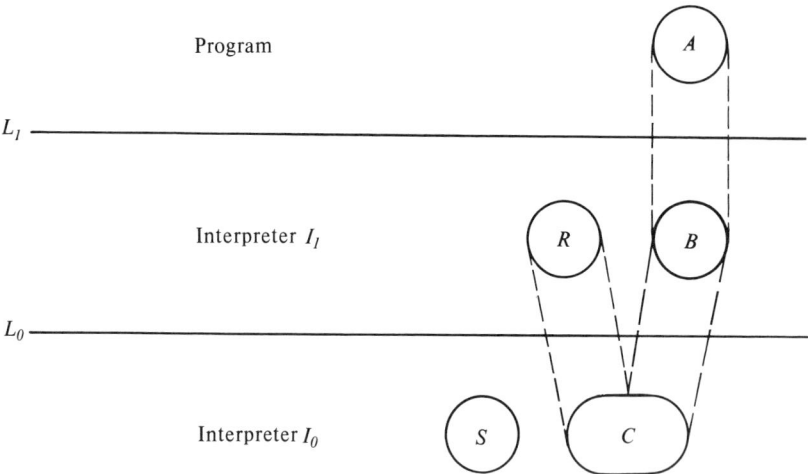

Figure 7.4 Representation Mappings in a Multilevel Interpreter System

Figure 7.4 depicts a multilevel system in which a program is executed on the L_1 interface supported by interpreter I_1. In turn, the interpreter I_1 is executed on the L_0 interface which is supported by interpreter I_0. The figure is intended to depict the *representation mappings* from 'abstract' data objects on one interface to their 'concrete' representations on the interface below. Thus, the set of abstract objects A manipulated by the program are represented by a set of objects B maintained for this purpose by interpreter I_1. In addition, the interpreter I_1 maintains data objects R so that, if necessary, the state of the (abstract) objects A can be restored by making suitable changes to their (concrete) representation B. That is, objects R retain the recovery data which the interpreter I_1 records in order to provide backward error recovery to the program. Similarly, the sets of abstract objects B and R are represented by a set of objects C maintained for this purpose by interpreter I_0. Objects S retain the recovery data which the interpreter I_0 records so that the state of the objects in B and R can be restored by updating C.

Because an interpreter is completely responsible for the interface it supports, it follows that each interpreter has complete responsibility for the provision of backward error recovery on the relevant interface. In Figure 7.4, backward error recovery is provided (to the program) on the interface L_1 by interpreter I_1. Similarly, the interpreter I_0 provides backward error recovery (to interpreter I_1) on the interface L_0. Note that the provision of backward error recovery on an interface does not imply that any other interfaces in the system are also recoverable. If the system in Figure 7.4 was changed so that no recovery data was recorded by the interpreter I_1 (i.e. R was omitted) then no backward error recovery would be provided to the program. Of course, if the interpreter I_1 was restored to a prior state by interpreter I_0 then this would necessarily effect a restoration of the corresponding prior state of the program. However, such a restoration would be in response to an exception occurring on the L_0 interface and would form a part of the provision of fault tolerance to the interpreter I_1 by interpreter I_0.

It is possible to envisage multilevel interpreter systems in which an underlying interpreter supports an interface which has been designed to facilitate the implementation of interpreters which themselves provide backward error recovery. Without going into details, the underlying interpreter would need to make available operations which assist in the preservation and management of recovery data, for example, operations to preserve and restore a copy of a specified data structure. Such techniques are best thought of as optimizations of the more direct construction (where each interpreter retains recovery data itself) and are not considered further.

Inclusive and Disjoint Recovery

As observed in Chapter 2, efficiency considerations impose severe limitations on the number of interpreters which can be utilized in a hierarchy. The remainder of this section is devoted to an examination of the issues involved in mechanizing the provision of backward error recovery for a system constructed as a hierarchy of interpreter extensions. Most of these issues can be discussed with respect to a simple system containing only a single interpreter extension as shown in Figure 7.5.

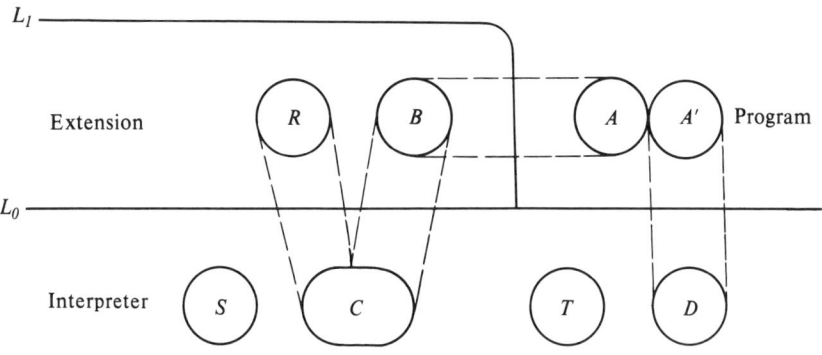

Figure 7.5 Representation Mappings in an Extended Interpreter System

In this system, a program executes on the L_1 interface, for which support is provided by an interpreter assisted by a single extension. The extension executes on the L_0 interface which is wholly supported by the interpreter. When an interpreter extension is used to implement a new interface in a system, support for that interface is provided by means of cooperation between the underlying interpreter and the extension. Thus, when backward error recovery is provided as a mechanism on such an interface the implementation of that mechanism is partly the responsibility of the interpreter and partly that of the extension. (The representation mappings shown in Figure 7.5 are therefore a little more complex than those of the interpretive multilevel system of Figure 7.4.)

Some of the abstract objects manipulated by the program will have their representations maintained by the interpreter; these abstract objects are identified in Figure 7.5 as objects A' with representations D. The remaining abstract objects manipulated by the program are shown as objects A, and these have representations B which are maintained by the extension. In order that backward error recovery can be provided to the program, additional sets of objects R and T are also maintained. Objects R retain the recovery data maintained by the extension so that the state of the objects in A can be restored, by updating their representations B. Objects T are the recovery data which the interpreter records so that the state of the objects in A' can be restored (by updating D). Furthermore, since the interpreter may be called upon to provide backward error recovery to the extension, the interpreter must record recovery data in objects S so that the state of the objects in R and B can be restored (by updating their representations C).

Thus, responsibility for restoring a recovery point established by the program is shared between the interpreter and the extension. Both record and maintain recovery data in order to discharge this responsibility. In addition, the interpreter must retain recovery data so that any recovery points established by the extension can be restored if necessary.

Clearly, the primary responsibility for recovery must rest with the interpreter. When the program establishes a recovery point, the interpreter takes appropriate action to ensure the recoverability of objects A' (relating to recovery data T) and must also ensure that the extension is invoked to do whatever is necessary to ensure the recoverability of objects A (relating to recovery data R). Similarly, when a recovery point is discarded by the program, the interpreter will make appropriate changes to T and ensure that the extension is given the opportunity to make changes to R. If the program raises an exception for which state restoration is needed for the objects in A and A', the interpreter must restore A' and invoke the extension to effect the restoration of A. Recovery for the extension is provided by the interpreter alone and is therefore straightforward.

Within the framework of multilevel backward error recovery presented here a further significant design decision must be made, which has a major impact on the way in which recovery is provided. In order to discuss this issue it is necessary to consider in more detail the operation of the multilevel system in Figure 7.5 when the abstract objects A are restored to a prior state. Since these objects are maintained by the extension, which manipulates their representations B, it has been suggested above that the extension will need to make changes to B (using recovery data R) in order to restore objects in A. If the objects B are all unrecoverable this will certainly be necessary. However, suppose that the objects B are all recoverable (i.e. they can all be restored by the underlying recovery mechanism implemented by the interpreter). An obvious optimization is then possible since restoration of a prior state of B will certainly also restore the corresponding prior state of A. To obtain this optimization, it is only necessary to stipulate that whenever a prior state of the program is to be restored, the prior state of the extension must also be restored.

A scheme of recovery in which program state restoration is accompanied by restoration of the state of the extension is termed an *inclusive recovery scheme* because the program is considered to be inclusive of the extension for recovery purposes. The recoverable file system implemented by Verhofstad[30] was based on an inclusive recovery scheme. A scheme of recovery in which the state of an extension is not restored when recovery is provided to the program is termed a *disjoint recovery scheme* since the program and the extension are considered to be disjoint for recovery purposes (in fact the extension is regarded as being part of the interpreter). In a disjoint recovery scheme an extension must restore the prior state of the abstract objects it supports without recourse to the recovery mechanism of the underlying interpreter.

Returning to the system of Figure 7.5, if objects B are all unrecoverable, then the behavior of the system is the same for both the inclusive and the disjoint schemes. When objects B are all recoverable the inclusive scheme enables R to be omitted since restoration of B automatically restores A; however the disjoint scheme requires the extension to re-implement recovery for the objects A. Given that one of the main aims of an interpreter extension is to extend an interface without incurring the inefficiency of re-implementing existing properties of the original interface, it seems natural to advocate use of the inclusive scheme.

Nevertheless, Shrivastava and Banatre[31] propose a system for reliably sharing scarce resources based on a disjoint recovery scheme. The main reason for not adopting inclusive recovery was that an extension in that system was used to provide abstract objects to more than one process. Thus recovery for one process could not be obtained by restoring the state of an extension because this would have had the effect of a partial state restoration on the other processes. (A direct comparison between inclusive and disjoint recovery is given below for a simple file system.)

The discussion so far has only considered the cases when objects B in Figure 7.5 are either all recoverable or all unrecoverable. Particular interest attaches to the situation, believed to be far more likely in practice, where some of these objects are recoverable and some are not. For a disjoint recovery scheme this has no impact; none of the objects used by the extension are restored when recovery of the program is needed. If an inclusive scheme for recovery is used then the extension must ensure that any necessary changes are made to the unrecoverable objects in B so that the overall effect of these changes, together with the automatic restoration of the prior state of those objects in B which are recoverable, is to restore the prior abstract state of the objects A.

A further decision to be made in the implementation of an inclusive recovery scheme is whether the restoration of the recoverable objects in B by the interpreter should precede or follow the changes made to B by the extension. The only possible advantage of having the interpreter perform restoration first is that this would permit the extension to make adjustments to some of the updated recoverable objects as well as to the unrecoverable objects. It is unlikely that this would be useful in practice. There is a much stronger reason for suggesting that the extension should make its changes to B first and this is because the extension would then have available to it the state of all its objects at the time the exception was raised by the program. The unrestored values of the recoverable objects in B may be significant, but again this is unlikely in practice. What will be significant for the extension are the unrestored values of the objects R (the recovery data), carefully recorded so that the extension can ensure that the state of the objects A is restored. If the extension makes use of recoverable objects to record recovery data, then an inclusive scheme of recovery must not allow these preserved values to be lost because of state restoration by the interpreter. A simple way to achieve this is to defer restoration by the interpreter until after the extension has completed its recovery actions. Otherwise some other method must be employed, such as only recording recovery data in unrecoverable objects, or by extending the inclusive scheme to distinguish objects (such as recovery data) for which disjoint recovery is the appropriate recovery regime.

To illustrate the differences between a disjoint and an inclusive scheme of recovery, an outline of a simple multilevel system is presented. This system is of the form shown in Figure 7.5, and provides a rudimentary single-user filing system. Full details of recovery in a similar multilevel system have been published elsewhere.[32] The interface L_0 supported by the interpreter makes available variables (held in main memory) and disk pages (held on secondary storage). A single extension conceals the disk pages from the user program and instead provides files consisting of numbered lines of text. Thus the interface L_1 provides the user program with variables (maintained by the interpreter) and files (maintained by the extension).

Figure 7.6 represents the data structures which are used by the extension to implement files. The contents of each file are stored in a set of disk pages, and in order to expedite access to a file the extension also maintains a copy of the most recently accessed disk page in main memory. In addition, the extension makes use of a number of variables to specify the current status of the file system and to record the mapping from file name and line number to addresses on disk. Whenever the user program accesses a

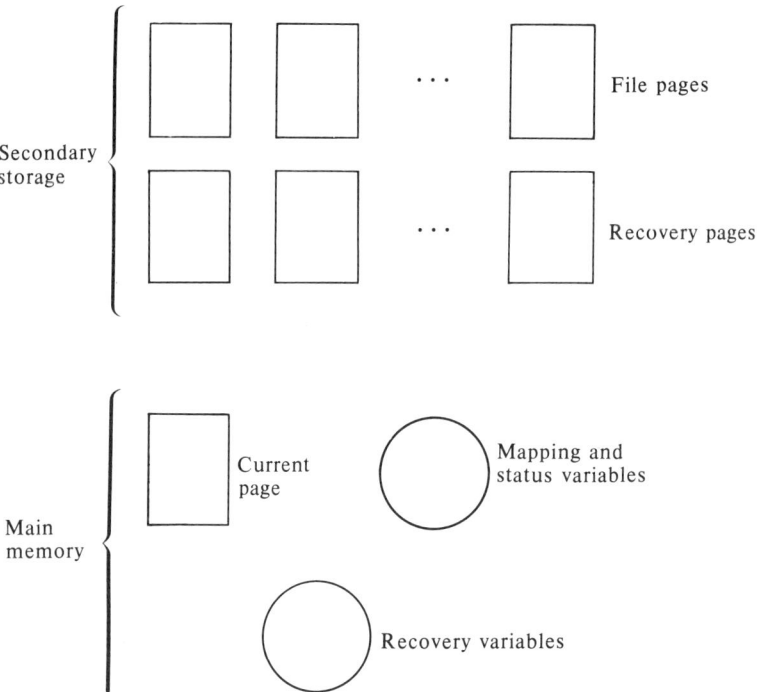

Figure 7.6 Data Structures in an Extension

line of a file the extension checks whether the disk page currently in main memory contains that line, and if so the access is applied to the main memory page. Otherwise, the current main memory page is copied back to the disk (if it has been updated), the disk page containing the line is copied into main memory and the access is then applied to the copy in memory.

It will be assumed that in this example system the interpreter provides a backward error recovery mechanism for variables held in main memory, but that the disk pages are unrecoverable. The extension retains recovery data so that it can provide backward error recovery for files used by the program. A simple strategy which enables the extension to restore a single recovery point is now described. (This strategy is very similar to the use of shadow pages in System R.)

Assume initially that the interpreter implements a disjoint recovery scheme. When the recovery point is established, the contents of the page held in main memory are copied out to the disk (this ensures that the pages on disk represent an up-to-date version of the file at the recovery point). Subsequently, whenever the page in main memory would be copied back to the disk, instead of overwriting the original disk page an unused disk page is acquired and used to store the current version (this is only necessary the first time a disk page is to be overwritten after a recovery point). The address of the preserved original page is recorded as recovery data, and the mapping variables are adjusted to reference the newly acquired page. With a disjoint recovery scheme no assistance in providing recovery for files can be obtained from the recoverability of the main memory variables, and so the extension must (in principle) ensure that the memory page, the mapping variables and the status variables can all be restored if recovery is needed. However, since it is only the abstract state of the files which must be restored, certain optimizations are possible. For example, it is simple to arrange that the page held in memory need not be restored. Instead, an internal status variable is set to indicate that the memory page is empty. Any subsequent access to a file by the program will then result in the appropriate disk page being copied into memory. A subset (possibly all) of the status variables would need to be restored and, most importantly, the mapping variables must be restored. By restoring the mapping variables to their values at the time the recovery point was established the original disk pages once again represent the files, which are thereby returned to their prior state. Thus the extension must preserve recovery data for the mapping variables and (some of) the status variables.

In contrast, if the interpreter implements an inclusive recovery scheme, the recovery actions of the extension can be greatly simplified. All that is necessary is for the extension to avoid overwriting the original disk pages (by acquiring a new page whenever the memory page is copied back to disk, exactly as described for the disjoint scheme). No direct action by the extension is then needed to restore the prior state of the files. With inclusive recovery in operation, the interpreter will restore the values of all variables used by the program and the extension. Thus, the prior values of the memory page and the mapping and status variables will be restored. Restoration of the mapping variables will, as in the disjoint scheme, restore all files to their prior state since the mapping variables will once again refer to the original disk pages.

On the basis of this simple example it would appear that the inclusive recovery scheme has much to commend it in preference to the disjoint recovery scheme. Unfortunately, a decision as to which scheme is preferable is not as straightforward as the above discussion might seem to imply. Even in the above example the decision would not be so simple if consideration were given to the issues of acquisition and release of disk pages (the example implicitly assumes that these are recoverable operations provided by the interpreter). With the inclusive scheme of recovery the extension in the example does not need to record recovery data in recoverable main memory variables, and thus evades the problem of ensuring that recovery data is not lost because of recovery performed by the interpreter. An inclusive scheme of recovery should certainly provide more efficient recovery than a disjoint scheme, but the benefits will often be less than might be expected. This is because optimization of the recovery actions of an extension is usually possible for a disjoint scheme by exploiting opportunities to restore the abstract (and not the concrete) state of a program (as was done in the example system to avoid having to restore the memory page). Finally, difficulties can be expected if inclusive recovery is used when an extension has to provide abstract objects to concurrently executing programs.

In summary, inclusive recovery provides a major benefit; it eliminates the needless re-implementation of recovery for objects represented by objects which are themselves recoverable. Disjoint recovery has the advantage of simplicity; by accepting full responsibility for recovery of the objects it supports, the provision of recovery by an extension is analogous to the provision of recovery by an interpreter in a fully interpretive multilevel system.

If a multilevel system is constructed by means of a sequence of extensions, the representation mappings for abstract objects manipulated by a program executing in the system can be much more complicated than those of Figure 7.5. However, the implementation of backward error recovery in such a system is only slightly more complex than for a system with only a single extension. To see why this is so it is only necessary to recall that each extension can legitimately regard any preceding extensions as an integral part of the interpreter, while subsequent extensions may be regarded as part of the user program. Anderson *et al.*[33] presented a model of recoverability for multilevel systems in which they discuss the provision of recovery in systems with more than one extension.

RECOVERY IN CONCURRENT SYSTEMS

When a system contains a number of concurrently active processes and one of these processes raises an exception it is necessary to consider the extent to which the provision of fault tolerance to that process impacts other processes in the system. Chapter 6 discusses the difficulties of assessing the spread of damage from the process in which the exception is raised to other processes in the system. Similar problems, and related solutions, are addressed in this section, which examines techniques for error recovery in a system of concurrently executing processes. As in previous sections, the principal emphasis will be placed on techniques for backward error recovery because of their power and generality, and because they can be mechanized. Forward error recovery techniques can also be used but because of their system specific nature not much can be said about their general application.

Concurrent Processes

It is helpful to classify a set of concurrent processes as being in one of three categories, namely *independent, competing* or *cooperating*.[34,35] The first of these categories is a trivial case; concurrent processes are said to be *independent* if the sets of abstract objects accessed by each process are disjoint, since the activity of each process must then be completely private from any other process. Clearly, the provision of error recovery to one of a number of independent processes is identical to the provision of error recovery to a single sequential process. Error recovery can be forward or backward, by means of measures in the process itself or mechanized by an underlying interpreter.

The simplest form of independent processes occurs when the processes are physically separate. For example, if a number of unconnected microprocessors each supporting a single process were considered to form a single system, the concurrent processes in that system would certainly be independent. Error recovery for each process could be provided without regard for the actions of the other processes. Only slightly more complicated is the case of a single CPU supporting the pseudo-parallel execution of a number of processes in fixed memory partitions with dedicated input and output devices. Such a multiprocessing system can naturally be regarded as containing a set of independent processes, for which error recovery can be provided as for sequential processes. However, the processes are not allowed to have shared access to any objects in the system, not even to a set of CPU registers. Either the computer has no registers, or the processes do not use them, or registers are dedicated to separate processes in the same way as devices. Otherwise, shared access to the registers would violate the requirement (for independence) that the objects accessed by the processes are disjoint.

The second category of concurrent processes removes this rather restrictive requirement. Concurrent processes are said to be *competing* if there are objects in the system which are accessed by more than one process but for which the shared access is solely because of the need to increase the utilization of scarce resources; the usage of the resources must be private in that *no* information flow results from the sharing (not even via 'covert channels').[36] Conventional operating systems are frequently used to support competing processes in multi-access computer systems. Objects which are shared in these systems include general purpose registers and peripheral devices. The saving and restoring of the registers and the allocation of devices by the operating system for the user processes can ensure that no information flow is possible and hence the processes can be classified as competing. Recovery for competing processes is discussed in the next sub-section.

The third category of concurrent processes imposes no constraints on information flow. *Cooperating processes* have shared access to objects which are used directly for inter-process communication. Information flow is usually a necessary feature of transaction processing systems, so the transactions in these systems normally constitute a set of cooperating processes. Unfortunately, information flow between processes implies interdependency between processes and this impinges on the provision of error recovery, as will be discussed after the next sub-section.

Recovery for Competing Processes

In defining the notion of competing processes, the possibility of information flow was carefully excluded and this enables the adoption of a relatively simple recovery strategy for processes in this category. The approach depends on the use of shared resources by competing processes being entirely private. In consequence, it will be completely immaterial to the operation of each individual process that the resource is actually shared and hence the processes must surely behave just as if they were independent (under an appropriate abstraction they *are* independent). Therefore recovery can be provided for each process as if it were a single sequential process, without regard for other processes in the system, as was proposed for independent processes.

Thus, in principle, the provision of recovery for competing processes is no more difficult than for independent processes. In practice, however, there are complications. The first of these relates to the definition of competing processes. This was prompted by the large class of systems in which there is no direct requirement for communication between concurrent processes, but in which scarce resources have to be shared between the processes. The problem is that in many of these systems there *is* communication between processes, but only for the purpose of coordinating the resource sharing. Nevertheless, this ancillary communication clearly involves a flow of information, albeit limited and for a specific purpose. (The strict definition of competing processes therefore excludes these systems.)

A second difficulty is more pragmatic and concerns the actual techniques needed for recovery, particularly when mechanized backward error recovery is to be supported. The problem is that when competing processes are involved, the resources for which they compete may require more sophisticated strategies for effective and efficient error recovery than those usually necessary for the objects manipulated by sequential processes. Much of the discussion on backward error recovery for a single process concerned the provision of recovery for objects which are normally represented in the main memory of a computer, whereas the objects manipulated by competing processes will often be represented by secondary memory or peripheral devices. A recovery cache device designed to make main memory recoverable is not likely to be appropriate for secondary memory and so objects such as files would normally be unrecoverable, as would devices used for input and output. The difficulties caused by these unrecoverable objects are increased when they are utilized by a set of competing processes.

Both of these difficulties are best resolved within the framework of a multilevel system. The previous section discusses the organization of recovery in systems constructed using interpreter extensions, and the means by which recoverable abstract objects could be provided having representations which included unrecoverable objects. An interpreter extension which supports concurrent processing can provide recoverable abstract objects to the processes by using these techniques. Furthermore, the extension can ensure that, at the interface on which the processes execute, no inter-process communication is needed for the harmonious sharing of resources between competing processes. The only necessary 'communication' takes place between the individual processes and the extension, in the form of requests for the acquisition and subsequent release of the shared objects. This is achieved by conventional methods of controlling the allocation of resources, as performed in practice by many operating systems and as discussed theoretically by Hoare[37] in relation to monitors.

When an interpreter extension supports concurrent processes by an implementation which precludes information flow between the processes, then they can certainly be classed as competing processes and recovery can therefore be provided separately for each process. This approach is adequate for many systems of concurrent processes and can be adopted, for example, in systems which support shared objects by implementing virtual memory and spooled input and output devices.

In order to facilitate the implementation of an interpreter extension providing recovery to competing processes, Shrivastava and Banatre[31] propose a programming language construct which they call a **port**. In their approach, access to shared objects is controlled by a monitor (presumed to be reliable in its own operation). In turn, access to the monitor can only be obtained through an instance of a port, which is a special form of encapsulated abstract data type. The body of a port has the form:

<prelude>; **inner**; <postlude>

The prelude and postlude invoke the monitor in order to acquire and release the resource. Use of the **inner** notation from SIMULA[38] ensures that any usage of the resource will be enclosed within the prelude and postlude of the port. Such usage can be a series of operations selected from those defined as procedures of the port. Recovery is implemented in the port by a recovery procedure which must be capable of undoing the effects of a sequence of normal operations, and can be invoked automatically when required. A simple example of a port used to control access to a pool of shared line-printers is presented in Figure 7.7. In addition to invoking the monitor to acquire a printer, the prelude in this example ensures that printed output is uniquely identifiable by printing an initial header page. This enables the recovery procedure to undo the effects of any subsequent use of the printer simply by requesting the operator to discard the printed output with that header page.

When ports are used to control access to shared resources, backward error recovery can be supported by a

line-printer = **port**;
begin ...
    procedure *print page (p:page);*
      begin
        print p on printer LP;
      end;
    recovery procedure *undo;*
      begin
        write to operator ('discard current output on printer', LP, 'for job', job number);
      end;

    acquire printer (LP, job number);   ⎫
    prepare header page h for job job number; ⎬ *"prelude"*
    print page (h);   ⎭
      inner;
    release printer (LP);   *"postlude"*
end;

Figure 7.7 The Port Notation

modified recovery cache mechanism. Shrivastava[39] describes how this was achieved for an implementation of Concurrent Pascal extended with the port facility. A companion paper[40] provides further examples of the use of ports.

Recovery for Cooperating Processes

When processes cooperate (that is communication takes place with the explicit aim of exchanging information) the simple approach to recovery advocated for competing and independent processes is no longer adequate. In particular, attempts by individual cooperating processes to achieve backward error recovery can result in the problem which has come to be known as the *domino effect*.[41] This effect is illustrated in its simplest form in Figure 7.8.

The two processes P_1 and P_2 independently establish recovery points; each '[' marks an active recovery point to

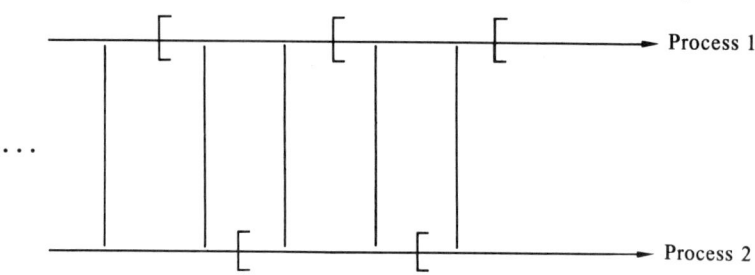

Figure 7.8 The Domino Effect

which the state of the corresponding process can be restored. Vertical lines in Figure 7.8 indicate the occurrence of communication between the processes. No difficulty is encountered if an exception is raised by process P_1 since restoration of its most recent recovery point provides satisfactory recovery. However, if process P_2 raises an exception, backward error recovery is more difficult to achieve since its most recent recovery point precedes an interchange of information with P_1. To effect recovery, not only must process P_2 be restored to a prior state but recovery must also be initiated for P_1, to its penultimate recovery point. Since this recovery point precedes further intercommunication, the states of the processes will still not be consistent and further recovery of P_2 must be initiated. Thus, an uncontrolled 'roll-back' is precipitated, with recovery points being restored in sequence like a line of toppling dominos. In this way a fault in a single process can result in each process of a set of cooperating processes using up many, if not all, of its active recovery points.

The propagation of recovery between a set of cooperating processes is necessitated by the flow of information between processes. If one process performs recovery after having received information from some other process, then it may need to receive another copy of the information. If a process performs recovery after having transmitted information to another process then the transmitted information may well have been erroneous, in which case recovery of the recipient will be necessary. Propagation of recovery, and hence the domino effect, does not arise for independent and competing processes because no information flows between such processes.

If backward error recovery is required for a set of cooperating processes then, in general, a penalty must be incurred. This penalty can be paid in terms of loss of activity (due to extensive roll-back) or of additional storage (due to frequently established recovery points). Alternatively, restrictions may be placed on concurrency, on communication or on recovery capability. A number of different techniques have been devised, each having a different trade-off of the inevitable penalties and restrictions. Some of these techniques will now be described.

All strategies for providing backward error recovery to a set of cooperating processes have a common goal: when an exception is raised by one of the processes, the aim is to identify a subset of the processes which includes the erroneous process and for which a set of active recovery points can be found to provide a consistent restart point for the processes. As can be seen by considering the domino effect, recovery points for a set of processes only lack consistency when communication between processes occurs during the period from one recovery point to the next. In order to formulate a precise definition, consider a subset $P_1, \ldots, P_n$ of the processes of a system and suppose that these have established recovery points at times $t_1, \ldots, t_n$ respectively. This set of recovery points is *consistent* at some later time t if the following conditions hold for all processes P_i and P_j in the subset:

(i) in the period t_i to t_j, processes P_i and P_j do not communicate,

(ii) in the period t_i to t, process P_i does not communicate with any process not in the subset.

Thus, for the set of recovery points to be consistent, each process P_i after having established its recovery point may only communicate with other processes in the subset that have also established their recovery points.

Consistent sets of recovery points are illustrated in Figure 7.9, which represents the activity of five processes *(P_1, ..., P_5)* with inter-process communication indicated by vertical lines and recovery points labelled $R_1, \ldots, R_8$. Sets of

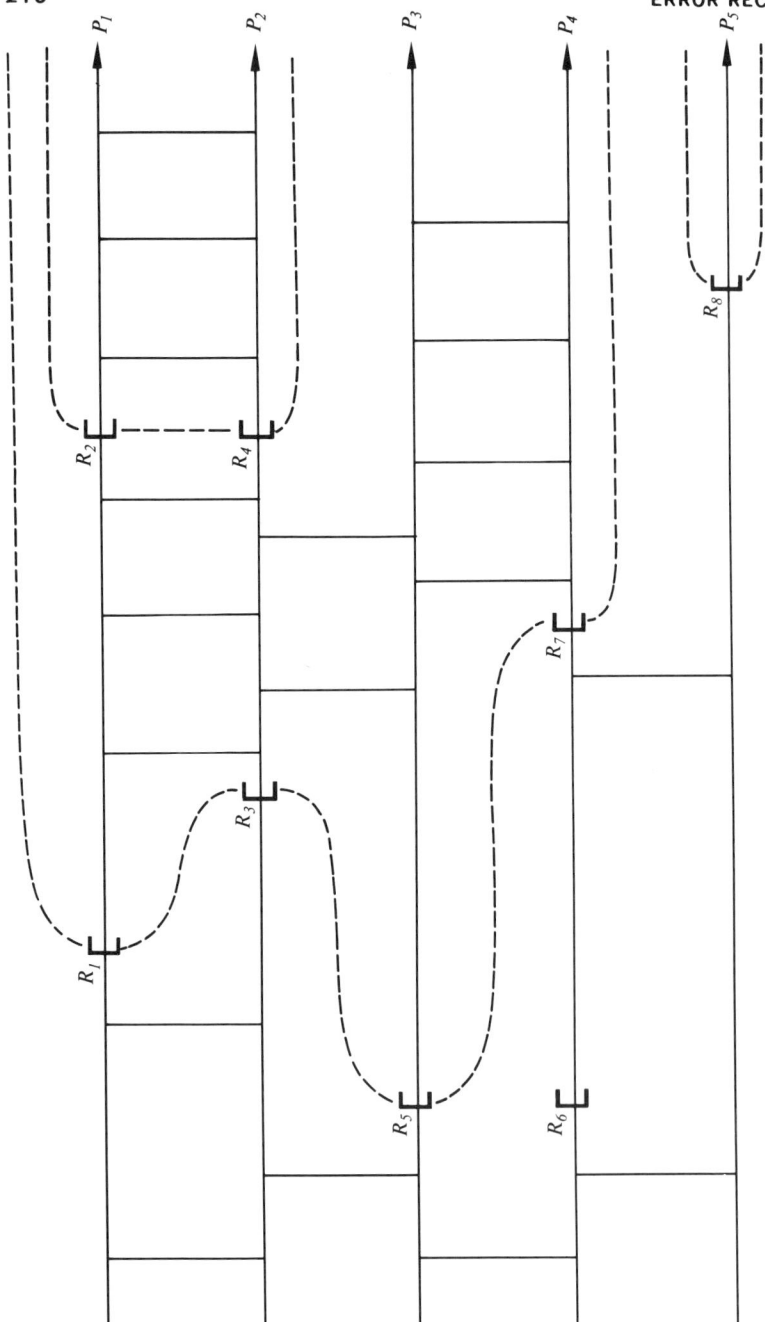

Figure 7.9 Recovery Lines

recovery points will be considered which are consistent at the time corresponding to the right hand edge of the figure. The simplest example is the singleton set $\{R_8\}$, which is consistent since process P_5 does not communicate with any other process after R_8 is established. Another simple example is the set $\{R_2, R_4\}$, which is consistent because these two recovery points are established simultaneously and, from then on, processes P_1 and P_2 only communicate with each other. The set $\{R_1, R_3, R_5, R_7\}$ provides a more general example of a consistent set of recovery points.

Note that a set of recovery points which is initially consistent can subsequently become inconsistent. The set $\{R_1, R_3, R_5, R_6\}$ is consistent from when R_3 is established until communication takes place between P_4 and P_5. Thereafter the set is inconsistent.

If two sets of recovery points have no process in common and are both consistent at time t say, then (from the definition of consistency) the union of the two sets must also be consistent (at time t). Thus sets $\{R_2, R_4, R_8\}$ and $\{R_1, R_3, R_5, R_7, R_8\}$ are consistent.

A consistent set of active recovery points is said to form a *recovery line* for the processes involved since if one of these processes raises an exception, backward error recovery can be provided by restoring all of the recovery points in the consistent set. Each broken line in Figure 7.9 connects recovery points forming a recovery line, and encapsulates the activity of a group of processes for which recovery can be obtained. The notion of a recovery line is closely related to that of an atomic action, introduced in Chapter 2. Recovery lines in Figure 7.9 also delineate the boundaries of atomic actions; hence no vertical communication lines can cross a broken line indicating a recovery line. Of course, it is not always possible to indicate a recovery line by connecting its constituent recovery points (e.g. consider the recovery line $\{R_2, R_4, R_8\}$).

The provision of backward error recovery in a system of cooperating processes requires that when a process raises an exception, a recovery line containing a recovery point for that process can be found. It is clearly preferable that the recovery line should contain as few other recovery points as possible and that these should have been established as recently as possible. Fortunately these two desiderata are compatible.

The first approach to be considered for locating a recovery line is that of designing a system so that an appropriate recovery line is always available, and known to the system in advance. This approach is based on the use of *planned recovery lines,* and in most systems requires constraints to be imposed on the communication between processes as well as enforcing some form of synchronization on the processes. In certain systems it may be possible to dispense with these restrictions, but substantial penalties are likely to be incurred either in terms of loss of system activity or in costs for maintaining recovery data.

For example, one extreme strategy would be to require that whenever any process in the system establishes a recovery point then all of the other processes must do the same. Certainly, these system-wide sets of recovery points provide a very convenient set of planned recovery lines such that roll-back of the system in any situation could be minimized. However, the large quantity of recovery data to be retained and the overheads involved in recording so much data are likely to prohibit adoption of what would otherwise be a simple and attractive solution.

At the opposite extreme, a system could be constructed such that recovery points are only established when each process in the system is initiated. In this way the overheads of preserving recovery data could be minimized at the cost of greatly increasing the roll-back needed to return the system to a prior state. For most applications the loss of activity would probably be too expensive; furthermore, very few systems could regress to this extent and still conform to their specifications.

Strategies intermediate to these two extremes can be devised. For some systems a straightforward approach based on periodically establishing recovery points for all processes (perhaps after fixed intervals of time) could provide a satisfactory compromise between the overheads of recording and retaining recovery data and the extent of the roll-back needed for recovery. However, such approaches are likely to incur unacceptable overheads of both roll-back and recovery data.

To obtain effective utilization of planned recovery lines it will usually be necessary to link the provision of recovery lines to the structure of the internal activity of a system. For this to be successful the desired structure must be enforced on the operation of the system by imposing restrictions on inter-process communication so as to constrain the flow of information within the system. The appropriate concept for structuring system activity is that of an atomic action. A set of recovery points established on entry to an atomic action will form a recovery line until one of them is discarded, or one of the processes leaves the atomic action (to communicate with a process external to the action). An atomic action is said to form a *restorable action* if:

(i)   on entry to the atomic action all processes establish a recovery point,

(ii) these recovery points are not discarded within the atomic actions,

(iii) processes leave the atomic action simultaneously.

If an exception is raised by any process within a restorable action, backward error recovery can be provided by restoring all of the recovery points in the recovery line established on entry to the action. Once processes have left the restorable action the recovery line is no longer available since the processes are then at liberty to discard their recovery points. For this reason, the recovery points should all be discarded on exit.

The concept of a restorable action is closely related to that of a *sphere of control* introduced by Davies[42,43] and Bjork.[44] However, spheres of control are also used to delineate process boundaries for purposes other than recovery, such as auditing, privacy, and resource allocation.

Randell[41] discusses how recovery blocks (see Chapter 9) can be extended for use with interacting processes. Restrictions are imposed which ensure that an extended recovery block, referred to as a *conversation,* encompasses a restorable action. A linguistic framework for conversations, and a discussion of the necessity for synchronization on exiting from a conversation, is presented by Russell and Tiedeman.[45]

The full generality of restorable actions may not be needed for the provision of backward error recovery in practical systems. Recoverable *transactions*[18] in a data base system constitute restorable actions, but usually involve only a single process. A limited form of a restorable action termed an *exchange*[8] has been proposed for use in real-time systems; processes in an exchange must have entered (establishing a recovery point) as soon as they were initiated, and must terminate on exit from the exchange.

Backward error recovery for a process involved in a conversation, transaction or exchange is straightforward because of the existence of the recovery line established on entry to the restorable action. Of course, the recovery mechanism must ensure that the planned recovery line is indeed a consistent set of active recovery points, by establishing and maintaining the recovery points, synchronizing processes on exit from the restorable action, and enforcing atomicity. (Details of mechanisms which enforce atomicity are given in the preceding chapter, where atomic actions provide the basis for damage assessment.)

The second approach for locating a recovery line, which must be adopted in the absence of planned recovery lines, is that when an exception is raised the recovery mechanism must search for an appropriate set of recovery points. For this to be possible, the recovery mechanism must monitor inter-process communication and maintain a record of information flow in the system so that the consistency of recovery points can be determined. In this way the recovery mechanism may be able to discover an *unplanned recovery line*.

The approach to providing backward error recovery for cooperating processes based on planned recovery lines has the following advantages:

(i) it ensures the existence of appropriate recovery lines;

(ii) relatively simple mechanisms can be used;

(iii) the overheads incurred are bounded, and under the control of the system designer.

Against these benefits must be set the degradation in system performance which is likely to result from imposing scheduling and communication constraints on processes. Conversely, the approach of searching for an unplanned recovery line has the advantage that no restrictions are imposed on processes, which is likely to mean that higher levels of concurrency and resource utilization can be achieved. The corresponding drawbacks to this approach are:

(i) an appropriate recovery line may not even exist;

(ii) a complex mechanism is needed to locate recovery lines, coupled with a costly mechanism for monitoring communication between processes;

(iii) there is a severe risk that the onset of the domino effect will result in an excessive loss of system activity - in consequence, the overheads of this approach are (potentially) unbounded, and beyond the control of the system designer.

In other words, the basic technique of searching for unplanned recovery lines is very expensive and may not even work. Two refinements to the basic method can be adopted in order to obtain a viable recovery technique.

The first of these refinements is for the recovery mechanism to establish additional recovery points, over and above those requested by individual processes, so as to dynamically construct recovery lines. Additional recovery points are needed when earlier recovery points become inconsistent due to information flow between processes. Although this technique can be used to ensure the existence of suitable recovery lines, this is only achieved at the cost of recording additional recovery data (in extreme cases, system-wide recovery points could be necessary).

The second refinement is for the recovery mechanism to take into account some aspects of the nature and purpose of the communication between processes. In this context, the most important aspect of any communication is that it is *directed;* for each instance of communication there is a *sender* and a *recipient* of information. In certain situations, the information received by a process has no influence on the subsequent activity of that process (e.g. the information could be ignored completely, or be recorded but not utilized). Such information has been termed 'insignificant information'[46] since the communication involved can be ignored by the recovery mechanism. If the sender of insignificant information subsequently transmits a correction (after state restoration of the sender), the recipient only needs to update any record of the information that it retains; state restoration of the recipient is not required.

The concept of insignificant information may be of limited practical value since most communications between cooperating processes can be expected to generate a significant flow of information. However, similar (though lesser) benefits can be obtained with regard to arbitrary communications if one crucial assumption is made: namely that any information received by a process is *validated* before any dependence is placed on that information. That is, information received by a process must either be rejected as invalid before any use is made of it, or be accepted irrevocably as being valid (and cannot then be regarded as a source of error propagation). Given this assumption, state restoration of a recipient of information need not involve restoration of the sender. The recovery mechanism must ensure, however, that a copy of the validated information is retained for reprocessing by the recipient after recovery.

As a simple example, consider a system in which every process either sends or receives messages, but not both. Assume that a recovery mechanism maintains copies of all messages, and that each message is validated by its recipient. If an exception is raised by a recipient process, error recovery can be provided simply by restoring the most recently established recovery point of that process. Messages sent to the process subsequent to the recovery point must be retransmitted by the recovery mechanism. If an exception is raised by a sending process its most recent recovery point should be restored; recovery will also be required (to an earlier recovery point) for any process that received any messages from the sending process subsequent to the restored recovery point.

Russell[47] establishes that various classes of system are 'domino-free' (i.e. a recent recovery line can always be found) if information validation is assumed. (In an earlier paper[48] he presents a detailed analysis of a producer-consumer system.) Explicit bounds are determined for the amount of unnecessary restoration which can occur in these systems. In related work, Kim[49] discusses systems of cooperating processes in which all communication is via recoverable monitor processes. A complex scheme is described which ensures that a recent recovery line can always be found. Information validation is assumed and additional recovery points are established by the recovery mechanism as necessary.

Distributed Systems

The problems of providing recovery in concurrent systems are exacerbated in loosely coupled distributed systems with decentralized control. Inter-process communication in such systems is performed by sending messages from node to node in the system; consequently messages are subject to significant delay between their dispatch and receipt. Message delay can impinge on the provision of recovery since, in the absence of any central control mechanism (such as a single underlying interpreter), processes have to cooperate in exchanging control information as well as to communicate data. In order to avoid confusion (if not chaos) arising from delay to (or even loss of) recovery control messages, recent work has concentrated on devising communication protocols for recovery which can identify recovery lines despite the lack of any central recovery authority.

If a strategy based on planned recovery lines is to be utilized in a distributed system, the only difficulty is in ensuring that a set of processes can coordinate their exit from what is intended to form a restorable action. An algorithm to solve this problem is presented by Gray[18] which employs a separate process called the 'coordinator'. The coordinator enquires of each process whether it is ready to exit from the restorable action. If every process is ready then all is well and the coordinator informs each process that it can leave the action (after returning an acknowledgement). However, if *any* process requests backward error recovery then the coordinator instructs *all* processes to restore their recovery points. The algorithm is known as the "two phase commit protocol".

Merlin and Randell[50] present a formal treatment of the problem of searching for an unplanned recovery line in a distributed system. A historical record of dependencies due to information flow between processes is represented using a directed graph termed an 'occurrence graph'. Each process in the system must keep a record of that part of the graph in which it is involved. If a recovery point is to be restored for a process then it must send 'FAIL' messages to any other process which must be restored for consistency (as determined by the occurrence graph). Any process receiving a FAIL message must cease its normal activity in preparation for state restoration, and send out further FAIL messages as necessary. Assuming that FAIL messages propagate faster than normal messages, a recovery line will eventually be identified. The mechanism is referred to as the "chase protocol" but is not claimed to be practicable, being highly prone to the domino effect. Further developments in this area are reported by Wood.[51]

SUMMARY

This chapter examines techniques for forward and backward error recovery - two approaches which an exception handler can adopt in order to remove errors from the state of a system. *Forward error recovery* attempts to make further use of the state found to be erroneous after making selective corrections to remove errors. This approach can be very efficient, but is system specific and only appropriate when damage can be anticipated (and will only succeed if predictions are accurate). In contrast, *backward error recovery* relies on restoring the system to a prior state, thereby discarding all of the current (erroneous) state. State restoration is a more profligate approach than forward error recovery, and can therefore be expensive to implement, but has the enormous advantage that it provides recovery even from unanticipated damage. Thus, backward error recovery can be used to cope with the errors generated by any fault whatsoever, including design faults.

SUMMARY

The later sections of the chapter concentrate on backward error recovery mechanisms because of their importance for fault tolerance. These mechanisms fall into three categories: *checkpointing* mechanisms, which save a copy of all (or part) of the system state; *audit trail* techniques, which record all modifications made to the state; *recovery* cache mechanisms, which compromise by incrementally forming a copy of just that part of the state which is changed.

The provision of a state restoration mechanism is straightforward in a single-level, single-process system, but more complicated for a system which contains a hierarchy of extensions or concurrent processes. Recovery schemes for multilevel systems can be either *inclusive* or *disjoint*: in an inclusive scheme extensions are linked to processes for efficiency; in a disjoint scheme the extensions are linked to the interpreter for simplicity. Multiprocess systems, however, present more difficult problems. Although the cases of *independent* and *competing* processes are tractable, a solution for *cooperating* processes inevitably imposes additional overheads on the operation of a system.

REFERENCES

1. W.W. Peterson and E.J. Weldon Jr, *Error-Correcting Codes*, MIT Press, Cambridge (MA) (1972).
2. W.N. Toy, "Fault-Tolerant Design of Local ESS Processors," *Proceedings of the IEEE* **66**(10), pp.1126-1145 (October 1978).
3. D.J. Taylor, D.E. Morgan, and J.P. Black, "Redundancy in Data Structures: Improving Software Fault Tolerance," *IEEE Transactions on Software Engineering* **SE-6**(6), pp.585-594 (November 1980).
4. D.J. Taylor, D.E. Morgan, and J.P. Black, "Redundancy in Data Structures: Some Theoretical Results," *IEEE Transactions on Software Engineering* **SE-6**(6), pp.595-602 (November 1980).

5. J.P. Black, D.J. Taylor, and D.E. Morgan, "A Case Study in Fault Tolerant Software," *Software - Practice and Experience* **11**(2), pp.145-157 (February 1981).
6. J.R. Connet, E.J. Pasternak, and B.D. Wagner, "Software Defenses in Real-Time Control Systems," *Digest of Papers: 1972 International Symposium on Fault-Tolerant Computing*, Newton (MA), pp.94-99 (June 1972).
7. R.P. Almquist et al., "Software Protection in No. 1 ESS," *International Switching Symposium Record*, Cambridge (MA), pp.565-569 (June 1972).
8. T. Anderson and J.C. Knight, "Practical Software Fault Tolerance for Real-Time Systems," ICASE Report 81-10, NASA Langley Research Center, Hampton (VA) (May 1981).
9. J.M. Taylor, "Redundancy and Recovery in the HIVE Virtual Machine," *Proceedings European Conference on Software System Engineering*, London, pp.263-293 (September 1976).
10. P.J. Kennedy and T.M. Quinn, "Recovery Strategies in the No. 2 Electronic Switching System," *Digest of Papers: 1972 International Symposium on Fault-Tolerant Computing*, Newton (MA), pp.165-169 (June 1972).
11. F. Cristian, "Exception Handling and Software-Fault Tolerance," *Digest of Papers FTCS-10: 10th International Symposium on Fault-Tolerant Computing Systems*, Kyoto, pp.97-103 (October 1980).
12. J.W. Young, "A First Order Approximation to the Optimum Checkpoint Interval," *Communications of the ACM* **17**(9), pp.530-531 (September 1974).
13. K.M. Chandy et al., "Analytic Models for Rollback and Recovery Strategies in Data Base Systems," *IEEE Transactions on Software Engineering* **SE-1**(1), pp.100-110 (March 1975).
14. E. Gelenbe and D. Derochette, "Performance of Rollback Recovery Systems under Intermittent Failures," *Communications of the ACM* **21**(6), pp.493-499 (June 1978).

15. E. Gelenbe, "On the Optimum Checkpoint Interval," *Journal of the ACM* **26**(2), pp.259-270 (April 1979).
16. A.B. Tonik, "Checkpoint, Restart and Recovery: Selected Annotated Bibliography," *SIGMOD FDT Bulletin* **7**(3-4), pp.72-76 (1975).
17. L.A. Bjork, "Generalized Audit Trail Requirements and Concepts for Data Base Applications," *IBM Systems Journal* **14**(3), pp.229-245 (1975).
18. J.N. Gray, "Notes on Data Base Operating Systems," pp. 393-481 in *Lecture Notes in Computer Science 60*, ed. R. Bayer, R.M. Graham and G. Seegmuller, Springer-Verlag, Berlin (1978).
19. R.M. Curtice, "Integrity in Data Base Systems," *Datamation* **23**(5), pp.64-68 (May 1977).
20. R. Boyd, "Restoral of a Real Time Operating System," *Proceedings of 1971 ACM Annual Conference*, Chicago (IL), pp.109-111 (August 1971).
21. J.S.M. Verhofstad, "Recovery Techniques for Data Base Systems," *Computing Surveys* **10**(2), pp.167-195 (June 1978).
22. A.G. Fraser, "Integrity of a Mass Storage Filing System," *Computer Journal* **12**(1), pp.1-5 (February 1969).
23. D.G. Severance and G.M. Lohman, "Differential Files: their Application to the Maintenance of Large Databases," *ACM Transactions on Database Systems* **1**(3), pp.256-267 (September 1976).
24. M.M. Astrahan *et al.*, "System R: Relational Approach to Database Management," *ACM Transactions on Database Systems* **1**(2), pp.97-137 (June 1976).
25. J.N. Gray *et al.*, "The Recovery Manager of a Data Management System," Report RJ2623, IBM Research Laboratory, San Jose (CA) (August 1979).
26. J.J. Horning *et al.*, "A Program Structure for Error Detection and Recovery," pp. 171-187 in *Lecture Notes in Computer Science 16*, ed. E. Gelenbe and C. Kaiser, Springer-Verlag, Berlin (1974).

27. P.A. Lee, N. Ghani, and K. Heron, "A Recovery Cache for the PDP-11," *IEEE Transactions on Computers* **C-29**(6), pp.546-549 (June 1980).
28. R. Kerr, "An Experimental Processor Architecture for Improved Reliability," pp. 199-212 in *State of the Art Report on System Reliability and Integrity*, Infotech, Maidenhead (1978).
29. T. Anderson and R. Kerr, "Recovery Blocks in Action: A System Supporting High Reliability," *Proceedings of 2nd International Conference on Software Engineering*, San Francisco (CA), pp.447-457 (October 1976).
30. J.S.M. Verhofstad, "The Construction of Recoverable Multi-Level Systems," Ph.D. Thesis, Computing Laboratory, University of Newcastle upon Tyne (1977).
31. S.K. Shrivastava and J-P. Banatre, "Reliable Resource Allocation Between Unreliable Processes," *IEEE Transactions on Software Engineering* **SE-4**(3), pp.230-241 (May 1978).
32. T. Anderson and P.A. Lee, "The Provision of Recoverable Interfaces," *Digest of Papers FTCS-9: Ninth Annual International Symposium on Fault-Tolerant Computing*, Madison (WI), pp.87-94 (June 1979).
33. T. Anderson, P.A. Lee, and S.K. Shrivastava, "A Model of Recoverability in Multilevel Systems," *IEEE Transactions on Software Engineering* **SE-4**(6), pp.486-494 (November 1978).
34. J.J. Horning and B. Randell, "Process Structuring," *Computing Surveys* **5**(1), pp.5-30 (March 1973).
35. C.A.R. Hoare, "Parallel Programming: An Axiomatic Approach," pp. 11-42 in *Lecture Notes in Computer Science 46*, ed. F.L. Bauer and K. Samelson, Springer-Verlag, Berlin (1976).
36. B.W. Lampson, "A Note on the Confinement Problem," *Communications of the ACM* **16**(10), pp.613-615 (October 1973).
37. C.A.R. Hoare, "Monitors: An Operating System Structuring Concept," *Communications of the ACM* **17**(10), pp.549-557 (October 1974).

38. G.M. Birtwistle et al., *SIMULA BEGIN*, Van Nostrand Reinhold, New York (1973).
39. S.K. Shrivastava, "Concurrent Pascal with Backward Error Recovery: Implementation," *Software - Practice and Experience* **9**(12), pp.1021-1033 (December 1979).
40. S.K. Shrivastava, "Concurrent Pascal with Backward Error Recovery: Language Features and Examples," *Software - Practice and Experience* **9**(12), pp.1001-1020 (December 1979).
41. B. Randell, "System Structure for Software Fault Tolerance," pp. 195-219 in *Current Trends in Programming Methodology, Vol. 1*, ed. R.T. Yeh, Prentice-Hall, Englewood Cliffs (NJ) (1977).
42. C.T. Davies, "Recovery Semantics for a DB/DC System," *Proceedings of 1973 ACM Annual Conference*, Atlanta (GA), pp.136-141 (August 1973).
43. C.T. Davies, "Data Processing Integrity," pp. 288-354 in *Computing Systems Reliability*, ed. T. Anderson and B. Randell, Cambridge University Press, Cambridge (1979).
44. L.A. Bjork, "Recovery Scenario for a DB/DC System," *Proceedings of 1973 ACM Annual Conference*, Atlanta (GA), pp.142-146 (August 1973).
45. D.L. Russell and M.J. Tiedeman, "Multiprocess Recovery Using Conversations," *Digest of Papers FTCS-9: Ninth Annual International Symposium on Fault-Tolerant Computing*, Madison (WI), pp.106-109 (June 1979).
46. B. Randell, P.A. Lee, and P.C. Treleaven, "Reliability Issues in Computing System Design," *Computing Surveys* **10**(2), pp.123-165 (June 1978).
47. D.L. Russell, "State Restoration in Systems of Communicating Processes," *IEEE Transactions on Software Engineering* **SE-6**(2), pp.183-194 (March 1980).
48. D.L. Russell, "Process Backup in Producer-Consumer Systems," *Proceedings of Sixth ACM Symposium on Operating Systems Principles*, West Lafayette (IN), pp.151-157 (November 1977).

49. K.H. Kim, "An Approach to Programmer-Transparent Coordination of Recovering Parallel Processes and its Efficient Implementation Rules," *Proceedings of International Conference on Parallel Processing*, Detroit (MI), pp.58-68 (August 1978).
50. P.M. Merlin and B. Randell, "State Restoration in Distributed Systems," *Digest of Papers FTCS-8: Eighth Annual International Conference on Fault-Tolerant Computing*, Toulouse, pp.129-134 (June 1978).
51. W.G. Wood, "Recovery Control of Communicating Processes in a Distributed System," Technical Report 158, Computing Laboratory, University of Newcastle upon Tyne (November 1980).

8

FAULT TREATMENT AND CONTINUED SERVICE

By means of techniques for error detection, damage assessment and error recovery a fault tolerant system aims to ensure that any errors introduced into the system state are removed. If these techniques succeed in placing the system in an error free state, the system can return to normal operation since the immediate danger of failure has been averted. However, this may not be enough to ensure reliability. Measures and mechanisms employed in the first three phases of fault tolerance are (necessarily) concerned with errors in the system, but errors are merely the symptoms produced by a fault; techniques which cope with errors, such as those described in the previous chapter, leave the fault which produced those errors untreated. Given that a fault has already inflicted damage on the system state there is clearly a possibility that the fault will continue to produce errors. Repeated manifestations of a fault can force a system to fail despite the efforts of the fault tolerance techniques described so far, either because the consequences of the fault become more and more serious, or because the system is so heavily engaged in coping with recurring errors that it fails to maintain its specified service.

This chapter examines what is usually the final phase of fault tolerance, describing techniques which attempt to eradicate faults from a system so that service can be maintained. These techniques provide *treatment* for the fault itself (rather than for errors, the symptoms of a fault) and can be divided into two stages, namely *fault location* and *system repair* (analogous to the treatment of errors which requires damage assessment and error recovery). Also covered in this chapter are issues relating to the resumption of normal operation, so that *continued service* can be provided by the system.

Almost all of the techniques for fault treatment described in the next two sections are implemented as measures in hardware systems. Mechanisms provide only limited assistance for fault treatment because the difficulty of the task results in most approaches being system specific. On-line treatment of faults in software systems is so difficult that it is hardly ever attempted. However, software systems usually provide much more flexible ways of returning to normal operation; these are briefly examined in the third section.

In view of the difficulties in implementing effective automatic techniques for fault treatment, it is tempting to adopt the 'strategy' of simply ignoring a fault and hoping for the best. There are three circumstances in which this minimal approach will be successful:

(i) if recovery from the errors generated by the fault is sufficiently powerful to cope with recurring fault manifestations;

(ii) if the future operation of the system fortuitously avoids the fault;

(iii) if the fault is transient.

Component faults in physical systems can often be transient due to temporary physical phenomena. In contrast, faults in software systems, and design faults in general, are almost always permanent. For a system with high reliability requirements it can be expected that equally high standards of design combined with thorough validation of the system will ensure that the number of residual design faults is small and their manifestation infrequent. In consequence, the operational characteristics of design faults will often match those of transient faults. Nevertheless, attempts to provide fault tolerance for design faults will

FAULT TREATMENT AND CONTINUED SERVICE

need to embody some means of fault treatment since the only viable recovery technique for errors generated by such faults is backward error recovery. If no further action is taken after the restoration of a recovery point and the system merely attempts to follow the same course of action as before then the same errors will again be generated. In particular, if a program raises an exception because of a fault in its design it will be futile to restore a prior state and try again with exactly the same program. Approaches which encompass treatment for software faults are discussed in Chapter 9.

FAULT LOCATION

Before a system can attempt to deal with a fault, it must first make an assessment of its location. The presence of a fault is indicated by the raising of an exception, and in many systems no further information is available to assist fault location. When this is the case, automatic repair of the system will only be possible if the exception provides an accurate guide to the location of the fault. It is therefore important to ensure that failure exceptions clearly identify a faulty component and (if possible) that all other exceptions are a consequence of design faults.

The characteristics of an exception will enable an initial estimate to be formed of the location of a fault. If further refinement of this estimate is required then this can either be attempted by means of exploratory measures, or deferred for manual attention. Any exploratory approach to fault location will be similar to the exploratory techniques for damage assessment which are examined in Chapter 6. However, the task of fault location is more difficult since even a perfect knowledge of the errors which are present in a system may not suffice to identify the fault which produced them.

The most important exploratory technique used to locate faults is that of *diagnostic checking*. As described in Chapter 5, a diagnostic check involves invoking a component with a set of inputs for which the correct outputs are known. If the outputs actually produced by the component differ from those expected then it can be assumed that a fault is present within that component. If the component produces the expected outputs then the fault is assumed to lie elsewhere. Although diagnostic checks are primarily used to locate hardware faults, they could be applied in software systems as a means of indicating whether or not a program had become corrupted.

Extensive use is made of diagnostic checking in the ESS No. 1A system to locate hardware faults. Initial error detection in the ESS No. 1A is often by the detection of a mismatch between the active and the stand-by CPUs. Following this, fault location occurs in two stages. In the first stage a simple and quick diagnostic check is performed to determine which CPU is suspect. The CPU suspected of being faulty is taken out of the on-line system and continued system service is provided using the remaining CPU. The second stage of fault location endeavors to locate the fault more accurately so that the faulty CPU can be repaired and then re-introduced into the on-line system. More extensive diagnostic checks are used in this second stage to generate a set of fault symptoms. The goal set for these checks was that they should be able to detect the presence of 95% of all possible faults (earlier experience indicated that a 95% rate of detection was feasible, although expensive to attain). By means of extensive simulation and testing of ESS No. 1A systems, the designers have constructed a massive data base of faults and their symptoms.[1] When the diagnostic programs uncover a set of fault symptoms these are summarized in what is called a 'signature' of the fault which produced them. Pattern matching techniques are then used to compare the signature with the entries in the data base, producing a list of likely faults. In this way, faults in the ESS No. 1A can normally be located to within three replaceable components (the design aim was for this to be achieved for 90% of all faults).

Diagnostic checks also play an important role in the Space Shuttle computer complex, which contains five identical general purpose computers. Initially, four of these are linked in an NMR configuration but this may be reduced to a TMR or duplex configuration by the crew if faults arise. Fault location between four or three computers follows directly from the voting checks which compare checksums of the outputs from the computers. Comparing the outputs from a duplex configuration will not identify which of the computers is faulty in the event of a disagreement. To resolve such disagreements each computer contains diagnostic checking facilities - hardware and timing checks which operate continuously, and micro-coded 'self-test' programs which can be executed when required. These checks are intended to locate 89% of all faults causing a disagreement to within a single computer.[2] Software diagnostic checks are also available, but are too time consuming for use by an operational computer and are only used for checking a computer off-line before it is allocated to an NMR configuration.

The time required to execute software implemented diagnostic checks usually militates against their frequent or extensive use in most systems because of the disruption in service this would entail. However, systems which are constructed to have excess capacity in the form of redundancy (e.g. Pluribus and Tandem) can be designed to take components out of service, subject them to diagnostic checks, and if all is well return them to service. This can be done when the system is operating normally as a form of on-line preventive maintenance, hoping to detect trouble before it occurs.

Some systems try to perform on-line the various checks which a manual fault location attempt would employ. For this purpose, each processor in the PRIME system contained a programmable control panel which could be accessed and operated by other processors.[3] Facilities provided by this control panel included access to registers and the ability to 'single-step' the processor. In this way, a suspect processor could be forced to execute a set of diagnostic routines by another processor.

To reduce the cost of designing diagnostic checks, a replication check can be used as a diagnostic. The results obtained from a specific component in a suspect system are compared with the results from the corresponding component in another copy of the system. In the event of a discrepancy the fault is assumed to be in the component of the suspect system; otherwise further tests must be performed.

The presence of a fault in FTMP is indicated by the replication checks performed by the voters, while fault location is based on reallocating components to different buses and monitoring the subsequent pattern of errors. When the voter of a processor observes a disagreement between the values it receives over a bus triad, all of the components which can transmit on the conflicting triad are noted and then allocated to different buses. If the fault is permanent the defective component (or bus) can be quickly identified. Although transient faults are likely to elude immediate location using this approach, they can be tracked down by maintaining for each component a count of demerits which is incremented every time the component is involved in a disagreement. As soon as any count exceeds a threshold value the corresponding component is removed from active service. As a final check a suspect component can be temporarily disabled to see if this stops the occurrence of disagreements.

Although fault location usually precedes system repair, a pessimistic and cautious alternative approach defers fault location until system repair is under way. The approach is exemplified in the next section, but is summarized here. It is a pessimistic approach in that initially all but a small trusted set of components are assumed to be faulty. Subsequently, only components which pass appropriate diagnostic checks are accepted as not being faulty. Thus the diagnostics attempt to locate fault-free components, while unchecked components continue to be considered faulty.

SYSTEM REPAIR

When fault location has been successfully performed, one or more components of the system will be considered to be faulty. To prevent these suspect components from impinging on the future operation of the system some means of repairing the system is needed. It is assumed here that *system* repair does not involve making repairs internal to a suspect component. Any such repairs would have to perform further fault location internal to the component and then adopt repair techniques such as those described in this section.

Techniques for system repair will necessarily be based on *reconfiguring* the system in such a way that the characteristics of use of suspect components are modified to some extent. (The standard approach is to make no further use of the suspect components.) Reconfiguration techniques have been classified[3] as:

manual when all actions are performed by some agency external to the system (usually human);

dynamic when actions are performed by the system, but only in response to instructions from its environment;

spontaneous when all actions are initiated and performed by the system itself.

Because of the difficulty and cost involved in constructing systems capable of making effective repairs to their own structure, dynamic and spontaneous reconfiguration techniques are only found in systems which either are inaccessible to manual techniques (e.g. JPL-STAR) or have reliability requirements such that the delays usually incurred by manual methods are unacceptable (e.g. SIFT and FTMP).

Manual reconfiguration clearly includes making physical changes to a system, such as altering the interconnections between components or substituting a new component in place of an old one. Dynamic and spontaneous reconfiguration techniques attempt to automate these actions by making use of some form of switching network to change interconnections or components. It could certainly be argued that switching from the use of one component to another does not actually constitute a change to the system since the components and their interfaces must remain unchanged. As illustrated in Figure 8.1, a switch is a component having an interface with both switched components. Switching from one component to the other has an effect on the interactions within the system, but the system itself (i.e. its components and design) remains unchanged. Nevertheless, since the effect of switching from the old to the new component is intended to be exactly the same as if the system had been physically changed by actually removing the

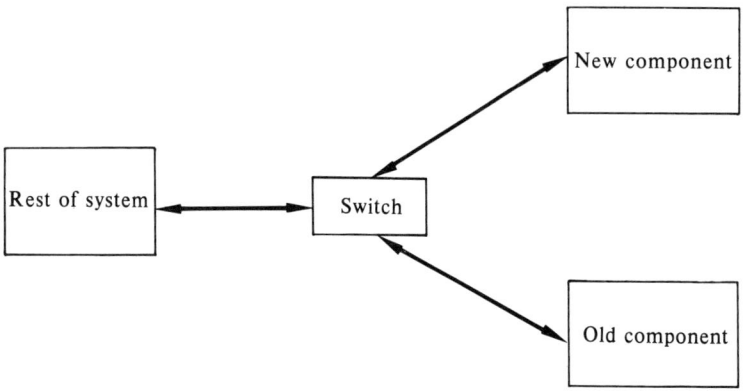

Figure 8.1 Reconfiguration by Switching

old component and substituting the new one, it is convenient to consider switching as a means by which reconfiguration can be performed by a system.

When manual reconfiguration is inadequate or unavailable, dynamic rather than spontaneous reconfiguration may be employed for one of two related reasons. The first is simply that for many systems fault location may have to be performed manually and hence spontaneous reconfiguration is impossible. The second reason is that even when a system does perform automatic fault location, the system designer may insist that manual confirmation must be given before the system is permitted to reconfigure itself. Since the possibility of an inaccurate determination of the location of a fault can never be eliminated, a manual check may be considered a wise precaution before reconfiguring a system.

The simplest strategy for reconfiguring a system to prevent the use of a component which is suspected of being faulty is to *replace* the component by a stand-by spare. A *stand-by spare* is a component which is surplus to the normal requirements of the system (i.e. it is redundant) but which is available when needed to take over from the component it is intended to replace. For example, in the ESS No. 1A, memory units called 'rover stores' are available as stand-by spares for the program stores. Since hardware spares can be maintained in an unpowered condition they can have an increased life expectancy over the functioning components in the system, a factor which influenced the designers of the JPL-STAR. Spare components have to be designed to meet the same specification as those they replace. A stand-by spare for a hardware component will usually be of identical design and construction since protection against design faults is rarely considered necessary. If repair of design faults is required then the stand-by spares must be of independent design. Independently designed spares are necessary for providing fault treatment in software systems and are an essential element of recovery blocks and N-version programming, which are discussed in detail in the next chapter.

Several systems (e.g. FTMP, Pluribus, PRIME and SIFT) have attempted to derive some benefit from the presence of spare components by adopting an alternative approach. In these systems none of the components are kept idle and all are initially available to provide service. The resulting excess capacity of the system can enable it to provide a better response at times of heavy loading, or to support a higher than specified level of fault tolerance. If a component is subsequently suspected of being a source of faults it is simply disabled. This can lead to a *graceful degradation* in the standard of service provided by the system, as the remaining components take on the duties of any components which are switched out of the system. For instance, in the Space Shuttle[2] the initial set of four identical computers can be reduced by the crew to three, then two, and even to one, with no loss of facilities but with a (rapidly) decreasing ability to provide fault tolerance. A more mundane example of graceful degradation would be a system in which a faulty memory module is removed from the set of operational modules, with a consequent reduction in the size of main memory available. Implementation of such a reconfigurable memory is greatly simplified by a virtual memory organization (this is exploited in the fault tolerant memory scheme proposed by Brandwajn and Joly.)[4]

In principle it would seem that the more accurately a fault can be located the better it will be for system repair. In practice, no additional benefit is gained by locating a fault more accurately than to a single replaceable component; it is the selection of the size of these components which has most impact on the effort needed for fault location (and on the cost of the overall system). Selecting a large unit of replacement makes fault location easier, but imposes a correspondingly larger redundancy overhead on the system. Small replaceable units contain fewer subcomponents and as a result (in physical systems at least) can be designed to have a (theoretically) lower Mean Time Between Failure (MTBF) than larger units. However, if a system is to be capable of being reconfigured from a large number of small components then the switching network required to interconnect all of those components will of necessity be a complex part of the system. Concern will then attach to the MTBF of that network which becomes a factor limiting the size of the replaceable components.

Another factor which influences the size of a replaceable component is the necessity for, and availability of, manual repairs to the system. The SIFT system provides an excellent illustration that there is little to be gained from locating faults any more accurately than is necessary for reconfiguration. No diagnostic checking is performed within a processing module (including memory) in an operational SIFT system because the unit of replacement is an entire processing module. No attempt is made to repair a faulty module while the system is operational, so the processing modules have to be adequately replicated. Repairs to a SIFT system are deferred until the current flight (which can last up to 10 hours) is over and can then take place at leisure. In contrast, a much smaller grain of replacement is adopted in the ESS No. 1A where, because the system consists of only two processors, a design objective is that the Mean Time To Repair for a faulty processor should not exceed two hours. This necessitates relatively accurate fault location, a small unit of replacement, and the substantial investment in diagnostic checking facilities described in the previous section.

For a system to be able to perform non-manual reconfiguration some form of switching must be available so that faulty components can be removed from the operational system, and new components incorporated. The fault tolerant systems used as examples in this book adopt different methods to achieve this. Hardware reconfiguration in the ESS No. 1A is the responsibility of special purpose 'processor configuration' circuitry (discussed below). In the SIFT system, if two or more processors inform the (replicated) global executive task that a particular processor appears to be faulty then all local executives will be instructed to remove that processing module from their scheduling tables. Subsequent actions of the faulty processor are completely disregarded by all other processors, and since processors cannot transmit information over the buses the faulty processor cannot by itself disrupt system operation. In the FTMP system a module *can* corrupt bus transmission so faulty modules have to be switched off. This switching is performed by the bus guardian units in response to commands sent by processor triads. The JPL-STAR used power switching to activate and deactivate components, under the control of the special purpose hardware in the TARP. Modules in the Pluribus system are interconnected by means of 'bus couplers'; these incorporate software-controlled enabling switches which can be used to disconnect a processor from the rest of the system.

The ESS No. 1A embodies a range of reconfiguration strategies with the aim of expediting, whenever possible, the tasks of fault location and system repair. First, an attempt is made to obtain a working system by replacing with stand-by spares only those components which are identified as suspect by a localized set of diagnostic checks. More comprehensive (global) reconfiguration is initiated if replacement proves inadequate, if no spare is available, or if checking circuits indicate a complete loss of control in the processor. The processor configuration circuits are activated to assemble a minimal processor configuration capable of performing diagnostics on all components in the system (components which were previously 'removed' from the system are re-checked in the hope that the rest may have done them some good). Components which pass the tests are added to the minimal configuration until normal operation can be restored. Global reconfiguration is attempted in three stages; the first relies on the current contents of memory, the second verifies all data before use, while the third applies *less* stringent checks in an attempt to configure a system capable of performing only very basic functions. Finally, provision has also been made for dynamic reconfiguration invoked from the master console and, of course, for manual repair.

The global reconfiguration strategies of the ESS No. 1A provide an example of fault location performed in combination with system repair. Initially only the 'processor configuration' circuits are relied upon and then diagnostic checks are used to locate components which appear to be free from faults. Other systems, including PRIME and Pluribus, have also adopted this strategy of starting from a trusted minimal system (usually termed the *hardcore* of the system) and bootstrapping up to a working system by systematically incorporating those components which satisfy their diagnostic checks. The PRIME approach[3] was to have the hardcore select a processor which was not under suspicion and establish it as the control processor with responsibility for completing the reconfiguration. In Pluribus, reconfiguration is performed under the control of a small operating system and proceeds in a sequence of predefined stages. At each stage further resources of the original system are tested and, if satisfactory, added to the reconfigured system. In this way, a local processor is augmented in turn by internal software, a clock, memory, buses and input/output devices.

Reconfiguration of a system is normally implemented as a measure although the switching that is needed can be supported by a mechanism. This is the case in the Pluribus and FTMP systems where software reconfiguration measures make use of mechanized hardware switching facilities (the enabling switches and bus guardian units respectively). In contrast, reconfiguration in the SIFT and JPL-STAR systems is performed without the assistance of underlying switching mechanisms, by measures implemented in software and hardware respectively. Caution is necessary when switching is provided as a mechanism since the ability to reconfigure a system is a very potent one and should only be used with circumspection. Precautions must be taken to ensure that the switching mechanism is not activated by accident (or by malicious intent). For example, access to the reconfiguration switches in Pluribus is controlled by a password mechanism, while FTMP relies upon the triplicated execution of the reconfiguration software to ensure that only legitimate reconfiguration takes place.

In order to minimize problems caused by faults in the switching network used for reconfiguration it is sensible to design the network so that a fault in one part does not adversely effect the operation of the rest. The reconfiguration scheme of the PRIME system made use of a distributed interconnection network which was designed so that a fault in the network would have the same effect as a failure of the system component attached to the faulty part of the network. Reconfiguration of the system to remove that component would also remove the faulty portion of the switching network.

Even though a system may be capable of spontaneous or dynamic reconfiguration, the need for manual repair will remain. The supply of stand-by spares, or the surplus of active components, will eventually be consumed by replacement and reconfiguration. To restore a full fault tolerant capability to the system the depletion of these resources must be made good, and this can only be done manually. For the Bell ESS and Tandem 16 systems, which are intended to maintain 24 hour service, provision had to be made for manual system maintenance to proceed in parallel with on-line operation. This is most easily achieved for systems which operate with a duplex or higher level of redundancy (as do the Bell, Pluribus and Tandem systems) since changes can be made to the redundant components. A problem which arose with an early design of Pluribus was that manual repairs were hampered by a lack of information; extensive recovery had destroyed all evidence of faults in the system. Exactly the same difficulty occurred in connection with an experimental implementation[5] of a backward error recovery mechanism. When the state restoration capability of the experimental system was extended to encompass output to the line-printer (by means of spooling) all error messages from the system were lost because backward error recovery ensured that they were never printed. The need for an independent and unrecoverable output stream for recording the erroneous behavior of the system was swiftly recognized.

RESUMING NORMAL SERVICE

Having dealt with the errors in a system and attempted to locate the fault responsible and effect an appropriate repair, it is necessary to return the system to its normal mode of operation. One simple method of achieving this would be to include a fixed restart point in the system. If recovery can be achieved by means of a fixed reset then this would probably be adequate. Otherwise, some means of restarting which is dependent upon the current computation of the system will be needed.

For hardware systems, a retry is frequently attempted and in this context the term has its usual meaning of restarting the system so as to repeat the operation which resulted in the exception being raised. Retry is the cheapest form of redundancy in every commodity except time - hence the phrase 'temporal redundancy'. Examples of the use of retry are when a direct memory access overruns in C.mmp,[6] and for hardware faults in the interpretation of instructions executed by the JPL-STAR (and indeed by commercial computers such as the IBM 370 series). After restoring a recovery point, the COPRA system[7] attempts to continue by performing a simple retry of a sequence of instructions. The advantages of (and obstacles to) instruction retry are examined by Maestri.[8]

In a software system there is considerable flexibility of action when an exception handler terminates. If the exception handler has successfully averted failure then control can be transferred to an appropriate location in the software in order to maintain continued service. Otherwise, if fault tolerance within the system is considered to be inadequate, the exception handler should terminate by signalling a failure exception.

An important decision must be made when a system returns to normal operation after handling an exception which was signalled by a component (or an interpreter or extension). The issue in question is whether the internal activity of the component can be *resumed* after the exception has been handled by the system. If the component cannot be resumed then the signalling of an exception effectively *terminates* the activity of the component. Liskov and Snyder[9] discuss this issue, distinguishing between a *resumption model* and a *termination model* for the semantics of an exception handling scheme. They argue cogently that the termination model is to be preferred on the grounds of simplicity, and have therefore adopted it for exception handling in the CLU language. However, the resumption model is acknowledged to have more expressive power; Levin[10] describes a powerful mechanism based solely on resumption. Goodenough's earlier proposals[11] include facilities for both termination and resumption.

Termination and resumption can be illustrated in terms of the Mesa language,[12] which provides **goto**, **exit**, **retry**, **continue** and **resume** as constructs by which an exception handler may complete its activity. Suppose that statement S of a Mesa program raises an exception, signalled from within a routine invoked by S. Each of the first four constructs conforms to the termination model and ensures that the activity of the routine invoked by S is terminated. A **retry** repeats the execution of statement S, **continue** continues with the next statement after S, **exit** terminates the nearest enclosing iterative statement, and **goto** explicitly specifies to where control should be transferred. Use of **retry** would be appropriate if the exception was thought to be due to a transient fault, or was a consequence of errors which the exception handler had eliminated. Use of **continue** would be appropriate if the operations being performed by S were no longer necessary, either because the actions of the handler subsumed those operations or because the requirements on the system were such that occasional deficiencies in service were acceptable (e.g. loss of a single call from a telephone exchange). Since **goto** and **exit** were also provided in Mesa they have presumably been found to be convenient. The fifth construct, **resume**, is based on the resumption model and therefore requires that the routine which signalled the exception is not terminated, but resumed at the point from which the exception was signalled. Use of **resume** would be appropriate if the exception handler was able to make adjustments such that the operations being performed by the routine which signalled the exception could then be successfully completed.

Despite the greater expressive power of a framework providing both resumption and termination, it is recommended that exception handling should be based solely on the termination model, particularly when exception handlers are used exclusively for fault tolerance. There are two main reasons for making this recommendation.

Firstly, a mechanism implementing only termination is very simple to construct (and hence more reliable) since the signalling of an exception can be regarded as an abnormal return from the component. A mechanism implementing resumption has to support a more complex pattern of interaction: the system invokes a component which in turn can invoke the system by signalling an exception. The provision of termination as well as resumption can give rise to further complications. For example, a component signalling an exception may be expecting the handler to execute **resume**, but the handler may decide that resumption is not necessary. However, the signalling component cannot simply be terminated since its internal state may require further 'cleaning-up' to return it to a consistent state. To alleviate this difficulty, Goodenough proposes a 'CLEANUP' exception (and Mesa includes an 'UNWIND' exception) which can be signalled from a handler to give the component which signalled the original exception a chance to tidy up.

Secondly, resumption seems an entirely inappropriate response to an exception indicating the presence of a fault. No information should be available to a system concerning the internal operation of a component. In particular, an exception handler in a system should not be able to make adjustments to the internal state of a component. Moreover, further use of the abstract objects and operations supported by that component is unlikely to be successful since its internal state could be inconsistent - indeed, further use of the component is very likely to result in new exceptions being signalled. Thus, it is difficult to see what could be achieved by a system before resuming the activity of a component (which might well contain the fault).

A final point can be made by analogy with most modern programming languages, in which it is illegal to 'jump' into an inner block of a program. The resumption model involves transferring control back into a potentially faulty component - for example, a procedure, an extension, or even the underlying interpreter. Surely resumption should also be illegal.

SUMMARY

In most fault tolerant systems, the location and repair of faults is achieved (if at all) by system specific techniques. Nevertheless, fault treatment in these systems often proceeds in two distinct phases. The first of these phases is intended to provide a rather coarse estimate of the location of the fault, which is obtained as quickly as possible, and is usually derived directly from the error detection which resulted in an exception being raised. On the basis of this estimate, an equally crude replacement strategy may be adopted to repair the fault and keep the system operational. Time is thereby gained for the second phase.

The second phase of fault treatment attempts to locate the fault much more accurately so that an economical repair can be achieved and the system restored to full working order. This phase can operate more leisurely, and is often postponed until it can be performed manually. Diagnostic checks are used to determine which components of the system are faulty, isolating faults to replaceable components. On-line repair of the system may entail replacing the faulty components by stand-by spares. Alternatively, the system may have sufficient capacity in reserve that (a possibly degraded) service can be maintained by merely disabling the faulty components. Critical components of the system known as the hardcore are responsible for applying diagnostic checks and performing the reconfiguration needed for system repair.

REFERENCES

1. Bell Laboratories, "LAMP: Logic Analyser for Maintenance Planning," *Bell System Technical Journal* **53**(8), pp.1431-1555 (October 1974).
2. J.R. Sklaroff, "Redundancy Management Technique for Space Shuttle Computers," *IBM Journal of Research and Development* **20**(1), pp.20-28 (January 1976).

3. B.R. Borgerson, "Spontaneous Reconfiguration in a Fail Softly Computer Utility," *Datafair 73 Conference Papers*, Nottingham, pp.326-333 (April 1973).
4. A. Brandwajn and R. Joly, "A Scheme for a Fault-Tolerant Virtual Memory," *Information Processing Letters* **10**(2), pp.99-103 (March 1980).
5. T. Anderson and R. Kerr, "Recovery Blocks in Action: A System Supporting High Reliability," *Proceedings of 2nd International Conference on Software Engineering*, San Francisco (CA), pp.447-457 (October 1976).
6. D. Siewiorek et al., "A Case Study of C.mmp, Cm* and C.vmp: Part 1 - Experiences with Fault Tolerance in Multiprocessor Systems," *Proceedings of the IEEE* **66**(10), pp.1178-1199 (October 1978).
7. C. Meraud, F. Browaeys, and G. Germain, "Automatic Rollback Techniques of the COPRA Computer," *Proceedings FTCS-6: 1976 International Symposium on Fault-Tolerant Computing*, Pittsburgh (PA), pp.23-29 (June 1976).
8. G.H. Maestri, "The Retryable Processor," *AFIPS Conference Proceedings 1972 FJCC* **41**, Anaheim (CA), pp.273-277 (December 1972).
9. B.H. Liskov and A. Snyder, "Exception Handling in CLU," *IEEE Transactions on Software Engineering* **SE-5**(6), pp.546-558 (November 1979).
10. R.A. Levin, "Program Structures for Exceptional Condition Handling," Ph.D. Thesis, Carnegie Mellon University, Pittsburgh (PA) (1977).
11. J.B. Goodenough, "Exception Handling: Issues and a Proposed Notation," *Communications of the ACM* **18**(12), pp.683-696 (December 1975).
12. J.G. Mitchell, W. Maybury, and R. Sweet, "Mesa Language Manual (Version 5.0)," CSL-79-3, Xerox Palo Alto Research Center (CA) (April 1979).

9

SOFTWARE FAULT TOLERANCE

Fault tolerance techniques for coping with the occurrence and effects of anticipated hardware component failures are now well established and form a vital part of any reliable computing system. However, it is unusual to find that strategies for fault tolerance have been included in a system for coping with *design faults*. Such faults may not have been a problem in hardware systems (or at least not recognized as such) but are of major concern in software systems.

Software is a crucial component of all computing systems. Indeed, the major proportion of the complexity of most systems is to be found in the software. Given the evident fallibility of software designers and programmers (some examples are discussed in Chapter 1) and the lack of any technique which can guarantee that a complex software system does not contain residual design faults, it is somewhat surprising that the provision of tolerance to software faults has rarely been considered necessary, even in systems with extremely stringent reliability requirements. One reason for this may have been the absence of suitable fault tolerance techniques, since it is clear that the standard techniques used to cope with (anticipated) hardware component failures are not directly appropriate for the unanticipated situations which result from design faults. The preceding chapters have shown that appropriate techniques are available (and in many cases are obvious when the characteristics of design faults have been recognized). The purpose of this chapter is to draw together the relevant techniques in order to describe coherent approaches to achieving software fault tolerance in particular, and design fault tolerance in general.

It is worth stating more precisely what is meant by software fault tolerance since two interpretations are possible. One interpretation is that software fault tolerance is concerned with techniques designed to tolerate the effects of faults in the underlying (hardware) interpreter, but which are implemented in software.[1,2] However, in this book software fault tolerance is considered to embrace all of the techniques necessary to enable a system to tolerate *software faults,* that is, faults in the design and construction of the software itself. Thus, in the term 'software fault tolerance', 'software' is taken to be a qualification of 'fault' and not of 'fault tolerance'. Since the implementation in software of the fault tolerance techniques discussed in the previous chapters raises few new issues, this chapter will concentrate on the more novel problems of providing tolerance to software faults.

Two main methods have been proposed for structuring a software system, and providing software fault tolerance: *recovery blocks,* and *N-version programming.* Because this is a new and important application for fault tolerance, each of these approaches will be examined in detail. Both approaches make the fundamental assumption that despite all of the fault prevention techniques which may have been used, a complex software system will always contain residual faults when it is put into operation, and software fault tolerance will be necessary if these faults are not to lead to failures of the overall system. Neither method can provide an absolute guarantee that the fault tolerance provided will be successful. Such a guarantee would require identification of the faults before they occurred, coupled with a demonstration that the tolerance provided was effective. Since residual software faults are by their nature unanticipatable this identification cannot be achieved. (Moreover, it seems unwise to use fault tolerance to cope with any software faults which have been identified - such faults should be removed from the system). As should be the case for any proposed technique for tolerating design faults, the two schemes provide 'last-resort' defenses against faults. They should be regarded as complementary to, and *not* as a substitute for, other techniques (such as testing) which remove faults before the software is put into operation.

THE RECOVERY BLOCK SCHEME

The recovery block scheme for providing software fault tolerance in sequential programs was introduced by Horning *et al.* in 1974.[3] This section will present the syntax and semantics of recovery blocks by examining the application to a software system of the four constituent phases of fault tolerance discussed in the preceding chapters. Implementation issues will then be discussed.

Consider a task that has to be performed reliably by a software system, and assume that a non-redundant software module has been designed and implemented with the aim of satisfying the authoritative specification of this task. This module will be referred to as the *primary module* in the following discussion; the reason for qualifying the module as 'primary' will become clear subsequently. It is assumed that this module has been tested and debugged as much as was practicable. However, it is recognized that the module may still contain residual design faults which could lead to (unacceptable) system failures. It is therefore necessary to construct a software system which can tolerate such faults.

The first stage in providing fault tolerance is to detect errors arising from the execution of the *primary module*. During its execution the module will be subjected to the interface checks provided by the underlying system. These checks could detect the consequences of faults in the module and hence signal an exception. However, this cannot be guaranteed since interface checks can only check for correctness of use of an interface and cannot check whether any usage corresponds to that of a correct program - it is quite possible that the execution of the module could be completed without any exceptions being signalled, despite faults in that module. Therefore it will be necessary to include error detection measures within the software system itself. Some measures could be included within the *primary module*. The disadvantages (and advantages) of such internal checks are explored in Chapter 5, from which it can be concluded that one particularly appropriate place for error detection is such that a 'last moment' check is provided, just before any of the results calculated by the module are used by subsequent program modules. Another desirable aspect of such a check is that correctness of operation of the system should be guaranteed if the check does not reveal any errors. In practice, checks for correctness are rarely feasible, and a check can only determine whether the outputs of the module appear to be acceptable (see Chapter 5). Thus, a first addition to the non-redundant system is to include measures for error detection in the form of a check (denoted by *acceptance test*) on the reasonableness of the results calculated, which follows the execution of the *primary module*:

primary module
acceptance test

The *acceptance test* will consist of a sequence of statements which will raise an exception if the state of the system is not acceptable. For the purposes of this chapter a module will be said to have *failed* if any exception is raised by the acceptance test or signalled by the underlying system during the execution of the module or acceptance test.

The next stage in providing a fault tolerant software system is to consider the damage assessment and error recovery that will have to be provided if the *primary module* fails. In Chapter 7 it is argued that the only appropriate technique for coping with the damage resulting from design faults is backward error recovery. Given that a design fault in the *primary module* could have caused arbitrary damage to the system state, and that the exact time at which errors were generated cannot be identified, the most suitable prior state for restoration is the state that existed just before the *primary module* was entered. This would require a recovery point to be established at that point. Since backward error

THE RECOVERY BLOCK SCHEME

recovery is most suitably implemented by a mechanism provided to the system rather than by measures within the system itself it will be assumed that a mechanism such as the recovery cache (see Chapter 7) is provided and that an *establish recovery point* instruction is available to the software system:

>   *establish recovery point*
>   *primary module*
>   *acceptance test*

In the event of the *primary module* failing and recovery having taken place, a strategy which enables the software system to continue to provide service must be devised. Clearly a retry of the *primary module* is not appropriate since the fault will again result in an exception being raised. What is needed is an alternative (stand-by spare) software module designed to satisfy the same *acceptance test* as the *primary module*, but which has a different design in the hope that it will not suffer from the same fault. Thus, representing this stand-by spare module as *alternate module*, the system will now consist of:

>   *establish recovery point*
>   *primary module*
>   *acceptance test*
>   *alternate module*
>   *acceptance test*

The strategy for continuing to provide service from the system will be to use the *alternate module* as a stand-by spare, to be executed if the primary module fails. Clearly there is no reason to limit the number of alternate modules to one, and multiple stand-by spares can be provided to provide extra confidence in there being a module which will generate results acceptable to the acceptance test.

The above scenario is the basis of the recovery block scheme, although a recovery block is usually expressed using the syntax shown in Figure 9.1. With this syntax the acceptance test, which is common to all modules, is situated at the beginning of the recovery block, identified by the keyword **ensure**. Following the acceptance test is the primary module, identified by the keyword **by**, and a (possibly empty) set of alternate modules each of which is preceded by

```
ensure   <acceptance test>
by       <primary module>
else by  <alternate module 1>
else by  <alternate module 2>
  .
  .
  .
else by  <alternate module n>
else error
```

Figure 9.1 Recovery Block Outline

else by. The final **else error** clause emphasizes the fact that no further alternate modules remain.

The execution of a recovery block proceeds as follows: on initial entry a recovery point is (implicitly) established and the primary module is entered. On completion of the module the acceptance test is evaluated - if this test (or the execution of the module) does not raise any exceptions then the results of the module are assumed to be acceptable and the recovery block is exited. However, if an exception is raised then automatic restoration of the recovery point occurs. (The recovery cache mechanism described in Chapter 7 was designed to provide this automatic recovery for the recovery block scheme.) Following recovery, the sequence of execution described above is repeated except that the next module is used in place of the module that failed. If all of the modules fail then this is regarded as a failure of the recovery block and an appropriate exception will be signalled. Recovery blocks can be nested so that one recovery block can form part of a module of an enclosing recovery block - an exception resulting from a failure of an inner recovery block will simply cause termination of the enclosing module in the same manner as any other exception. For example, Figure 9.2 illustrates two nested recovery blocks, with the inner recovery block forming part of the primary module of an outer recovery block. If the primary and alternate modules of this inner recovery block fail then the **else error** clause will be reached and an exception will be

THE RECOVERY BLOCK SCHEME

signalled. In consequence, recovery will take place and the alternate module <another module> of the outer recovery block will be executed.

```
ensure    <acceptance test for outer recovery block>
by        .
          .
          .
          ensure    <acceptance test for inner recovery block>
          by        <primary module>
          else by   <alternate module>
          else error
          .
          .
          .
else by   <another module>
          .
          .
          .
else error
```

Figure 9.2 Nested Recovery Blocks

The recovery block scheme does not impose any constraints on the programming style, methodology and language used to implement the modules and the acceptance test. Clearly, the use of structured programming techniques and high level languages is to be encouraged, and the recovery block scheme can be easily incorporated into most present day programming languages, the only changes required being those which allow the recovery block structure to be expressed. For example, Shrivastava[4] reports on a Pascal system that was extended to incorporate recovery blocks. However, the recovery block approach could be used with other forms of programming language (such as a data base query language or a job control language) or with low level assembler languages.

The aim of a recovery block is (like all fault tolerant systems) to mask the effects of internal faults from the system of which it is a part. In consequence, no provision is made (or is necessary) for informing any enclosing software system as to which module actually produced the outputs that satisfied the acceptance test. However, it is advisable to preserve a record of the execution history of a recovery block in which 'debugging' information such as the exceptions that were raised and the acceptance tests and modules that failed are noted, so that off-line manual fault diagnosis and repair of modules can take place to eliminate the faults that were uncovered.

Since the primary module is the first module in a recovery block to be executed, it is normal to use as the primary a module which has characteristics that make it more desirable than those modules selected as the alternates. (Hence, this first module is qualified as being the *primary* module.) For example, the primary module might have the shortest execution time or use a minimum of main storage (or both!). The alternate modules might attempt to perform exactly the same functions as the primary but in some different, perhaps less efficient, manner. The modules in the fault tolerant sort program shown in Figure 9.3 illustrate this characteristic. This recovery block is intended to sort an array A into ascending order. The primary module uses what is hoped will be the most efficient (and thereby most complex) sorting algorithm. Successive alternate modules also aim to sort A correctly, but using less and less efficient algorithms. Hopefully, these less efficient algorithms will be simpler than the algorithm employed by the primary module and hence will be less prone to design faults.

ensure $A[j + 1] \geq A[j]$ **for** $j = 1, 2, \ldots, n-1$
by   sort A using quicksort
else by   sort A using Shell sort
else by   sort A using insertion sort
else error

Figure 9.3 Fault Tolerant Sort Program

This form of use of a recovery block, where the modules all aim to provide identical service, parallels the use of spontaneous replacement in hardware systems. However, two differences should be noted. Firstly, it is normal in hardware systems to use a replacement component with design and construction identical to that of the failing component; this is not the case in a recovery block. Secondly, the replacement in hardware systems is usually permanent - the stand-by spare component becomes the primary once it has been switched into operation. In a recovery block a failing module is only replaced temporarily, just for that execution of the block. On subsequent entries to the recovery block all of the modules will again be used in the hope that the new set of inputs does not cause a further manifestation of the fault.

It is not necessarily the case that all of the modules in a recovery block produce exactly the same results; the constraint on the modules is that they produce acceptable results, as defined by the acceptance test. Thus, while the primary module attempts to produce the desired results, the second and subsequent modules may only attempt to provide an increasingly degraded (but acceptable) service. A recovery block can therefore be used to provide what may be termed *gracefully degrading software*. The more degraded the service, the simpler the module may be and consequently the greater the hope that it does not contain any design faults. As an example of a recovery block designed in this manner, Figure 9.4 shows the outline of a program which has to enter a disk-to-core transfer request into a queue of outstanding requests.

    ensure   *consistency of disk transfer queue*
    by   *enter request in optimal queue position*
    else by *enter request at end of queue*
    else by *send warning message 'request ignored'*
    else error

Figure 9.4 Gracefully Degrading Program

The acceptance test for this recovery block simply checks that the transfer queue is consistent. The primary module attempts to place the new transfer request in the optimal position in the queue, for example, to minimize disk head movement. The first alternate module avoids the complications of the primary module by simply placing the request at the end of the queue. The second alternate module is more desperate and leaves the queue unchanged, providing a warning that the request has been ignored. While this may cause problems for the program requesting the transfer, at least the rest of the system is allowed to proceed without disruption. If this module fails, indicating that the queue was inconsistent when the recovery block was entered, then recovery would have to take place at a more global level.

Implementation of Recovery Blocks

The main mechanisms required to support recovery blocks are those which implement recovery and manage the flow of control within a recovery block program. The implementation of mechanisms for recovery is discussed in Chapter 7 and is not considered further here.

The flow of control between the modules of a recovery block can be directly supported by the interpreter by means of special purpose instructions tailored to suit the characteristics of recovery blocks. Anderson and Kerr[5] report on an experimental architecture providing such specific instructions, together with a recovery cache mechanism.

An alternative implementation of the flow of control can be based on an exception handling mechanism, with all exceptions being diverted to a handler which initiates recovery and switches control to the next alternate module (or raises an exception if no further alternates exist). An example of a system supporting recovery blocks in this manner is described by Lee et al.[6]

So far it has been assumed that all exceptions occurring during the execution of a recovery block program will result in backward error recovery and a transfer of control to the next alternate module. However, there is nothing to prevent the use of exception handling within a module of a recovery block. For example, a module could enable a handler to provide efficient forward error recovery from a specific erroneous situation (based on assumptions about the consequences of the fault which led to this exception) in order to avoid the more costly but general backward error recovery provided within the recovery block framework (where no such assumptions are made). For example, if arithmetic underflow occurred in a computation, a handler might simply set the result of the offending calculation to the smallest number available, and the computation could then be allowed to proceed. However, such specific recovery actions are inappropriate for and ineffective against errors caused by design faults. Recovery blocks are intended to form a 'back-stop' which can handle unanticipated situations caused by design faults in programs, exceptions for which handlers had not been provided, and even faults in exception handlers themselves. Indeed, support for the recovery block scheme can (and preferably should) be provided as a default form of exception handling by an interpreter. These points are discussed by Cristian,[7] and by Melliar-Smith and Randell[8] who provide an example of a program incorporating recovery blocks for backward error recovery and exception handling with specific (forward) error recovery measures.

The above discussion has introduced the general ideas behind the recovery block scheme. While the scheme is simple in concept, consideration of its practical utility gives rise to several important and interesting questions. The following sections will examine in detail the issues that these questions raise.

The Utility of Recovery Blocks

Since the recovery block scheme increases the overall size of a programming task in that additional software must be designed and implemented for the alternate modules (and for the acceptance test), it might be argued that the use of recovery blocks will increase the complexity of a software system and will therefore detract from, rather than increase, the overall reliability of the system. However, it is not the case that the complexity of a recovery block is dependent upon the number of alternate modules. Because of the backward error recovery that is provided, each alternate module will start execution from exactly the same state, just as if the other modules were not in existence. Thus, although the modules have to be designed to satisfy the same acceptance test, the designer of one module need have no knowledge of the design of any of the other modules, leave alone any responsibility for coping with any damage that a previously executed module may have caused. (Equally, the designer of a program containing recovery blocks does not need to be concerned with which of the various alternate modules actually produced acceptable results at run-time.) It therefore follows that the alternate modules can (and preferably should) be independent from each other, and that the complexity of a recovery block containing multiple alternate modules should be no greater than that of a single non-redundant module.

The execution of the acceptance test, however, contributes an increase in the complexity of a recovery block program when compared to a program without provision for fault tolerance, since such error detection measures are unlikely to be included in a program which could derive no benefit from their deployment. However, for a system with high reliability requirements, error detection will be of vital importance, and the acceptance test of a recovery block is unlikely to be more complex than the measures in a comparable system. In fact, the structure of recovery blocks provides a means for *reducing* the complexity found in systems which have extensive ad hoc error detection (and recovery) facilities.

The strength of the recovery block scheme (and of the N-version programming scheme to be discussed in a following section) derives from the provision of modules which do not contain common faults. This requirement gives rise to two important and inter-related questions. Firstly, is it possible to generate alternate modules for a particular problem? Secondly, can it be ensured that the modules do not contain common faults?

Unfortunately, the characteristics of design faults means that a general answer to these questions cannot be given. However, there are several reasons why the answer to both questions is likely to be 'yes' for many applications. These questions will be examined first with respect to recovery blocks containing alternate modules designed to produce the same results. Issues arising from using recovery blocks for gracefully degrading software will then be considered.

For some problems it is comparatively easy to obtain different algorithms for a module - obvious examples are combinatorial problems (such as sorting) and numerical problems (such as root finding). Knuth[9] and the *Collected Algorithms of the Association for Computing Machinery* provide a rich source of alternative algorithms for problems such as these.

The complexity of many algorithms is compounded by the need to optimize performance. It might be feasible to provide alternate modules whose run-time characteristics make them less suitable for use as the primary module but which are simpler and therefore less prone to design faults. For example, one readily available source of alternate modules might be the prior versions of a module which have been replaced by a newer (more complex) version with superior run-time performance. It might even be feasible to use the recovery block scheme as a method of introducing new versions of modules into systems which cannot be halted, even momentarily, with the knowledge that the old versions would be available as back-ups if (when) the new module failed.

When a source of alternatives is not readily available it will certainly be difficult for an individual programmer to design different yet usefully independent modules. Having 'solved' a problem once, a programmer will be conditioned to considering the problem in a particular manner which may preclude the (lateral) thinking necessary for the design of other independent solutions. Also, having designed, implemented and tested one module, it is psychologically difficult for many programmers to accept the fact that the module still contains bugs and that another module has to be provided, since this constitutes an admission of failure (of the programmer). Another consequence of the programmer not being able to identify the residual faults in a first version of a module is that it will be difficult to prevent the same faults from being present in subsequent versions. For example, a mistaken interpretation of the specification of the problem from which the programmer is working will result in a common fault in all versions.

For these reasons it will be necessary to use separate programmers or teams of programmers, each working independently from a specification of the problem to generate a set of modules to be incorporated in the final recovery block program. Given the already high cost of software production this is not a suggestion to be made (or taken) lightly.

The suggestion of using independent programming teams is not unique to the proponents of the recovery block scheme and has been advocated by others.[10,11,12,13,14,15] Moreover, it is not necessarily the case that using, say, two independent teams results in a doubling of the costs of the overall software system. Gilb[10] has stated that coding a program twice using different teams of programmers only results in an extra (coding) cost of about 10%, and rarely exceeds 25%.

There are additional benefits to be derived from using independent programming teams. Hecht[13] has argued that one of the major contributions to the overall cost of a system is the testing and validation that has to be performed (particularly when high reliability is required) and that the adoption of the recovery block scheme provides a way of reducing these costs. This argument is based on the assumption that in order to achieve the same high reliability the recovery block modules do not need to be tested to the same extent as a module in a non-redundant software system. Similar views are put forward by Gilb,[10] and by Fischler et al.[12] who also noted that an additional benefit of using independent programming teams was that the derivation of a complete and accurate specification of the problem for use by the teams itself resulted in the exposure of a larger number of problems than might otherwise have been the case. It also seems likely that the independent examination of the specification by multiple teams will uncover further ambiguous situations which could have given rise to design faults in the operational program had they not been exposed. Gilb[10] also cites programmer motivation as a side benefit of the adoption of multiple programming teams, suggesting that the teams will compete to produce the best (i.e. least faulty) module and this competition will spur the development of better modules.

The availability of multiple modules can also aid the testing which occurs before the software system is put into operation.[12,16] The modules can be exercised with the same input data and their outputs compared (manually) in order to show up design faults in the modules. In fact, this was the sole motivation proposed by Long et al.[14] for the use of dual programming teams in the implementation of critical nuclear plant control software.

When alternate modules have been designed to provide gracefully degrading service, the algorithm for each module will be different (e.g. as is the case in Figure 9.4) and hence it is less likely that a design fault will be repeated in all of the modules, whether produced by the same programmer or not. As noted previously, the more degraded the service, the simpler the module should be, and the opportunities for introducing design faults should be reduced.

As a final point on the provision of independent alternate modules, it should be noted that while the recovery block scheme enables redundancy to be specified for program code it does not provide for redundancy in the data structures of programs. Thus, while an alternate module can define local data structures to be of any form, data structures which are global to the recovery block must be fixed and their format invariant. Therefore there may be situations in which the static structure of global data limits the ability of the programmer to design alternate modules.

Acceptance Tests

Another major influence on the effectiveness of a recovery block will be the acceptance test. The acceptance test is a programmer-provided error detection measure and can therefore be as cursory or as comprehensive as the programmer wishes. This is perhaps its strength and weakness. On the one hand it is desirable to have as comprehensive a test as is possible. However, this may well lead to a large and complex acceptance test. On the other hand there is a need to keep the acceptance test simple so that its run-time overheads are reasonable, and the test itself is not prone to design faults. Residual design faults in acceptance tests can have two main effects: either a test could erroneously reject acceptable results, or it could fail to reveal actual errors in the state being checked. If there were further alternate modules, occurrence of the former will not necessarily cause the recovery block to fail because a subsequent alternate module could produce results which passed the acceptance test. Since failing checks are recorded for off-line analysis, it is likely that such faults in the acceptance test will be quickly identified and remedied. Failing to detect actual errors is of course more insidious and difficult to deal with. If this occurs it can only be hoped that subsequent checks will reveal the ensuing damage.

The general form of error detection measures was discussed in Chapter 5. From that discussion it follows that a useful test could be based on a full replication check: the acceptance test could incorporate what would essentially be an alternate module to replicate the execution of the other modules in the recovery block for comparison purposes. However, it can be appreciated that this form of check is not really suited to the recovery block approach, for three reasons. Firstly, since it is assumed that modules inevitably contain design faults, it is likely that such a complex acceptance test would also contain design faults (the effects of which were discussed above). Secondly, only duplication (between the acceptance test and a module) can be easily achieved within the recovery block structure - this is sufficient if the acceptance test and the module being checked are in agreement, but is less satisfactory when disagreement occurs since it will not be apparent whether it is the acceptance test or the module at fault. (Moreover, assuming that the acceptance test is the least suspect immediately raises the question as to why the algorithm used in the acceptance test was not used in the primary module; alternatively, always doubting results calculated by an acceptance test (e.g. because the primary contains the 'best' algorithm) suggests that it is not worth having the acceptance test at all!). Thirdly, when the alternate modules are producing different (gracefully degrading) results it is clear that the exact comparison of results implied for a replication check is not appropriate. Thus, it can be seen that the recovery block scheme was never intended to be used to provide an NMR-like system, and such systems are better implemented using the N-version programming scheme described in a subsequent section. There are further problems with voting checks in software fault tolerant systems, but discussion of this point is best postponed until the section on N-version programming.

The acceptance test in a recovery block is expected to take one of the other forms of check described in Chapter 5; a description of these forms is not repeated here. As its name suggests, the acceptance test is not intended to guarantee complete correctness, but is meant to be a check on the acceptability of the results produced by a module or, more comprehensively, on the acceptability of the system state following the execution of a module. Furthermore, as is discussed below, acceptance tests are meant to complement rather than replace other forms of error detection.

The recovery cache mechanism can provide two forms of run-time assistance to aid the design and implementation of acceptance tests, both with respect to detecting errors in the system state resulting from the faulty module and to detecting the consequences of faults in the acceptance test itself. (These forms of assistance could also be provided by some of the other backward error recovery mechanisms described in Chapter 7.) Firstly, since the recovery cache ensures that the prior values of variables updated by a module are available for recovery purposes, the prior values can also be made available for access by the acceptance test. The usual notation employed to illustrate this read-only operation is:

prior *variable name*

(A similar operation is supported in System R which allows access to the NEW and OLD values of updated tuples.) For example, the acceptance test on the sorting program outlined in Figure 9.3 is the obvious check on the order of the array elements. However, this check would not detect errors caused by the loss or modification of items from the original unsorted array. A more stringent acceptance test could also employ a checksum comparison of the elements of the array before and after execution of a module. The prior checksum is most rigorously obtained through the use of the **prior** operation by the acceptance test. The **prior** operation can also be used to check that any variables which should have been updated have in fact been changed.

The second form of assistance that can be provided to acceptance tests by the recovery cache mechanism is also concerned with the variables that have been updated by a module. Since all updated variables are noted in the recovery cache, an exception can be signalled by the cache mechanism if an acceptance test does not access all of the global variables that have been modified. This can ensure that the acceptance test performs at least some minimal checking of the new state of all updated variables, and that the system state following the execution of a module contains no variables which have been updated unintentionally. For example, a comprehensive test would have to check that *all* of the system state was acceptable following the execution of a recovery block, even if that recovery block should only have changed a small isolated part of the state. An acceptance test which uses the recovery cache to check which variables have been updated can provide most of the benefits of such a comprehensive test without incurring the excessive execution time penalties which would normally preclude its adoption. In this way the recovery cache can provide an efficient solution to a restricted form of the frame problem.[17] Faults in the acceptance test as well as in the module can be revealed by this recovery cache imposed check. Faults in the acceptance test can also be revealed by imposing the sensible requirement that an acceptance test should not change the state (i.e. should have no side effects); the recovery cache (or a protection mechanism) can signal an exception should an acceptance test attempt to violate this restriction.

When the alternate modules of a recovery block have been designed to provide gracefully degrading results the acceptance test can only be as rigorous as a check on the results from the weakest module. This has led to the suggestion that there should be a separate acceptance test for each module. However, a recovery block will usually form only part of a program, and the acceptance test provides a check on the consistency of the results which are to be used by the rest of that program. Hence, it is likely that a single test of acceptability will be required whether the alternate modules attempt to produce the same or different results. On the rare occasions when multiple acceptance tests are required, nested recovery blocks[18] or assertion statements[19] can be used to obtain the desired effect.

Although the acceptance test is an important error detection measure in a recovery block, it will not be the only form of error detection. Interface checks provided by the underlying interpreter will also enable some errors to be detected during the execution of the recovery block. Furthermore, extra 'internal' checks can be utilized within each module through the use of **assert** statements as discussed in Chapter 5. While **assert** statements can form a useful error detection measure there is nothing to force a programmer to include them in a program. (Indeed, there are usually many pressures which ensure that such checks are *not* included in operational programs - for example, programmers usually have constraints to meet such as strict deadlines and limitations on the execution time and storage requirements of the final product, constraints which do not encourage the inclusion of (redundant) error detection measures.) In contrast, the recovery block scheme explicitly requires a check to be considered and included; **ensure true** stands out as a decision not to include a proper test.

It is felt that further advantages accrue from the explicit requirement for a check, because the programmer is forced to think about the structure of the overall program, and where and what can (and should) be tested - indeed, it can be argued that the acceptance tests should be the first part of a program to be designed. The formulation of acceptance tests can lead to the programmer giving additional consideration to the likely behavior of a module (e.g. its behavior for special cases) and can lead to the uncovering of more faults during the design and implementation stages than might otherwise have been the case.[20] Putting this another way, it may be expected that a primary module of a recovery block will contain less faults than a module designed for the same problem but not within the recovery block framework.

Against all of these points, it must not be overlooked that the acceptance test is a critical component of a recovery block program, whose reliability directly impinges on the overall reliability of the program; an unreliable acceptance test will lead to an unreliable recovery block however many alternate modules are provided. Hopefully, an acceptance test will be much simpler than the modules it is intended to check, and fault prevention techniques (e.g. proving and extensive testing) and fault tolerance techniques (e.g. the acceptance test could incorporate a recovery block) can be used to increase its reliability.

To summarize, while the requirement for an acceptance test imposes extra burdens on the programmers, it seems likely that the advantages, not only at run-time but also during the design and construction of the program, of requiring a check far outweigh any disadvantages. While acceptance tests for specific problems can often be formulated there are no hard and fast guidelines which can be specified to aid the programmer. For software systems which are decomposed into hierarchies of modules, the module boundaries form obvious places at which acceptance tests can be deployed, and the development of formal specification languages for describing the interfaces to modules is one line of research from which a general methodology for constructing acceptance tests may develop.

Some further guidance for the selection and placement of acceptance tests may be obtained from attempts at formally verifying the correctness of programs,[21] by exploiting the relationship between run-time assertions (such as acceptance tests) and the inductive assertions used in the verification process. Verification is usually concerned with formally establishing that a module will satisfy a specified postcondition when executed with a particular precondition. Establishing that the postcondition holds may be difficult for some modules, and for such modules it may be possible to confirm at run-time that the postcondition holds by incorporating it in the acceptance test of a recovery block containing the module. Similarly, when two modules are to be executed consecutively it is necessary for verification to show that the postcondition of the first module implies the precondition of the second module. Again, a run-time check of that precondition by an acceptance test in a recovery block incorporating the first module can provide an alternative to formal verification. Clearly, if part of a system is not amenable to formal verification then it is very sensible to deploy run-time checks to test the operation of those parts.

Many of the assertions used as pre- and postconditions will not be directly suitable for run-time testing. However, it will always be possible to test some weaker form of an assertion and this may still be useful. Formal verification cannot yet be expected to guarantee the absence of faults in software, since the task of verification is as complex and error-prone as the design and construction of software.[22,23] Run-time checks such as acceptance tests may therefore be useful even in software systems which have been subjected to verification. The verification of fault tolerant programs has received little attention[24,25] and is an important area for further research.

Run-Time Overheads

The last major area of contention raised by the recovery block scheme concerns the run-time overheads that their use incurs. As with any system that utilizes redundancy to provide fault tolerance, the use of recovery blocks involves space and execution time overheads which may not be present in programs with no provision for tolerating faults.

The space overheads stem from the extra storage required for the recovery data, the alternate modules and the acceptance test. When compared to the overall costs of most highly reliable systems (and given the decreasing cost of storage) these overheads should be minimal and not of major concern. In systems where the memory cost may be more significant (e.g. in aerospace applications the main memory has to be highly reliable with a small volume and minimal power requirements) the alternate modules could be considered as candidates for swapping out to secondary storage.

The recovery cache was in fact specifically designed to minimize the amount of storage required for recording recovery data. It is expected that for most applications the recovery data will only be a small percentage of the total data space of a program. Shrivastava and Akinpelu[19] report on experiments in which figures for programs containing a single recovery block are between 3% and 39% (with an average of 17%) which are considerably less than the 100% overhead that recording the complete data space of a program would entail. When multiple recovery points can be active, as is likely with the recovery block scheme, the efficiency of the recovery cache becomes more desirable. (Optimizations which can be applied to the recording of recovery data are covered in Chapter 7.)

The execution time of a recovery block will naturally depend on the characteristics of the particular application for which it is being used. Some general remarks can be made, although this application dependency should be borne in mind. Given that recovery blocks are intended to form a last-resort attempt at preventing system failure, it can be expected that in many situations a recovery block will execute without any exceptions being raised. This leads to the question of how much extra overhead does this 'normal' execution of a recovery block incur when compared to the same primary module executing outside the recovery block framework.

The extra overhead will consist of the time required to execute the recovery block specific instructions (e.g. establish and discard a recovery point) and the acceptance test, and the delays imposed because of the need to retain recovery data. The recovery block specific instructions are only expected to form a small percentage of the total number of instructions executed. Hence the extra delays caused by their execution should not be significant.

The time required to execute the acceptance test will obviously be application dependent. Kim and Ramamoorthy[26] have proposed an architecture to mitigate this overhead by executing the acceptance test in parallel with subsequent modules. In the experiments reported by Andrews[20] the inclusion of run-time assertions as acceptance tests in programs resulted in execution time overheads of 12% (which included time for forward error recovery). For the programs monitored by Shrivastava and Akinpelu[19] the time to evaluate acceptance tests "turned out to be negligibly small".

As far as overheads for recording recovery data are concerned, the recovery cache is intended to be provided as part of the underlying machine (e.g. implemented in hardware). Its operation should therefore be fast, particularly as many of its operations can be performed in parallel with the normal execution of a module. The majority of instructions executed by the interpreter should not be affected at all by a recovery cache mechanism, and the only instructions incurring any extra overhead will be those that write to an object (typically, only 1 instruction in 10 is a write instruction)[6] and therefore require intervention by the mechanism. Lee et al.[6] describe a hardware implemented recovery cache which was designed to be added to a PDP-11 system, imposing a delay of approximately 15%. Shrivastava and Akinpelu[19] report overheads ranging between 1% and 11%. Since neither of these systems was fully optimized these figures should be regarded as conservative.

For normal applications, in which a recovery block is expected to execute without modules failing, the recovery cache algorithm based on saving the original value of updated objects is the most satisfactory since it optimizes the progress of a module at the expense of the extra time required to restore a prior state if recovery is invoked. Because the recovery time may be relatively long it has been suggested that the recovery block scheme will not be suitable for systems such as real-time systems. Since recovery can be provided by a fast underlying mechanism, this may not be the case. In fact, several algorithms are known for the recording of recovery data, each of which has different space/time tradeoffs (see Chapter 7). An algorithm which inhibited the updating of an object and recorded the new value of the object in the recovery cache would optimize the time required for recovery. Indeed, with this organization the recovery cache could also act as a high-speed buffer store and thereby increase the speed of the normal execution of modules. Thus it is felt that for a given set of constraints, a suitable implementation of the recovery cache can be specified.

The programmer also has some control over the recovery time - since recovery blocks can be nested to provide as fine a grain of recovery as is desired, the recovery time can be minimized at the expense of an overall increase in recovery data recording.

Against all of this optimism about the recovery block scheme, the overheads of providing recovery in concurrent systems and multilevel systems with unrecoverable objects cannot be overlooked. The general problem of providing backward error recovery is usually raised as a drawback of the recovery block scheme. In fact this is not an intractable problem, and will be discussed further in a following section in which the N-version programming scheme is compared with the recovery block scheme. Until much more practical experience with recovery blocks is obtained, it must remain a conjecture, albeit a very plausible conjecture, that the use and implementation of recovery blocks can be organized so that the overheads are tolerable and acceptable for many software systems.

Summary of Recovery Blocks

The recovery block scheme provides a unifying framework for the implementation of fault tolerant software, incorporating strategies for *error detection* by the acceptance test and interface checks provided by the underlying system; *backward error recovery* provided automatically by a mechanism; and *fault treatment* which simply uses an alternate module as a temporary stand-by spare. No strategy for *damage assessment* is needed since the backward error recovery is assumed to remove all of the damage caused by a faulty module.

As yet there is not a great deal of experience with the use of recovery blocks for providing software fault tolerance. Nevertheless, it does seem that the recovery block scheme provides a coherent framework for the inclusion of redundancy in a software system, avoiding many of the disadvantages that other ad hoc solutions might encounter. There are few conceptual reasons why the scheme should not fulfill its objectives of enabling software faults to be tolerated.

While the number of reported experiments demonstrating the utility of recovery blocks is limited[5] some experiments have been conducted by students at the University of Newcastle upon Tyne.[27] The results of these experiments, while not providing a definitive answer to whether the use of recovery blocks can significantly improve the reliability of a software system, have been very encouraging and have failed to reveal any shortcomings of the scheme. This is still a subject of on-going research, and it remains to be seen whether these results will be reinforced by larger and more realistic experiments in constructing software systems using recovery blocks.

THE DEADLINE MECHANISM

A variation of the recovery block scheme called the *deadline mechanism* has been proposed by Campbell et al.[28] The deadline mechanism is intended to support software fault tolerance in real-time applications where a program has to satisfy requests for service with a given time limit (deadline) or else system failure is likely to ensue.

Figure 9.5, adapted from the above paper, shows an example of how a navigation program could be specified for the deadline mechanism, and will be used to illustrate the way in which fault tolerance is provided.

every	second	
within	ten milliseconds	
calculate by	read sensors;	*"primary module"*
	calculate new position	
else by	approximate new position from	*"alternate module"*
	old position	

Figure 9.5 Outline of Fault Tolerant Navigation Program

In this notation, the **every** statement is used to specify the maximum frequency with which the program is invoked. (This quantity is not of direct relevance here but can be used, in conjunction with other timing figures, to ensure that a set of such programs does not exceed the computational capacity of the system on which they are to be executed.) The **within** statement determines the deadline that must be met by the program, by specifying the maximum amount of time that can elapse before results must be provided. Following this are the primary module, and a single alternate module used to provide a degraded service should the primary fail. It is assumed that the alternate module is free from faults.

Since the program must provide its service before the deadline elapses, it is necessary for the program designer to estimate the execution time of the program accurately. The deadline mechanism requires only that a guaranteed upper bound can be placed on the time needed to execute the (simple) alternate module (how the execution time for the alternate module is communicated to the deadline mechanism is not made clear by Campbell *et al.*). No such bound need be determined for the more complex and possibly faulty primary module. To ensure that the overall program meets the deadline, a scheduling mechanism operates in the manner described below with respect to the above program being executed on a single CPU. The timing constraints for this program are diagramatically represented in Figure 9.6.

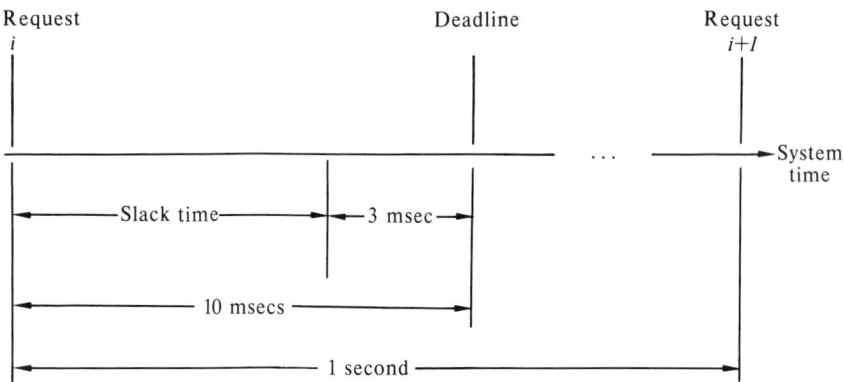

Figure 9.6 Timing Constraints for Navigation Program

Assume that the maximum execution time for the alternate module is 3 msecs. When the program is entered the scheduler can reserve 3 msecs of time before the deadline during which the alternate could be executed to ensure that the program did not fail. During the remaining time, referred to as the slack time, the execution of the primary module can be attempted. If the primary produces satisfactory results within the slack time, the program can be exited. However, if the execution of the primary module is not completed within this time because, say, of a design fault then its execution can be terminated and the alternate module invoked.

The scheduling algorithm described above is optimistic in the sense that it executes the possibly faulty primary module first and hence time is wasted if that module fails. An alternative (pessimistic) scheduling algorithm could execute the alternate first, although this execution would be redundant if the primary module subsequently produced acceptable results. The tradeoff between the two scheduling algorithms becomes important when the set of deadline programs in a system is considered, since time wasted by one program will reduce the time available for the execution of others. Some simple simulation results demonstrating this tradeoff are given by Campbell *et al.*

No explicit provisions appear to be made for checking that the results produced by a primary module are in fact acceptable. An **assert** statement or a recovery block could presumably be used in the primary module. Also, Campbell *et al.* do not discuss whether a backward error recovery mechanism is required (presumably it is), and how this mechanism (or the modules) should be organized so that the recovery time overhead can be predicted. The recovery cache algorithm based on saving updated variables and leaving the system state unchanged would be the obvious way of making the recovery time minimal and predictable. Nevertheless, the deadline mechanism is an interesting variation of the recovery block scheme for real-time systems where high reliability is often of paramount importance.

THE N-VERSION PROGRAMMING SCHEME

Since NMR structures have proved to be an effective form of fault tolerance in hardware systems, an obvious extension is to apply the same structuring to sequential software systems in order to provide software fault tolerance. Some investigations in this area, under the title of *N*-version programming, have been carried out by Chen and Avizienis.[29] This section will concentrate on the scheme as presented in that paper.

The semantics of *N*-version programming are as might be expected - *N*-versions of a program ($N > 1$) which have been independently designed to satisfy a common specification are executed and their results compared by some form of replication check. Based on a majority vote, this check can eliminate erroneous results (i.e. the minority) and pass on the presumably correct results calculated by the majority to the rest of the system.

Implementation of N-Version Programming

Control of the N-versions of a program is provided by what is termed the driver program. The driver program is responsible for:

(i)   invoking each of the versions;
(ii) waiting for the versions to complete their execution;
(iii) comparing and acting upon the N sets of results.

It can be seen that mechanisms are required to synchronize the actions of the driver and the versions, and to communicate outputs from the versions to the driver. The scheme also requires that each version is executed atomically and has access to the same input space. Each of these points will be examined below.

A synchronization mechanism is an important aspect of N-version programming. The scheme proposed by Chen and Avizienis is fairly simple, based essentially on the use of **wait** and **send** primitives. The versions **wait** and do not commence processing until a **send** is executed by the driver. Similarly, the driver **waits** until **send** responses have been received from all N versions to indicate that their outputs are complete. The voting check on the sets of results can then be evaluated. The synchronization scheme has to allow for different execution times of the modules, in particular for modules which do not complete their execution, for example due to an infinite loop caused by a design fault. This requires some form of timeout mechanism to be added to the synchronization mechanism used by the driver.[30] A different approach to synchronization is adopted in the SIFT and Space Shuttle systems which both adopt an NMR structure for executing programs. The problem of versions which do not complete is overcome in these systems by performing the voting check at a predetermined fixed time rather than waiting for completion signals from the versions. (The problem of different execution times does not occur in these systems since all of their versions are identical.) As a result both systems contain a complex synchronization scheme to ensure that the executions of the versions on multiple processors do not get out of step. Describing this approach using N-version programming terminology, synchronization in these systems is effected by the driver whereas in the N-version programming scheme the synchronization is driven by the versions.

The results from each version have to be communicated in an identical format to the driver program for use in the voting check. Provision is made in the proposed scheme to send a vector of values containing the results to the driver, together with status flags which provide information about the execution which produced those results. For instance, the status values might be used to mechanize the signalling of a failure exception from a version to the driver, should any exception occur during the execution of the version for which actions provided by a local handler were ineffective.

In some applications the vector of output values may be large and result in a significant volume of communication traffic, for example, if the N versions were sorting a large file. That this may be a problem is exemplified by the SIFT and Space Shuttle systems, which both attempt to minimize the amount of communication necessary for the voting check, for example, in the Space Shuttle by voting on a checksum of the results rather than on individual values.

A requirement for hardware and software NMR systems is that each version executes atomically with respect to the other versions, that is, without any communication with or interference from the other versions. In hardware systems this is usually implemented by physically separating the versions. Clearly, this is also appropriate for N-version programming. Multiprocessor systems (such as SIFT and FTMP) would be suitable for executing such programs since it could then be arranged to execute each version in parallel on independent hardware. Execution of an N-version program on a single processor system is possible so long as the isolation of separate versions can be maintained.

When executed, each version must have access to an identical set of input values (how this is achieved is not described by Chen and Avizienis). One method of implementing this would be for the driver to communicate the set of input values to each version, although there is the danger of there being a large set of input values, for example, as the input to the sort operation mentioned above. Another possibility would be to allow the versions to access the input values from a shared, global data structure. As exemplified by the SIFT system, such structures must be read-only if the atomicity criterion is not to be violated. The proposed scheme allows a version to retain private data in structures local to its instantiation, to be used in subsequent executions of that version, which could reduce the amount of input required. Further ramifications of this are discussed below.

Voting Check

Probably the most important aspect of the N-version programming scheme is the voting check performed by the driver program. It might be expected that the NMR structure of N-version programming would enable a simple, application-independent equality check to be used (as is provided in NMR hardware systems), and that such a check could be provided by an underlying mechanism rather than by measures in the driver program. Unfortunately, this is not always the case.

For some applications (e.g. programs manipulating characters or performing integer arithmetic), where versions can be expected to produce identical results if their execution is without fault, an equality voting check can be used with the majority being selected as the correct result. However, for other computations an exact comparison check cannot be used, since the inexact hardware representation of real numbers coupled with the different algorithms used can lead to minor discrepancies between valid sets of results. For this reason, "inexact voting" has been investigated, that is, a check which can identify a consensus even though small discrepancies occur between the sets of results being compared. The obvious approach is to use some form of range check, expecting that the results will be within a certain range of each other. As noted by Chen and Avizienis, the maximum allowable range used in a check may be difficult to determine and may change between executions of a version. Even if the range can be determined and all of the versions produce results, the inexact vote requires a non-trivial algorithm to identify the erroneous values in a set and to then evaluate a result derived from the remaining (differing) values. The algorithm will be combinatorial in nature, based on evaluating the differences between all of the N results; its execution time will therefore be dependent upon the number of versions in use, and may be significant when each version produces a large number of results to be voted upon. The detailed characteristics of the algorithm may be application dependent - indeed, it is noted that "there is no inexact voting approach which can be applied successfully to all cases".[29]

Summary of N-Version Programming

When a voting check can be successfully implemented, the NMR structure of N-version programming is a simple and attractive framework for fault tolerance. *Error detection* is provided by the voting check; *damage assessment* is not required if the activities of the versions are atomic; *error recovery* involves ignoring the values identified as erroneous by the check; and *fault treatment* simply results in the versions determined to have produced erroneous results being ignored. Of course, if a majority of versions do not produce equivalent results then further fault tolerance measures will be needed to avert failure. Two-version systems are one instance of this situation since a voting check, while satisfactory if the two sets of results are in agreement, can only provide error detection when the two sets differ. (Although Chen and Avizienis do not preclude the construction of 2-version programs their discussion of implementation issues assumes 3-version programs, the schemes for which are not appropriate for the 2-version case.) The 2-version system described by von Linde[15] relies on manual intervention when the check detects an error. If fault tolerance in a 2-version system had to be provided without manual assistance, some form of acceptance test (as in the recovery block scheme) would be necessary to apply other criteria in an attempt to differentiate between the (possibly) good and bad sets of results.

Comparison with the Recovery Block Scheme

As in recovery blocks, the strength of N-version programming depends upon the ability of the system implementors to provide multiple versions of a program which are functionally equivalent but which do not contain common design faults. Thus, the arguments as to whether this is feasible are essentially the same as those presented in the prior section on recovery blocks, and will not be repeated here. However, the N-version programming scheme has one potential advantage over the recovery block scheme, stemming from the fact that a version can define its own private data structures which are retained between successive executions. When versions do use data structures with different formats, the algorithms needed for their manipulation will be different, and hence the provision of independent versions may be simplified. For example, three versions maintaining a symbol table for a compiler could use an array structure, a hash table and a linked list to retain information, each of which would require different algorithms to insert, search for and delete entries. It must be noted, however, that the retention of private data structures between executions can cause further problems, as is discussed subsequently.

For those applications in which a suitable exact or inexact voting check can be implemented, the N-version programming scheme has some clear advantages over the recovery block scheme. As discussed in Chapter 5, this type of replication check is very powerful and can go a long way towards providing a check for correctness of operation, rather than the acceptability check usually found in recovery blocks. If the overhead of executing the multiple versions are ignored, a voting check is likely to be more efficient in execution time than an acceptance test, although experimentation with inexact voting checks will be required to substantiate this.

However, while the simplicity of the voting check adopted by the N-version programming scheme is an attractive way of overcoming the difficulties associated with the acceptance tests of recovery blocks, there are situations for which such a check is inappropriate or impractical. The problems with inexact voting are discussed above.

Furthermore, Chen and Avizienis note that a voting check cannot be used if there are multiple distinct solutions to a problem. A similar situation arises when gracefully degrading results are acceptable as the outputs from a program. In these situations N-version programming would not be appropriate, although the recovery block scheme could be used.

The NMR structure of N-version programming is attractive for fault tolerance because of the simple and quick strategies that can be adopted for damage assessment, error recovery and fault treatment, and delays such as those caused by the recovery cache mechanism should not be incurred. However, this assumes that sufficient hardware resources are available to enable the N versions to be executed in parallel, although the overall requirement for system resources will then be greater than for a corresponding recovery block. Indeed, the requirement for resources is likely to limit the extent to which N-version programs can be nested within each other. Even with sufficient parallelism, the execution time of an N-version program will be constrained by the slowest version - there may be a substantial difference in the execution speeds of the fastest and slowest versions because of the need to generate independent designs. In contrast, the time required to execute a recovery block will normally be constrained by the execution time of the primary module.

Chen and Avizienis suggest that one disadvantage of the recovery block scheme when compared with the N-version programming scheme stems from the requirement of the former for backward error recovery, which can be expensive in the case of interacting processes, or unavailable in the case of unrecoverable objects. These situations may not appear to be a problem in the N-version programming scheme. However, this is only because the execution of each version must be constrained to be atomic with respect to the other versions and to have no effect on the enclosing system - the only allowable results from a version are the results sent to the driver which can then select the 'correct' results and then update global system variables as necessary.

In contrast, the recovery block scheme does not impose any constraints on the execution of a module, although the price paid is that backward error recovery must be available, as is discussed below. (In fact, backward error recovery may be regarded as a method of achieving atomicity between the modules of a recovery block.) If constraints similar to those placed on the execution of versions were applied to the recovery block modules then the recovery mechanism would not be required and the difficulties alluded to above would not arise. Similarly, if the constraints applied to the execution of versions could not be guaranteed then it would be necessary to include a recovery mechanism in the N-version programming scheme, similar to that of the recovery block scheme but with extra complications to cope with the possible damage caused by the parallel execution of several versions.

The provision of backward error recovery for recovery block programs which progress by manipulating objects other than those which reside in the main memory is often raised as a potential drawback of the scheme. Chapter 7 has discussed why this may in fact not be too great a problem, since the abstraction of recovery can often be provided even when restoration of a concrete state is not available. The solutions to this problem are best exemplified by an example of how the recovery block scheme and the N-version programming scheme cope with unrecoverable objects. Consider the primary module of a recovery block which has launched a rocket on an erroneously calculated trajectory. Recovery to the prior concrete state (with the rocket back on its concrete launch pad) would be somewhat difficult. However, the same problem would occur if the versions in an N-version program were allowed to launch a rocket before the voting check on the calculated trajectories. Clearly, the versions would have to be constrained not to do so (again, to satisfy the atomicity requirement) and the solution would be to only perform the trajectory calculations in the versions, with the launching of the rocket being undertaken after the voting check on the trajectory provided by the versions. A similar structure could be imposed on the recovery block program;[19] the launching of the rocket could follow the successful execution of the acceptance test.

However, for both schemes it must be ensured that the rocket launching is not part of any enclosing recovery block or *N*-version program, since the problem of recovery would still prevail. One approach would be to carefully design the software system to ensure that this situation did not arise. While this is not impossible to achieve, it imposes yet another constraint on the construction of a software system.

For the recovery block scheme there is an alternative approach which removes constraints on the construction of recovery blocks by resolving the recovery problem exemplified by the rocket launching. While restoration of the prior concrete state is difficult, restoration of the prior abstract state may be simple. For instance, triggering a self-destruct mechanism in the rocket may suffice. Yet another solution would be to implement the 'launch rocket' operation so that the launch was delayed until the outermost recovery block had been successfully completed (since there would be no recovery requirement after this point). The construction of multilevel systems which automatically cover both of these solutions to the problems of unrecoverable objects is discussed in Chapter 7.

Thus, it can be seen that the problems of providing recovery when unrecoverable objects are being manipulated affects both the recovery block scheme and the *N*-version programming scheme and does not provide an advantage to the latter over the former. In fact, the flexibility in construction of software systems that only the recovery block scheme can offer may well be a significant advantage over the *N*-version programming scheme.

It was noted in the previous section that the *N*-version programming scheme allows a version to retain some record of its previous execution in local data structures. Thus subsequent executions of a version can and probably will depend on earlier executions, and there is the danger that the cumulative effect of small discrepancies will give rise to erroneous results from a version. Once erroneous, the state of a version will stay erroneous unless some means of recovery is provided. In the proposed scheme, no such recovery is envisaged, and the driver makes no further use of a version when its results have been found to be erroneous. The subsequent reduction in redundancy will of course reduce the effectiveness of the fault tolerance provided, especially when a 3-version system is reduced to 2-versions.

In contrast, errors generated by a failing module in a recovery block are recovered from and cannot affect future executions of that module. Thus a failing module is discarded only for the execution which was detected to be erroneous - subsequent executions of the recovery block can safely reuse a module which had failed previously. The N-version programming scheme could operate in a similar manner if the versions were programmed to be memoryless.

While not of primary concern for this chapter, it should be noted that both the recovery block and the N-version programming schemes can provide some protection against faults in the underlying system (e.g. against hardware component faults) although this is not their main purpose. For example, suppose that a 'CPU-fault' exception was raised during the execution of a recovery block program. After running diagnostic checks, an exception handler may conclude that the fault was transient. However, to guard against any as yet undetected errors that may have been introduced into the state of the recovery block program, facilities of the recovery block scheme can be used to provide a *retry* - the error recovery can be invoked to rectify any damage, and the same module of the recovery block can then be re-entered. The N-version programming scheme could also provide effective tolerance against such transient faults.

A similar use of the features of recovery blocks occurred in a student project,[27] where the system on which the student was programming supported recovery blocks but provided no explicit means for exception handling. The student proceeded to use recovery blocks to handle failure exceptions from the underlying machine as illustrated in Figure 9.7.

ensure true
by *print file on line printer*
else by *spool file;*
print warning message on terminal
else error

Figure 9.7 Exception Handling by a Recovery Block

While it was recognized that this was not the most effective method of handling the exception, the student was happy to do so because the backward error recovery increased his confidence that all of the possible errors had been recovered from (and the scheme also provided a neat structuring of the control flow in the absence of an exception mechanism).

If either scheme was implemented on a single CPU then permanent component faults in that CPU would be unlikely to be tolerated (unless an alternate module or another version fortuitously avoided the faulty part of the CPU). An implementation of N-version programming using multiple processors would obviously be much more likely to tolerate such faults.

In summary, N-version programming and recovery blocks are in many ways similar approaches to providing software fault tolerance, although each has features which complement deficiencies in the other. For systems which have replicated hardware resources available and for which simple voting checks can be implemented, the N-version programming scheme seems the most natural approach. For systems with more limited hardware resources or with characteristics which make a voting check inappropriate, the recovery block scheme offers certain advantages.

Only limited experiments with N-version programming have been undertaken. The simple experiments reported,[29,30] consisting of running sets of student programs as 3-version programs on an IBM 360/91, were of a mixed nature; not unnaturally, the scheme worked for some sets of programs. Unfortunately, other combinations of programs failed to provide the necessary tolerance and in one case a version caused the operating system to abort the execution of the 3-version program of which it was a part. Given the limited nature of the experiments these negative results are not really surprising - one would not expect to use inexperienced programmers to generate versions of a program for an application with high reliability requirements. To quote the latter paper: "it is believed that at the present stage of the investigation N-version programming remains an interesting and potentially effective approach to software fault-tolerance".

SUMMARY

This chapter has discussed in detail the two main schemes that have been suggested for the provision and support of software fault tolerance, that is, tolerance of the effects and consequences of design faults in software systems. The concepts and implementation of the recovery block scheme and the N-version programming scheme have been examined in depth in an attempt to answer the questions which most frequently arise when the schemes are discussed. Since the recovery block scheme has been under investigation for the longer period of time the issues it raises are perhaps better understood than those of N-version programming. Nevertheless, both schemes present a coherent approach for attacking the problems of software fault tolerance.

The discussion has concentrated on the tolerance of design faults in the software of computing systems. Given the increasing complexity of hardware systems as a consequence of improving integration techniques it seems likely that design faults in the hardware circuits of the future will not be as uncommon as they appear to be in present day systems. The structures proposed for providing software fault tolerance, particularly that of using N independently designed modules working in parallel and voting on the outputs, could be adopted for use in VLSI chips. Some steps along these lines are suggested by Sedmak and Liebergot[31] who discuss a generalized VLSI chip in which the logic is duplicated using normal and complemented voltage values, although this structure is proposed principally to tolerate faults attributable to the manufacturing process.

While it seems widely recognized that software is inevitably the cause of many reliability problems in computing systems in general, and in systems with high reliability requirements in particular, it does not seem to be widely accepted that fault tolerance is an appropriate solution to these problems. Certainly, at the many presentations of the recovery block scheme that the authors have been involved with, the audience reaction has been most favorable but few people think (or admit) that the scheme could be of use in their system. Perhaps one reason for this reluctance is the

SUMMARY

lack of quantified estimates of the enhancement in reliability to be expected from using recovery blocks or N-version programming. Perhaps people do not wish to concede that their systems contain design faults, and would regard the adoption of the schemes as an admission of defeat.

A parallel can be drawn between the use of these fault tolerance schemes and the launch escape tower which was included as part of the Apollo launch vehicles. The escape tower was a last resort mechanism to allow the astronauts to (attempt to) escape should any faults affect the early launch stages of the rocket. If the rocket designers could have guaranteed that no launch problems would occur then the expense of the development of the escape tower could have been avoided. However, nobody regarded the provision of the escape tower as an indictment of the skills of the rocket designers. Rather, it was accepted that the escape tower provided some increase in confidence that the lives of the astronauts would not be lost if any problem arose. The fact that the tower was never used operationally indicates that the design was as good as had been hoped for. Nevertheless, it would have been difficult to convince the astronauts beforehand that the tower was redundant!

The recovery block and N-version programming schemes should be regarded in the same light as the launch escape tower. They can provide a last-resort attempt to tolerate design faults, which it is hoped will never be exercised in the operational system. However, the incorporation of one (or both) of the schemes should lead to increased confidence in the reliability of the system.

Examples of the use of software fault tolerance in practical systems are already beginning to emerge. Hecht reports that an alternate module was provided in the Titan III space launch vehicle as a backup for an attitude control module.[13] Von Linde briefly describes the use of a 2-version software system for controlling railway traffic,[15] and confirms the view that testing can never reveal all of the faults in a software system. He also notes that several dangerous situations would have occurred had the 2-version programming scheme not been adopted.

There are probably many examples of software faults leading to system failures although information on such faults is rarely documented, for obvious reasons. Unfortunately, it may take some kind of computer-controlled disaster to bring about recognition that fault prevention techniques are not sufficient for high software reliability, and that software fault tolerance can and should be provided in application areas which have high reliability requirements. There are few theoretical reasons for not adopting fault tolerance in software systems, although practical justification must await the results of on-going research efforts.

REFERENCES

1. J.G. Robinson and E.S. Roberts, "Software Fault-Tolerance in the Pluribus," *AFIPS Conference Proceedings 1978 NCC* **47**, Anaheim (CA), pp.563-569 (June 1978).
2. J.H. Wensley et al., "SIFT: Design and Analysis of a Fault-Tolerant Computer for Aircraft Control," *Proceedings of the IEEE* **66**(10), pp.1240-1255 (October 1978).
3. J.J. Horning et al., "A Program Structure for Error Detection and Recovery," pp. 171-187 in *Lecture Notes in Computer Science 16*, ed. E. Gelenbe and C. Kaiser, Springer-Verlag, Berlin (1974).
4. S.K. Shrivastava, "Sequential Pascal with Recovery Blocks," *Software - Practice and Experience* **8**(2), pp.177-185 (March 1978).
5. T. Anderson and R. Kerr, "Recovery Blocks in Action: A System Supporting High Reliability," *Proceedings of 2nd International Conference on Software Engineering*, San Francisco (CA), pp.447-457 (October 1976).
6. P.A. Lee, N. Ghani, and K. Heron, "A Recovery Cache for the PDP-11," *IEEE Transactions on Computers* **C-29**(6), pp.546-549 (June 1980).
7. F. Cristian, "Exception Handling and Software-Fault Tolerance," *Digest of Papers FTCS-10: 10th International Symposium on Fault-Tolerant Computing Systems*, Kyoto, pp.97-103 (October 1980).

8. P.M. Melliar-Smith and B. Randell, "Software Reliability: The Role of Programmed Exception Handling," *SIGPLAN Notices* **12**(3), pp.95-100 (March 1977).
9. D.E. Knuth, *The Art of Computer Programming Vols.1-3*, Addison-Wesley, Reading (MA) (1968-).
10. T. Gilb, "Distinct Software: A Redundancy Technique for Reliable Software," pp. 117-133 in *State of the Art Report on Software Reliability*, Infotech, Maidenhead (1977).
11. H. Kopetz, "Software Redundancy in Real Time Systems," *IFIP Congress 74*, Stockholm, pp.182-186 (August 1974).
12. M.A. Fischler, O. Firschein, and D.L. Drew, "Distinct Software: An Approach to Reliable Computing," *Proceedings of Second USA-Japan Computer Conference*, Tokyo, pp.573-579 (August 1975).
13. H. Hecht, "Fault Tolerant Software for Real-Time Applications," *Computing Surveys* **8**(4), pp.391-407 (December 1976).
14. A.B. Long et al., "A Methodology for the Development and Validation of Critical Software for Nuclear Power Plants," *Proceedings COMPSAC 77*, Chicago (IL), pp.620-626 (November 1977).
15. O.B. von Linde, "Computers Can Now Perform Vital Functions Safely," *Railway Gazette International* **135**(11), pp.1004-1006 (November 1979).
16. T. Gilb, *Software Metrics*, Winthrop, Cambridge (MA) (1977).
17. E. Sandewall, "An Approach to the Frame Problem, and its Implementation," pp. 195-204 in *Machine Intelligence 7*, ed. B. Meltzer and D. Michie, Edinburgh University Press, Edinburgh (1972).
18. P.A. Lee, "A Reconsideration of the Recovery Block Scheme," *Computer Journal* **21**(4), pp.306-310 (November 1978).
19. S.K. Shrivastava and A.A. Akinpelu, "Fault Tolerant Sequential Programming Using Recovery Blocks," *Digest of Papers FTCS-8: Eighth Annual International Conference on Fault-Tolerant Computing*, Toulouse, p.207

(June 1978).

20. D.M. Andrews, "Using Executable Assertions for Testing and Fault Tolerance," *Digest of Papers FTCS-9: Ninth Annual International Symposium on Fault-Tolerant Computing*, Madison (WI), pp.102-105 (June 1979).

21. E. Best and F. Cristian, "Systematic Detection of Exception Occurrences," Technical Report 165, Computing Laboratory, University of Newcastle upon Tyne (April 1981).

22. S.L. Gerhart and L. Yelowitz, "Observations of Fallibility in Applications of Modern Programming Methodologies," *IEEE Transactions on Software Engineering* **SE-2**(3), pp.195-207 (September 1976).

23. A.S. Tanenbaum, "In Defense of Program Testing or Correctness Proofs Considered Harmful," *SIGPLAN Notices* **11**(5), pp.64-68 (May 1976).

24. T. Anderson and R.W. Witty, "Safe Programming," *BIT* **18**, pp.1-8 (1978).

25. F. Cristian, "Robust Data Abstractions," *Acta Informatica* (To Appear).

26. K.H. Kim and C.V. Ramamoorthy, "Failure-Tolerant Parallel Programming and its Supporting System Architecture," *AFIPS Conference Proceedings 1976 NCC* **45**, New York, pp.413-423 (June 1976).

27. E.J. Salzman, "An Experiment in Producing Highly Reliable Software," M.Sc. Dissertation, Computing Laboratory, University of Newcastle upon Tyne (1978).

28. R.H. Campbell, K.H. Horton, and G.G. Belford, "Simulations of a Fault-Tolerant Deadline Mechanism," *Digest of Papers FTCS-9: Ninth Annual International Symposium on Fault-Tolerant Computing*, Madison (WI), pp.95-101 (June 1979).

29. L. Chen and A. Avizienis, "N-Version Programming: A Fault-Tolerance Approach to Reliability of Software Operation," *Digest of Papers FTCS-8: Eighth Annual International Conference on Fault-Tolerant Computing*, Toulouse, pp.3-9 (June 1978).

30. A. Avizienis and L. Chen, "On the Implementation of N-Version Programming for Software Fault-Tolerance During Program Execution," *Proceedings COMPSAC 77*, Chicago (IL), pp.149-155 (November 1977).
31. R.M. Sedmak and H.L. Liebergot, "Fault-Tolerance of a General Purpose Computer Implemented by Very Large Scale Integration," *IEEE Transactions on Computers* **C-29**(6), pp.492-500 (June 1980).

10

CONCLUSION

If computing systems could be designed and built so as to be free from faults throughout their operational life, then this book would be redundant. Or would it? Constructing a perfect system, even if this could be achieved in practice, is not necessarily the most cost-effective approach for producing high reliability. The law of diminishing returns (and its quantitative variant, the 80:20 rule) suggests that optimal solutions are rarely obtained by placing all one's eggs in one basket. A well-engineered approach to building highly reliable systems is likely to be based on striving to attain perfection, but acknowledges that imperfections will remain and that fault tolerance will be needed to cope with them.

In any case, both physical reality and human nature make fault tolerance necessary by ensuring that perfect systems are something to be aspired to rather than achieved. Physical components inevitably deteriorate and give rise to faults, while human fallibility coupled with the inherent complexity of hardware and software make the complete absence of design faults from practical computing systems an unattainable goal. When operation without failure is required despite the presence of faults, the adoption of strategies for fault tolerance cannot be avoided.

This book has presented the principles and practice of fault tolerance, identifying the basic principles which can form a coherent strategy for fault tolerance, and examining the various techniques by which those principles can be and have been implemented in practice. The aim has been to present general principles and techniques, applicable to all levels in computing systems and not just to the hardware or software.

Particular attention has been given to the problems associated with tolerating *unanticipated faults*, that is, faults which were not foreseen when the system was being designed (except for recognition that such faults will indeed affect the system). Design faults are probably the most important category of unanticipated faults, and are a consequence of unmastered complexity in a system. In computing systems, design faults have largely been encountered in software rather than hardware. Software is prone to design faults because, despite modern software construction methodologies, most software systems continue to be enormously complex. In contrast, the elimination of design faults from hardware systems has (in the past) been a viable approach because such systems are comparatively simple, and hence amenable to techniques such as disciplined design practices and thorough testing. However, as the scale of integration available continues to increase through advances in semiconductor technology, it seems inevitable that future hardware systems will become ever more complex, and therefore increasingly prone to design faults. Already, VLSI techniques have produced individual integrated circuits having a degree of complexity much more akin to that of early software systems than to many hardware systems. Existing hardware design and testing techniques are known to be inadequate for the prevention of design faults in VLSI circuitry. Furthermore, the specific fault tolerance techniques currently prevalent in hardware systems rely on a knowledge of component failure modes and are therefore inappropriate for dealing with the consequences of unanticipated faults. Effective fault tolerance for complex hardware and software systems requires new and more general techniques, such as those advocated in this book.

Any provision for fault tolerance in a system must be based on the inclusion of redundancy within the system. Unfortunately, redundancy added to a system is a two-edged sword. On the one hand, system reliability can be enhanced because of tolerance to faults, but on the other, the increase in the size and complexity of the system could result in new faults and lead to an overall reduction in reliability. Ad hoc approaches to the provision of fault tolerance run the risk of doing more harm than good. The next section therefore outlines a methodical approach to fault tolerance (re-iterating points made in earlier chapters) by illustrating the exception handling framework presented in Chapter 3.

METHODOLOGY AND FRAMEWORK FOR FAULT TOLERANCE

What should a process do if it detects an error while trying to load a backup copy of a recovery program from magnetic tape, which was needed because of a read error in a copy of the recovery program held on disk, which was invoked because, due to a design fault, the process made an illegal access to a magnetic tape? The answer is straightforward: very little - any attempt to design a process so that it can cope completely automatically with such complex and obscure situations is doomed to failure.

The purpose of this admittedly contrived example is to highlight the need for a systematic and structured approach to the design and provision of fault tolerance. Two issues are felt to be of vital importance. Firstly, it is essential that the system itself is designed by carefully identifying appropriate *structure* so that the interactions between the various components in the system can be understood, in order to retain mastery over the complexity of the system. The principle element of most methodologies for system construction is *modular decomposition,* that is, factoring the design task for the overall system into a set of subtasks each involving the design of a simpler and more manageable component (or module). In turn, these components may need to be decomposed further, leading to a hierarchical structuring of the system (which can be modelled by an assembly tree as discussed in Chapter 2). Each component supports interactions on the interface with its environment, and provides responses to requests for service by means of internal activity, relying on facilities provided by lower level components.

Secondly, this understanding and mastery of complexity must be achieved not only for normal interactions but also for the abnormal interactions which occur when component or design faults affect the system. For this to be possible it is highly desirable that a framework is adopted in which the normal activity of the system is clearly distinguished from its abnormal (i.e. fault tolerance) activity, and which includes provision for the automatic invocation of fault tolerance and subsequent return to normal processing. In order to maintain a clear separation between the normal and abnormal activity of a system, *exception handling* (described in Chapter 3) has been adopted throughout this book as the framework for implementing fault tolerance. The detection of an error results in the raising of an exception followed by automatic invocation of the appropriate exception handler. The other three phases of fault tolerance, namely damage assessment, error recovery and fault treatment, can then be provided by the handler with the aim of returning the system to normal operation.

Exception handling concepts are frequently applied to software systems and to the interpretive interface between hardware and software. However, it is felt that these concepts are equally applicable to the hardware of a system, even though they are rarely used in descriptions of hardware fault tolerance techniques. As far as software systems are concerned, exception handling facilities should be mechanized, since it is only then that the benefits to be obtained from the framework can be readily achieved. A computer architecture in which the interpreter supports an exception handling mechanism with the characteristics described in earlier chapters would be of major benefit to the implementation in software of fault tolerance for dealing with failures of both hardware and software components.

Exception handling and modular decomposition are important notions in their own right. However, these notions should not be considered in isolation for a fault tolerant system; it is necessary to consider the way in which they interact and can be combined. This combination leads to a unified model of exception handling in any system (hardware or software), and to the derivation of the characteristics of what will be referred to as an *ideal component*, that is, a component which is ideally suited to the coherent provision of fault tolerance, and whose characteristics should therefore be mirrored by the components from which a fault tolerant system is constructed. These characteristics are the subject of the next sub-section.

Ideal Fault Tolerant Components

The characteristics of an ideal component will be described with respect to the component illustrated in Figure 10.1. (This approach is a development of that presented by Wulf.)[1] An ideal component is, like any other component, part of some containing system (assumed to be at the top of Figure 10.1). As a result of the activity of that system the ideal component will receive requests to provide service. By means of normal activity, the ideal component will endeavor to provide this service, in accordance with its specification, and in order to do so will generate requests for service to its own internal sub-components. If these sub-components (assumed to be at the bottom of Figure 10.1) respond normally, and if no errors are detected by the ideal component, then a legal 'service request' will produce a 'normal response'.

Figure 10.1 shows the way in which different categories of exceptions fit into this framework. Consider first the exceptions which can be signalled by the ideal component to the containing system. The simplest case occurs when the ideal component receives an illegal request for service. As part of its normal activity the component is required to detect illegal service requests, and will then signal an *interface exception* to the containing system (which is assumed to be in error).

The situations which lead to the ideal component signalling a *failure exception* are more complex. Errors in the state of the component detected during its normal activity can be reported as any of three categories of exception (shown at the bottom of Figure 10.1): interface or failure exceptions signalled to the ideal component by a sub-component, or exceptions explicitly raised (i.e. by the **raise**

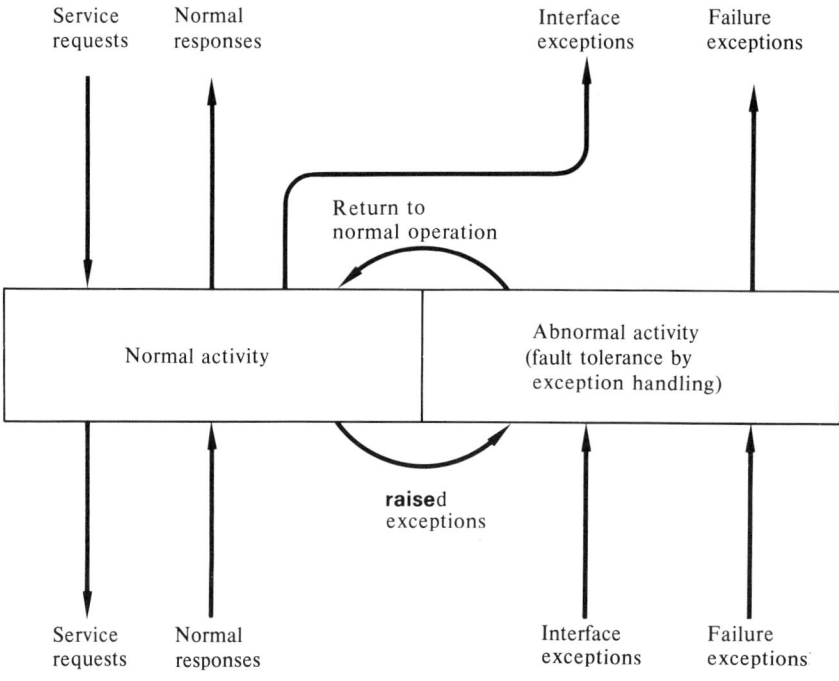

Figure 10.1 Ideal Fault Tolerant Component

instruction) when measures within the ideal component detect an error. Any of these exceptions will result in an exception handler (part of the abnormal activity of an ideal component) being invoked to provide fault tolerance. If the exception handler is successful the effects of the fault which caused the exception will be masked and the ideal component can return to normal operation without its service being impaired. Unfortunately, there may be circumstances in which this masking cannot be achieved, either because of

METHODOLOGY AND FRAMEWORK FOR FAULT TOLERANCE 299

inadequate provision for fault tolerance (e.g. no handler for a particular exception) or because of lack of service from sub-components. When it is recognized that normal activity cannot be resumed the ideal component must signal a *failure exception* to indicate that it cannot provide its normal service. The failure exception will indicate that the component is either about to fail, or has already failed. The significance of failure exceptions will be discussed further in the next sub-section.

It must be emphasized that only interface and failure exceptions from the ideal component are signalled to the containing system. None of the exceptions at the bottom of Figure 10.1 are allowed to pass directly to that system, and all are handled by the ideal component (as is advocated in Chapter 3). This is as it should be - when a system makes use of the service provided by a component it need not (and should not) have any information about how that service is implemented. Thus exceptions explicitly raised by the ideal component or signalled by sub-components would be meaningless to the containing system. For example, a software system providing users with facilities for statistical data analysis should not be expected to provide fault tolerance to cope with an exception such as 'Unit 4F not on-line' from a lower level component.

During the abnormal activity of an ideal component a number of interactions can occur which, for clarity, have been omitted from Figure 10.1. The provision of fault tolerance will certainly involve requests for service to, and response from, sub-components - the response can be normal or via interface or failure exceptions. Also, an exception handler can explicitly raise a further exception, either because it detects a new error or because it has performed diagnostic checking of sub-components for fault treatment.

In the framework presented here, a containing system can only issue requests for service to a component; it is not possible to request the component to resume some earlier request - a new request must be issued. In consequence, when an ideal component signals an exception its own activity is terminated, as advocated in Chapter 8. On termination, the internal state of the component must be consistent so that future requests for service do not generate further exceptions unnecessarily. One requirement which ensures consistency in a very disciplined fashion stipulates that when a component does not provide a normal response to a request for service it must revert to the (external) state it had at the time of the request. Thus a request for service must either be successfully completed by the component or appear to have had no effect on the component, which remains in its prior state. A simple method of meeting this requirement is for an ideal component to establish a recovery point when the request for service is received and then either discard or restore that recovery point as necessary.

Failure Exceptions

Although the signalling of failure exceptions has been an essential element of the above discussion it should be realized that their occurrence is to be prevented if at all possible. Ideally, of course, *faults* should be prevented; a truly ideal component is one which is always fault free. However, if the inevitable presence of faults leads to errors then (ideally) these should always be detected and fault tolerance employed to ensure that the ideal component never fails. It is much more appropriate and effective for errors in a component to be handled within the component, than for the containing system to have to try to deal with the problem of a failing component.

One of the problems in the provision of fault tolerance is precisely identifying the cause of an exception (the difficulties of which were discussed in Chapter 5). If in designing a system it can be assumed that components will never fail (either because of fault prevention or fault tolerance) then the provision of fault tolerance in that system will be greatly simplified - the only faults which can affect the system are design faults. Indeed, any exception raised by the system must be a consequence of a design fault, and appropriate strategies can be adopted by the exception handlers without further investigation.

In practice, however, component failures will occur. When fault prevention has not been wholly successful and fault tolerance within a component is unable to cope with the consequences, an ideal component will as a last resort acknowledge its deficiencies by signalling a failure exception to the containing system. For example, components containing only dynamic redundancy will have to signal a failure exception if an error is detected. Again this leads to a significant simplification of the fault tolerance in the containing system since, in the absence of failure exceptions, the system can rely upon its components. Moreover, the association of faults with exceptions is straightforward: component faults are directly identified by their failure exceptions; as before, other exceptions must be a consequence of design faults in the system. Diagnostic checks, usually necessary if the cause of errors is uncertain, will never need to be applied in a system constructed from components which always signal failure exceptions appropriately.

One practical situation in which the provision of failure exceptions is particularly important is on the interpretive interface between software and hardware. (The hardware interpreter can be regarded as a component providing services to a software process.) If it can be assumed that any fault in the interpreter is either successfully tolerated or results in the signalling of a failure exception to the process then the provision of fault tolerance in the process can be greatly simplified. The process will not need to execute diagnostic programs to ascertain whether an exception was due to a design fault or a failure of the interpreter since, in the absence of failure exceptions, all other exceptions can be attributed to design faults in the process itself. For anticipated failure exceptions, it is particularly convenient to provide handlers in an extension of the interpreter and thereby mask all faults of the interpreter from the process.

What can be done if an unanticipated failure exception is signalled to a system? Once again the answer is straightforward: not a lot. However, three general 'strategies' can be suggested.

(i) The pessimistic approach: the system signals a failure exception and then stops, ceasing to provide service. The rationale is that an unexpected situation will only get worse if attempts are made to continue; the failure exception requests intervention (usually manual) from a higher authority. (Divine intervention may be requested by signalling the exception higher still.)

(ii) The optimistic approach: the system proclaims 'business as usual' and attempts to carry on regardless. The hope here is that the component signalling the failure exception should not have done so and will not actually fail, or that even if it does fail it may not damage the system (much).

(iii) The pragmatic approach: the system explicitly raises an exception for which the handler provides fault tolerance appropriate for a design fault in the system. It may be that state restoration and the substitution of alternative algorithms will successfully avoid any recurrence of the component failure. They may not succeed, but what is there to lose?

Critical Components

Any fault tolerant system will be totally dependent upon the correct functioning of some critical components which are usually referred to as the *hardcore* of the system. In particular, it is vital that the measures and mechanisms provided for fault tolerance are themselves reliable, otherwise little confidence can be placed in the ability of the system to withstand faults. For example, the voter in a TMR system and the recovery cache in a system utilizing recovery blocks can be regarded as hardcore. In view of its critical role in the system, the hardcore must be designed to operate very reliably indeed. This can only be achieved by adopting fault prevention techniques to minimize the number of faults in the hardcore, or by incorporating further internal fault tolerance. By clearly separating the normal and abnormal activities of a system, the framework for fault tolerance adopted in this book ensures that the hardcore can be readily identified and hence efforts concentrated on improving its reliability.

There are two obvious difficulties though. Firstly, at some level the system must be built from components which are not fault tolerant (after all, to the best of current knowledge the operation of the Universe does not rely on the use of recovery points). Secondly, why should it be possible to achieve high reliability for the hardcore of a system any more easily than for the system itself? The resolution of these difficulties is simple. Indeed, simplicity is the key. The hardcore of a well-designed system must be simple; at least it must be much less complex than the rest of the system which depends on it. For example, the acceptance test of a recovery block needs to be simpler, and therefore less prone to faults, than the modules it checks. Juvenal[2] posed the question "But who is to guard the guards themselves?" to which the answer must (eventually) be "No one". Some guards, like some system components, just have to be trusted. All that can be done is to select honest guards and simple components.

THE FUTURE

It is inconceivable that the role of fault tolerance in computing systems will diminish; its importance can only increase. While most of the large-scale applications of fault tolerance have so far been in systems designed for specialized applications, there are clear indications of a widespread and growing demand for increased reliability in many areas, as witnessed by the commercial success of the Tandem 16 corporation.

Fault tolerance is already implemented in some of the components of current general-purpose computers. Many systems with semiconductor memory employ redundancy and fault tolerance to provide single-bit error correction and to signal a failure exception if multiple-bit errors occur. The advance of VLSI technology can only increase the extent to which fault tolerance is provided in systems, since the reductions in hardware costs that are available through VLSI are making the provision of redundancy, even massive redundancy, a much more economical proposition. For example, a complete check on the operation of a CPU would in the past have been a major and expensive undertaking, whereas the provision of replicated microprocessors now yields a straightforward, cheap and effective solution. This approach has been adopted in the Sperry Univac 1100/60 processor[3] at the microprogram level, where the arithmetic and logical operations required when a microinstruction is executed are performed by duplicated sub-processors connected to separate data buses. Outputs on the buses are compared and an exception is signalled if any discrepancy is detected.

A further opportunity for the effective utilization of fault tolerance is a consequence of pin limitations on VLSI circuits. The design of a VLSI circuit is more often constrained by the number of pins possible than by the permitted logic density. As a result, surplus silicon surface can be available within an integrated circuit and can be utilized by extra logic elements for fault tolerance (since very few, if any, extra pins will be needed). This could greatly increase the reliability of the components, or (more crudely) serve as a means of improving the yield from the manufacturing process. A generalized VLSI chip has been proposed by Sedmak and Liebergot[4] which uses additional internal logic to check the operation of the normal activity of the chip.

While VLSI may provide the basis for solutions to the problem of failing hardware components, software is and will remain a cloud on the reliability horizon. In the absence of fault prevention techniques which can guarantee the 'correctness' of software, faults in software systems (and hardware design faults) will have to be tolerated if failures are to be averted. For this reason, the previous chapter has discussed at length two proposed schemes for software fault tolerance. The application and effectiveness of these schemes in practical systems has yet to be demonstrated. However, the authors firmly believe that the importance of design fault tolerance in general, and software fault tolerance in particular, will soon be much more widely recognized. In consequence, design fault tolerance will become an essential part of systems for which high reliability is a prime requirement.

REFERENCES

1. W.A. Wulf, "Reliable Hardware/Software Architecture," *IEEE Transactions on Software Engineering* **SE-1**(2), pp.233-240 (June 1975).
2. Juvenal, p. 139 in *Bartlett's Familiar Quotations (14th edition)*, ed. E.M. Beck, Little Brown and Co., Boston (MA) (1968).
3. L.A. Boone, H.L. Liebergot, and R.M. Sedmak, "Availability, Reliability, and Maintainability Aspects of the Sperry Univac 1100/60," *Digest of Papers FTCS-10: 10th International Symposium on Fault-Tolerant Computing*, Kyoto, pp.3-8 (October 1980).
4. R.M. Sedmak and H.L. Liebergot, "Fault-Tolerance of a General Purpose Computer Implemented by Very Large Scale Integration," *IEEE Transactions on Computers* **C-29**(6), pp.492-500 (June 1980).

REFERENCES

1. J.A. Abrahams and D.P. Siewiorek, "An Algorithm for the Accurate Reliability Evaluation of Triple Modular Redundancy Networks," *IEEE Transactions on Computers* **C-23**(7), pp.652-692 (July 1974).
2. A.K. Agrawala and T.G. Rauscher, *Foundations of Microprogramming*, Academic Press, New York (1976).
3. R.P. Almquist et al., "Software Protection in No. 1 ESS," *International Switching Symposium Record*, Cambridge (MA), pp.565-569 (June 1972).
4. T. Anderson and R. Kerr, "Recovery Blocks in Action: A System Supporting High Reliability," *Proceedings of 2nd International Conference on Software Engineering*, San Francisco (CA), pp.447-457 (October 1976).
5. T. Anderson and J.C. Knight, "Practical Software Fault Tolerance for Real-Time Systems," ICASE Report 81-10, NASA Langley Research Center, Hampton (VA) (May 1981).
6. T. Anderson and P.A. Lee, "The Provision of Recoverable Interfaces," *Digest of Papers FTCS-9: Ninth Annual International Symposium on Fault-Tolerant Computing*, Madison (WI), pp.87-94 (June 1979).
7. T. Anderson, P.A. Lee, and S.K. Shrivastava, "A Model of Recoverability in Multilevel Systems," *IEEE Transactions on Software Engineering* **SE-4**(6), pp.486-494 (November 1978).
8. T. Anderson and B. Randell (eds.), *Computing Systems Reliability*, Cambridge University Press, Cambridge (1979).
9. T. Anderson and R.W. Witty, "Safe Programming," *BIT* **18**, pp.1-8 (1978).
10. D.M. Andrews, "Using Executable Assertions for Testing and Fault Tolerance," *Digest of Papers FTCS-9: Ninth Annual International Symposium on Fault-Tolerant Computing*, Madison (WI), pp.102-105 (June 1979).
11. Anon., "Blown Balloons," *Aviation Week & Space Technology*, p.17 (September 20 1971).
12. M.M. Astrahan et al., "System R: Relational Approach to Database Management," *ACM Transactions on Database Systems* **1**(2), pp.97-137 (June 1976).
13. A. Avizienis, "Arithmetic Error Codes: Cost and Effectiveness Studies for Applications in Digital Systems Design," *IEEE Transactions on Computers* **C-20**(11), pp.1322-1331 (November 1971).

14. A. Avizienis, "Arithmetic Algorithms for Error-Coded Operands," *IEEE Transactions on Computers* **C-22**(6), pp.567-572 (June 1973).
15. A. Avizienis, "Fault-Tolerant Systems," *IEEE Transactions on Computers* **C-25**(12), pp.1304-1312 (December 1976).
16. A. Avizienis, "Fault-Tolerance: The Survival Attribute of Digital Systems," *Proceedings of the IEEE* **66**(10), pp.1109-1125 (October 1978).
17. A. Avizienis and L. Chen, "On the Implementation of N-Version Programming for Software Fault-Tolerance During Program Execution," *Proceedings COMPSAC 77*, Chicago (IL), pp.149-155 (November 1977).
18. A. Avizienis and D.A. Rennels, "Fault-Tolerance Experiments with the JPL-STAR Computer," *Digest of Papers COMPCON 72*, San Francisco (CA), pp.321-324 (September 1972).
19. A. Avizienis et al., "The STAR (Self-Testing and Repairing) Computer: An Investigation of the Theory and Practice of Fault-Tolerant Computer Design," *IEEE Transactions on Computers* **C-20**(11), pp.1312-1321 (November 1971).
20. J.M. Ayache, P. Azema, and M. Diaz, "Observer: A Concept for On-Line Detection of Control Errors," *Digest of Papers FTCS-9: Ninth Annual International Symposium on Fault-Tolerant Computing*, Madison (WI), pp.79-86 (June 1979).
21. R.E. Barlow and F. Proschan, *Mathematical Theory of Reliability*, Wiley, New York (1965).
22. R.E. Barlow and F. Proschan, *Statistical Theory of Reliability and Life Testing*, Holt Rinehart and Winston, New York (1975).
23. J.F. Bartlett, "A 'NonStop' Operating System," *Proceedings of Eleventh Hawaii International Conference on System Sciences*, Honolulu (HA), pp.103-117 (January 1978).
24. H.B. Baskin, B.R. Borgerson, and R. Roberts, "PRIME - A Modular Architecture for Terminal-Oriented Systems," *AFIPS Conference Proceedings 1972 SJCC* **40**, Atlantic City (NJ), pp.431-437 (May 1972).
25. L.A. Belady and M.M. Lehman, "A Model of Large Program Development," *IBM Systems Journal* **15**(3), pp.225-252 (1976).
26. Bell Laboratories, "LAMP: Logic Analyser for Maintenance Planning," *Bell System Technical Journal* **53**(8), pp.1431-1555 (October 1974).
27. Bell Laboratories, "ESS No. 1A Processor," *Bell Systems Technical Journal* **56**(2) (February 1977).

28. E. Best, "Atomicity of Activities," pp. 225-250 in *Lecture Notes in Computer Science 84*, ed. W. Brauer, Springer-Verlag, Berlin (1980).
29. E. Best and F. Cristian, "Systematic Detection of Exception Occurrences," Technical Report 165, Computing Laboratory, University of Newcastle upon Tyne (April 1981).
30. G.M. Birtwistle et al., *SIMULA BEGIN*, Van Nostrand Reinhold, New York (1973).
31. L.A. Bjork, "Recovery Scenario for a DB/DC System," *Proceedings of 1973 ACM Annual Conference*, Atlanta (GA), pp.142-146 (August 1973).
32. L.A. Bjork, "Generalized Audit Trail Requirements and Concepts for Data Base Applications," *IBM Systems Journal* **14**(3), pp.229-245 (1975).
33. J.P. Black, D.J. Taylor, and D.E. Morgan, "A Case Study in Fault Tolerant Software," *Software - Practice and Experience* **11**(2), pp.145-157 (February 1981).
34. S. Bloom, M.J. McPheters, and S.H. Tsiang, "Software Quality Control," *Record of 1973 IEEE Symposium on Computer Software Reliability*, New York, pp.107-116 (May 1973).
35. B.W. Boehm, "Software and its Impact: A Quantitative Assessment," *Datamation* **19**(5), pp.48-59 (May 1973).
36. L.A. Boone, H.L. Liebergot, and R.M. Sedmak, "Availability, Reliability, and Maintainability Aspects of the Sperry Univac 1100/60," *Digest of Papers FTCS-10: 10th International Symposium on Fault-Tolerant Computing*, Kyoto, pp.3-8 (October 1980).
37. B.R. Borgerson, "A Fail-Softly System for Time-Sharing Use," *Digest of Papers: 1972 International Symposium on Fault-Tolerant Computing*, Newton (MA), pp.89-93 (June 1972).
38. B.R. Borgerson, "Spontaneous Reconfiguration in a Fail Softly Computer Utility," *Datafair 73 Conference Papers*, Nottingham, pp.326-333 (April 1973).
39. B.R. Borgerson and R.F. Freitas, "An Analysis of PRIME Using a New Reliability Model," *Digest of Papers FTC-4: Fourth Annual International Symposium on Fault-Tolerant Computing*, Urbana (IL), pp.2.26-2.31 (January 1974).
40. W.G. Bouricius et al., "Reliability Modeling Techniques for Fault Tolerant Computers," *IEEE Transactions on Computers* **C-20**(11), pp.1306-1311 (November 1971).
41. P.W. Bowman et al., "Maintenance Software," *Bell System Technical Journal* **56**(2), pp.255-287 (February 1977).
42. R. Boyd, "Restoral of a Real Time Operating System," *Proceedings of 1971 ACM Annual Conference*, Chicago (IL), pp.109-111 (August 1971).

43. A. Brandwajn and R. Joly, "A Scheme for a Fault-Tolerant Virtual Memory," *Information Processing Letters* **10**(2), pp.99-103 (March 1980).
44. J.K. Buckle, *The ICL 2900 Series*, Macmillan, London (1978).
45. D.D. Burchby, L.W. Kern, and W.A. Sturm, "Specification of the Fault-Tolerant Spaceborne Computer," *Proceedings FTCS-6: 1976 International Symposium on Fault-Tolerant Computing*, Pittsburgh (PA), pp.129-133 (June 1976).
46. R.H. Campbell, K.H. Horton, and G.G. Belford, "Simulations of a Fault-Tolerant Deadline Mechanism," *Digest of Papers FTCS-9: Ninth Annual International Symposium on Fault-Tolerant Computing*, Madison (WI), pp.95-101 (June 1979).
47. W.C. Carter, "Hardware Reliability," pp. 211-263 in *Computing Systems Reliability*, ed. T. Anderson and B. Randell, Cambridge University Press, Cambridge (1979).
48. W.C. Carter et al., "Cost Effectiveness of a Self Checking Computer Design," *Proceedings FTCS-7: Seventh Annual International Conference on Fault-Tolerant Computing*, Los Angeles (CA), pp.117-123 (June 1977).
49. K.M. Chandy et al., "Analytic Models for Rollback and Recovery Strategies in Data Base Systems," *IEEE Transactions on Software Engineering* **SE-1**(1), pp.100-110 (March 1975).
50. L. Chen, "Improving Software Reliability by N-Version Programming," UCLA-ENG-7843, Computer Science Department, University of California at Los Angeles (CA) (August 1978).
51. L. Chen and A. Avizienis, "N-Version Programming: A Fault-Tolerance Approach to Reliability of Software Operation," *Digest of Papers FTCS-8: Eighth Annual International Conference on Fault-Tolerant Computing*, Toulouse, pp.3-9 (June 1978).
52. G.F. Clement and R.D. Royer, "Recovery from Faults in the No. 1A Processor," *Digest of Papers FTC-4: Fourth Annual International Symposium on Fault-Tolerant Computing*, Urbana (IL), pp.5.2-5.7 (January 1974).
53. E.G. Coffman, M.J. Elphick, and A. Shoshani, "System Deadlocks," *Computing Surveys* **3**(2), pp.67-78 (June 1971).
54. E. Cohen and D. Jefferson, "Protection in The Hydra Operating System," *Operating Systems Review* **9**(5), pp.141-160 (November 1975).
55. R.B. Conn, N.A. Alexandridis, and A. Avizienis, "Design of a Fault-Tolerant, Modular Computer with Dynamic Redundancy," *AFIPS Conference Proceedings 1972 FJCC* **41**, Anaheim (CA), pp.1057-1067 (December 1972).

REFERENCES

56. J.R. Connet, E.J. Pasternak, and B.D. Wagner, "Software Defenses in Real-Time Control Systems," *Digest of Papers: 1972 International Symposium on Fault-Tolerant Computing*, Newton (MA), pp.94-99 (June 1972).
57. A.E. Cooper and W.T. Chow, "Development of On-Board Space Computer Systems," *IBM Journal of Research and Development* **20**(1), pp.5-19 (January 1976).
58. D.C. Cosserat, "A Capability Oriented Multi-Processor System for Real-Time Applications," *First International Conference on Computer Communications*, Washington (DC), pp.282-289 (October 1972).
59. F. Cristian, "Exception Handling and Software-Fault Tolerance," *Digest of Papers FTCS-10: 10th International Symposium on Fault-Tolerant Computing Systems*, Kyoto, pp.97-103 (October 1980).
60. F. Cristian, "Robust Data Abstractions," *Acta Informatica* (To Appear).
61. R.M. Curtice, "Integrity in Data Base Systems," *Datamation* **23**(5), pp.64-68 (May 1977).
62. O.-J. Dahl, E.W. Dijkstra, and C.A.R. Hoare, *Structured Programming*, Academic Press, London (1972).
63. C.T. Davies, "Recovery Semantics for a DB/DC System," *Proceedings of 1973 ACM Annual Conference*, Atlanta (GA), pp.136-141 (August 1973).
64. C.T. Davies, "Data Processing Spheres of Control," *IBM Systems Journal* **17**(2), pp.179-198 (1978).
65. C.T. Davies, "Data Processing Integrity," pp. 288-354 in *Computing Systems Reliability*, ed. T. Anderson and B. Randell, Cambridge University Press, Cambridge (1979).
66. D. DeAngelis and J.A. Lauro, "Software Recovery in the Fault-Tolerant Spaceborne Computer," *Proceedings FTCS-6: 1976 International Symposium on Fault-Tolerant Computing*, Pittsburgh (PA), pp.143-147 (June 1976).
67. P.J. Denning, "Fault Tolerant Operating Systems," *Computing Surveys* **8**(4), pp.359-389 (December 1976).
68. E.W. Dijkstra, "Cooperating Sequential Processes," pp. 43-112 in *Programming Languages*, ed. F. Genuys, Academic Press, London (1968).
69. E.W. Dijkstra, "The Structure of the 'THE' Multiprogramming System," *Communications of the ACM* **11**(5), pp.341-346 (May 1968).
70. E.W. Dijkstra, *A Discipline of Programming*, Prentice-Hall, Englewood Cliffs (NJ) (1976).

71. R.W. Downing, J.S. Nowak, and L.S. Tuomenoksa, "The No. 1 ESS Maintenance Plan," *Bell System Technical Journal* **43**(5), pp.1961-2020 (September 1964).
72. W.R. Elmendorf, "Fault-Tolerant Programming," *Digest of Papers: 1972 International Symposium on Fault-Tolerant Computing*, Newton (MA), pp.79-83 (June 1972).
73. D.M. England, "Operating System of System 250," *International Switching Symposium Record*, Cambridge (MA), pp.525-529 (June 1972).
74. D.M. England, "Capability Concept Mechanisms and Structure in System 250," *International Workshop on Protection in Operating Systems*, Rocquencourt, pp.63-82 (August 1974).
75. K.P. Eswaran and D.D. Chamberlin, "Functional Specification of a Subsystem for Database Integrity," *Proceedings of International Conference on Very Large Data Bases* **1**(1), Framingham (MA), pp.48-68 (September 1975).
76. K.P. Eswaran et al., "The Notion of Consistency and Predicate Locks in a Data Base System," *Communications of the ACM* **19**(11), pp.624-633 (November 1976).
77. R.S. Fabry, "Dynamic Verification of Operating System Decisions," *Communications of the ACM* **16**(11), pp.659-668 (November 1973).
78. E.A. Feustel, "The Rice Research Computer - A Tagged Architecture," *AFIPS Conference Proceedings 1972 SJCC* **40**, Atlantic City (NJ), pp.369-377 (May 1972).
79. E.A. Feustel, "On The Advantages of Tagged Architecture," *IEEE Transactions on Computers* **C-22**(7), pp.644-656 (July 1973).
80. M.A. Fischler, O. Firschein, and D.L. Drew, "Distinct Software: An Approach to Reliable Computing," *Proceedings of Second USA-Japan Computer Conference*, Tokyo, pp.573-579 (August 1975).
81. A.G. Fraser, "Integrity of a Mass Storage Filing System," *Computer Journal* **12**(1), pp.1-5 (February 1969).
82. J. Gall, *Systemantics: How Systems Work and Especially How They Fail*, Pocket Books, New York (1978).
83. E. Gelenbe, "On the Optimum Checkpoint Interval," *Journal of the ACM* **26**(2), pp.259-270 (April 1979).
84. E. Gelenbe and D. Derochette, "Performance of Rollback Recovery Systems under Intermittent Failures," *Communications of the ACM* **21**(6), pp.493-499 (June 1978).
85. S.L. Gerhart and L. Yelowitz, "Observations of Fallibility in Applications of Modern Programming Methodologies," *IEEE Transactions on Software Engineering* **SE-2**(3), pp.195-207 (September 1976).

86. T. Gilb, "Parallel Programming," *Datamation* **20**(10), pp.160-161 (October 1974).
87. T. Gilb, "Distinct Software: A Redundancy Technique for Reliable Software," pp. 117-133 in *State of the Art Report on Software Reliability*, Infotech, Maidenhead (1977).
88. T. Gilb, *Software Metrics*, Winthrop, Cambridge (MA) (1977).
89. J.B. Goodenough, "Exception Handling: Issues and a Proposed Notation," *Communications of the ACM* **18**(12), pp.683-696 (December 1975).
90. J.N. Gray, "Notes on Data Base Operating Systems," pp. 393-481 in *Lecture Notes in Computer Science 60*, ed. R. Bayer, R.M. Graham and G. Seegmuller, Springer-Verlag, Berlin (1978).
91. J.N. Gray et al., "Granularity of Locks and Degrees of Consistency in a Shared Data Base," pp. 365-394 in *Modelling in Data Base Management Systems*, ed. G.M. Nijssen, North-Holland, Amsterdam (1976).
92. J.N. Gray et al., "The Recovery Manager of a Data Management System," Report RJ2623, IBM Research Laboratory, San Jose (CA) (August 1979).
93. A. Grnarov, J. Arlatt, and A. Avizienis, "On the Performance of Software Fault-Tolerance Strategies," *Digest of Papers FTCS-10: 10th International Symposium on Fault-Tolerant Computing*, Kyoto, pp.251-253 (October 1980).
94. J.V. Guttag and J.J. Horning, "Formal Specification as a Design Tool," *Conference Record of Seventh Annual ACM Symposium on Principles of Programming Languages*, Las Vegas (NV), pp.251-261 (January 1980).
95. D. Halton, "Hardware of the System 250 for Communications Control," *International Switching Symposium Record*, Cambridge (MA), pp.530-536 (June 1972).
96. K.J. Hamer-Hodges, "Fault Resistance and Recovery Within System 250," *First International Conference on Computer Communications*, Washington (DC), pp.290-296 (October 1972).
97. P. Brinch Hansen, *Operating System Principles*, Prentice-Hall, Englewood Cliffs (NJ) (1973).
98. F.E. Heart et al., "A New Minicomputer/Multiprocessor for the ARPA Network," *AFIPS Conference Proceedings 1973 NCC and Exposition* **42**, New York, pp.529-537 (June 1973).
99. H. Hecht, "Fault Tolerant Software for Real-Time Applications," *Computing Surveys* **8**(4), pp.391-407 (December 1976).

100. H. Hecht, "Fault-Tolerant Software," *IEEE Transactions on Reliability* **R-28**(3), pp.227-232 (August 1979).

101. C.A.R. Hoare, "Monitors: An Operating System Structuring Concept," *Communications of the ACM* **17**(10), pp.549-557 (October 1974).

102. C.A.R. Hoare, "Parallel Programming: An Axiomatic Approach," pp. 11-42 in *Lecture Notes in Computer Science 46*, ed. F.L. Bauer and K. Samelson, Springer-Verlag, Berlin (1976).

103. R.C. Holt, "Some Deadlock Properties of Computer Systems," *Computing Surveys* **4**(3), pp.177-196 (September 1972).

104. A.L. Hopkins and T.B. Smith, "The Architectural Elements of a Symmetric Fault-Tolerant Multiprocessor," *IEEE Transactions on Computers* **C-24**(5), pp.498-505 (May 1975).

105. A.L. Hopkins, T.B. Smith, and J.H. Lala, "FTMP - A Highly Reliable Fault-Tolerant Multiprocessor for Aircraft," *Proceedings of the IEEE* **66**(10), pp.1221-1240 (October 1978).

106. J.J. Horning and B. Randell, "Process Structuring," *Computing Surveys* **5**(1), pp.5-30 (March 1973).

107. J.J. Horning *et al.*, "A Program Structure for Error Detection and Recovery," pp. 171-187 in *Lecture Notes in Computer Science 16*, ed. E. Gelenbe and C. Kaiser, Springer-Verlag, Berlin (1974).

108. IBM, "An Application-Oriented Multiprocessing System," *IBM Systems Journal* **6**(2), pp.78-132 (1967).

109. H. Ihara *et al.*, "Fault-Tolerant Computer System with Three Symmetric Computers," *Proceedings of the IEEE* **66**(10), pp.1160-1177 (October 1978).

110. J.K. Iliffe, *Basic Machine Principles*, Macdonald, London (1968).

111. K. Jackson and C.I. Moir, "Parallel Processing in Software and Hardware - the MASCOT Approach," *Proceedings of 1975 Sagamore Computer Conference on Parallel Processing*, Sagamore (NY), pp.71-78 (August 1975).

112. A.K. Jones, "Protection Mechanisms and The Enforcement of Security Policies," pp. 228-251 in *Lecture Notes in Computer Science 60*, ed. R. Bayer, R.M. Graham and G. Seegmuller, Springer-Verlag, Berlin (1978).

113. W.C. Jones and S.H. Tsiang, "Reliability Experience of a Fault Tolerant Switching System," *National Telecommunications Conference Record*, New Orleans (LA), pp.5.1-5.7 (December 1975).

114. Juvenal, p. 139 in *Bartlett's Familiar Quotations (14th edition)*, ed. E.M. Beck, Little Brown and Co., Boston (MA) (1968).

115. D. Katsuki et al., "Pluribus - An Operational Fault-Tolerant Multiprocessor," *Proceedings of the IEEE* **66**(10), pp.1146-1159 (October 1978).

116. J.A. Katzman, "A Fault-Tolerant Computing System," *Proceedings of Eleventh Hawaii International Conference on System Sciences*, Honolulu (HA), pp.85-102 (January 1978).

117. P.J. Kennedy and T.M. Quinn, "Recovery Strategies in the No. 2 Electronic Switching System," *Digest of Papers: 1972 International Symposium on Fault-Tolerant Computing*, Newton (MA), pp.165-169 (June 1972).

118. R. Kerr, "An Experimental Processor Architecture for Improved Reliability," pp. 199-212 in *State of the Art Report on System Reliability and Integrity*, Infotech, Maidenhead (1978).

119. K.H. Kim, "An Approach to Programmer-Transparent Coordination of Recovering Parallel Processes and its Efficient Implementation Rules," *Proceedings of International Conference on Parallel Processing*, Detroit (MI), pp.58-68 (August 1978).

120. K.H. Kim and C.V. Ramamoorthy, "Failure-Tolerant Parallel Programming and its Supporting System Architecture," *AFIPS Conference Proceedings 1976 NCC* **45**, New York, pp.413-423 (June 1976).

121. K.H. Kim et al., "Strategies for Structured and Fault-Tolerant Design of Recovery Programs," *Proceedings COMPSAC 78*, Chicago (IL), pp.651-656 (November 1978).

122. D.E. Knuth, *The Art of Computer Programming Vols.1-3*, Addison-Wesley, Reading (MA) (1968-).

123. H. Kopetz, "Software Redundancy in Real Time Systems," *IFIP Congress 74*, Stockholm, pp.182-186 (August 1974).

124. J.H. Lala and A.L. Hopkins, "Survival and Dispatch Probability Models for the FTMP Computer," *Digest of Papers FTCS-8: Eighth Annual International Conference on Fault-Tolerant Computing*, Toulouse, pp.37-43 (June 1978).

125. B.W. Lampson, "A Note on the Confinement Problem," *Communications of the ACM* **16**(10), pp.613-615 (October 1973).

126. P.A. Lee, "A Reconsideration of the Recovery Block Scheme," *Computer Journal* **21**(4), pp.306-310 (November 1978).

127. P.A. Lee, N. Ghani, and K. Heron, "A Recovery Cache for the PDP-11," *IEEE Transactions on Computers* **C-29**(6), pp.546-549 (June 1980).

128. R.A. Levin, "Program Structures for Exceptional Condition Handling," Ph.D. Thesis, Carnegie Mellon University, Pittsburgh (PA) (1977).

129. O.B. von Linde, "Computers Can Now Perform Vital Functions Safely," *Railway Gazette International* **135**(11), pp.1004-1006 (November 1979).

130. T.A. Linden, "Operating System Structures to Support Security and Reliable Software," *Computing Surveys* **8**(4), pp.409-445 (December 1976).

131. B.H. Liskov, "The Design of the Venus Operating System," *Communications of the ACM* **15**(3), pp.144-149 (March 1972).

132. B.H. Liskov and A. Snyder, "Exception Handling in CLU," *IEEE Transactions on Software Engineering* **SE-5**(6), pp.546-558 (November 1979).

133. B.H. Liskov and S.N. Zilles, "An Introduction to Formal Specifications of Data Abstractions," pp. 1-32 in *Current Trends in Programming Methodology, Vol. 1*, ed. R.T. Yeh, Prentice-Hall, Englewood Cliffs (NJ) (1977).

134. B. Littlewood, "A Bayesian Differential Debugging Model for Software Reliability," *Workshop on Quantitative Software Models*, Kiamesha Lake (NY), pp.170-181 (October 1979).

135. B. Littlewood, "How to Measure Software Reliability and How Not To," *IEEE Transactions on Reliability* **R-28**(2), pp.103-110 (June 1979).

136. D.B. Lomet, "Process Structuring, Synchronization and Recovery Using Atomic Actions," *SIGPLAN Notices* **12**(3), pp.128-137 (March 1977).

137. D.B. Lomet, "Subsystems of Processes with Deadlock Avoidance," *IEEE Transactions on Software Engineering* **SE-6**(3), pp.297-304 (May 1980).

138. A.B. Long et al., "A Methodology for the Development and Validation of Critical Software for Nuclear Power Plants," *Proceedings COMPSAC 77*, Chicago (IL), pp.620-626 (November 1977).

139. D.C. Luckham and W. Polak, "Ada Exception Handling: An Axiomatic Approach," *ACM Transactions on Programming Languages and Systems* **2**(2), pp.225-233 (April 1980).

140. M.D. MacLaren, "Exception Handling in PL/I," *SIGPLAN Notices* **12**(3), pp.101-104 (March 1977).

141. D. Mackie, "The Tandem 16 NonStop System," pp. 145-161 in *State of the Art Report on System Reliability and Integrity*, Infotech, Maidenhead (1978).

142. G.H. Maestri, "The Retryable Processor," *AFIPS Conference Proceedings 1972 FJCC* **41**, Anaheim (CA), pp.273-277 (December 1972).

143. F.P. Maison, "The MECRA: A Self-Reconfigurable Computer for Highly Reliable Processes," *IEEE Transactions on Computers* **C-20**(11), pp.1382-1388 (November 1971).

144. M.E. Majster, "Treatment of Partial Operations in the Algebraic Specification Technique," *Proceedings of Conference on Specifications of Reliable Software*, Boston (MA), pp.190-197 (April 1979).

145. W.F. Mann, S.M. Ornstein, and M.F. Kraley, "A Network-Oriented Multiprocessor Front-End Handling Many Hosts and Hundreds of Terminals," *AFIPS Conference Proceedings 1976 NCC* **45**, New York, pp.533-540 (June 1976).

146. P.M. Melliar-Smith, "System Specification," pp. 19-65 in *Computing Systems Reliability*, ed. T. Anderson and B. Randell, Cambridge University Press, Cambridge (1979).

147. P.M. Melliar-Smith and B. Randell, "Software Reliability: The Role of Programmed Exception Handling," *SIGPLAN Notices* **12**(3), pp.95-100 (March 1977).

148. C. Meraud, F. Browaeys, and G. Germain, "Automatic Rollback Techniques of the COPRA Computer," *Proceedings FTCS-6: 1976 International Symposium on Fault-Tolerant Computing*, Pittsburgh (PA), pp.23-29 (June 1976).

149. C. Meraud and P. Lloret, "COPRA: A Modular Family of Reconfigurable Computers," *Proceedings of IEEE 1978 National Aerospace and Electronics Conference*, Dayton (OH), pp.822-827 (May 1978).

150. P.M. Merlin and B. Randell, "State Restoration in Distributed Systems," *Digest of Papers FTCS-8: Eigth Annual International Conference on Fault-Tolerant Computing*, Toulouse, pp.129-134 (June 1978).

151. M.N. Meyers, W.A. Roult, and K.W. Yoder, "No. 4 ESS: Maintenance Software," *Bell System Technical Journal* **56**(7), pp.1139-1167 (September 1977).

152. G.E. Migneault, "Software Reliability and Advanced Avionics," *AFIPS Conference Proceedings 1980 NCC* **49**, Anaheim (CA), pp.715-720 (May 1980).

153. J.G. Mitchell, W. Maybury, and R. Sweet, "Mesa Language Manual (Version 5.0)," CSL-79-3, Xerox Palo Alto Research Center (CA) (April 1979).

154. P.B. Moranda, "Software Quality Technology," *Computer* **11**(11), pp.72-78 (November 1978).

155. A. de Morgan, *A Budget of Paradoxes*, Longmans Green, London (1872).

156. D.E. Morgan and D.J. Taylor, "A Survey of Methods of Achieving Reliable Software," *Computer*, pp.44-53 (February 1977).

157. D.R. Musser, "Abstract Data Type Specification in the AFFIRM System," *IEEE Transactions on Software Engineering* **SE-6**(1), pp.24-32 (January 1980).

158. G.J. Myers, *Software Reliability: Principles and Practices*, Wiley, New York (1976).
159. G.J. Myers, *Advances in Computer Architecture*, Wiley, New York (1978).
160. P. Naur, "Software Reliability," pp. 243-251 in *State of the Art Report on Software Reliability*, Infotech, Maidenhead (1977).
161. R.M. Needham, "Protection," pp. 264-287 in *Computing Systems Reliability*, ed. T. Anderson and B. Randell, Cambridge University Press, Cambridge (1979).
162. R.M. Needham and R.D.H. Walker, "The Cambridge CAP Computer and its Protection System," *Proceedings of 6th Symposium on Operating System Principles*, West Lafayette (IN), pp.1-10 (November 1977).
163. J. von Neumann, "Probabilistic Logics and the Synthesis of Reliable Organisms from Unreliable Components," pp. 43-98 in *Automata Studies*, ed. C.E. Shannon and J. McCarthy, Princeton University Press, Princeton (NJ) (1956).
164. Y-W. Ng and A. Avizienis, "A Reliability Model for Gracefully Degrading and Repairable Fault-Tolerant Systems," *Proceedings FTCS-7: Seventh Annual International Conference on Fault-Tolerant Computing*, Los Angeles (CA), pp.22-28 (June 1977).
165. F.J. O'Brien, "Rollback Point Insertion Strategies," *Proceedings FTCS-6: 1976 International Symposium on Fault-Tolerant Computing*, Pittsburgh (PA), pp.138-142 (June 1976).
166. E.I. Organick, *Computer System Organization: The B5700/6700 Series*, Academic Press, New York (1973).
167. S.M. Ornstein et al., "Pluribus - A Reliable Multiprocessor," *AFIPS Conference Proceedings 1975 NCC* **44**, Anaheim (CA), pp.551-559 (May 1975).
168. D.L. Parnas, "On The Criteria to be Used in Decomposing Systems Into Modules," *Communications of the ACM* **15**(12), pp.1053-1058 (December 1972).
169. D.L. Parnas, "On a Buzzword: Hierarchical Structure," *IFIP Congress 74*, Stockholm, pp.336-339 (August 1974).
170. W.W. Peterson and E.J. Weldon Jr, *Error-Correcting Codes*, MIT Press, Cambridge (MA) (1972).
171. B. Randell, "System Structure for Software Fault Tolerance," pp. 195-219 in *Current Trends in Programming Methodology, Vol. 1*, ed. R.T. Yeh, Prentice-Hall, Englewood Cliffs (NJ) (1977).
172. B. Randell, P.A. Lee, and P.C. Treleaven, "Reliability Issues in Computing System Design," *Computing Surveys* **10**(2), pp.123-165 (June 1978).

REFERENCES

173. J.-C. Rault, "The Many Facets of Quantitative Assessment of Software Reliability," *Workshop on Quantitative Software Models*, Kiamesha Lake (NY), pp.224-231 (October 1979).
174. D.D. Redell and R.S. Fabry, "Selective Revocation of Capabilities," *International Workshop on Protection in Operating Systems*, Rocquencourt, pp.197-210 (August 1974).
175. R.M. Reiss, "A Prediction Experiment with Three Software Reliability Models," *Workshop on Quantitative Software Models*, Kiamesha Lake (NY), pp.190-200 (October 1979).
176. D.A. Rennels, "Architectures for Fault-Tolerant Spacecraft Computers," *Proceedings of the IEEE* **66**(10), pp.1255-1268 (October 1978).
177. C.S. Repton, "Reliability Assurance for System 250, A Reliable, Real-Time Control System," *First International Conference on Computer Communications*, Washington (DC), pp.297-305 (October 1972).
178. J.G. Robinson and E.S. Roberts, "Software Fault-Tolerance in the Pluribus," *AFIPS Conference Proceedings 1978 NCC* **47**, Anaheim (CA), pp.563-569 (June 1978).
179. J.A. Rohr, "STAREX Self-Repair Routines: Software Recovery in the JPL-STAR Computer," *Digest of Papers FTC/3: 73 International Symposium on Fault-Tolerant Computing*, Palo Alto (CA), pp.11-16 (June 1973).
180. D.T. Ross, "Structured Analysis (SA): A Language for Communicating Ideas," *IEEE Transactions on Software Engineering* **SE-3**(1), pp.16-34 (January 1977).
181. D.L. Russell, "Process Backup in Producer-Consumer Systems," *Proceedings of Sixth ACM Symposium on Operating Systems Principles*, West Lafayette (IN), pp.151-157 (November 1977).
182. D.L. Russell, "State Restoration in Systems of Communicating Processes," *IEEE Transactions on Software Engineering* **SE-6**(2), pp.183-194 (March 1980).
183. D.L. Russell and M.J. Tiedeman, "Multiprocess Recovery Using Conversations," *Digest of Papers FTCS-9: Ninth Annual International Symposium on Fault-Tolerant Computing*, Madison (WI), pp.106-109 (June 1979).
184. J.H. Saltzer, "Protection and the Control of Information Sharing in Multics," *Communications of the ACM* **17**(7), pp.388-402 (July 1974).
185. J.H. Saltzer and M.D. Schroeder, "The Protection of Information in Computer Systems," *Proceedings of the IEEE* **63**(9), pp.1278-1308 (September 1975).

186. E.J. Salzman, "An Experiment in Producing Highly Reliable Software," M.Sc. Dissertation, Computing Laboratory, University of Newcastle upon Tyne (1978).
187. E. Sandewall, "An Approach to the Frame Problem, and its Implementation," pp. 195-204 in *Machine Intelligence* 7, ed. B. Meltzer and D. Michie, Edinburgh University Press, Edinburgh (1972).
188. M.D. Schroeder and J.H. Saltzer, "A Hardware Architecture for Implementing Protection Rings," *Communications of the ACM* 15(3), pp.157-170 (March 1972).
189. R.M. Sedmak and H.L. Liebergot, "Fault-Tolerance of a General Purpose Computer Implemented by Very Large Scale Integration," *IEEE Transactions on Computers* C-29(6), pp.492-500 (June 1980).
190. D.G. Severance and G.M. Lohman, "Differential Files: their Application to the Maintenance of Large Databases," *ACM Transactions on Database Systems* 1(3), pp.256-267 (September 1976).
191. C.T. Sheridan, "Space Shuttle Software," *Datamation* 24(7), pp.128-140 (July 1978).
192. M.L. Shooman, *Probabilistic Reliability: An Engineering Approach*, McGraw-Hill, New York (1968).
193. R.A. Short, "The Attainment of Reliable Digital Systems Through the Use of Redundancy - A Survey," *IEEE Computer Group News* 2(2), pp.2-17 (March 1968).
194. S.K. Shrivastava, "Sequential Pascal with Recovery Blocks," *Software - Practice and Experience* 8(2), pp.177-185 (March 1978).
195. S.K. Shrivastava, "Concurrent Pascal with Backward Error Recovery: Implementation," *Software - Practice and Experience* 9(12), pp.1021-1033 (December 1979).
196. S.K. Shrivastava, "Concurrent Pascal with Backward Error Recovery: Language Features and Examples," *Software - Practice and Experience* 9(12), pp.1001-1020 (December 1979).
197. S.K. Shrivastava and A.A. Akinpelu, "Fault Tolerant Sequential Programming Using Recovery Blocks," *Digest of Papers FTCS-8: Eighth Annual International Conference on Fault-Tolerant Computing*, Toulouse, p.207 (June 1978).
198. S.K. Shrivastava and J-P. Banatre, "Reliable Resource Allocation Between Unreliable Processes," *IEEE Transactions on Software Engineering* SE-4(3), pp.230-241 (May 1978).
199. D.P. Siewiorek, M. Canapa, and S. Clark, "C.vmp: The Architecture and Implementation of a Fault Tolerant Multiprocessor," *Proceedings FTCS-7: Seventh Annual International Conference on Fault-Tolerant Computing*, Los Angeles (CA), pp.37-43

(June 1977).

200. D. Siewiorek et al., "A Case Study of C.mmp, Cm* and C.vmp: Part 1 - Experiences with Fault Tolerance in Multiprocessor Systems," *Proceedings of the IEEE* **66**(10), pp.1178-1199 (October 1978).

201. J.R. Sklaroff, "Redundancy Management Technique for Space Shuttle Computers," *IBM Journal of Research and Development* **20**(1), pp.20-28 (January 1976).

202. D.J. Smith, *Reliability Engineering*, Pitman, London (1972).

203. R.A. Snowdon and P. Henderson, "The TOPD System for Computer Aided System Development," pp. 338-354 in *Tutorial: Software Design Strategies*, ed. G.D. Bergland and R.D. Gordon, IEEE Computer Society, Long Beach (CA) (1979).

204. J.J. Stiffler, "Architectural Design For Near - 100% Fault Coverage," *Proceedings FTCS-6: 1976 International Symposium on Fault-Tolerant Computing*, Pittsburgh (PA), pp.134-137 (June 1976).

205. J.J. Stiffler, N.G. Parke, and P.C. Barr, "The SERF Fault-Tolerant Computer," *Digest of Papers FTC/3: 73 International Symposium on Fault-Tolerant Computing*, Palo Alto (CA), pp.23-31 (June 1973).

206. A.N. Sukert, "Empirical Validation of Three Software Error Prediction Models," *IEEE Transactions on Reliability* **R-28**(3), pp.199-204 (August 1979).

207. R.S. Swarz, "Reliability and Maintainability Enhancements for the VAX-11/780," *Digest of Papers FTCS-8: Eighth Annual International Conference on Fault-Tolerant Computing*, Toulouse, pp.24-28 (June 1978).

208. D. Swearingen and J. Donahas, "Quantitive Software Reliability Models - Data Parameters: A Tutorial," *Workshop on Quantitative Software Models*, Kiamesha Lake (NY), pp.143-153 (October 1979).

209. A.S. Tanenbaum, "In Defense of Program Testing or Correctness Proofs Considered Harmful," *SIGPLAN Notices* **11**(5), pp.64-68 (May 1976).

210. D.J. Taylor, D.E. Morgan, and J.P. Black, "Redundancy in Data Structures: Improving Software Fault Tolerance," *IEEE Transactions on Software Engineering* **SE-6**(6), pp.585-594 (November 1980).

211. D.J. Taylor, D.E. Morgan, and J.P. Black, "Redundancy in Data Structures: Some Theoretical Results," *IEEE Transactions on Software Engineering* **SE-6**(6), pp.595-602 (November 1980).

212. J.M. Taylor, "Redundancy and Recovery in the HIVE Virtual Machine," *Proceedings European Conference on Software System Engineering*, London, pp.263-293 (September 1976).

213. A.B. Tonik, "Checkpoint, Restart and Recovery: Selected Annotated Bibliography," *SIGMOD FDT Bulletin* **7**(3-4), pp.72-76 (1975).
214. W.N. Toy, "Fault-Tolerant Design of Local ESS Processors," *Proceedings of the IEEE* **66**(10), pp.1126-1145 (October 1978).
215. E. Ulsamer, "Computers - Key to Tomorrow's Air Force," *Air Force Magazine* **56**(7), pp.46-52 (July 1973).
216. V. Vemuri, "The Current State of Software Reliability Modeling," *Workshop on Quantitative Software Models*, Kiamesha Lake (NY), pp.232-238 (October 1979).
217. J.S.M. Verhofstad, "The Construction of Recoverable Multi-Level Systems," Ph.D. Thesis, Computing Laboratory, University of Newcastle upon Tyne (1977).
218. J.S.M. Verhofstad, "Recovery Techniques for Data Base Systems," *Computing Surveys* **10**(2), pp.167-195 (June 1978).
219. J.F. Wakerly, "Microcomputer Reliability Improvement Using Triple-Modular Redundancy," *Proceedings of the IEEE* **64**(6), pp.889-895 (June 1976).
220. M. Ward and J.C.D. Nissen, "Software Security in a Stored Program Controlled Switching System," *International Switching Symposium Record*, Cambridge (MA), pp.570-576 (June 1972).
221. A.Y. Wei et al., "Application of the Fault-Tolerant Deadline Mechanism to a Satellite On-Board Computer System," *Digest of Papers FTCS-10: 10th International Symposium on Fault-Tolerant Computing*, Kyoto, pp.107-109 (October 1980).
222. C.B. Weinstock, "SIFT: System Design and Implementation," *Digest of Papers FTCS-10: 10th International Symposium on Fault-Tolerant Computing*, Kyoto, pp.75-77 (October 1980).
223. C.B. Weinstock and M.W. Green, "Reconfiguration Strategies for the SIFT Fault-Tolerant Computer," *Proceedings COMPSAC 78*, Chicago (IL), pp.645-650 (November 1978).
224. J.H. Wensley, "SIFT - Software Implemented Fault Tolerance," *AFIPS Conference Proceedings 1972 FJCC* **41**, Anaheim (CA), pp.243-253 (December 1972).
225. J.H. Wensley et al., "The Design, Analysis and Verification of the SIFT Fault Tolerant System," *Proceedings of 2nd International Conference on Software Engineering*, Long Beach (CA), pp.458-469 (October 1976).
226. J.H. Wensley et al., "SIFT: Design and Analysis of a Fault-Tolerant Computer for Aircraft Control," *Proceedings of the IEEE* **66**(10), pp.1240-1255 (October 1978).
227. M.V. Wilkes, *Time-Sharing Computer Systems*, Macdonald, London (1972).

REFERENCES

228. M.V. Wilkes and R.M. Needham, *The Cambridge CAP Computer and its Operating System*, North-Holland, New York (1979).
229. N. Wirth, *Systematic Programming: An Introduction*, Prentice-Hall, Englewood Cliffs (NJ) (1973).
230. W.G. Wood, "Recovery Control of Communicating Processes in a Distributed System," Technical Report 158, Computing Laboratory, University of Newcastle upon Tyne (November 1980).
231. W.A. Wulf, "Reliable Hardware/Software Architecture," *IEEE Transactions on Software Engineering* **SE-1**(2), pp.233-240 (June 1975).
232. W. Wulf et al., "HYDRA: The Kernel of a Multiprocessor Operating System," *Communications of the ACM* **17**(6), pp.337-345 (June 1974).
233. R.T. Yeh and K.M. Chandy (eds.), *Current Trends in Programming Methodology (Volumes 1-4)*, Prentice-Hall, Englewood Cliffs (NJ) (1978).
234. J.W. Young, "A First Order Approximation to the Optimum Checkpoint Interval," *Communications of the ACM* **17**(9), pp.530-531 (September 1974).

ANNOTATED BIBLIOGRAPHY

Each chapter of this book contains its own extensive set of references relevant to the material covered in that chapter. This annotated bibliography contains three sections, providing supplementary material and references. (A complete list of all references is presented after Chapter 10.) The first section, entitled 'Multiple Sources', references the books, conference proceedings and journals which contain high-quality research papers on fault tolerance. Also included in this section are survey papers on this topic. The second section provides a comprehensive annotated list of references to all of the major computing systems known to the authors in which hardware and software fault tolerance techniques together play a major role. The final section of this bibliography, on software fault tolerance topics, has been included because of its comparative novelty and because of the importance attached in this book to the problems of tolerating design faults in general, and software faults in particular. Papers on exception handling in software systems are also covered in this section.

MULTIPLE SOURCES

1. *Digest of Papers of the International Symposia on Fault Tolerant Computing (FTCS).*
   This conference has been held annually since 1971 and is the major conference on and source of references for fault tolerance. The early conference proceedings reflect the hardware oriented view of fault tolerance prevalent in the early 1970s. Software topics have received much more attention in recent years, although hardware issues still dominate the proceedings.

2. *IEEE Transactions on Computers.*
   Papers covering hardware reliability are to be found in this journal, with special issues (e.g. June 1980) being devoted to fault tolerance approximately once per year.

3. *IEEE Transactions on Reliability.*
   This journal covers reliability in all forms of system; in particular, it contains papers concerned with modeling and with reliability calculations. Papers covering computer-related topics are to be found occasionally.

4. T. Anderson and B. Randell (eds.), *Computing Systems Reliability*, Cambridge University Press, Cambridge (1979).

   This book contains a revised set of papers which were originally prepared as lecture notes for an advanced course, covering all aspects of reliability in computing systems, including: system structure, specifications, program validation, programming languages, and hardware and software fault tolerance. An annotated bibliography with over 90 entries is also provided.

5. B. Randell, P.A. Lee, and P.C. Treleaven, "Reliability Issues in Computing System Design," *Computing Surveys* **10** (2), pp.123-165 (June 1978).

   This survey paper presents an analysis of the various problems involved in achieving high reliability from complex computing systems, highlighting the role played by system structure in mastering complexity. A unified description of three fault tolerant computing systems is included in this paper. (The original version of the paper covering eight fault tolerant systems appeared in Lecture Notes in Computer Science **60**, Springer-Verlag, Berlin, pp. 282-388 (1978).)

6. A. Avizienis, "Fault-Tolerance: The Survival Attribute of Digital Systems," *Proceedings of the IEEE* **66** (10), pp.1109-1125 (October 1978).

   Professor Avizienis has long been one of the foremost researchers into fault tolerance, particularly for hardware systems, and has published a sequence of survey papers over the years. This is one such survey paper, discussing fault tolerance in general terms and noting the existence of "man-made" faults (i.e. what this book has referred to as design faults) as well as physical component faults. However, the techniques for achieving fault tolerance are mostly described with respect to hardware systems and physical faults. The paper also discusses the evolution of fault tolerant systems and provides an extensive list of 80 references.

FAULT TOLERANT SYSTEMS

COMTRAC

COMTRAC (COMputer-aided TRAffic Control system) is the name given to the computing system introduced in 1975 to control Shinkasen (the Japanese 'bullet' train). Essentially, the system consists of three symmetrically interconnected computers. Normally two computers operate synchronously with their results being compared by a voting unit, while the third computer acts as a stand-by spare.

1. H. Ihara et al., "Fault-Tolerant Computer System with Three Symmetric Computers," *Proceedings of the IEEE* **66** (10), pp.1160-1177 (October 1978).

    This paper describes the organization and operation of the COMTRAC system, covering the manual methods adopted to provide error recovery in the system, the hardware controlling the dual system, the operation of the reconfiguration control program, and the various levels of degraded service that can be provided if failures occur. Results from the operational system are also given: the total system had gone down only seven times during 1975-1977 - once because of a hardware fault, once for reasons unknown, and *five* times because of software faults.

COPRA

COPRA is a reconfigurable multiprocessor system being developed in France for aerospace applications. The system consists of three main kinds of replicated modules: processors, memory modules and I/O units. These modules are fully interconnected via a switching matrix. All modules are permanently powered up, with the computing load being shared between the available CPUs by the operating system. Each processor consists of two identical halves which operate synchronously with a comparison check on their outputs for error detection. Parity checks form the other main error detection measure.

1. F.P. Maison, "The MECRA: A Self-Reconfigurable Computer for Highly Reliable Processes," *IEEE Transactions on Computers* **C-20** (11), pp.1382-1388 (November 1971).

    The MECRA was apparently one of the original architecture studies which lead to the design of COPRA, although there appear to be few features in common between the two systems. MECRA was a microprogrammed machine, relying on coding techniques and some duplication for error detection. The microprogram for the machine was resident in main memory, and it was possible to modify this microprogram in an attempt to reconfigure the system if hardware failures occurred. For instance, the algorithms for logical operations could be altered to account for, say, failure of the AND functional unit. Presumably this was felt to be more effective than replication of the relevant critical units.

2. C. Meraud, F. Browaeys, and G. Germain, "Automatic Rollback Techniques of the COPRA Computer," *Proceedings FTCS-6: 1976 International Symposium on Fault-Tolerant Computing*, Pittsburgh (PA), pp.23-29 (June 1976).

    Following a brief outline of the structure of COPRA, this paper discusses the recovery techniques that were investigated. Essentially, backward error recovery was provided (with a single extant recovery point) to assist the system to tolerate hardware faults. The paper discusses (but not very clearly) the problems of providing backward error recovery when unrecoverable objects are being manipulated, and describes where instructions establishing recovery points can be planted by a compiler to ensure that a program can be divided into sequences of instructions for which recovery can be provided (e.g. a recovery point must not be established before an unrecoverable I/O operation).

3. C. Meraud and P. Lloret, "COPRA: A Modular Family of Reconfigurable Computers," *Proceedings of IEEE 1978 National Aerospace and Electronics Conference*, Dayton (OH), pp.822-827 (May 1978).

    This paper discusses the architecture of COPRA. Brief details of the error detection mechanisms are given (comparison checks on replicated CPUs; parity check on memory) and the various possible system configurations are described.

C.vmp

Carnegie-Mellon University has been investigating multiprocessor systems since 1970, and its C.mmp and Cm* systems are well known. Multiprocessor systems with replicated resources form a natural basis for a fault tolerant system, and although the operating systems for these two systems provide some tolerance to hardware component failures (particularly the Hydra operating system in C.mmp) fault tolerance was not a primary research goal. C.vmp is a more recent multiprocessor system which has been designed specifically to tolerate hardware faults. Basically, C.vmp has a TMR organization. Three CPUs are connected to triplicated sets of memory and peripheral units by three buses attached to a voter which can act on the information being sent or received by the processors. This bus voter can operate in three modes (under operator or program control): voting mode; independent mode, essentially with the voter inoperative and the system operating as three separate computers; and broadcast mode, where one CPU is taken to be the master and its requests are broadcast onto all three buses.

1. D.P. Siewiorek, M. Canapa, and S. Clark, "C.vmp: The Architecture and Implementation of a Fault Tolerant Multiprocessor," *Proceedings FTCS-7: Seventh Annual International Conference on Fault-Tolerant Computing*, Los Angeles (CA), pp.37-43 (June 1977).

    This paper describes and analyzes the C.vmp architecture. The system is designed to satisfy the following objectives: tolerance of permanent and transient hardware failures, achieved without program intervention; suitable for use in systems with real-time constraints; use of off-the-shelf components; and provisions to tradeoff performance for reliability dynamically (i.e. through programmed use of the three modes of voter operation discussed above). The organization of the bus voter is described in detail, and the approach taken to provide TMR operation of peripherals which cannot operate in tight synchronization (such as floppy disks) is discussed. An analysis of the reliability and performance of C.vmp with permanent and transient hardware faults is also presented.

2. D. Siewiorek et al., "A Case Study of C.mmp, Cm* and C.vmp: Part 1 - Experiences with Fault Tolerance in Multiprocessor Systems," *Proceedings of the IEEE* **66** (10), pp.1178-1199 (October 1978).

This paper covers three multiprocessor systems operational at Carnegie-Mellon University, discussing their design goals and architectures, and the experience gained from their use. Special emphasis is given to the reliability features of the systems, describing the strategies adopted (mainly software-implemented in the case of C.mmp and Cm*) and presenting reliability data obtained from operational use. The C.vmp voting scheme is described in detail, and the issues of processor synchronization in that system discussed. Some performance measurements of C.vmp are given showing that the voter introduces a degradation of the order of 14% in processor performance.

ESS Systems (Bell Laboratories)

Few computer systems have higher reliability requirements than those imposed on systems controlling telephone switching systems, where the cumulative down-time is expected not to exceed 2 hours over a 40 year lifetime. To satisfy these requirements, fault tolerance has been a major aspect of the Bell System Electronic Switching Systems (ESS) since their inception, and introduction into service in 1965. Few fault tolerant systems have been documented as comprehensively as the various ESS systems - for this reason the ESS No. 1A has been extensively examined in this book. The following papers (or preferably this book) should be mandatory reading for all designers of reliable computing systems.

1. J.R. Connet, E.J. Pasternak, and B.D. Wagner, "Software Defenses in Real-Time Control Systems," *Digest of Papers: 1972 International Symposium on Fault-Tolerant Computing*, Newton (MA), pp.94-99 (June 1972).

An important part of the ESS systems are the so-called 'audit programs', used to detect errors arising in the data base of the system (particularly those errors caused by software faults), and to provide recovery from those errors. This paper describes the salient redundancy features which have been incorporated into data structures (e.g. backup copies, redundantly linked lists, type checking information). The figures cited for the effectiveness of these techniques provide a convincing case for the inclusion of software measures in a fault tolerant system: "installations are experiencing a rate of 10 to 100 errors detected and corrected per day with rates of several hundred occasionally recorded", despite "intensive effort made over the last three years to correct the program troubles". The paper also notes that "if numerous program corrections had not been made ... the level would have been much higher. Indeed, at the time of cutover the error rate was in the range of 100 to 300 per day". Those who still believe large programs can be completely tested and debugged should take heed of these figures.

2. P.J. Kennedy and T.M. Quinn, "Recovery Strategies in the No. 2 Electronic Switching System," *Digest of Papers: 1972 International Symposium on Fault-Tolerant Computing*, Newton (MA), pp.165-169 (June 1972).

   This paper provides an overview of the No. 2 ESS which was designed for small telephone offices. (A detailed discussion of all aspects of the No. 2 ESS can be found in the BSTJ, **48**(8) (October 1969).) The system is comprised essentially of two processors operating in parallel to detect errors. Because of the small size of the No. 2 telephone office, economic issues were particularly important considerations in the design of the system. In consequence, each processor consists of a CPU, a read-only program store and a read-write call store, which together form a single replaceable unit. This may be contrasted with the structure adopted in ESS systems serving larger telephone offices where each processor is more complex and has to be configured from multiple replaceable units to meet the reliability requirements. This paper concentrates on the software measures adopted to provide fault tolerance in the No. 2 ESS, and describes the degrees of error recovery that are attempted, ranging from (simple) initialization of hardware registers to (desperate) clearing of all transient data in the call stores. Experience derived from some in-service systems is also included.

3. S. Bloom, M.J. McPheters, and S.H. Tsiang, "Software Quality Control," *Record of 1973 IEEE Symposium on Computer Software Reliability*, New York, pp.107-116 (May 1973).

   Any practical software system will have to undergo changes during its lifetime, to correct faults and also to introduce new features. An important (and often neglected) aspect of a reliable system is the manner in which these changes are introduced into an operational system. This problem is particularly acute in the ESS systems, where changes have to be introduced into a working system without disruption of its service. This paper discusses various (and often rather mundane) aspects of the software administration and maintenance for the generic ESS1 programs, and the methods by which troubles were reported and changes introduced. Figures are presented on the software development statistics, showing again the fallibility of programmers.

4. G.F. Clement and R.D. Royer, "Recovery from Faults in the No. 1A Processor," *Digest of Papers FTC-4: Fourth Annual International Symposium on Fault-Tolerant Computing*, Urbana (IL), pp.5.2-5.7 (January 1974).

   This paper provides an easily read overview of the techniques for fault tolerance in the ESS No. 1A processor. The organization of the redundancy provided in the No. 1A processor is described, and the design of the 1A is related to the experience gained from earlier ESS developments.

5. Bell Laboratories, "LAMP: Logic Analyser for Maintenance Planning," *Bell System Technical Journal* **53** (8), pp.1431-1555 (October 1974).

This issue of the BSTJ is devoted to the LAMP system, and contains five papers describing the overall system, the logic circuit simulators, automatic test generation, COMET (Controllability, Observability and Maintenance Engineering Technique) - a technique for organizing a system design to enhance diagnosability, and an application of LAMP to the design of the 1A processor subsystems. Of particular relevance to fault tolerance are the circuit and fault simulation capabilities of LAMP which were used to develop the extensive diagnostics in use in the 1A system for detecting the effects of classical hardware faults (e.g. stuck-at-1 and stuck-at-0).

6. W.C. Jones and S.H. Tsiang, "Reliability Experience of a Fault Tolerant Switching System," *National Telecommunications Conference Record*, New Orleans (LA), pp.5.1-5.7 (December 1975).

This paper reports on the experience gained from 8 years of ESS No. 1 operation (up to 1973), and analyses the reasons for system down-time during those years. While the ESS No. 1 was not reaching its design objective of 2 hours down-time over 40 years, the percentage up-time in 1973 of 99.9973% (equivalent to 9 hours down-time in 40 years) is still most impressive. The paper also notes that the high degree of reliability of the ESS No. 1 has itself caused some problems: since the maintenance staff assigned to a single system get very little opportunity to exercise their skills they are less able to deal efficiently with trouble when it does arise. Thus centralization of maintenance to cover a number of sites was introduced and considerable effort was expended to improve documentation and also to reduce dependence on humans.

7. Bell Laboratories, "ESS No. 1A Processor," *Bell Systems Technical Journal* **56** (2) (February 1977).

This issue of the BSTJ is devoted to the 1A Processor. The first paper provides an overview of the 1A processor, describing its organization and objectives, and presenting some field data obtained from in-service systems. The next three papers provide a detailed description of the major hardware units of the system, covering the CPU, the memory systems, the bus systems, and the technology used in their construction. The next two papers are concerned with software aspects, describing the structure of the operating system and the maintenance software. Of particular interest in these papers are a discussion of the expected sources of unreliability in the system (hardware unreliability 20%, software deficiencies 15%, procedural (manual) faults 30%, fault tolerance deficiencies 35%), and a description of the extensive and impressive diagnostic software that is used to locate hardware faults. The final paper describes the testing that the system was subjected to before being put into service.

8. W.N. Toy, "Fault-Tolerant Design of Local ESS Processors," *Proceedings of the IEEE* **66** (10), pp.1126-1145 (October 1978).

A good overview of the development and structure of ESS processors is presented in this paper, covering the first generation machines (the No.s 1 and 2) and the most recent (the 1A and 3A). The paper then describes in detail the hardware design of the 3A processor. A major change in the 3A is the absence of a replication check between the duplicated CPUs. Instead, the 3A has been designed to be self-checking, with error detection hardware designed as an integral part of the microprogrammed processor.

Fault Tolerant Multiprocessor (FTMP)

FTMP is one of two architectures (the other is SIFT) developed for critical aircraft control applications, and sponsored by the US National Aeronautics and Space Administration. Such applications have extremely high reliability requirements - more than 10^{-9} failures per hour is unacceptable. As described in this book, the main features of FTMP are the provision of multiple hardware modules (processes with some private memory; main memory modules; buses; input/output access logic) which operate in TMR configurations with standby spares. Special hardware units called bus guardians implement the TMR structure.

1. A.L. Hopkins and T.B. Smith, "The Architectural Elements of a Symmetric Fault-Tolerant Multiprocessor," *IEEE Transactions on Computers* **C-24** (5), pp.498-505 (May 1975).

For Symmetric Fault-Tolerant Multiprocessor read FTMP - the architecture presented in this paper led directly to the FTMP design, and provides a good description of the rationale behind the FTMP approach.

2. J.H. Lala and A.L. Hopkins, "Survival and Dispatch Probability Models for the FTMP Computer," *Digest of Papers FTCS-8: Eighth Annual International Conference on Fault-Tolerant Computing*, Toulouse, pp.37-43 (June 1978).

The various mathematical models used to estimate the reliability of FTMP are described in this paper. Several different models were used to cope with the different types of hardware failure that could affect a system. For example, combinatorial methods were used to model system failures resulting from exhaustion of spares, while Markov processes were used to model the behavior of a system when dealing with faults. Intermittent hardware faults were also taken into account in the models. The results show that a system failure rate of 10^{-9} per hour can be attained only if the probability of a fault being present initially is less than 10^{-6} The models show that scheduling maintenance at 200 hour intervals can be expected to be adequate.

3. A.L. Hopkins, T.B. Smith, and J.H. Lala, "FTMP - A Highly Reliable Fault-Tolerant Multiprocessor for Aircraft," *Proceedings of the IEEE* **66** (10), pp.1221-1240 (October 1978).

This paper provides the best summary of FTMP. The first part of the paper discusses the theory behind FTMP and the general system organization. There then follows a fairly detailed description of an engineering prototype which was then under construction. The Markov models developed for analyzing the reliability of the system (see above) are also presented.

Fault Tolerant Spaceborne Computer (FTSC)

Development of FTSC, a system intended for long (e.g. 5 year) unattended space missions, has been funded by the US Air Force since 1971. The project started by commissioning two independent architecture studies which were then evaluated by analysis and simulation in order to derive a single design for implementation as the FTSC.

1. R.B. Conn, N.A. Alexandridis, and A. Avizienis, "Design of a Fault-Tolerant, Modular Computer with Dynamic Redundancy," *AFIPS Conference Proceedings 1972 FJCC* **41**, Anaheim (CA), pp.1057-1067 (December 1972).

The Modular Spacecraft Computer was one of the two architecture studies which eventually led to the FTSC. The first part of the paper describes an initial design which was very similar to that of the JPL-STAR. An analysis of this architecture "illustrated that the modularization overhead, for the proposed technology, was high enough to question the idealized theoretical conclusion that increased partitioning leads to greater reliability" and a new design was formulated, the main difference being the replacement of separate functional units by a general-purpose CPU module. However, many similarities with the JPL-STAR remain: stand-by spare modules with reconfiguration by power switching; error detecting codes on instructions and data words forming the main method of error detection; a centralized control unit protected by TMR; duplication of read-write memory modules for recovery.

2. J.J. Stiffler, N.G. Parke, and P.C. Barr, "The SERF Fault-Tolerant Computer," *Digest of Papers FTC/3: 73 International Symposium on Fault-Tolerant Computing*, Palo Alto (CA), pp.23-31 (June 1973).

This two part paper describes the conceptual design, implementation and analysis of the SERF system, which was the other architecture study initiated for the FTSC project. SERF was a single bus computer with an arithmetic processing unit (APU), a control unit, main memory modules, I/O interfaces and a configuration control unit which assumed control of the system when an error was detected. Reliable operation of these main modules was achieved through the deployment of internal redundancy (the acronym SERF abbreviates Sub Element Redundant Fault tolerance) under the (theoretical) assumption that for a given amount of redundancy, the best reliability characteristics are achieved by increased partitioning of the system. Thus, the APU consisted of four 8-bit modules with two stand-by spares, with each module containing two identical halves and a voter. The main memory modules contained spare bit lines, with parity checks and a reversal check on the word selection address lines. Special hardware switching mechanisms called ripplers were designed to effect the appropriate reconfiguration, automatically in the case of the APU and under program control for memory reconfiguration.

3. D.D. Burchby, L.W. Kern, and W.A. Sturm, "Specification of the Fault-Tolerant Spaceborne Computer," *Proceedings FTCS-6: 1976 International Symposium on Fault-Tolerant Computing*, Pittsburgh (PA), pp.129-133 (June 1976).

This paper describes the development of the specification for the FTSC from the two earlier architectural investigations, giving a very brief overview of the two designs and the reasons for the final choice of features (FTSC contains features from both designs).

4. J.J. Stiffler, "Architectural Design For Near - 100% Fault Coverage," *Proceedings FTCS-6: 1976 International Symposium on Fault-Tolerant Computing*, Pittsburgh (PA), pp.134-137 (June 1976).

Some details of the error detection and reconfiguration hardware of the FTSC are presented in this paper. Only hardware faults are considered, even though a goal for FTSC was to tolerate "all faults having a non-negligible probability of occurring". The main hardware modules are: four CPUs (one active, one monitoring the active CPU, two unpowered); up to 24 memory modules; three Configuration Control Units (CCU) used primarily for reconfiguration; and a single bus system (with some internal redundancy). Heavy reliance is placed on the use of coding checks for error detection. The coding redundancy can also be used, under program control, to perform single bit correction. The three CCUs operate in a TMR mode (with no spares) to initiate reconfiguration activities in the CPU and to provide a first stage reconfiguration of the hardware modules.

5. F.J. O'Brien, "Rollback Point Insertion Strategies," *Proceedings FTCS-6: 1976 International Symposium on Fault-Tolerant Computing*, Pittsburgh (PA), pp.138-142 (June 1976).

An applications task in the FTSC can establish a single recovery point. This paper provides some details on how recovery to that recovery point is implemented. The strategy is based on four major assumptions: (i) hardware faults are immediately noticed;

(ii) memory modules are non-volatile; (iii) simultaneous module faults are unlikely; (iv) most importantly, the application program has no design faults. Thus the recovery can only provide protection against hardware faults. Memory modules containing programs and constants can be protected by maintaining copies in spare modules or on backing store, by maintaining a single module containing a coded version (exclusive-or) of all such modules so that the contents of a single faulty module can be re-created, or by reloading over a radio link. State restoration for program variables has to be performed explicitly. Variables are assumed to be redundantly stored by the application program itself. However, since write operations are unrecoverable, the program has to ensure that, following the establishment of the recovery point, these variables are not updated (since recovery would not then be possible). The paper discusses the complications of organizing programs to achieve this effect. Damage assessment in the FTSC seems to be based on the a priori decision that recovery will remove all errors. This decision results in recovery being invoked even in situations where it seems unnecessary, for instance, when another copy of a faulty memory module is available.

6. D. DeAngelis and J.A. Lauro, "Software Recovery in the Fault-Tolerant Spaceborne Computer," *Proceedings FTCS-6: 1976 International Symposium on Fault-Tolerant Computing*, Pittsburgh (PA), pp.143-147 (June 1976).

    This paper discusses the software implemented strategies for fault treatment and error recovery in FTSC. The program responsible resides in read-only memory within each CPU module, with the CCUs attempting to ensure that a fault-free CPU is used to execute this program. The first action of the program is to locate faulty modules. If a fault has occurred in a memory module two courses of action are available. If a faulty bit or bit line is suspected the spare bit lines can be used to replace the faulty line (and recovery can be achieved by invoking the hardware provided single-error correction facility). Otherwise the whole memory module will be replaced by a spare. This replacement (and that of other faulty modules) is achieved by power switching. Finally, backward error recovery of the programs in the system is invoked (see the paper above).

7. K.H. Kim et al., "Strategies for Structured and Fault-Tolerant Design of Recovery Programs," *Proceedings COMPSAC 78*, Chicago (IL), pp.651-656 (November 1978).

    A difficulty in reading the previous two papers stems from the unstructured, implementation-driven presentation of the FTSC features, particularly those of the so-called recovery program. This paper examines the design techniques and implementation strategies that were found to be "useful in obtaining an easily understandable recovery program", briefly illustrated with respect to the FTSC recovery program. The paper proposes a sensible structuring of the recovery program into multiple levels, with the program at a given level validating untested parts of the system but only making use of modules which have already been checked. (A similar strategy is implemented in the Pluribus operating system.) The paper also advocates the use of recovery blocks, with an acceptance test forming a last check on a reconfigured system and the alternate modules attempting other more global (or drastic) fault tolerance actions.

HIVE

The HIVE (High Integrity Virtual Environment) project at the Royal Signals and Radar Establishment (U.K. Ministry of Defence) was concerned with the design and development of a system for implementing high integrity, dedicated transaction processing systems such as communicattions switching. The HIVE virtual machine provided an arbitrary number of virtual processes (VPs) which could access the resources of the system through a software-implemented capability mechanism and which could communicate through a message passing scheme. A static structuring of VPs was defined at system build time, each VP being dedicated to one particular program which was executed cyclically at run-time. Thus a request for service from the environment of a HIVE system results in a 'transaction' being passed from VP to VP, to be processed in stages.

1. J.M. Taylor, "Redundancy and Recovery in the HIVE Virtual Machine," *Proceedings European Conference on Software System Engineering*, London, pp.263-293 (September 1976).

    As its title suggests, this paper concentrates on the redundancy used in the HIVE virtual machine to provide recovery; the other constituent phases of fault tolerance are not discussed. HIVE aims to provide backward error recovery to cope with hardware faults, the strategy for which is based on the static nature of a system (i.e. a static permanent set of VPs and data base objects). All permanent objects (code and data) are maintained in at least four replicated versions distributed across the storage media of the system: two read-only (for the most drastic recovery when the system is restarted with no record of its previous activity), and two read-write versions. Each VP starts execution when a message arrives, is then given a capability for one of the read-write versions of all of the data base objects it requires, and these objects are locked - in effect, this establishes a recovery point. If the VP completes its execution, commitment occurs - the other read-write versions are updated and the locks released (hopefully, after all such updating has completed). Otherwise recovery takes place and a retry is attempted. The normal send message procedure of a VP is buffered: messages will not be sent until a VP has completed its execution. If a VP only made use of this procedure then its actions would be atomic. Unfortunately another (unbuffered) send message procedure is provided which means that this may not be the case. Providing recovery for non-atomic VPs is not discussed. Recovery was complicated by the fact that the processing of each transaction was not implemented as an atomic action encompassing all of the VPs involved. Thus, while a special checkpointing VP could ensure that the data received by a HIVE system was regenerated following a system crash, the rest of the data base could then be inconsistent since some VPs may already have processed their part of the transaction and committed the results. HIVE provided a mechanism - a bit in each message - to allow the checkpointing VP to indicate that a transaction was being regenerated. However, there seems to be no method of preventing other VPs from accessing and acting upon the inconsistent data base.

IBM 9020

The IBM 9020 is a modular multiprocessor computer system designed to suit the requirements of the Federal Aviation Administration for air traffic control applications. The 9020 is constructed from IBM/360 units; a typical system would consist of three CPUs, nine memory units, and associated peripherals, with a complex interconnection network. The units have been modified to support the multiprocessor nature and fault tolerance activities of the system. For instance, the standard IBM/360 instruction set has been extended with instructions for configuration control, controlling accesses to shared storage and signalling exceptions between CPUs.

1. IBM, "An Application-Oriented Multiprocessing System," *IBM Systems Journal* **6** (2), pp.78-132 (1967).

    This issue contains six papers describing the IBM 9020 system, the overall title emphasizing the fact that the system was designed for one specific application rather than as a general purpose fault tolerant system. After a brief introductory paper the second paper covers the hardware characteristics of the system, describing the main units and the mechanisms provided to enable programs to control the system configuration - for instance, the units can be configured into a single system or into multiple separate systems each executing in isolation. The special instructions (and hardware) for achieving atomic accesses to shared storage are also described. The third paper briefly describes the control program of the 9020 which manages system resources (e.g. storage allocation and task scheduling) and controls the execution of the diagnostic and application programs. The on-line and off-line diagnostic programs are the subjects of the next two papers. The failure exceptions that are signalled by the hardware are handled by these programs, which attempt to classify faults as solid or intermittent and to take the necessary reconfiguration actions. The final paper covers the programs required for air traffic control.

JPL-STAR Computer

The Jet Propulsion Laboratory Self-Testing And Repairing (JPL-STAR) computer was the result of studies initiated in 1961 into the design of fault tolerant computer systems. The research was sponsored by the US National Aeronautics and Space Administration. The JPL-STAR was intended for a long (10 year) mission to the outer planets. The prospective mission was eventually cancelled and the development of the JPL-STAR ceased. However, a prototype was built and subjected to some experiments. The main features of the JPL-STAR were its modular architecture with unpowered standby-spares available for replacing faulty modules, and the use of a special hard-wired TMR Test And Repair Processor (the TARP) which implemented the fault tolerance strategies.

1. A. Avizienis et al., "The STAR (Self-Testing and Repairing) Computer: An Investigation of the Theory and Practice of Fault-Tolerant Computer Design," *IEEE Transactions on Computers* **C-20** (11), pp.1312-1321 (November 1971).

    One of the most widely referenced papers on fault tolerant computing systems, describing the design of the JPL-STAR, the principal objective of which was "to attain fault tolerance for a variety of faults: transient, permanent, random and catastrophic". The paper discusses the techniques used in the JPL-STAR to tolerate such (hardware) faults, providing further details of some of the techniques which have been examined in this book.

2. A. Avizienis and D.A. Rennels, "Fault-Tolerance Experiments with the JPL-STAR Computer," *Digest of Papers COMPCON 72*, San Francisco (CA), pp.321-324 (September 1972).

    Few papers discuss any experimental assessment of the JPL-STAR design, perhaps due to the curtailment of the project. This paper briefly describes some experiments that were carried out with the prototype system, consisting of the injection of permanent and transient hardware faults during the execution of a program. The only results presented are that the introduction of noise bursts on the buses "demonstrated 99.5-100% proper recovery" and that a limited test indicated that the coverage of the TARP for achieving successful fault tolerance was in the range 90-100%.

3. J.A. Rohr, "STAREX Self-Repair Routines: Software Recovery in the JPL-STAR Computer," *Digest of Papers FTC/3: 73 International Symposium on Fault-Tolerant Computing*, Palo Alto (CA), pp.11-16 (June 1973).

    STAREX was an operating system for the JPL-STAR. One of the main features of STAREX was the provision of a limited form of backward error recovery (for recovery after hardware faults), allowing a single recovery point to be established. The problem of providing recovery in the presence of unrecoverable operations (e.g. input/output) was recognized, and the paper describes how a program was able to perform its own recovery after automatic rollback had occurred.

4. A. Avizienis, "Arithmetic Algorithms for Error-Coded Operands," *IEEE Transactions on Computers* C-22 (6), pp.567-572 (June 1973).

All memory words in the JPL-STAR contained redundancy in the form of an arithmetic residue code. This coding enabled errors resulting from faulty storage, transmission or arithmetic manipulation of words to be detected. The paper describes the algorithms used to implement arithmetic operations in the JPL-STAR.

Plessey System 250

System 250 was designed in the early 1970s by the Plessey Company (UK), initially for stored program control of telephone switching. It is a multiprocessor system having up to eight CPUs, connected to all other memory and peripheral interface modules in the system by a dedicated bus. The main feature of the architecture is the provision of capability based protection which naturally plays a major role in the design and implementation of the fault tolerance actions of the system. It is surprising to note the absence, in the papers below, of references to any other fault tolerant system, especially the Bell ESS systems which were already in service and were designed for a similar application.

1. D.M. England, "Operating System of System 250," *International Switching Symposium Record*, Cambridge (MA), pp.525-529 (June 1972).

    This paper provides a brief summary of the levels of abstraction provided by the System 250 operating system, but contains nothing of interest for fault tolerance, and little about the capability mechanisms in the system even though other papers refer to it for this purpose.

2. D. Halton, "Hardware of the System 250 for Communications Control," *International Switching Symposium Record*, Cambridge (MA), pp.530-536 (June 1972).

    As its title suggests, details of the hardware implementation of System 250 are presented in this paper. The features most relevant to this book are the description of the capability mechanism and its implementation, and the checksum and parity redundancy used to protect this mechanism against faults.

3. D.C. Cosserat, "A Capability Oriented Multi-Processor System for Real-Time Applications," *First International Conference on Computer Communications*, Washington (DC), pp.282-289 (October 1972).

    This paper presents the (obvious) arguments in favor of a centralized computer controlled telephone switching system and discusses the design considerations that led to the System 250 architecture. The main requirements were: real-time constraints on programs; controlled protection and sharing of information; modular structure allowing for easy expansion; and of course high reliability. The two main architectural features discussed (briefly) are the capability mechanism and the absence of interrupts generated by peripherals, the latter as a way of minimizing the overheads of unnecessary process switching (overheads perhaps exacerbated by the capability mechanism).

4. K.J. Hamer-Hodges, "Fault Resistance and Recovery Within System 250," *First International Conference on Computer Communications*, Washington (DC), pp.290-296 (October 1972).

This paper provides more details of the hardware implementation of System 250. Some details are presented of the initial hardware implemented strategies for fault tolerance (although the error detection that initiates these strategies is not discussed): following the recognition of a fault condition, an interrupt is raised to force the processor into a hardware-implemented sequence which nullifies all capability registers and reloads the system capability table so that only the recovery program (see the paper below) can be executed. The title of this paper more accurately reflects the content of the following paper.

5. C.S. Repton, "Reliability Assurance for System 250, A Reliable, Real-Time Control System," *First International Conference on Computer Communications*, Washington (DC), pp.297-305 (October 1972).

This is the best paper on fault tolerance in System 250. The main forms of error detection in the system are: hardware checks; software consistency checks; and diagnostic programs. Three stages of error recovery are envisaged with increasing disruption to the system as a consequence. (Backward error recovery is usually the objective, obtained by program measures rather than by mechanisms.) Firstly, each process has a defined recovery action which can be activated if the process detects an error. This action could involve regenerating data areas or simply giving up. The second stage of error recovery uses a checkpoint (via duplicate files on backing store) to enable important processes to be restarted. The final stage of recovery is a restart with the current system state being abandoned. Naturally, damage assessment is based on the assumption that the capability mechanism provides tight constraints on the flow of information (even in the presence of faults). However, no mention is made of the problems caused by valid information flow between processes, and it is not made clear whether processes execute atomically. Fault treatment consists of hardware diagnostic programs and reconfiguration. Since all of these actions are software controlled it is essential that the programs are executed on a fault-free processor. Therefore the first step of the fault interrupt sequence (see the paper above) is to invoke a 'maze' program. Successful execution of this program is taken to indicate that the processor is fault-free. Unsuccessful execution causes the hardware to re-initiate the fault interrupt sequence, using another store module (the relevant programs are replicated in all store modules). Although the paper notes the likely existence of software faults it assumes that the process recovery discussed above will suffice to provide tolerance.

6. D.M. England, "Capability Concept Mechanisms and Structure in System 250," *International Workshop on Protection in Operating Systems*, Rocquencourt, pp.63-82 (August 1974).

   This paper is a collection of notes which provide a description of the implementation of capabilities in the Plessey System 250.

Pluribus

The Pluribus multiprocessor system was originally designed in 1972 by Bolt Beranek and Newman Inc. as a reliable, high capacity Interface Message Processor for use with the ARPANET. In common with the SIFT system, much of the fault tolerance in Pluribus is software controlled. However, Pluribus is used in a much more tolerant environment than that of SIFT - thus the main goal for Pluribus was to maximize system availability rather than aim for error-free operation. For example, if a packet from the network gets lost or corrupted then recovery of that packet is dealt with by the network and not by Pluribus.

1. F.E. Heart et al., "A New Minicomputer/Multiprocessor for the ARPA Network," *AFIPS Conference Proceedings 1973 NCC and Exposition* **42**, New York, pp.529-537 (June 1973).

   The first paper on Pluribus (before the system was named Pluribus) describing the modular multiprocessor structure of the hardware.

2. S.M. Ornstein et al., "Pluribus - A Reliable Multiprocessor," *AFIPS Conference Proceedings 1975 NCC* **44**, Anaheim (CA), pp.551-559 (May 1975).

   This paper discusses how the Pluribus software implements fault tolerance in the system and provides examples of how some software and hardware faults are coped with.

3. W.F. Mann, S.M. Ornstein, and M.F. Kraley, "A Network-Oriented Multiprocessor Front-End Handling Many Hosts and Hundreds of Terminals," *AFIPS Conference Proceedings 1976 NCC* **45**, New York, pp.533-540 (June 1976).

   This paper describes the design of Pluribus with respect to its application as an ARPANET front-end processor, discussing the hardware requirements and which network functions should be provided in the front-end. This is not the paper to read to learn about fault tolerance in Pluribus.

4. J.G. Robinson and E.S. Roberts, "Software Fault-Tolerance in the Pluribus," *AFIPS Conference Proceedings 1978 NCC* **47**, Anaheim (CA), pp.563-569 (June 1978).

   This paper describes how the Pluribus operating system tolerates faults arising in the hardware components of the system (not tolerance of software faults). Most of the sections of this paper are reprinted in the following paper by Katsuki et al.

5. D. Katsuki et al., "Pluribus - An Operational Fault-Tolerant Multiprocessor," *Proceedings of the IEEE* **66** (10), pp.1146-1159 (October 1978).

   This paper provides a good overview of the Pluribus system, describing the hardware structure and the organization of the operating system. Some field experience is also presented, quoting overall availability of eight systems over a 12 month period as being above 99.7% (and noting that "almost all of the downtime was caused by program bugs").

PRIME

PRIME was a system designed during the early 1970s at the University of California at Berkeley, although the implementation was never completed (presumably for funding reasons). PRIME was to be a general purpose, multi-access interactive system providing continuous availability to its (terminal) users. The system consisted of an interconnected set of replicated functional units (e.g. processors, memory, disks) which were to be dynamically allocated to users as required. At any time one processor in the system was designated as the Control Processor (CP) and executed the Central Control Monitor which implemented system-wide control functions such as resource allocation. Other processors were dedicated to executing user tasks, but also included a local operating system (actually implemented in microcode within the processor).

1. H.B. Baskin, B.R. Borgerson, and R. Roberts, "PRIME - A Modular Architecture for Terminal-Oriented Systems," *AFIPS Conference Proceedings 1972 SJCC* **40**, Atlantic City (NJ), pp.431-437 (May 1972).

   This paper discusses the rationale behind the design of the PRIME system and presents some implementation details; the fault tolerance characteristics of the system are described in much more detail in the papers below.

2. B.R. Borgerson, "A Fail-Softly System for Time-Sharing Use," *Digest of Papers: 1972 International Symposium on Fault-Tolerant Computing*, Newton (MA), pp.89-93 (June 1972).

   The main fault tolerance features incorporated in PRIME and the motivation for building a modular fail-softly system for use in a time sharing environment are outlined in this paper.

3. B.R. Borgerson, "Spontaneous Reconfiguration in a Fail Softly Computer Utility," *Datafair 73 Conference Papers*, Nottingham, pp.326-333 (April 1973).

   As its title suggests, this paper concentrates on the reconfiguration aspects of fault tolerance in the PRIME system. Reconfiguration in PRIME was spontaneous, controlled by the CP. The ability to reconfigure a system is a powerful one; steps have to be taken to minimize the possibility of a faulty processor

performing the reconfiguration. The paper describes the steps taken when: (i) a processor suspects that the CP is faulty; (ii) the CP detects an internal error; (iii) the CP suspects one of the other processors; (iv) the CP refuses to abdicate its role. In the first three situations, following the detection of an error a hardware implemented reconfiguration establishes a processor not involved in the detection as the CP. This processor then executes diagnostic checks on the suspect modules and removes those considered faulty from the tables of system resources. In situation (iv), two other processors can collaborate to force the CP to abdicate, if necessary by powering it down. The system reconfiguration can then proceed as in the first three situations.

4. R.S. Fabry, "Dynamic Verification of Operating System Decisions," *Communications of the ACM* **16** (11), pp.659-668 (November 1973).

Apart from continuous availability, one of the goals of PRIME was to guarantee that no single fault could compromise the privacy of a user's data. Thus there was no (simultaneous) sharing of memory resources in PRIME, and users could only communicate by explicit message passing. To ensure that this protection structure was maintained even in the presence of hardware and software faults, PRIME was designed with the aim that every operating system decision which could have compromised this structure was dynamically checked. This paper describes the error detecting checks that were performed on message passing, and when memory and disk pages were allocated, accessed and cleared after use. The paper notes the importance of independence between a decision and its check so that no single fault could compromise both.

5. B.R. Borgerson and R.F. Freitas, "An Analysis of PRIME Using a New Reliability Model," *Digest of Papers FTC-4: Fourth Annual International Symposium on Fault-Tolerant Computing*, Urbana (IL), pp.2.26-2.31 (January 1974).

For those that like reliability models, this paper presents a model that was used to analyze the reliability of PRIME. The effects of three classes of fault are analyzed with the model: faults affecting the fault tolerance strategies in the system; resource exhaustion; multiple faults and faults whose effects are undetected. Not surprisingly, the paper shows that the reliability of PRIME is significantly better than that of a system with no fault tolerance.

Software Implemented Fault Tolerance (SIFT)

SIFT is one of two systems (the other is FTMP) that have been designed for extremely reliable aircraft control applications. The main features of SIFT (which have been discussed in this book) are the minimal use of special purpose hardware (standard off-the-shelf minicomputers with no special fault tolerance features provide the main processing power), the implementation of fault tolerance solely in software, and replicated execution of tasks with voting on the outputs. The dependence on software for reliable system operation requires that there are no design faults in the software - the SIFT designers intend to verify the correctness of their system formally.

1. J.H. Wensley, "SIFT - Software Implemented Fault Tolerance," *AFIPS Conference Proceedings 1972 FJCC* **41**, Anaheim (CA), pp.243-253 (December 1972).

   This was the first major presentation of the SIFT system. At the level of detail discussed in this paper, the reader will find it difficult to spot any major differences between the architecture presented here and that described in the papers below, indicating the soundness of the early design.

2. J.H. Wensley et al., "The Design, Analysis and Verification of the SIFT Fault Tolerant System," *Proceedings of 2nd International Conference on Software Engineering*, Long Beach (CA), pp.458-469 (October 1976).

   A primary requirement in SIFT is that its software system is shown to be correct by means of rigorous, formal techniques. This paper describes the approaches being followed to achieve this goal (although the verification had not been completed at that time). The system has been hierarchically designed and specified, with modules at the top of the hierarchy providing a very abstract description of the system while modules at the lowest level describe the real hardware. Each module interface has been formally specified in terms of V-functions (which return the state of an abstract data structure) and O-functions (which cause a transition from one state to another). Every module has been implemented in terms of the O- and V-functions of the modules directly below, and these implementations are to be verified with respect to the specification of the module and those of the lower-level modules which it utilizes. By this approach, the proof of the complete SIFT system should be reduced to the proof of several small programs. The Markov-based reliability model developed for SIFT is also described, and has been formally related to the specification of the highest level modules in the hierarchy to show that the model accurately represents the behavior of the system.

3. J.H. Wensley et al., "SIFT: Design and Analysis of a Fault-Tolerant Computer for Aircraft Control," *Proceedings of the IEEE* **66** (10), pp.1240-1255 (October 1978).

   This paper provides the best overall description of the SIFT system. It describes the SIFT software and hardware organization, the Markov model that has been used to analyze the reliability of the system, and the approach to proving the correctness of SIFT.

4. C.B. Weinstock and M.W. Green, "Reconfiguration Strategies for the SIFT Fault-Tolerant Computer," *Proceedings COMPSAC 78*, Chicago (IL), pp.645-650 (November 1978).

This paper describes the reconfiguration software in SIFT. The salient sections also appear in the above paper.

5. C.B. Weinstock, "SIFT: System Design and Implementation," *Digest of Papers FTCS-10: 10th International Symposium on Fault-Tolerant Computing*, Kyoto, pp.75-77 (October 1980).

>The design of the SIFT operating system is briefly covered in this paper.

Space Shuttle Computer Complex

The Space Shuttle is the first manned spacecraft to be totally dependent on computer control for the safe operation of a mission. There is no provision for manual takeover of flight critical operations should the computers fail. Thus reliability and fault tolerance have been a major concern in the design of the Space Shuttle computer complex. The resulting system comprises five identical general purpose computers. Four of the computers operate together on critical tasks, receiving the same inputs and voting on their outputs (executing identical software, it should be noted). No provisions have been made for tolerating software (or hardware) design faults. The possible use of the fifth computer for fault tolerance is not addressed by these papers which instead suggest that it is to be used for non-critical tasks. Elsewhere it has been suggested that this computer was intended to be used as a backup, executing different software to that of the main set. This would be eminently sensible. However, it seems that most of the budget has been spent on the development of the software for the main system, and the backup (whose role would become critical if a software fault affects the main system) has received relatively little attention.

1. J.R. Sklaroff, "Redundancy Management Technique for Space Shuttle Computers," *IBM Journal of Research and Development* **20** (1), pp.20-28 (January 1976).

>This paper covers the hardware organization of the five Shuttle computers, and the strategies that are used when (computer) failures occur. Normally, four of the computers operate in an NMR configuration, each checking the results calculated by the others. The comparison check is based on a checksum of the outputs produced in a computational cycle rather than on the individual outputs in order to reduce the bus and processing overheads. When an error is detected, the aim is to identify the faulty hardware module sufficiently accurately that manual reconfiguration by the crew can take place (why reconfiguration is not performed automatically by the system is not made clear). The paper also describes the operation of the system when only three or two computers are available.

2. A.E. Cooper and W.T. Chow, "Development of On-Board Space Computer Systems," *IBM Journal of Research and Development* **20** (1), pp.5-19 (January 1976).

This paper provides an interesting overview of IBM's involvement over the last sixteen years in computer systems for spacecraft. The functions, characteristics, requirements and design approaches for computer systems for seven space vehicles are discussed in some detail. These systems vary from the simplex computers used in the unmanned Saturn 1 in the early 1960s, through TMR systems in the manned launches of the Apollo program, to the five computers used in the Space Shuttle. The growing dependence (now total in the Space Shuttle) on computers and their software is discussed. However, it seems that only hardware component failures are considered to be a reliability problem. Certainly, the problems of software are hardly mentioned.

3. C.T. Sheridan, "Space Shuttle Software," *Datamation* **24** (7), pp.128-140 (July 1978).

This is one of the few papers describing software developed for the Space Shuttle. The paper concentrates on the fairly complex method by which it is ensured that the four computers remain in synchronization (there is no common clock), which is one of the necessary conditions for the generation of identical results - a central feature of the reliability strategy of the Shuttle computers.

Tandem 16

The Tandem 16 computer system has been aimed at "offering the commercial market place an off-the-shelf, general purpose system with at least an order of magnitude better availability than existing off-the-shelf systems without charging a premium". The main application for such systems is expected to be on-line, data base transaction processing systems. As far as innovative ideas for fault tolerance are concerned, the Tandem system is conservative, providing redundancy of hardware units such that no single point of (hardware) failure can disable the entire system. The software is assumed to be free from faults. Briefly, a system consists of multiple processor modules (between 2 and 16), two interprocessor buses, peripheral controllers which can be attached to two processing modules, and periperals (disks can be attached to two controllers). The operating system has the prime responsibility for implementing fault tolerance in the system, providing the necessary reconfiguration actions to avoid faulty units and to permit on-line system maintenance and repair. The current commercial success of the Tandem systems demonstrates that fault tolerance is not just a requirement of specialized, critical applications, and that there are many applications awaiting the availability of cost-effective fault tolerant computing.

1. D. Mackie, "The Tandem 16 NonStop System," pp. 145-161 in *State of the Art Report on System Reliability and Integrity*, Infotech, Maidenhead (1978).
   This paper presents the main fault tolerance features of the Tandem system. The organization of the hardware and software, and the means by which single hardware failures are tolerated are described in some detail, albeit in the somewhat self-congratulatory manner normally encountered in sales brochures.

2. J.A. Katzman, "A Fault-Tolerant Computing System," *Proceedings of Eleventh Hawaii International Conference on System Sciences*, Honolulu (HA), pp.85-102 (January 1978).
   This paper concentrates on the design of the various hardware units in a Tandem system, describing the organization of: the system packaging and power distribution; the processor module; and the input/output system. The appendix to the paper presents some reliability mathematics to substantiate the claim that the system can provide an order of magnitude more availability than conventional systems.

3. J.F. Bartlett, "A 'NonStop' Operating System," *Proceedings of Eleventh Hawaii International Conference on System Sciences*, Honolulu (HA), pp.103-117 (January 1978).
   The operating system for the Tandem/16 system (NonStop is a trademark of Tandem Computers!) is described in this paper. The main facilities implemented by the operating system for the user are processes and a message passing system. The major fault tolerance application of processes and messages is to provide 'process-pairs': two processes are executed on separate processors and use the message system to try to ensure that a failure of a primary process (due to hardware failures) can be tolerated by a backup process. System wide access to input/output devices is implemented using the message system, and can be made fault tolerant by means of process-pairs. For example, two processes can cooperate to ensure that if a primary disk accessing process cannot operate then a backup process can take over. The cooperation takes the form of explicit message passing for synchronizing the processes and providing sufficient information to enable recovery points to be established. The operating system can also provide the user with an abstract disk which is implemented as two independent disk drives operating redundantly to provide tolerance against disk failures. Process-pairs can also be used by user programs, and the operating system provides functions to send state information concerning the primary process to the backup. However, the choice of which state information to send seems to be under the explicit control of the primary process and other complications arise when files are being manipulated (due to the inherent 'unrecoverability' of such objects). As the paper notes "the innovative aspects ... lie not in any new concepts introduced, but rather in the synthesis of pre-existing ideas". There are few general purpose operating systems supporting multiple communicating processes on multi-processor

systems, leave alone providing some tolerance to hardware failures.

SOFTWARE FAULT TOLERANCE

The development of software systems which incorporate redundancy to enable design faults to be tolerated is a relatively new area of research in fault tolerance. This section provides a comprehensive set of references on this topic. The references have been placed into four groups. The first three groups cover the recovery block scheme, the N-version programming scheme, and other papers advocating the adoption of similar approaches (although not always for fault tolerance). Finally papers describing exception handling in programming languages are covered.

Recovery Blocks

1. J.J. Horning et al., "A Program Structure for Error Detection and Recovery," pp. 171-187 in *Lecture Notes in Computer Science 16*, (ed. E. Gelenbe and C. Kaiser), Springer-Verlag, Berlin (1974).
   > This was the first document describing the recovery block scheme, describing the semantics of recovery blocks and presenting an algorithm for the implementation of the recovery cache (or recursive cache as it was called in this paper). The authors of the paper also foresaw the need for extending, by programmed means, the recovery provided by the cache, introducing the notion of 'recoverable procedures' to support programmer-provided recovery actions.

2. K.H. Kim and C.V. Ramamoorthy, "Failure-Tolerant Parallel Programming and its Supporting System Architecture," *AFIPS Conference Proceedings 1976 NCC* **45**, New York, pp.413-423 (June 1976).
   > This paper discusses an architecture for executing fault tolerant software such as recovery block programs. The architecture is intended to minimize the run-time overheads associated with recovery blocks by, for example, executing the acceptance test in parallel with subsequent modules.

3. T. Anderson and R. Kerr, "Recovery Blocks in Action: A System Supporting High Reliability," *Proceedings of 2nd International Conference on Software Engineering*, San Francisco (CA), pp.447-457 (October 1976).
   > This paper addresses three main topics. Firstly, a detailed description of an implementation of the recovery cache mechanism is presented. Secondly, the main features of a proposed computer architecture are described in detail. As well as supporting

the recovery block scheme this architecture provides a high level of error detection, based on a tagged memory and a novel control structure, which enables easy detection of corrupted programs and data. Thirdly, the paper discusses some simple experiments conducted with a prototype system implementing this architecture, in which recovery block programs were subject to the effects of genuine design faults, to deliberate corruption of the code and data, and to faults in the prototype system itself, but still executed without failures.

4. H. Hecht, "Fault Tolerant Software for Real-Time Applications," *Computing Surveys* **8** (4), pp.391-407 (December 1976).

This paper supports the view that recovery blocks provide a suitable framework for the implementation of software fault tolerance. Some outline programs are presented to illustrate the application of recovery block concepts to aircraft navigation programs. Since such applications have real-time requirements, the acceptance test is supplemented by the incorporation of a 'watchdog timer'. The paper also develops a model for analyzing the reliability of a software fault tolerant system which shows (under the given set of assumptions) the effectiveness of applying fault tolerance. The costs of producing a software system with redundancy for fault tolerance are compared against the costs incurred in testing a fault intolerant program to achieve a similar level of reliability, and the paper suggests that the costs are broadly comparable. The paper concludes that further experimental research into software fault tolerance is warranted.

5. B. Randell, "System Structure for Software Fault Tolerance," pp. 195-219 in *Current Trends in Programming Methodology, Vol. 1*, (ed. R.T. Yeh), Prentice-Hall, Englewood Cliffs (NJ) (1977).

This influential and widely referenced paper on software fault tolerance begins with a presentation of the recovery block scheme. The paper then discusses the problems of providing backward error recovery when processes interact, and introduces the concept of a 'conversation', a structuring of the activities of processes to avoid excessive recovery overheads. Finally, the paper discusses the structuring of systems into multiple levels and investigates some of the implications such structurings have on the provision of fault tolerance, in particular with respect to the provision of programmed recovery actions.

6. P.M. Melliar-Smith and B. Randell, "Software Reliability: The Role of Programmed Exception Handling," *SIGPLAN Notices* **12** (3), pp.95-100 (March 1977).

The paper discusses the role of exception handlers which provide specific recovery measures for achieving reliability in software systems, arguing that since such handlers are suitable for anticipated situations and inappropriate for coping with design faults (whereas the recovery block scheme is more suitable for the latter), exception handlers and recovery blocks are complementary techniques; both can and should be deployed in a system to achieve high reliability. An example of a program utilizing both approaches is presented. The paper is also noted for its definitions of fault, error and failure (from which the definitions adopted in this book were derived).

7. S.K. Shrivastava, "Sequential Pascal with Recovery Blocks," *Software - Practice and Experience* **8** (2), pp.177-185 (March 1978).

An implementation of recovery blocks in Brinch Hansen's Sequential Pascal system is described by this paper, covering the new instructions added to support recovery blocks and the organization adopted for the recovery cache.

8. S.K. Shrivastava and A.A. Akinpelu, "Fault Tolerant Sequential Programming Using Recovery Blocks," *Digest of Papers FTCS-8: Eighth Annual International Conference on Fault-Tolerant Computing*, Toulouse, p.207 (June 1978).

This short paper presents some statistics gathered from measuring the overheads incurred in executing several programs containing recovery blocks. These figures show that the overheads of recording recovery data ranged between 1% and 11% in time with a worst-case of 40% in space. The authors conclude "that the recovery cache could provide acceptable recovery performance for most applications".

9. P.A. Lee, "A Reconsideration of the Recovery Block Scheme," *Computer Journal* **21** (4), pp.306-310 (November 1978).

Presentations of the recovery block scheme usually generate a fairly standard set of questions about the scheme and its utility. This paper examines in detail the issues that these questions raise. The main questions covered include: the type of faults the scheme can provide tolerance for; the generation of alternate modules; the design of acceptance tests; the implementation of recovery; the run-time overheads; and the relationship between recovery blocks and exception handlers.

10. R.H. Campbell, K.H. Horton, and G.G. Belford, "Simulations of a Fault-Tolerant Deadline Mechanism," *Digest of Papers FTCS-9: Ninth Annual International Symposium on Fault-Tolerant Computing*, Madison (WI), pp.95-101 (June 1979).

The deadline mechanism (described in Chapter 9) is a variant of the recovery block scheme for real-time systems with critical timing constraints. The paper describes the intended operation of the scheme and presents some results obtained from simple simulations of the mechanism with different scheduling algorithms for the execution of the alternate modules.

11. H. Hecht, "Fault-Tolerant Software," *IEEE Transactions on Reliability* **R-28** (3), pp.227-232 (August 1979).

A short overview of recovery blocks and N-version programming.

12. S.K. Shrivastava, "Concurrent Pascal with Backward Error Recovery: Language Features and Examples," *Software - Practice and Experience* **9** (12), pp.1001-1020 (December 1979).

    This paper describes extensions made to the language Concurrent Pascal to support the 'port' facility discussed in Chapter 7. The paper presents the semantics of the recovery provided by ports, and gives examples of their use in a producer-consumer system, the well known dining philosophers problem (extended to include vomiting as a recovery action) and a filing system providing recoverable file updates.

13. S.K. Shrivastava, "Concurrent Pascal with Backward Error Recovery: Implementation," *Software - Practice and Experience* **9** (12), pp.1021-1033 (December 1979).

    This paper is a companion to that above, describing how Brinch Hansen's Concurrent Pascal system was extended to include the recovery mechanisms required by recovery blocks and ports.

14. P.A. Lee, N. Ghani, and K. Heron, "A Recovery Cache for the PDP-11," *IEEE Transactions on Computers* **C-29** (6), pp.546-549 (June 1980).

    The recovery cache mechanism for providing backward error recovery should ideally be designed as an integral part of a computing system. This paper describes the design of an 'add-on' recovery cache for a PDP-11 systems which enables efficient recovery to be performed for recovery block programs executed on that system. This recovery cache requires no hardware alterations to the host CPU, but intersects the bus between the CPU and the memory modules. Specially designed hardware enables the recovery cache to operate concurrently with the host system with the aim of minimizing the overheads imposed on the host (typically to about 15%). The paper describes the interface presented by the recovery cache to the host system, suggests yet another variation of the algorithms for recovery cache management, and provides an overview of the implementation.

15. A.Y. Wei *et al.*, "Application of the Fault-Tolerant Deadline Mechanism to a Satellite On-Board Computer System," *Digest of Papers FTCS-10: 10th International Symposium on Fault-Tolerant Computing*, Kyoto, pp.107-109 (October 1980).

    This short paper discusses the application of the deadline mechanism to a model of a satellite on-board computer system, showing the experimental constructs incorporated in the language Path Pascal. The authors claim that the mechanism has been shown to "successfully recover from the randomly generated timing errors", although the paper contains little to support this.

N-Version Programming

1. A. Avizienis and L. Chen, "On the Implementation of N-Version Programming for Software Fault-Tolerance During Program Execution," *Proceedings COMPSAC 77*, Chicago (IL), pp.149-155 (November 1977).
    > As this was the first publication on the N-version programming scheme, the paper discusses work in progress and some initial experimental results.

2. L. Chen and A. Avizienis, "N-Version Programming: A Fault-Tolerance Approach to Reliability of Software Operation," *Digest of Papers FTCS-8: Eighth Annual International Conference on Fault-Tolerant Computing*, Toulouse, pp.3-9 (June 1978).
    > This paper presents a full but concise description of the N-version programming scheme, the experiments that were carried out, the results from these experiments, and the conclusions that were drawn. The weaknesses and strengths of the scheme (discussed at length in Chapter 9), are expounded and some comparisons are made with the recovery block scheme. The paper concludes that "N-version programming remains an interesting and potentially effective approach to software fault-tolerance".

3. L. Chen, "Improving Software Reliability by N-Version Programming," UCLA-ENG-7843, Computer Science Department, University of California at Los Angeles (CA) (August 1978).
    > This report describes a (postgraduate) research project undertaken to investigate the N-Version programming scheme. The main results presented and conclusions drawn are the same as in the above two papers, but extra details are included for some programs which were unsuitable for N-version implementation.

4. A. Grnarov, J. Arlatt, and A. Avizienis, "On the Performance of Software Fault-Tolerance Strategies," *Digest of Papers FTCS-10: 10th International Symposium on Fault-Tolerant Computing*, Kyoto, pp.251-253 (October 1980).
    > This short paper presents queueing models for comparing the processing time and reliability performance of the recovery block and N-version programming schemes.

Other Software Fault Tolerance Papers

1. W.R. Elmendorf, "Fault-Tolerant Programming," *Digest of Papers: 1972 International Symposium on Fault-Tolerant Computing*, Newton (MA), pp.79-83 (June 1972).
    > The principles behind the N-version programming approach to software fault tolerance can be discerned in this paper.

2. M. Ward and J.C.D. Nissen, "Software Security in a Stored Program Controlled Switching System," *International Switching Symposium Record*, Cambridge (MA), pp.570-576 (June 1972).

   This perceptive early paper is concerned with the effects of residual faults in a computer controlled telephone switching system, in particular, faults in the software and unanticipated hardware faults. The paper stresses the importance of damage confinement and discusses the use of backward error recovery as a recovery technique suitable for the type of faults under consideration.

3. H. Kopetz, "Software Redundancy in Real Time Systems," *IFIP Congress 74*, Stockholm, pp.182-186 (August 1974).

   The overall structure of the redundacy necessary for software fault tolerance is briefly covered in this paper, namely stand-by spare modules (as in recovery blocks) and triple modular redundancy (as in N-version programming).

4. T. Gilb, "Parallel Programming," *Datamation* **20** (10), pp.160-161 (October 1974).

   This short note was one of the first to advocate the use of dual programming teams, albeit for testing and run-time error detection alone.

5. M.A. Fischler, O. Firschein, and D.L. Drew, "Distinct Software: An Approach to Reliable Computing," *Proceedings of Second USA-Japan Computer Conference*, Tokyo, pp.573-579 (August 1975).

   This paper is concerned with the undetected design faults that can affect a complex system, and argues that the concept of 'distinctness' - the use of independent teams generating solutions which can be compared - can be usefully applied throughout all stages of system design, from requirements and specification definition through to the operational system. The paper explores the use of distinct programming for fault prevention (e.g. debugging and testing by comparing independent implementations) and for fault tolerance (in a N-version programming scheme). Some results from informal experiments are presented which support the hypothesis that independently designed software modules can be economically produced, that improvements in the problem specification and the design of the modules can be derived, and that this approach results in design faults being exposed. The paper concludes that "distinct software can play an important role in all aspects of system design, and is a viable economic alternative to conventional methods of attaining system reliability".

6. P.J. Denning, "Fault Tolerant Operating Systems," *Computing Surveys* **8** (4), pp.359-389 (December 1976).

   This paper concentrates on capability based protection mechanisms and their use for fault tolerance, essentially for error detection and damage confinement. Error recovery in multilevel systems is also briefly covered.

7. T. Gilb, "Distinct Software: A Redundancy Technique for Reliable Software," pp. 117-133 in *State of the Art Report on Software Reliability*, Infotech, Maidenhead (1977).

    This paper presents the benefits that can be derived from using two independent designs at various stages in the implementation of a software system: at the development phase, as a means of spreading the risk and providing motivation between two competing teams; at the testing phase, as a way of reducing the high cost of testing and debugging software; and for fault tolerance during the operational phase. The latter case is not explored in depth, and a lack of distinction between fault (bug) and error adds some confusion in the section which discusses the "automatic correction of random bugs". The paper claims that the cost of dual coding is "probably between 5% and 10% of the project cost and probably rarely exceeds about 25%" (sic), and reports on several practical examples of the use of distinct software, most of which are during the testing phase.

8. A.B. Long et al., "A Methodology for the Development and Validation of Critical Software for Nuclear Power Plants," *Proceedings COMPSAC 77*, Chicago (IL), pp.620-626 (November 1977).

    The paper proposes the use of dual programming teams to generate independent software modules, but only to be used for software testing and not in the operational system for software fault tolerance. Indeed, despite the apparent criticality of the task, the authors do not reference any of the software fault tolerance research.

9. S.K. Shrivastava and J-P. Banatre, "Reliable Resource Allocation Between Unreliable Processes," *IEEE Transactions on Software Engineering* **SE-4** (3), pp.230-241 (May 1978).

    This paper addresses the problems of providing error recovery for interacting processes and suggest a program structure (called a "port") for providing backward error recovery for processes which interact only when competing for access to the (memoryless) resources of a system. A port enables a programmer to specify how a resource should be used and what recovery actions should be undertaken if recovery is invoked. Based on the **class** and **inner** concepts of Simula, a port consists of: (i) a set of procedures which can be called by the user of a port to manipulate a resource; (ii) a prelude which is executed when a port is initialized; (iii) a postlude which is executed when the user has completed use of the resource; (iv) a recovery procedure to be executed if the user invokes recovery. Depending on the point at which recovery is invoked, the prelude, recovery procedure and postlude can be automatically executed by the underlying system. Some examples of the uses of ports are presented in the paper, and the fairly complex rules governing the use of ports are given in an appendix.

10. T. Anderson, P.A. Lee, and S.K. Shrivastava, "A Model of Recoverability in Multilevel Systems," *IEEE Transactions on Software Engineering* **SE-4** (6), pp.486-494 (November 1978).

> The term 'multilevel' is often found in descriptions of computing systems. The first part of this paper discusses two distinct categories of multilevel system. The paper then goes on to examine the provision of backward error recovery in both types of system, with a level of software hiding the unrecoverable features of an interface by providing a new interface with recoverable objects to programs needing facilities for backward error recovery. Two recovery schemes termed "inclusive" and "disjoint" (see Chapter 7) and the ramifications of their implementation are described in detail.

11. T. Anderson and P.A. Lee, "The Provision of Recoverable Interfaces," *Digest of Papers FTCS-9: Ninth Annual International Symposium on Fault-Tolerant Computing*, Madison (WI), pp.87-94 (June 1979).

> This paper investigates an example of structuring a system into multiple levels, following the model presented in the paper above, so that backward error recovery can be provided. A simple file system is used to illustrate different organizations of recovery, and their advantages and disadvantages.

12. D.M. Andrews, "Using Executable Assertions for Testing and Fault Tolerance," *Digest of Papers FTCS-9: Ninth Annual International Symposium on Fault-Tolerant Computing*, Madison (WI), pp.102-105 (June 1979).

> The paper discusses the inclusion of assertion statements in programs to provide run-time error detection, and reports on some experiments in which this approach was used for both program testing and for fault tolerance, in the latter case by invoking simple recovery measures, for instance, correcting the value of a variable detected to be erroneous. Some performance figures on the overheads of assertions are supplied: when used solely for testing (one assertion per 10 executable statements) the increase in size and execution time were 8% and 4% respectively. When used in another program in conjunction with recovery actions the increases were 13.5% in size and 12% in execution time (approximately one assertion per five executable statements). The paper concludes that "executable assertions are practical for both testing and fault tolerance".

13. O.B. von Linde, "Computers Can Now Perform Vital Functions Safely," *Railway Gazette International* **135** (11), pp.1004-1006 (November 1979).

> This paper briefly presents a practical application of software fault tolerance to computer controlled railway interlocking systems and on-train signalling and speed control systems. The approach is essentially to use a 2-version programming scheme for error detection, with manual intervention for the remaining aspects of fault tolerance. If you do not believe that software fault tolerance is necessary or practicable, read this paper.

14. D.J. Taylor, D.E. Morgan, and J.P. Black, "Redundancy in Data Structures: Improving Software Fault Tolerance," *IEEE Transactions on Software Engineering* **SE-6** (6), pp.585-594 (November 1980).
    This paper describes some research into the effectiveness of systematically adding redundancy to data structures to enable some structural errors to be detected and recovered from. (This work is described in Chapters 5 and 7.) An overview and examples of the approach are presented and some experimental results given showing the effectiveness of the approach.
15. D.J. Taylor, D.E. Morgan, and J.P. Black, "Redundancy in Data Structures: Some Theoretical Results," *IEEE Transactions on Software Engineering* **SE-6** (6), pp.595-602 (November 1980).
    Some of the theoretical investigations of redundancy in data structures are presented in this companion paper to that above, describing a theory for evaluating the effectiveness of such redundancy.
16. J.P. Black, D.J. Taylor, and D.E. Morgan, "A Case Study in Fault Tolerant Software," *Software - Practice and Experience* **11** (2), pp.145-157 (February 1981).
    This paper provides some experimental results obtained from adding redundancy to the data structures of a small data base system (see the two papers above by the same authors), randomly overwriting parts of those structures and monitoring how well the system detected and recovered from the errors that were introduced. The storage overhead incurred by the addition of redundancy was less than 10% per record, and the authors conclude that "the incorporation of redundancy and audit programs can be done at an acceptable overhead cost for systems where fault tolerance is a significant requirement".

Exception Handling

1. J.B. Goodenough, "Exception Handling: Issues and a Proposed Notation," *Communications of the ACM* **18** (12), pp.683-696 (December 1975).
    This widely referenced paper on exception handling discusses the general role and uses of exception handling in programming languages. The basic requirements and issues of exception handling are described and language features proposed. However, the proposed approach is quite complex since it attempts to satisfy many objectives (e.g. exception handling for 'normal' and 'abnormal' programmming) within a single mechanism.
2. M.D. MacLaren, "Exception Handling in PL/I," *SIGPLAN Notices* **12** (3), pp.101-104 (March 1977).
    A generally critical analysis of exception handling facilities in PL/I, discussing the problems of using the facilities and of the compiler in implementing them.

3. R.A. Levin, "Program Structures for Exceptional Condition Handling," Ph.D. Thesis, Carnegie Mellon University, Pittsburgh (PA) (1977).

   This report contains an extensive survey of exception handling proposals and mechanisms, and proposes a new mechanism for languages supporting shared abstract objects. This mechanism is based on the "uses" hierarchy rather than the "calls" hierarchy normally adopted, and supports the resumption model (see Chapter 8) which allows a procedure to continue execution after an exception it has signalled has been handled. Issues concerning the verification of programs containing this new exception handling mechanism are also covered.

4. B.H. Liskov and A. Snyder, "Exception Handling in CLU," *IEEE Transactions on Software Engineering* **SE-5** (6), pp.546-558 (November 1979).

   Exception handling as a means of implementing fault tolerant programs is advocated in this paper which describes the exception handling mechanism in the CLU programming language, and which presents a clear description of the various issues. The CLU mechanism is based on a relatively simple model of exception handling, more constrained than that suggested by Goodenough, which the authors cogently argue leads to the development of well structured programs and is easy to use and implement. The mechanism is based on the association of exceptions with abstract data types. Exceptions are signalled across a single level of abstraction only (to the invoker of an abstract type) following which the signalling procedure is terminated. The paper presents several examples in CLU which highlight the drawbacks of the termination model and favor the resumption model, but argues that such examples are rare and do not justify implementing the more complex resumption model.

5. F. Cristian, "Exception Handling and Software-Fault Tolerance," *Digest of Papers FTCS-10: 10th International Symposium on Fault-Tolerant Computing Systems*, Kyoto, pp.97-103 (October 1980).

   This paper presents a model of programmed and default exception handling in software systems structured as hierarchies of data abstractions. Exceptions are defined in terms of weakest preconditions associated with operations, and an attempt is made to define precisely those parts of the system state which are inconsistent when an exception occurs. The model has many features in common with that advocated in this book, specifically the termination model and no automatic propagation of an exception. The paper also proposes the use of failure exceptions as last-resort responses from modules. Finally, the paper addresses the problems associated with tolerating design faults.

AUTHOR INDEX

Abrahams, J.A., 74
Agrawala, A.K., 31
Akinpelu, A.A., 266, 269-271, 282, 350
Alexandridis, N.A., 333
Almquist, R.P., 176
Anderson, T., 7, 56, 177, 196, 204, 208, 220, 243, 258, 269, 272, 326, 348, 355
Andrews, D.M., 130, 267, 270, 355
Arlatt, J., 352
Astrahan, M.M., 104, 189
Avizienis, A., 4, 9, 55, 56, 74, 105, 127, 275-281, 285, 326, 333, 338, 339, 352
Ayache, J.M., 121
Azema, P., 121

Banatre, J-P., 203, 212, 354
Barlow, R.E., 39, 42, 71, 74
Barr, P.C., 125, 333
Bartlett, J.F., 108, 347
Baskin, H.B., 342
Belady, L.A., 57
Belford, G.G., 124, 273-275, 350
Best, E., 38, 268
Birtwistle, G.M., 212
Bjork, L.A., 187, 219
Black, J.P., 132, 175, 176, 356
Bloom, S., 330
Boehm, B.W., 8
Boone, L.A., 303
Borgerson, B.R., 235, 237, 242, 342, 343
Bouricius, W.G., 74
Bowman, P.W., 74
Boyd, R., 188

Brandwajn, A., 239
Brinch Hansen, P., 161
Browaeys, F., 244, 327
Buckle, J.K., 136, 165
Burchby, D.D., 334

Campbell, R.H., 124, 273-275, 350
Canapa, M., 328
Carter, W.C., 6, 9, 141
Chamberlin, D.D., 137
Chandy, K.M., 7, 14, 186
Chen, L., 275-281, 285, 352
Chow, W.T., 346
Clark, S., 328
Clement, G.F., 94, 330
Coffman, E.G., 162
Cohen, E., 166
Conn, R.B., 333
Connet, J.R., 176, 329
Cooper, A.E., 346
Cosserat, D.C., 339
Cristian, F., 81, 82, 85, 88, 185, 259, 268, 269, 357
Curtice, R.M., 188

Dahl, O.-J., 14
Davies, C.T., 38, 219
DeAngelis, D., 335
de Morgan, A., 18
Denning, P.J., 353
Derochette, D., 186
Diaz, M., 121
Dijkstra, E.W., 14, 35, 161
Donahas, J., 75
Downing, R.W., 5
Drew, D.L., 262, 353

Elmendorf, W.R., 352
Elphick, M.J., 162
England, D.M., 168, 339, 341
Eswaran, K.P., 38, 137, 161

Fabry, R.S., 156, 160, 162, 343
Feustel, E.A., 136
Firschein, O., 262, 353
Fischler, M.A., 262, 353
Fraser, A.G., 189
Freitas, R.F., 343

Gall, J., 46
Gelenbe, E., 186
Gerhart, S.L., 269, 327
Germain, G., 244, 327
Ghani, N., 196, 197, 258, 271, 351
Gilb, T., 39, 262, 353, 354
Goodenough, J.B., 80, 88, 245, 356
Gray, J.N., 38, 162, 187, 189, 190, 220, 223, 356
Green, M.W., 344
Grnarov, A., 352
Guttag, J.V., 44

Halton, D., 339
Hamer-Hodges, K.J., 340
Heart, F.E., 341
Hecht, H., 262, 287, 349, 350
Henderson, P., 14
Heron, K., 196, 197, 258, 271, 351
Hoare, C.A.R., 14, 161, 208, 212
Holt, R.C., 162
Hopkins, A.L., 74, 99, 332, 333
Horning, J.J., 20, 44, 191, 195, 208, 251, 348
Horton, K.H., 124, 273-275, 350

Ihara, H., 327
Iliffe, J.K., 136

Jackson, K., 24
Jefferson, D., 166
Joly, R., 239
Jones, A.K., 157
Jones, W.C., 331
Juvenal, 303

Katsuki, D., 107, 134, 342
Katzman, J.A., 107, 347
Kennedy, P.J., 178, 330
Kern, L.W., 334
Kerr, R., 56, 136, 196, 243, 258, 272, 348
Kim, K.H., 223, 270, 335, 348
Knight, J.C., 177, 220
Knuth, D.E., 261
Kopetz, H., 262, 353
Kraley, M.F., 341

Lala, J.H., 74, 99, 332, 333
Lampson, B.W., 209
Lauro, J.A., 335
Lee, P.A., 39, 55, 196, 197, 204, 208, 222, 258, 266, 271, 326, 350, 351, 355
Lehman, M.M., 57
Levin, R.A., 85-87, 245, 357
Liebergot, H.L., 142, 286, 303, 304
Linden, T.A., 159
Liskov, B.H., 35, 44, 81, 85, 87, 88, 244, 357
Littlewood, B., 76
Lloret, P., 328
Lohman, G.M., 189
Lomet, D.B., 36, 38, 162
Long, A.B., 262, 263, 354
Luckham, D.C., 88

MacLaren, M.D., 88, 356
Mackie, D., 347
Maestri, G.H., 244
Maison, F.P., 327
Majster, M.E., 82

AUTHOR INDEX

Mann, W.F., 341
Maybury, W., 88, 245
McPheters, M.J., 330
Melliar-Smith, P.M., 17, 44, 259, 349
Meraud, C., 244, 327, 328
Merlin, P.M., 224
Meyers, M.N., 152
Migneault, G.E., 46
Mitchell, J.G., 88, 245
Moir, C.I., 24
Moranda, P.B., 76
Morgan, D.E., 7, 132, 175, 176, 356
Musser, D.R., 44
Myers, G.J., 7, 8, 39, 129, 136

Naur, P., 39
Needham, R.M., 129, 159, 168
Ng, Y-W., 74
Nissen, J.C.D., 353
Nowak, J.S., 5

O'Brien, F.J., 334
Organick, E.I., 136, 168
Ornstein, S.M., 341

Parke, N.G., 125, 333
Parnas, D.L., 14, 86
Pasternak, E.J., 176, 329
Peterson, W.W., 126, 175
Polak, W., 88
Proschan, F., 39, 42, 71, 74

Quinn, T.M., 178, 330

Ramamoorthy, C.V., 270, 348
Randell, B., 7, 17, 20, 39, 55, 208, 213, 219, 222, 224, 259, 326, 349
Rault, J.-C., 75
Rauscher, T.G., 31
Redell, D.D., 160
Reiss, R.M., 76

Rennels, D.A., 142, 338
Repton, C.S., 340
Roberts, E.S., 250, 341
Roberts, R., 250, 342
Robinson, J.G., 341
Rohr, J.A., 107, 338
Ross, D.T., 24
Roult, W.A., 152
Royer, R.D., 94, 330
Russell, D.L., 219, 222

Saltzer, J.H., 157, 158, 165, 166, 168
Salzman, E.J., 272, 284
Sandewall, E., 266
Schroeder, M.D., 157, 158, 165, 166
Sedmak, R.M., 142, 286, 303, 304
Severance, D.G., 189
Sheridan, C.T., 346
Shooman, M.L., 74
Short, R.A., 68
Shoshani, A., 162
Shrivastava, S.K., 203, 208, 212, 213, 255, 266, 269-271, 282, 350, 351, 354, 355
Siewiorek, D.P., 74, 244, 328, 329
Sklaroff, J.R., 121, 235, 239, 345
Smith, D.J., 74
Smith, T.B., 99, 332, 333
Snowdon, R.A., 14
Snyder, A., 81, 85, 87, 88, 245, 357
Stiffler, J.J., 125, 333, 334
Sturm, W.A., 334
Sukert, A.N., 76
Swarz, R.S., 127
Swearingen, D., 75
Sweet, R., 88, 245

Tanenbaum, A.S., 269

Taylor, D.J., 7, 132, 133, 175, 176, 356
Taylor, J.M., 156, 169, 178, 189, 336
Tiedeman, M.J., 219
Tonik, A.B., 186
Toy, W.N., 94, 175, 332
Treleaven, P.C., 39, 55, 222, 326
Tsiang, S.H., 330, 331
Tuomenoksa, L.S., 5

Ulsamer, E., 7

Vemuri, V., 75
Verhofstad, J.S.M., 188, 202
von Linde, O.B., 262, 279, 287, 355
von Neumann, J., 5

Wagner, B.D., 176, 329
Wakerly, J.F., 72
Walker, R.D.H., 168
Ward, M., 353
Wei, A.Y., 351
Weinstock, C.B., 344, 345
Weldon Jr, E.J., 126, 175
Wensley, J.H., 74, 99, 250, 344
Wilkes, M.V., 158, 168
Wirth, N., 14
Witty, R.W., 269
Wood, W.G., 224
Wulf, W.A., 169, 297

Yeh, R.T., 7, 14
Yelowitz, L., 269
Yoder, K.W., 152
Young, J.W., 186

Zilles, S.N., 44

SUBJECT INDEX

Acceptability. *See* Error detection, acceptability check
Acceptance test. *See* Recovery block, acceptance test
Apollo lunar missions, 7, 287
Arithmetic codes, 126-127. *See also* Parity
ARPANET, 107, 178
Assembly tree, 24-26, 28, 295
assert statement, 130, 267
Assertions, 130, 266-268, 270
 in System R, 137-138
Atomic action, 36-38, 138
 for damage confinement and assessment, 148-157, 168-169, 277-278, 281
 dynamically identified, 154
 implementation of, 148-151, 155-166, 168-169
 planned, 155-157
 for recovery, 217, 219-220, 282
Audit programs, 175-176. *See also* ESS, No. 1A, audit programs
Audit trail, 187-190, 225

Bell System. *See* ESS
Bolt Beranek and Newman, 107. *See also* Pluribus
Burroughs B1726, 31
Burroughs B6700, 136-137, 168

CAP computer, 168
Capability, 158-160, 166, 168-169
Careful replacement, 189
Chase protocol, 224. *See also* Recovery line

Checkpoint, 186-192, 194, 225
 incremental, 191-194
 partial, 188, 190-191, 194
Checksum. *See* Error detection, coding check
Cold start, 178
Commitment, 184, 223
Compensation, 182
Component. *See* System, component of
COMTRAC (COMputer-aided TRAffic Control), 326-327
Continued service, 65-66, 232, 244-246
Conversation, 219
COPRA, 244, 327-328
C.vmp, 328-329
Cyclic redundancy codes, 126, 127

Damage, 147
 anticipated, 152, 174-177, 179
 assessment, 65-66, 147-148, 152-155, 166-168
 exploratory, 154-155, 164
 confinement, 65-66, 148-151, 155-166, 168-169. *See also* Atomic action
 unanticipated, 174, 182
Data base recovery, 188-190
Deadline mechanism, 273-275
Deadlock, 162. *See also* Lock
Descriptor, 136, 158, 168
Design. *See* System, design of
Diagnostic. *See* Error detection, diagnostic check
Differential file, 189, 190

Disjoint recovery scheme, 202-204, 206-207, 225
Domino effect, 213-215, 221, 224
Draper, C.S., Laboratory, 99. *See also* FTMP

Error, 52-54, 58
Error correcting codes, 50, 68, 71, 126, 175
Error detection, 64-66, 113-142
  acceptability check, 116-117. *See also* Recovery block, acceptance test
  coding check, 126-127. *See also* Parity
  diagnostic check, 82, 133-134, 140, 141, 154, 164, 233. *See also* Fault location, diagnostic check
  ideal check, criteria for, 114-116
  interface check, 135-142, 157, 251, 266
  last-moment check, 117-119, 126, 138, 252
  matching check. *See* replication check
  reasonableness check, 128-130
  replication check, 118-123, 127, 142, 235-236, 264, 304. *See also* Voting
  reversal check, 124-126
  structural check, 130-133, 175
  timing check, 123-124, 141
  type check, 128, 132, 135, 136
  voting check. *See* replication check
Error recovery, 65-66, 173-225
  backward, 179-225, 233, 243, 252, 259, 281-284, 302. *See also* Recovery cache; Recovery point
  in data base systems, 188-190
  in distributed systems, 223-224
  forward, 179, 181, 182, 209, 224, 258-259
  in multilevel systems, 197-208, 211, 225, 283
ESS (Electronic Switching System), 329-332
  No. 1: 5, 94, 95, 98, 175, 331-332
  No. 1A, 94-98, 330-332
    audit programs, 98, 120, 124, 132, 154-155, 176
    damage assessment in, 152-155
    error detection in, 119-132 *passim*, 140, 141
    error recovery in, 176, 178
    exceptions in. *See* Exception, in ESS No. 1A
    fault treatment in, 234, 238, 240-243
    LAMP (Logic Analyzer for Maintenance Planning), 234, 331
    MTTR, 74, 240
    processor configuration circuits, 241, 242
    redundancy in, 95-96, 122, 331
    reliability requirements, 74, 94
  No. 2: 178, 330, 332
Exception, 77-88, 296-302, 356-357
  in Ada, 88
  attribution to:
    component fault, 80, 81, 139-142, 233. *See also* Exception, failure
    design fault, 80, 81, 135, 139-142, 301
  in CLU, 81, 85, 88, 245, 357
  declaration of, 82, 87, 137
  disable enable instructions, 83
  in ESS No. 1A, 98
  failure, 80-81, 138-142, 177, 233, 244, 284, 297-303
  in multilevel systems, 84-86, 142

handler, 79-88
  association with exception, 79, 82-83, 87-88
  invocation, 79, 85
  handling context, 83, 85-86, 88
  interface, 79-81, 84, 135-141, 185, 297-299. *See also* Error detection, interface check
  in JPL-STAR, 107
  in Mesa, 88, 245, 246
  in multilevel systems, 83-87, 142. *See also* Exception, propagation
  in PL/I, 88, 356
  propagation, 85-87, 299
    in calls hierarchy, 86-87
    in uses hierarchy, 86-87
  raise signal instructions, 82, 84-85, 114, 140, 252, 297-299
  raising, 78
  in SIFT, 101
  signalling, 78
    resumption after, 244-246
    termination after, 244-246, 299
  in System R, 137-138
  in Tandem 16: 124
Exchange, 220
Extension. *See* Interpreter, extension of

Failure, 40-42, 47, 54-55, 58
  of component, 47, 50-53
  of design, 47, 51-53
Fault, 53-58
  anticipated, 5-9
  component, 53-57
  design, 5-8, 53-57. *See also* Fault, software
  hardware, 5-8, 56, 296
  manifestation, 53
  permanent, 56, 232, 236

software, 7-8, 54, 56-57, 98, 250, 294. *See also* Fault, unanticipated
tolerance of, 121, 175, 249-291, 348-356
transient, 56, 122, 232, 236, 245
unanticipated, 5-9, 179-181, 294. *See also* Fault, design
Fault avoidance, 4
Fault intolerant, 4
Fault location, 232-236, 247
  diagnostic check, 233-236, 240-242, 247, 299, 301. *See also* Error detection, diagnostic check
  exploratory measures for, 233
Fault prevention, 3-10, 300, 302
Fault removal, 4
Fault treatment, 65-66, 231-243, 247, 299
FTMP (Fault Tolerant MultiProcessor), 98-99, 102-104, 277, 332-333
  bus guardian units, 103-104, 153, 241-242
  bus isolation units, 103-104
  damage assessment in, 153
  error detection in, 120-122. *See also* FTMP, voting unit
  fault treatment in, 236, 237, 239, 241, 242
  redundancy in, 99, 102-104, 122
  reliability models for, 74
  reliability requirements of, 99
  triad, 103, 120-121, 236, 241
  voting unit, 104
FTSC (Fault Tolerant Spaceborne Computer), 333-336

Graceful degradation, 239, 247
  in software, 257, 263, 264, 266, 281

Hamming codes, 126

Hardcore, 72, 242, 247, 302-303
HIVE, 156, 178, 189, 336-337

IBM, 104, 129, 142, 165. *See also* System R
9020: 337
ICL 2900: 136-137, 165
Ideal component, 297-300
IMP. *See* Pluribus
Inclusive recovery scheme, 202-204, 206-207, 225
Incremental dumping, 188
Information flow, 38, 147-151, 155-156, 209-215, 219-222, 224
  confinement of. *See* Damage, confinement
Information hiding, 14, 246, 299
Information validation, 222-223
Interaction diagram, 21-25, 96, 100, 103, 106, 109
Interface 16-17, 58
  interpretive, 29-30, 35
Interface check. *See* Error detection, interface check
Interpreter, 29-35
  diagram, 29-31
  extension of, 32-35
  in JPL-STAR, 107
  recovery by. *See* Error recovery, in multilevel systems
  in System R, 104
  in Tandem 16: 108

JPL-STAR (Jet Propulsion Laboratory—Self Testing and Repairing computer), 105-107, 333, 338-339
  damage assessment in, 153, 154
  error detection in, 121, 123, 125, 127
  error recovery in, 178
  exceptions in. *See* Exception, in JPL-STAR
  fault treatment in, 237, 239, 241, 242, 244
  redundancy in, 105-107
STAREX, 107
TARP (Test and Repair Processor), 105-107, 121, 123, 153, 241

Lock, 38, 160-162
Log. *See* Audit trail

MASCOT, 24
Mean Time Between Failures (MTBF), 42, 73, 240
Mean Time to Repair (MTTR), 74
Measure, 35-36, 58
Mechanism, 35-36, 58
MECRA computer, 327
Modular decomposition, 14, 295-296
Monitor, 20, 161, 212, 223
M-out-of-N codes, 126
Multics, 165, 168
Multilevel system, 29-35

NASA (National Aeronautics and Space Administration), 2, 98, 99
NMR, 120. *See also* TMR
  in SIFT, 101-102, 121
  in software. *See* N-version programming
  in Space Shuttle, 121, 234-235
N-version programming, 264, 275-285, 352
  comparison with recovery block, 280-285
  driver program for, 276-278
  exception handling within, 284
  inexact voting check in, 278-279
  voting check in, 276-281

Parity, 68, 69, 80, 126-127, 140
Pascal, 128, 136, 213, 255
Plessey PP250, 168, 339-341
PL/I, 129. *See also* Exception, in PL/I
Pluribus, 107, 341-342
  bus couplers, 241
  damage assessment in, 152
  error detection in, 124, 126, 127, 132, 134
  error recovery in, 178
  fault treatment in, 235, 239, 241-243
  reliability requirements, 107
Port notation, 212-213
PRIME, 156, 162, 235, 239, 242, 243, 342-343
prior. *See* Recovery block, **prior**
Processes, 20
  competing, 208-210
    recovery of, 210-213
  concurrent, 208-210
    recovery of, 209-224
  cooperating, 208-210
    recovery of, 213-223
  independent, 208-209
    recovery of, 209
Protection
  domain, 159
  mechanism, 137, 158-166. *See also* Damage, confinement; Capability

raise. *See* Exception, **raise** instruction
Reconfiguration, 237-243
  dynamic, 237, 238, 242, 243
  manual, 237-243 *passim*
  spontaneous, 237, 238, 243, 256
  by switching, 237-238, 240, 242, 243
Recoverable objects, 182, 202-204, 207, 211
Recovery. *See* Error recovery

Recovery block, 191, 194, 251-272, 348-351
  acceptance test, 252-254, 260, 263-269, 280, 303
  comparison with N-version programming, 280-285
  exception handling within, 258-259, 284-285
  prior, 265
Recovery cache, 191-197, 211, 213, 254, 265-266, 269-271, 275, 281, 302
  recovery field, 195-197
  recovery level, 196-197
  region, 191-197
Recovery data, 183-207 *passim,* 218, 221
Recovery line, 216-224
  planned, 218-220, 223
  unplanned, 220, 221, 224
Recovery point, 183-186. *See also* Recovery line
  active, 184
  consistent set of, 215, 217, 220
  discard, 183, 185, 191, 193-197, 201
  establish, 183, 185, 191-197, 201, 252-254
  interval between, 186
  restore, 183, 185, 191, 193-197, 201, 233, 244
Recovery region, 184, 193-195
Recursive cache. *See* Recovery cache
Redundancy, 67-72. *See also* Stand-by spare
  classification:
    dynamic, 68-72, 74, 80, 81, 117, 138-139, 301
    masking. *See* static
    static, 68-72, 74, 81. *See also* TMR
    temporal, 68-69, 121-122, 244
Reliability, 13, 15, 39-42

operational, 41-42
quantitative evaluation of, 42, 72-77
  software, 74-77
  requirements, 45, 46, 70, 74, 94, 99, 107
Reliance, 40
Repair. See Reconfiguration
Reset, 177-178, 182, 244. See also Error recovery, backward
Restorable action, 219-220
Resuming normal service. See Continued service
Retry, 244, 245

Self Checking Computer Module, 142
Semaphore, 20, 161
SERF (Sub Element Redundant Fault tolerance), 125, 333-334
SIFT (Software Implemented Fault Tolerance), 98-102, 121, 277, 343-345
  damage assessment in, 153
  error detection in, 121-122. See also SIFT, voting
  exceptions in. See Exception, in SIFT
  executive software, 101-102
  fault treatment in, 237, 239-242
  redundancy in, 99-101, 122
  reliability model for, 74
  reliability requirements of, 99
  voting in, 102, 276-278
signal. See Exception, **raise signal** instructions
Software faults. See Fault, software
Space Shuttle, 2, 121, 234-235, 239, 276-277, 345-346
Specification, 40-44, 46, 47
  checking against, 115-117
  exact, 43-44, 116

Sperry Univac 1100/60: 303
Sphere of control, 38, 219
SRI International, 99. See also SIFT
Stand-by spare, 238-239, 243
  in ESS No. 1A, 95, 238-239
  in JPL-STAR, 105, 239
  in software, 253, 257
STAR. See JPL-STAR
State. See System, state
State restoration. See Error recovery, backward
System, 16-19, 58
  abnormal activity, 77
  atomic, 18, 24, 25. See also component of, atomic
  component of, 17-19. See also Ideal component
    atomic, 24, 57, 70. See also System, atomic
    critical. See Hardcore
    replaceable, 234, 238-240
  design of, 17-19, 27, 28
  environment of, 16, 18-19
  normal activity, 77
  state:
    abnormal, 178-179
    erroneous, 46-54, 58
    external, 16, 47
    internal, 18, 47, 49
    normal, 178-179
    prior, 178-182, 233
    valid, 47-49
  structure, 13-38
System R, 104-105
  damage confinement in, 161-162
  error detection in, 137-138, 265
  error recovery in, 189-190, 206
  exceptions in. See Exception, in System R
  relational data interface (RDI), 105, 137, 138
  relational data system (RDS), 104-105

relational storage system (RSS), 104-105, 189-190
System repair. *See* Reconfiguration

Tandum 16: 107-109, 346-348
 dynabus, 108
 error detection in, 124, 126, 132
 error recovery in, 175
 exceptions in. *See* Exception, in Tandem 16
 fault treatment in, 235, 243, 303
 operating system, 108
Tagged storage, 136
TMR, 68-69, 71, 72, 75, 120, 150-151, 234. *See also* NMR; Voting
 in FTMP, 102-103, 120
 in JPL-STAR, 105
Transaction, 38, 138, 161, 189, 210, 220. *See also* Restorable action

Transition:
 erroneous, 46-53, 58
 valid, 47, 49, 52
Triple Modular Redundancy. *See* TMR
Two phase commit protocol, 223. *See also* Recovery line

Unrecoverable objects, 182, 202-205, 211, 243, 282-283

VLSI (Very Large Scale Integration), 6, 8, 14, 57, 151, 286, 294, 303, 304
Voting, 68, 72, 102, 104, 120, 151, 235, 276-281. *See also* TMR; Error detection, replication check

Watchdog timers, 124. *See also* Error detection, timing check

RAYMOND H. FOGLER LIBRARY

DATE DUE

BOOKS ARE SUBJECT TO
RECALL AFTER TWO WEEKS

MAY 1 1 1984

AUG 0 3 1984

JUL 3 0 1988